ART BY SADORU CHIBA
STORY BY NORIMITSU KAIHOU (NITROPLUS)
VOLUME 1

School-Live!

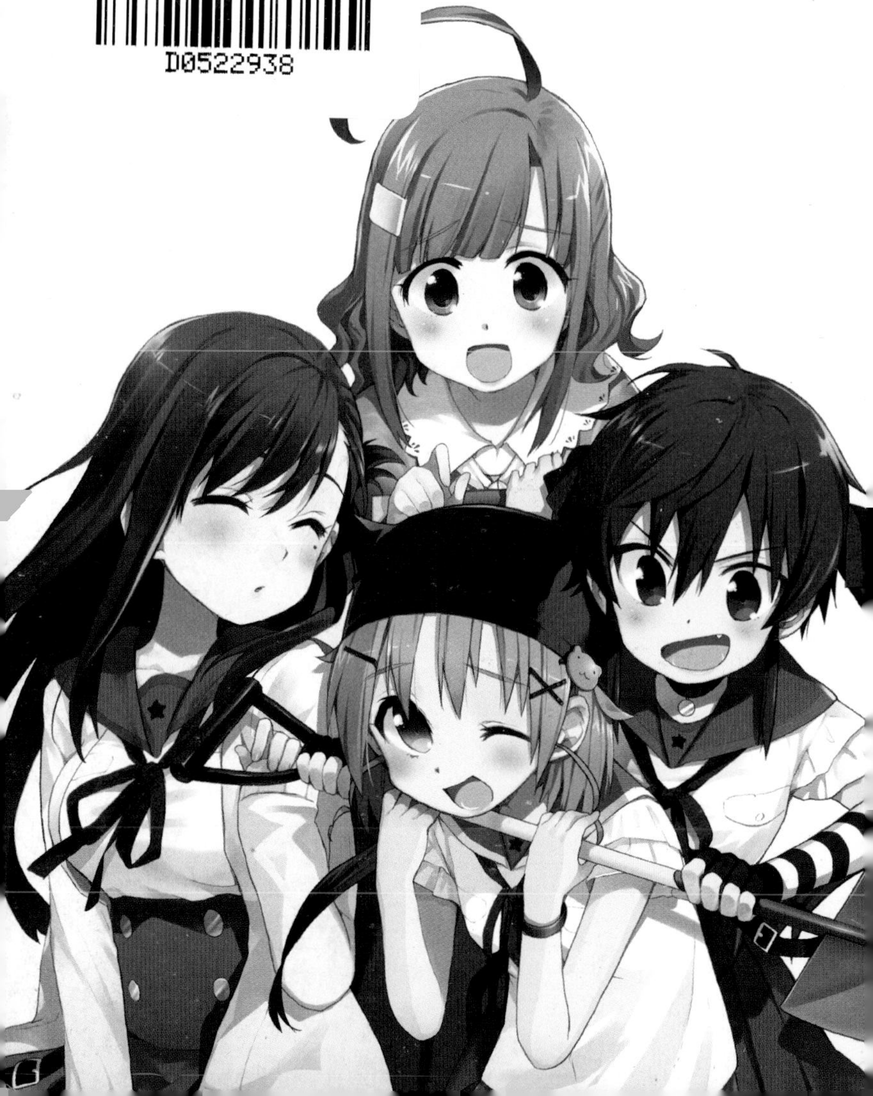

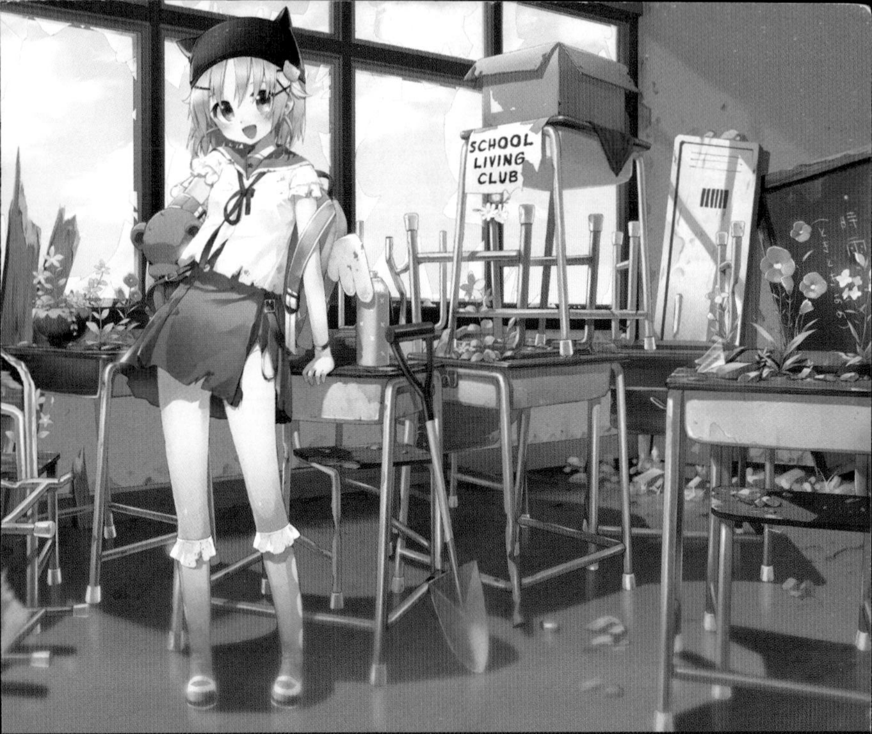
SCHOOL
LIVING
CLUB

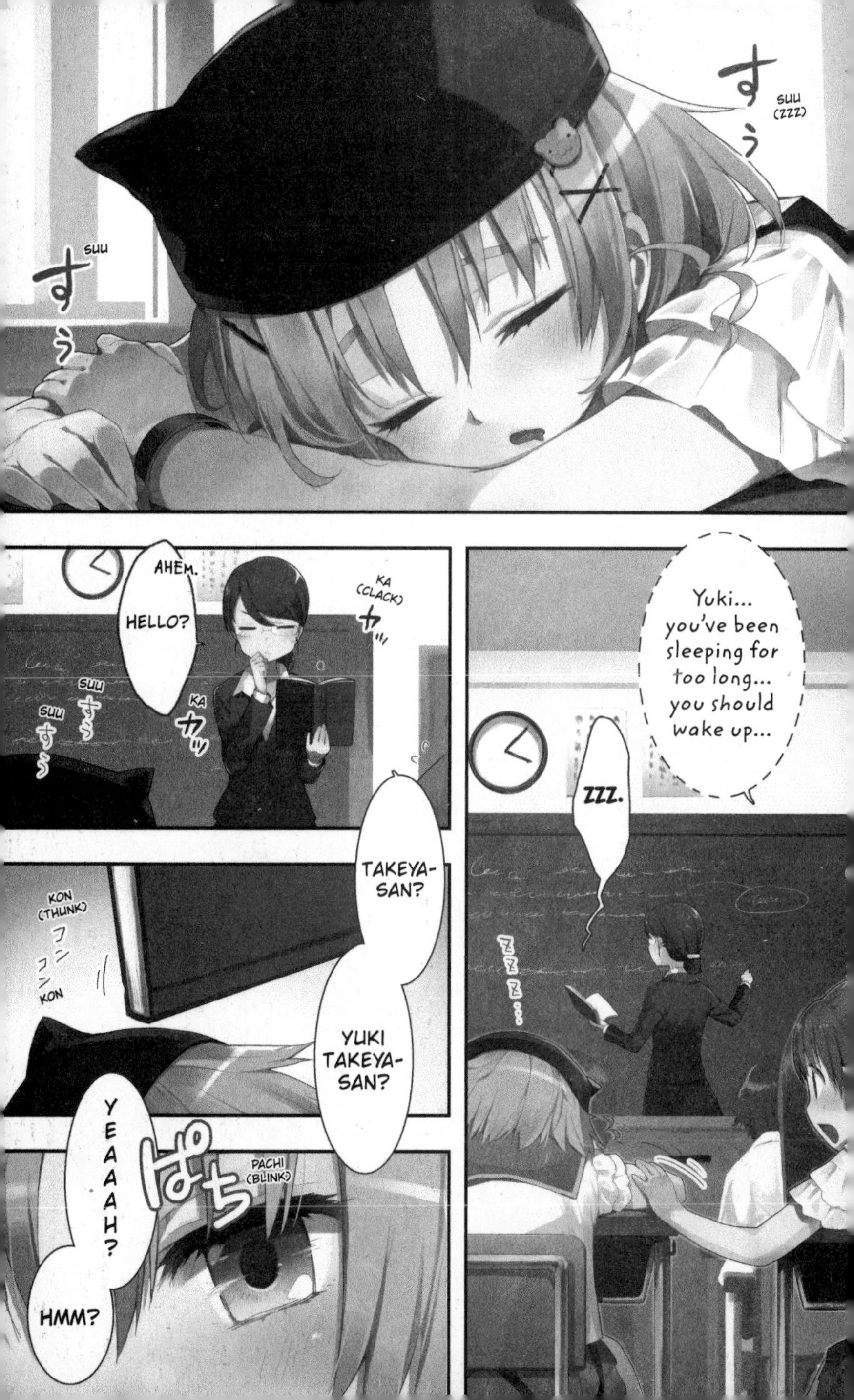

すう
SUU (ZZZ)
すう
SUU
Yuki... you've been sleeping for too long... you should wake up...
ZZZ.
ZZZ...
カ
KA (CLACK)
AHEM.
HELLO?
カッ
KA
すう
SUU
すう
SUU
TAKEYA-SAN?
YUKI TAKEYA-SAN?
コン
KON (THUNK)
コン
KON
ぱち
PACHI (BLINK)
YEAAAAH?
HMM?

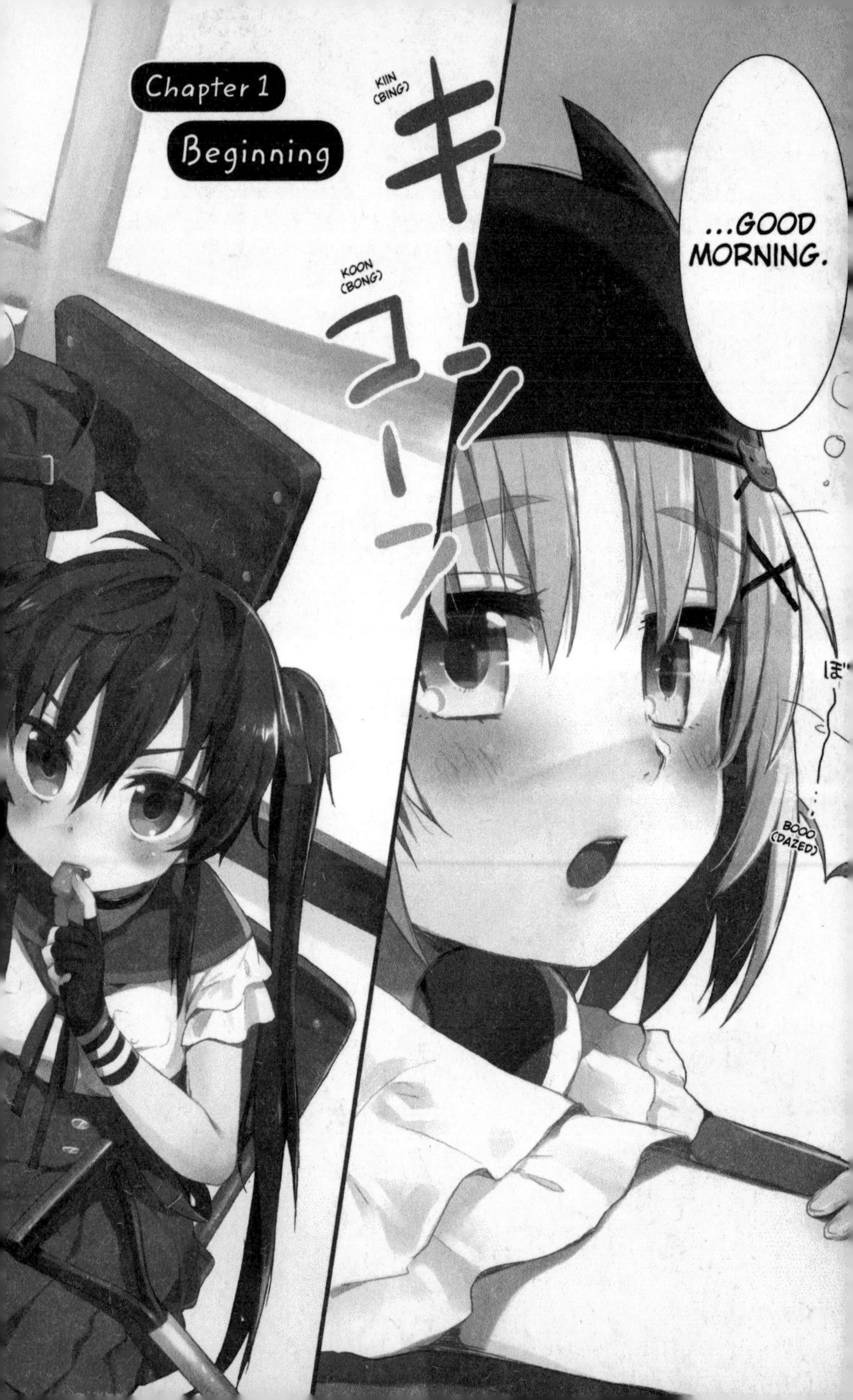
...GOOD MORNING.
ぼー
BOOO (DAZED)
KIIN (BING)
キーン
KOON (BONG)
コーン
Chapter 1
Beginning

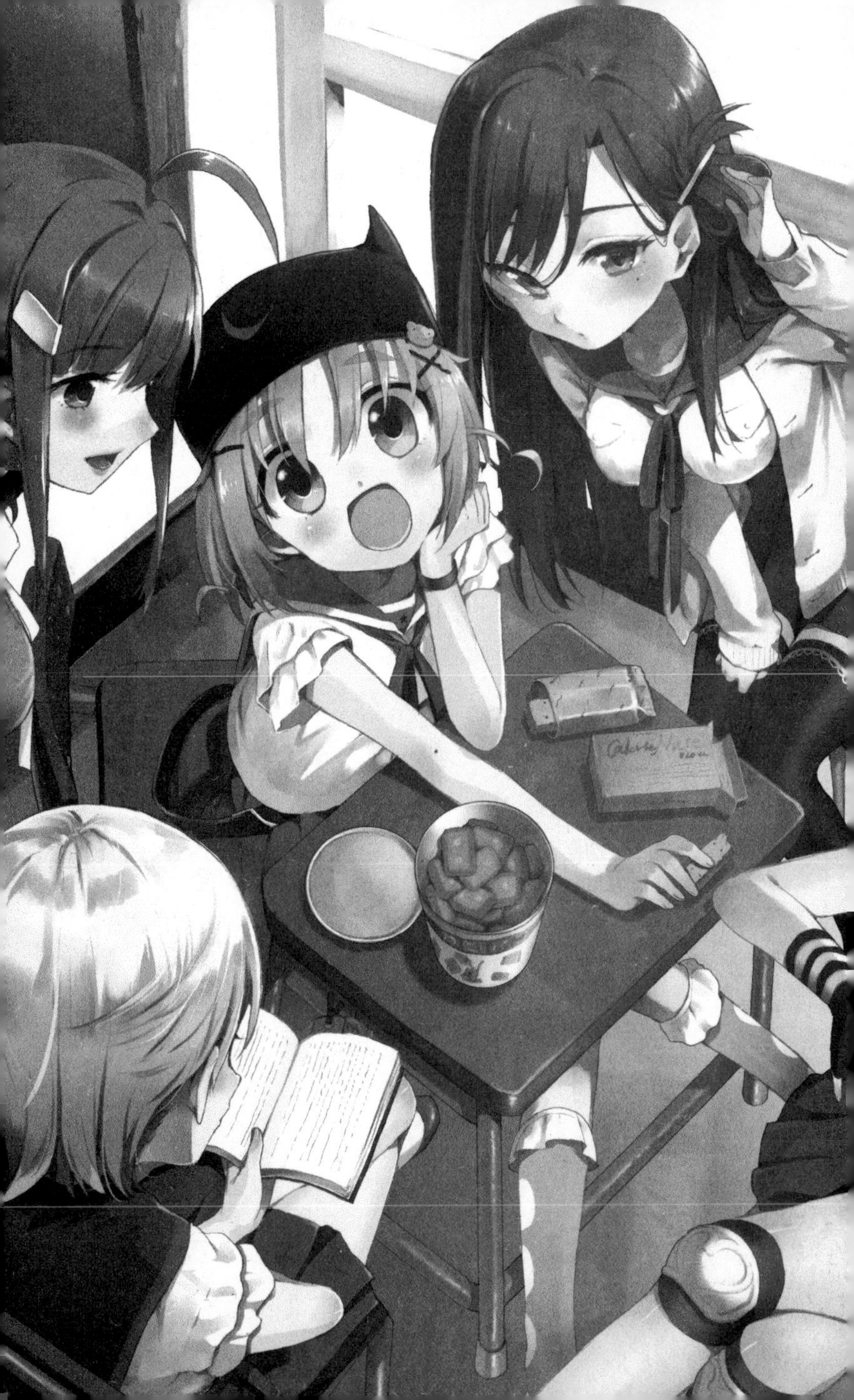

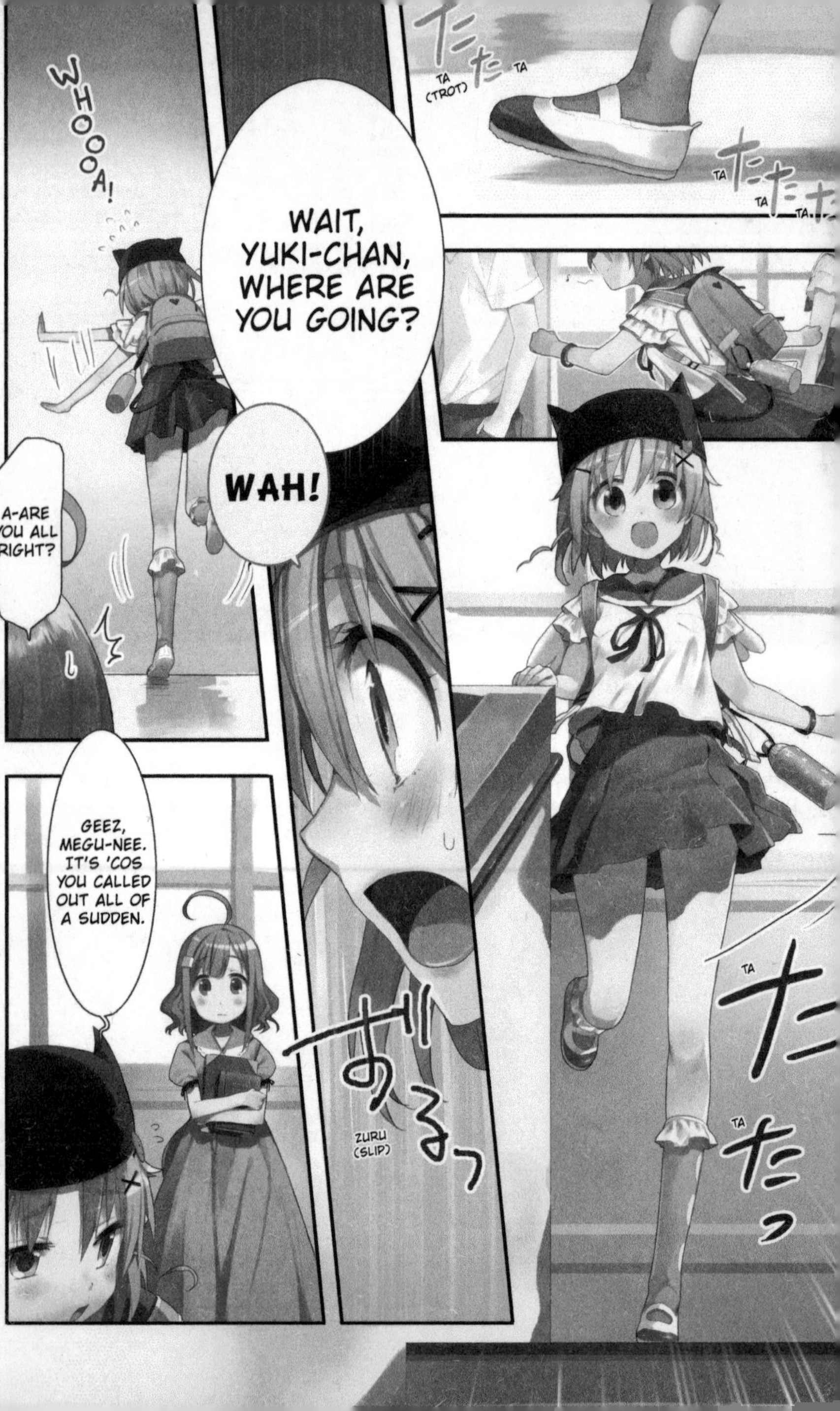
TA (TROT) TA
TA TA TA...
TA
TA
WAIT, YUKI-CHAN, WHERE ARE YOU GOING?
WAH!
ZURU (SLIP)
WHOOOA!
A-ARE YOU ALL RIGHT?
GEEZ, MEGU-NEE. IT'S 'COS YOU CALLED OUT ALL OF A SUDDEN.

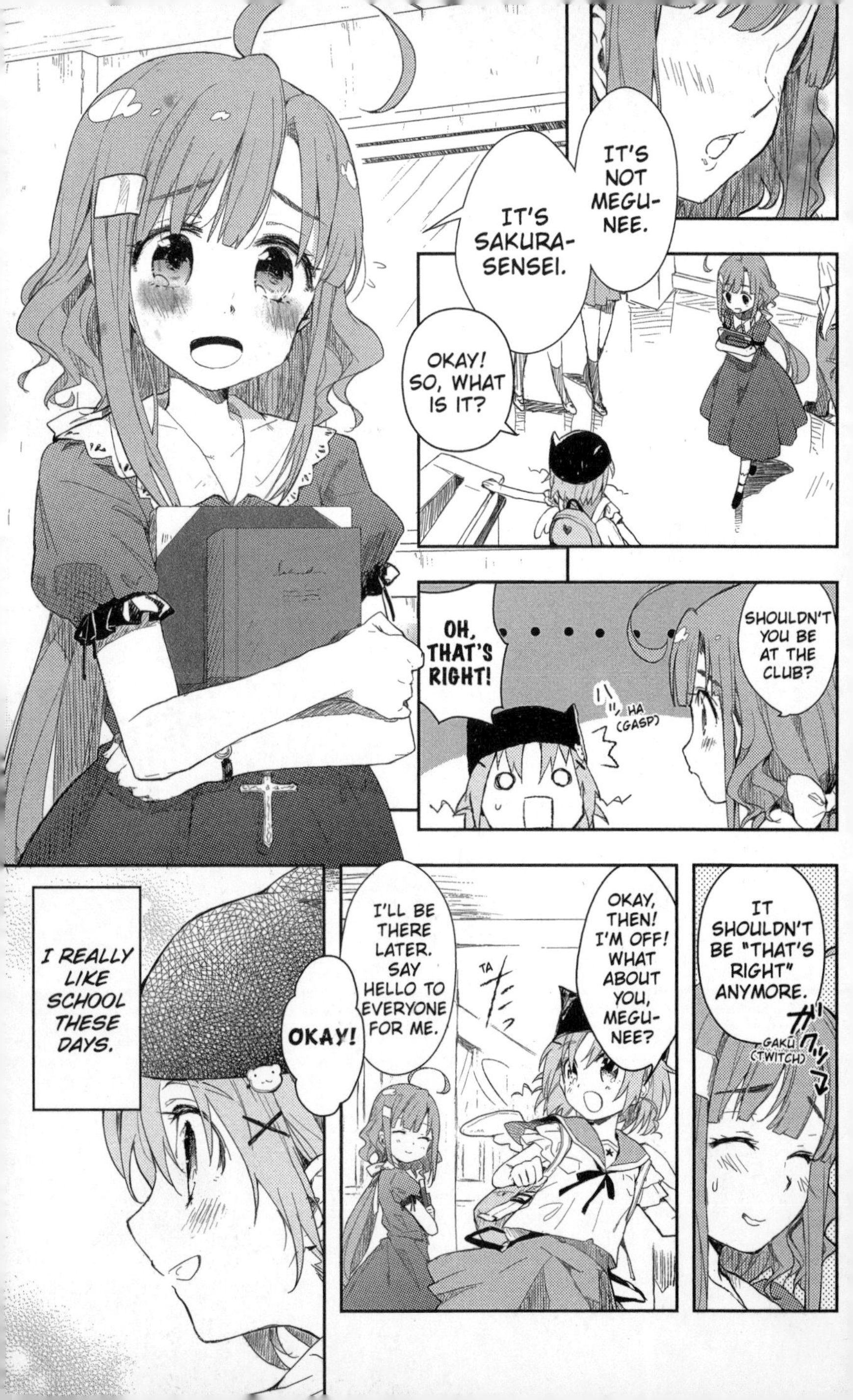
IT'S NOT MEGU-NEE.
IT'S SAKURA-SENSEI.
OKAY! SO, WHAT IS IT?
SHOULDN'T YOU BE AT THE CLUB?
. . . . . .
HA (GASP)
OH, THAT'S RIGHT!
IT SHOULDN'T BE "THAT'S RIGHT" ANYMORE.
GAKU (TWITCH)
OKAY, THEN! I'M OFF! WHAT ABOUT YOU, MEGU-NEE?
TA
I'LL BE THERE LATER. SAY HELLO TO EVERYONE FOR ME.
OKAY!
I REALLY LIKE SCHOOL THESE DAYS.

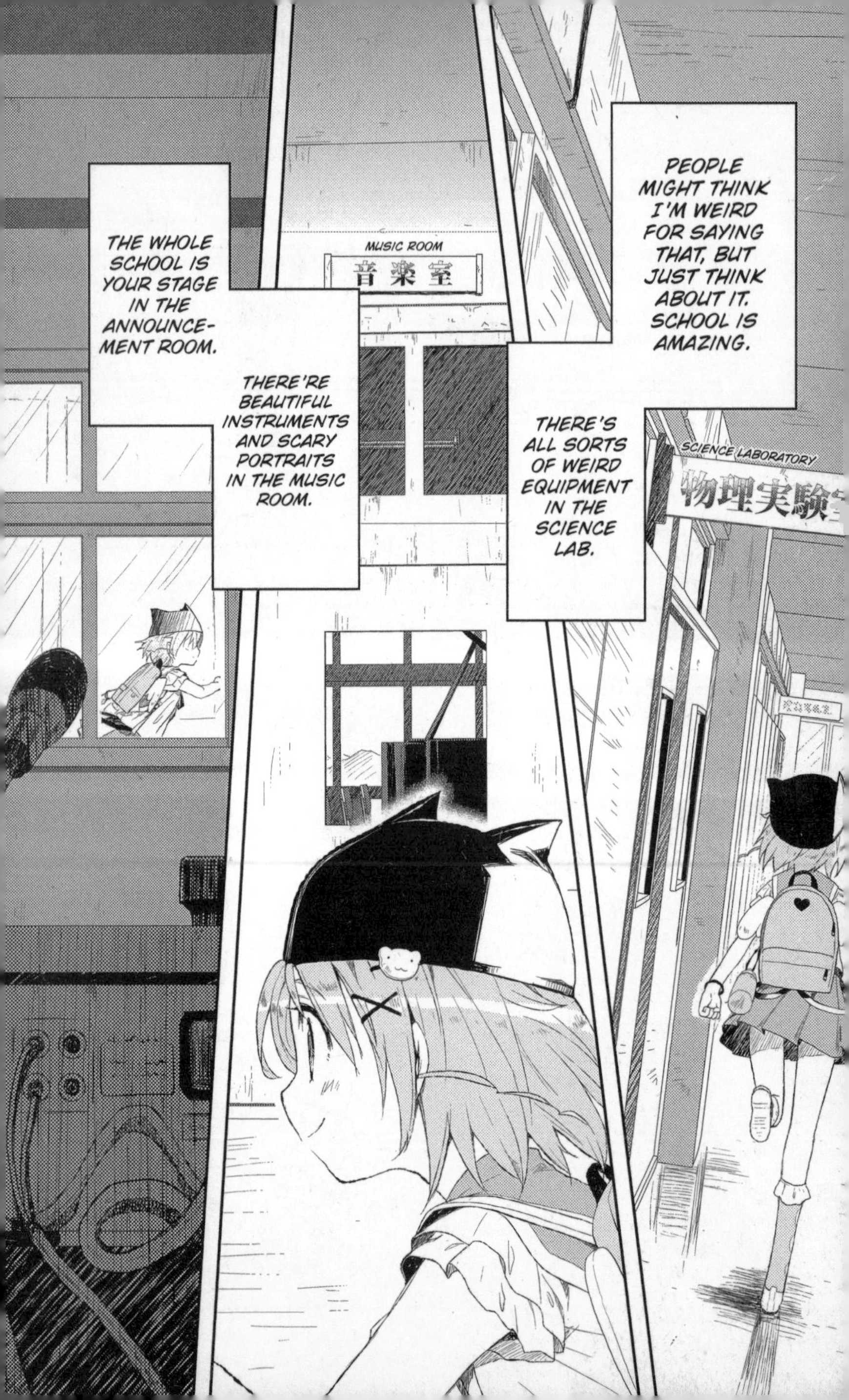
PEOPLE MIGHT THINK I'M WEIRD FOR SAYING THAT, BUT JUST THINK ABOUT IT. SCHOOL IS AMAZING.
SCIENCE LABORATORY
物理実験
THERE'S ALL SORTS OF WEIRD EQUIPMENT IN THE SCIENCE LAB.
MUSIC ROOM
音楽室
THERE'RE BEAUTIFUL INSTRUMENTS AND SCARY PORTRAITS IN THE MUSIC ROOM.
THE WHOLE SCHOOL IS YOUR STAGE IN THE ANNOUNCEMENT ROOM.

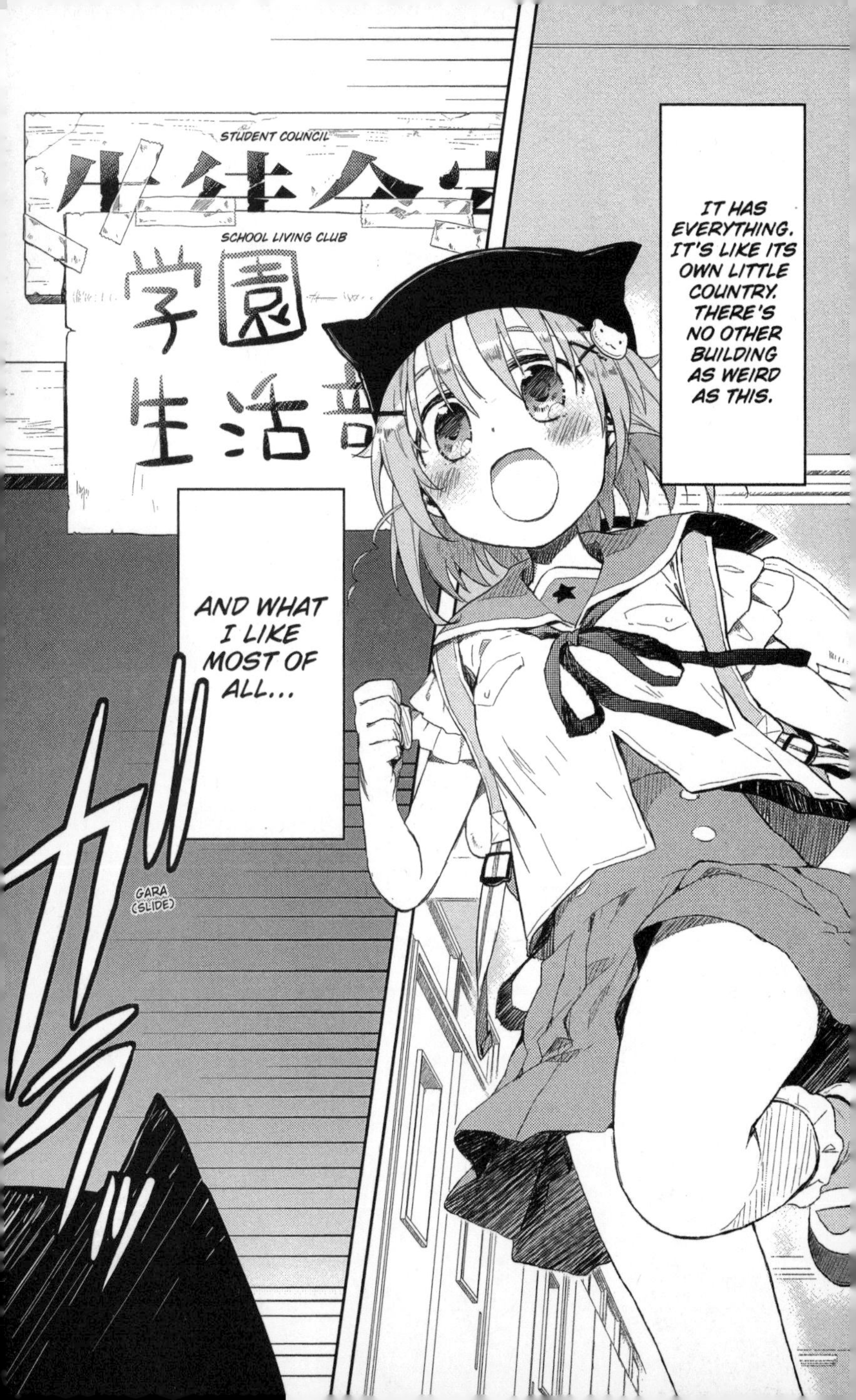

IT HAS EVERYTHING. IT'S LIKE ITS OWN LITTLE COUNTRY. THERE'S NO OTHER BUILDING AS WEIRD AS THIS.
STUDENT COUNCIL
SCHOOL LIVING CLUB
AND WHAT I LIKE MOST OF ALL...
GARA (SLIDE)

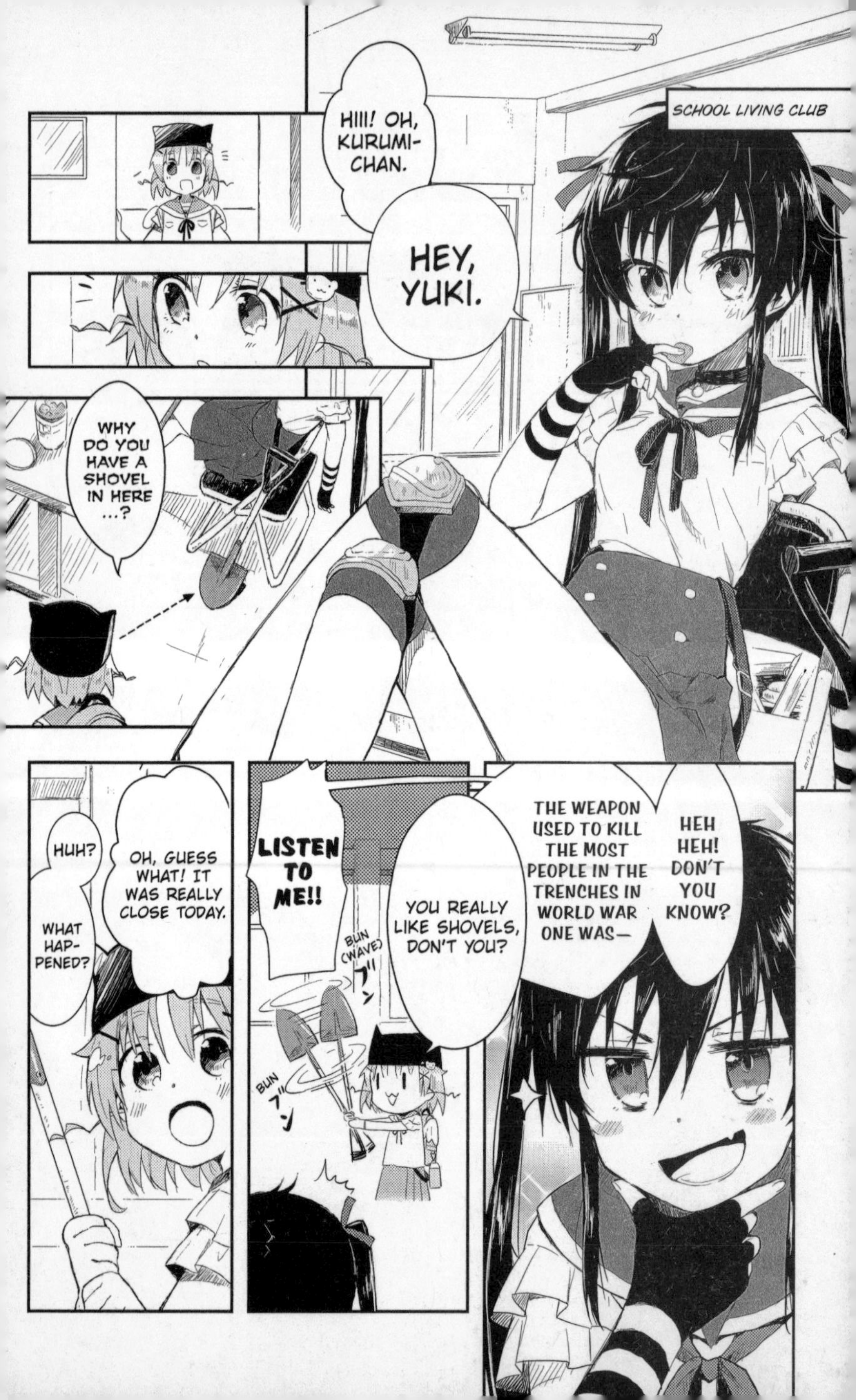
SCHOOL LIVING CLUB
HEY, YUKI.
HIII! OH, KURUMI-CHAN.
WHY DO YOU HAVE A SHOVEL IN HERE ...?
HEH HEH! DON'T YOU KNOW?
THE WEAPON USED TO KILL THE MOST PEOPLE IN THE TRENCHES IN WORLD WAR ONE WAS—
YOU REALLY LIKE SHOVELS, DON'T YOU?
BUN (WAVE) ブン
BUN ブン
LISTEN TO ME!!
OH, GUESS WHAT! IT WAS REALLY CLOSE TODAY.
HUH?
WHAT HAP-PENED?

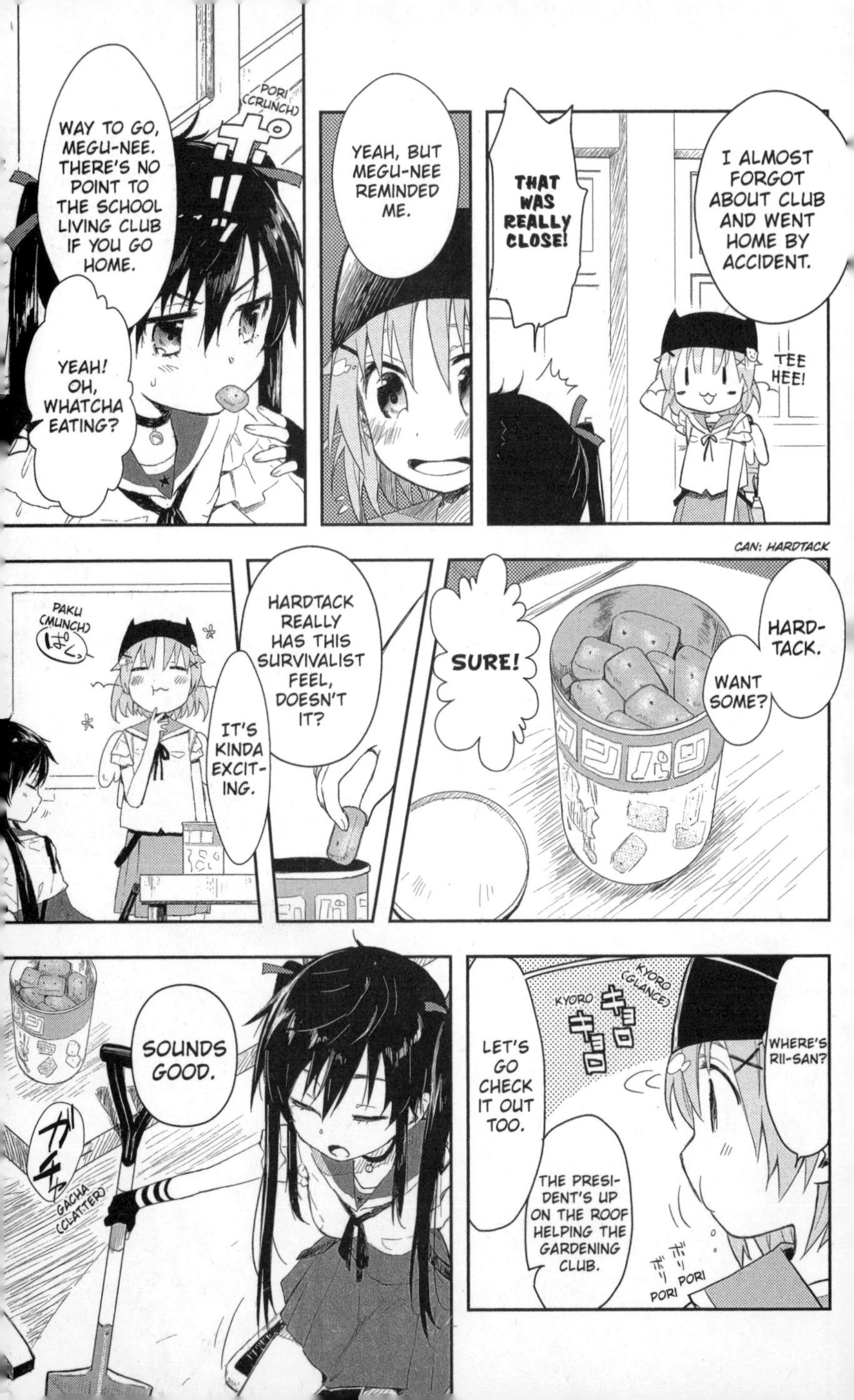
I ALMOST FORGOT ABOUT CLUB AND WENT HOME BY ACCIDENT.
THAT WAS REALLY CLOSE!
TEE HEE!
YEAH, BUT MEGU-NEE REMINDED ME.
PORI (CRUNCH)
WAY TO GO, MEGU-NEE. THERE'S NO POINT TO THE SCHOOL LIVING CLUB IF YOU GO HOME.
YEAH! OH, WHATCHA EATING?
CAN: HARDTACK
HARD-TACK.
WANT SOME?
SURE!
HARDTACK REALLY HAS THIS SURVIVALIST FEEL, DOESN'T IT?
IT'S KINDA EXCIT-ING.
PAKU (MUNCH)
KYORO (GLANCE)
KYORO
WHERE'S RII-SAN?
THE PRESI-DENT'S UP ON THE ROOF HELPING THE GARDENING CLUB.
PORI PORI
LET'S GO CHECK IT OUT TOO.
SOUNDS GOOD.
GACHA (CLATTER)

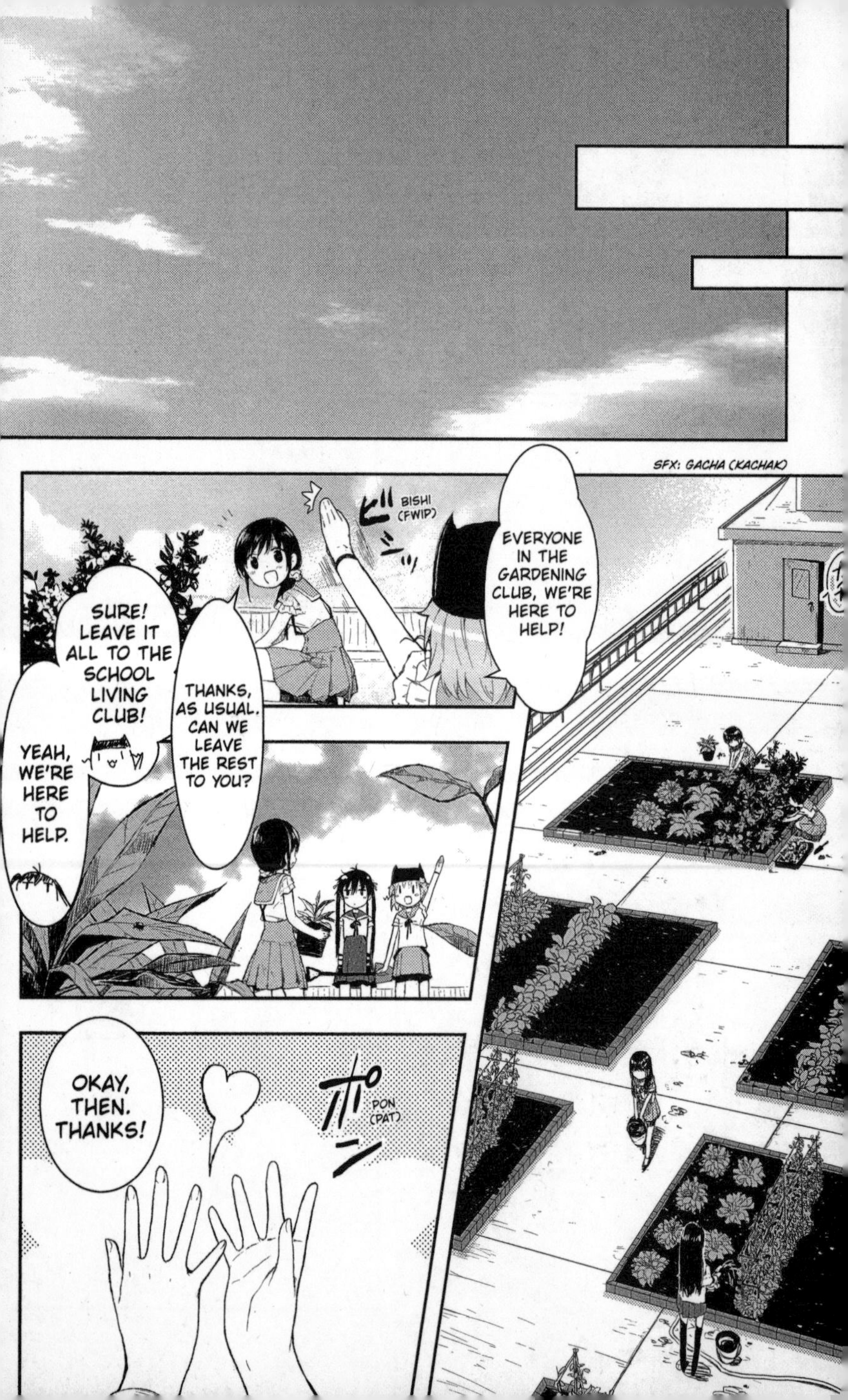
SFX: GACHA (KACHAK)
EVERYONE IN THE GARDENING CLUB, WE'RE HERE TO HELP!
BISHI (FWIP)
SURE! LEAVE IT ALL TO THE SCHOOL LIVING CLUB!
THANKS, AS USUAL. CAN WE LEAVE THE REST TO YOU?
YEAH, WE'RE HERE TO HELP.
PON (PAT)
OKAY, THEN. THANKS!

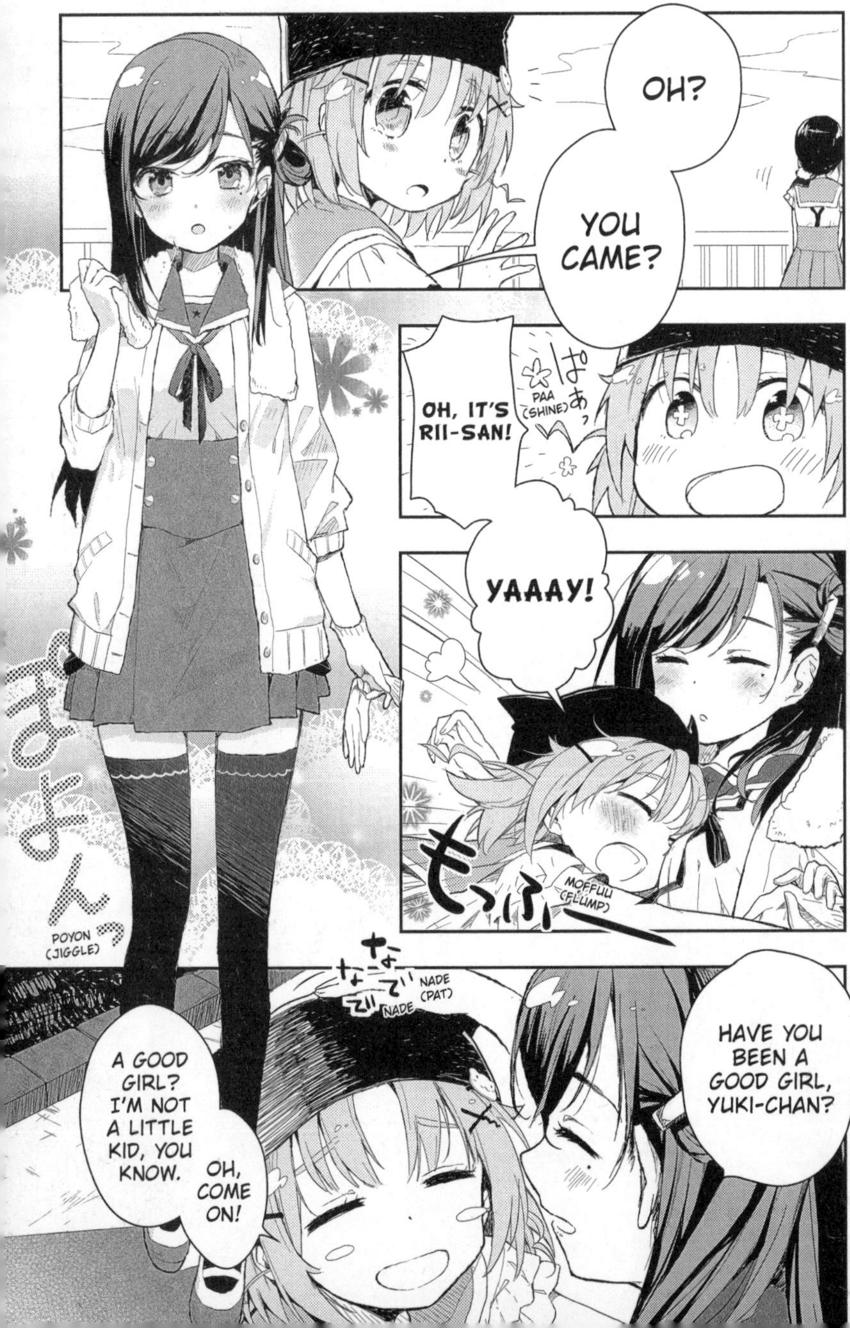
OH? YOU CAME?
ぱあ
PAA (SHINE)
OH, IT'S RII-SAN!
YAAAY!
もふっ
MOFFUU (FLUMP)
ぽよん
POYON (JIGGLE)
HAVE YOU BEEN A GOOD GIRL, YUKI-CHAN?
なでなで
NADE (PAT) NADE
A GOOD GIRL? I'M NOT A LITTLE KID, YOU KNOW.
OH, COME ON!

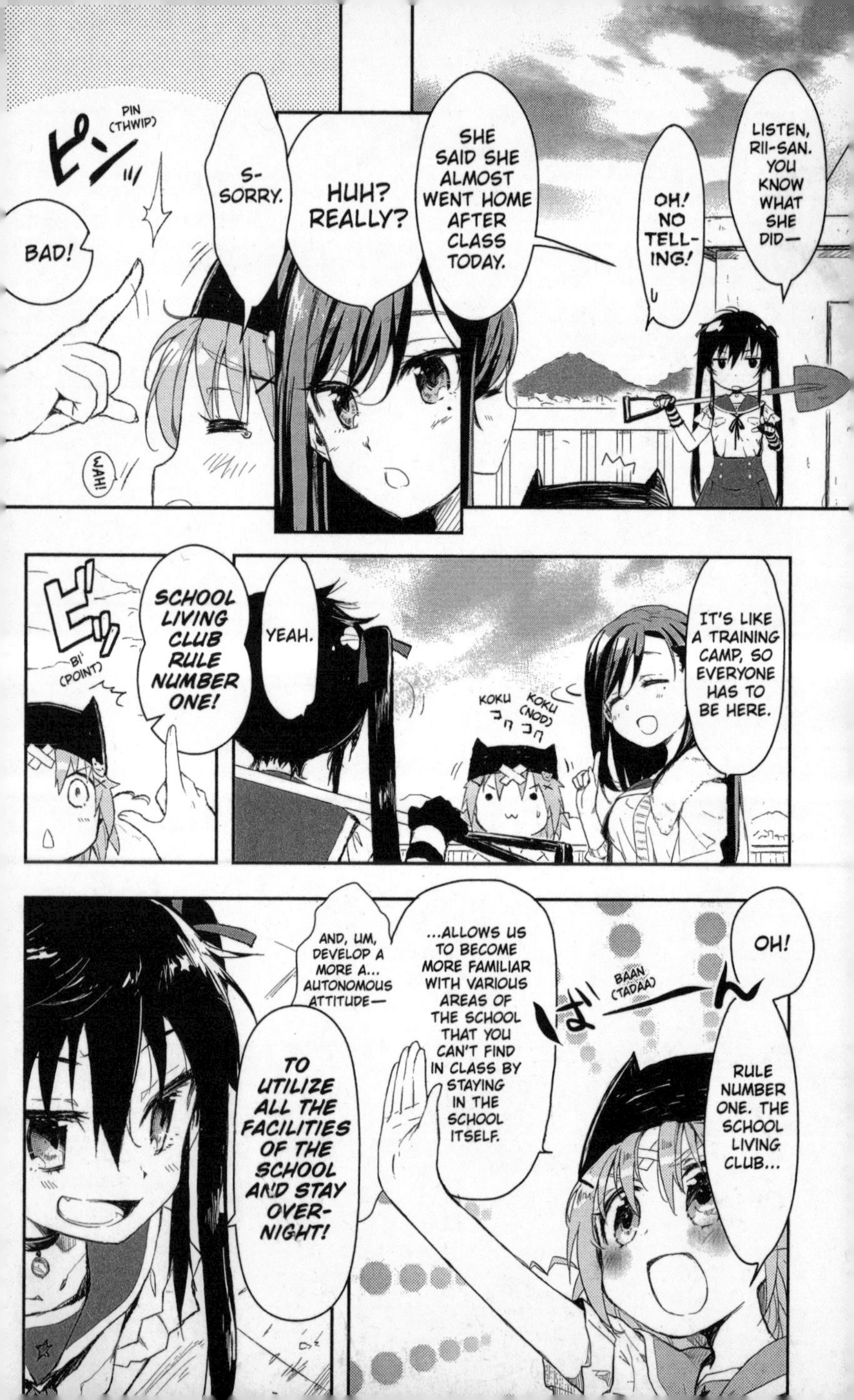
LISTEN, RII-SAN. YOU KNOW WHAT SHE DID—
OH! NO TELLING!
SHE SAID SHE ALMOST WENT HOME AFTER CLASS TODAY.
HUH? REALLY?
S-SORRY.
PIN (THWIP)
BAD!
WAH!
IT'S LIKE A TRAINING CAMP, SO EVERYONE HAS TO BE HERE.
KOKU KOKU (NOD)
YEAH.
SCHOOL LIVING CLUB RULE NUMBER ONE!
BI (POINT)
OH!
BAAN (TADAA)
RULE NUMBER ONE. THE SCHOOL LIVING CLUB...
...ALLOWS US TO BECOME MORE FAMILIAR WITH VARIOUS AREAS OF THE SCHOOL THAT YOU CAN'T FIND IN CLASS BY STAYING IN THE SCHOOL ITSELF.
AND, UM, DEVELOP A MORE A... AUTONOMOUS ATTITUDE—
TO UTILIZE ALL THE FACILITIES OF THE SCHOOL AND STAY OVER-NIGHT!

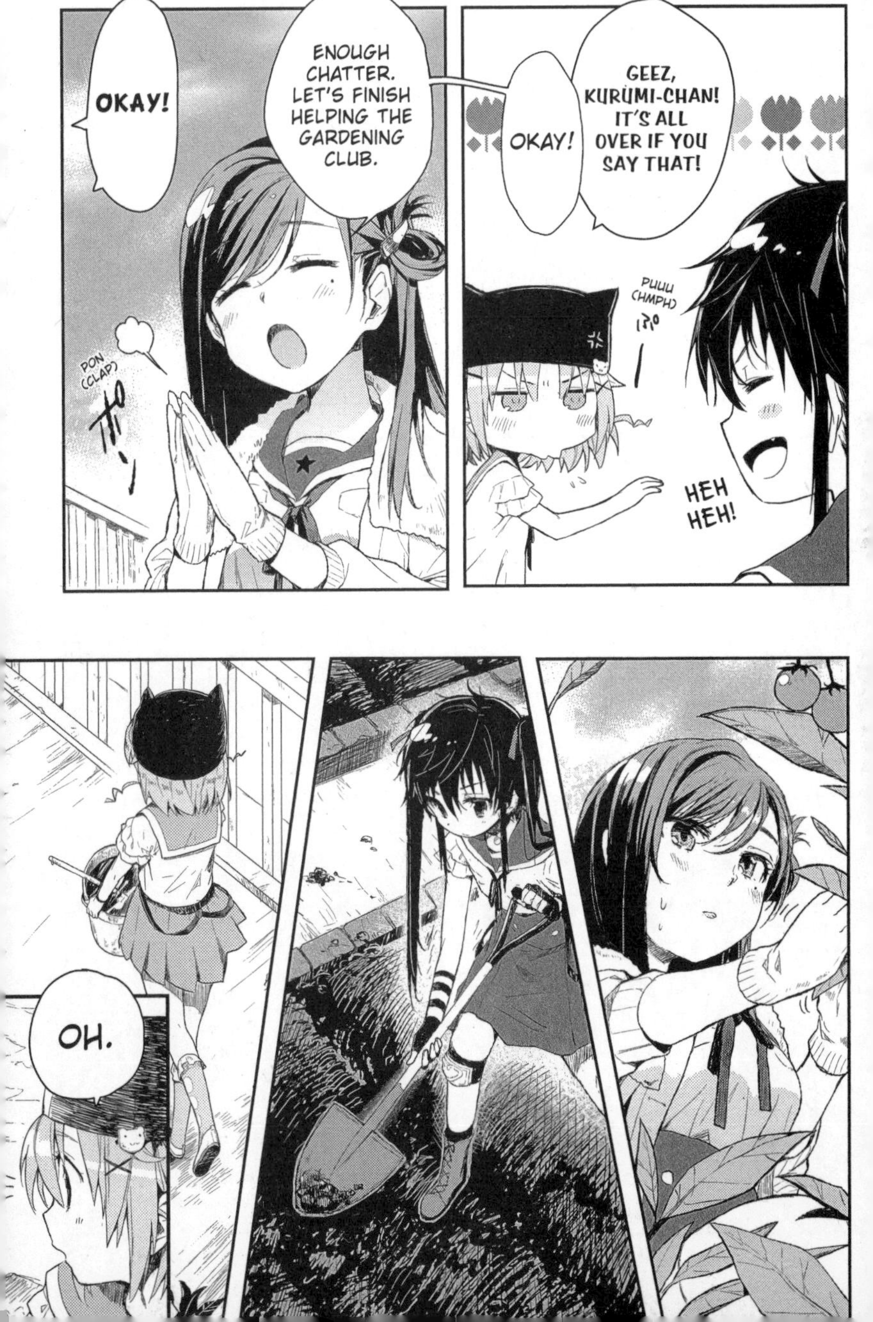
GEEZ, KURUMI-CHAN! IT'S ALL OVER IF YOU SAY THAT!
OKAY!
PUUU (HMPH)
HEH HEH!
ENOUGH CHATTER. LET'S FINISH HELPING THE GARDENING CLUB.
OKAY!
PON (CLAP)
OH.

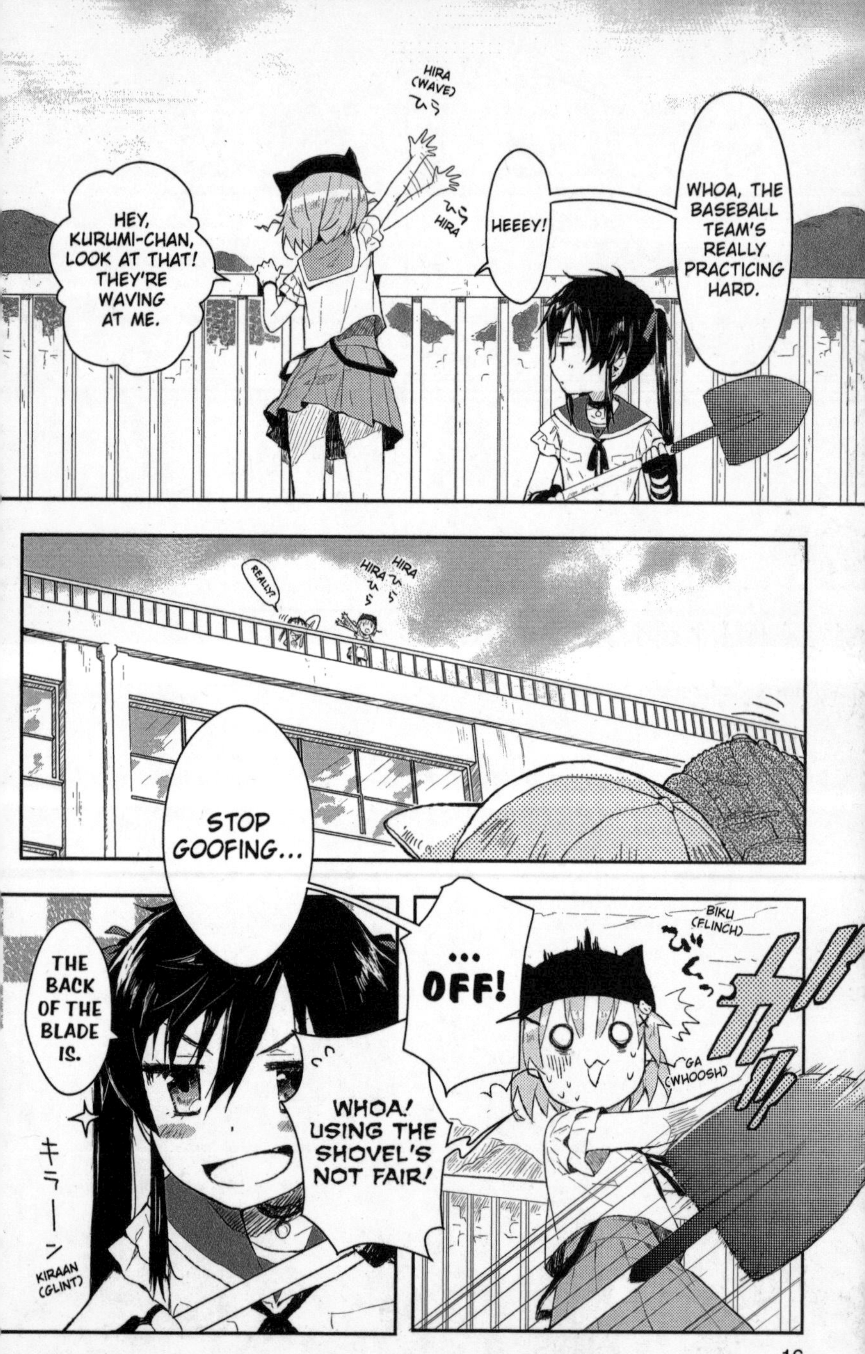
WHOA, THE BASEBALL TEAM'S REALLY PRACTICING HARD.
HEEEY!
HIRA (WAVE) ひら
ひら HIRA
HEY, KURUMI-CHAN, LOOK AT THAT! THEY'RE WAVING AT ME.
HIRA ひら
HIRA ひら
REALLY?
STOP GOOFING...
BIKU (FLINCH) びくっ
... OFF!
GA (WHOOSH)
WHOA! USING THE SHOVEL'S NOT FAIR!
THE BACK OF THE BLADE IS.
キラーン KIRAAN (GLINT)

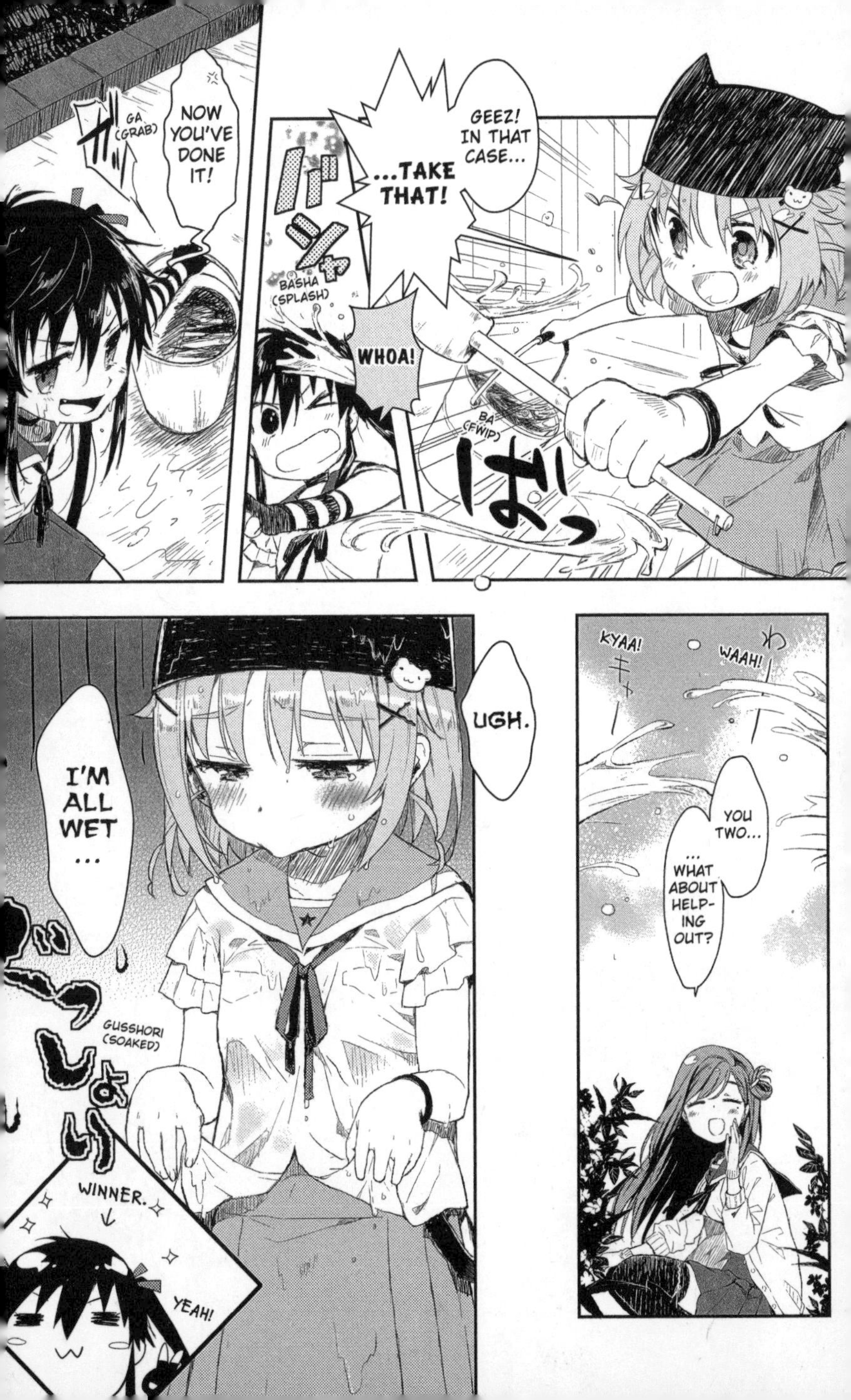
GEEZ! IN THAT CASE...
...TAKE THAT!
BA (FWIP)
BASHA (SPLASH)
WHOA!
GA (GRAB)
NOW YOU'VE DONE IT!
KYAA!
WAAH!
YOU TWO...
...WHAT ABOUT HELPING OUT?
UGH.
I'M ALL WET...
GUSSHORI (SOAKED)
WINNER.
YEAH!

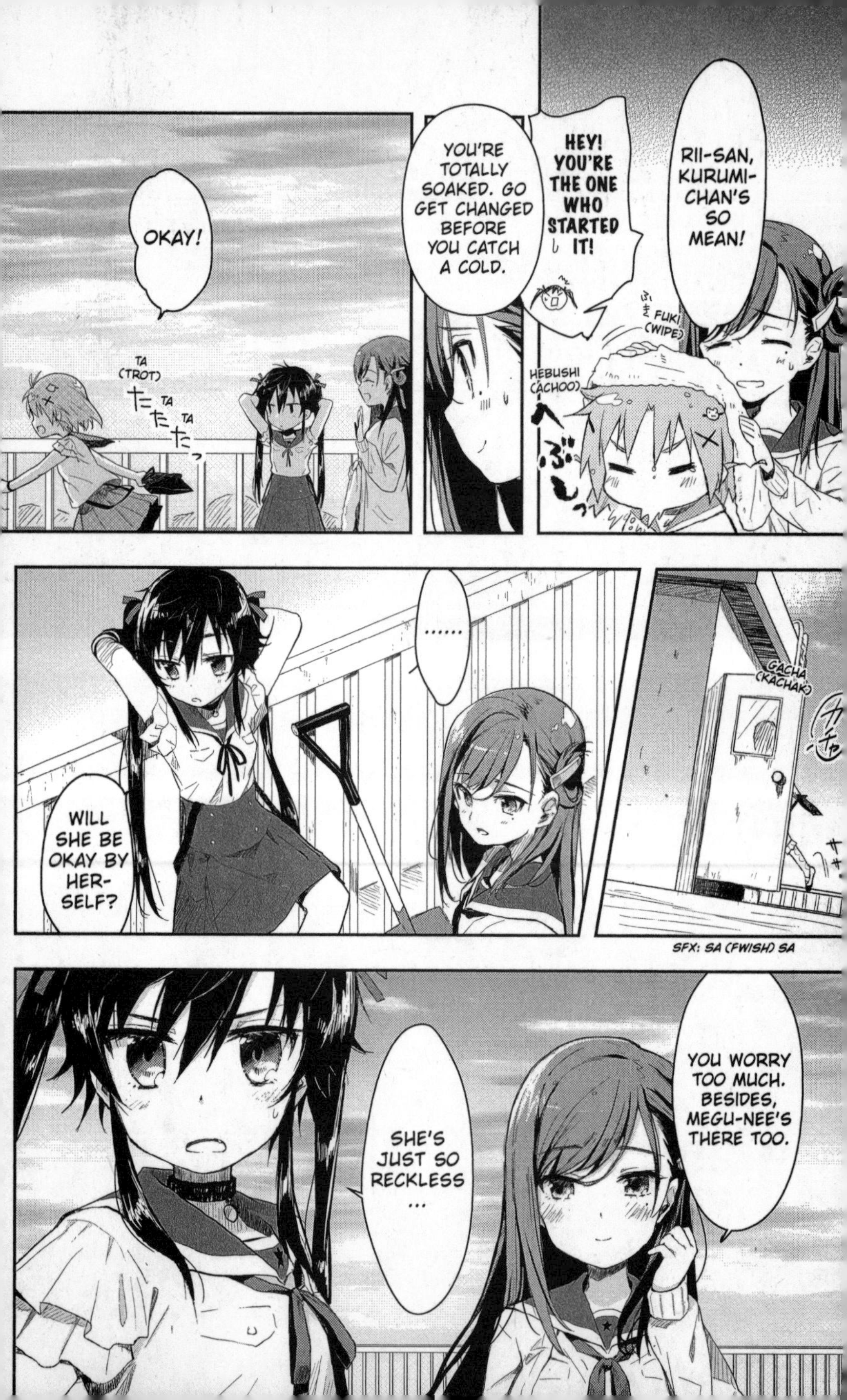
RII-SAN, KURUMI-CHAN'S SO MEAN!
HEY! YOU'RE THE ONE WHO STARTED IT!
FUKI (WIPE)
HEBUSHI (ACHOO)
YOU'RE TOTALLY SOAKED. GO GET CHANGED BEFORE YOU CATCH A COLD.
OKAY!
TA (TROT) TA TA
GACHA (KACHAK)
SFX: SA (FWISH) SA
......
WILL SHE BE OKAY BY HER-SELF?
YOU WORRY TOO MUCH. BESIDES, MEGU-NEE'S THERE TOO.
SHE'S JUST SO RECKLESS ...

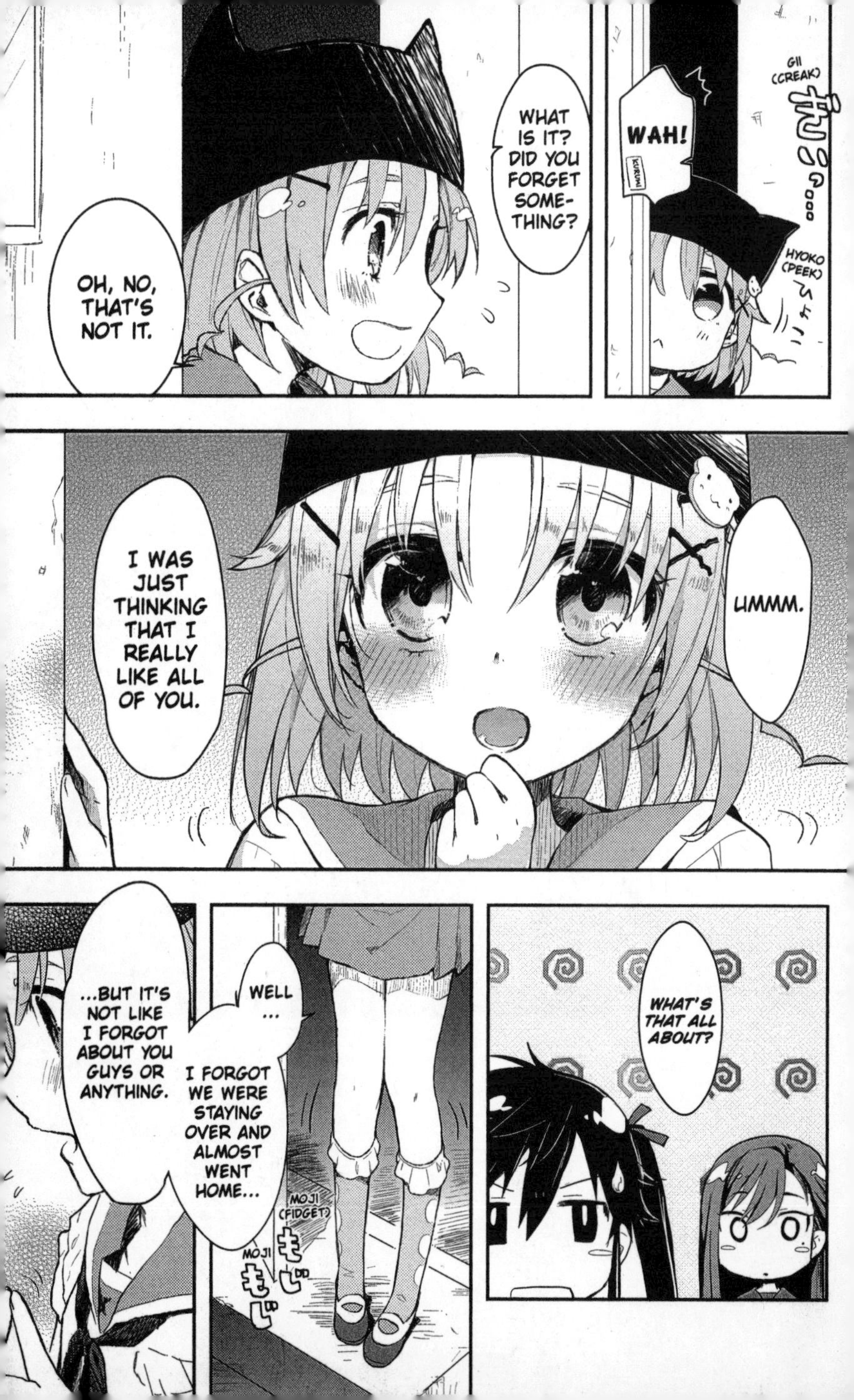
GII (CREAK)
ぎぃぃ…
WAH!
KURUMI
HYOKO (PEEK)
ひょこ
WHAT IS IT? DID YOU FORGET SOME-THING?
OH, NO, THAT'S NOT IT.
UMMM.
I WAS JUST THINKING THAT I REALLY LIKE ALL OF YOU.
WHAT'S THAT ALL ABOUT?
WELL...
I FORGOT WE WERE STAYING OVER AND ALMOST WENT HOME...
MOJI (FIDGET)
もじ
MOJI
もじ
...BUT IT'S NOT LIKE I FORGOT ABOUT YOU GUYS OR ANYTHING.

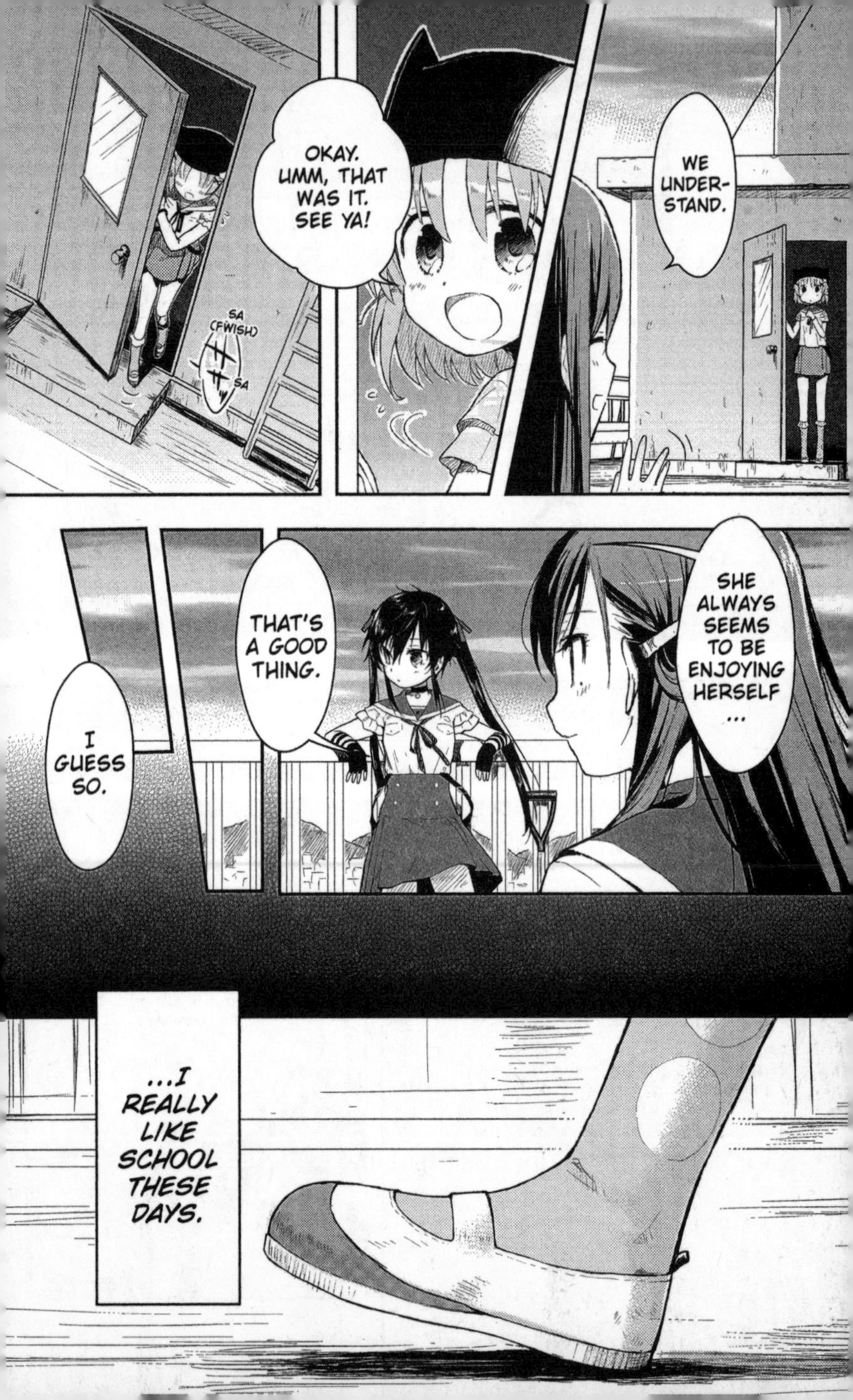
WE UNDER-STAND.
OKAY. UMM, THAT WAS IT. SEE YA!
SA (FWISH)
SA
SHE ALWAYS SEEMS TO BE ENJOYING HERSELF ...
THAT'S A GOOD THING.
I GUESS SO.
...I REALLY LIKE SCHOOL THESE DAYS.

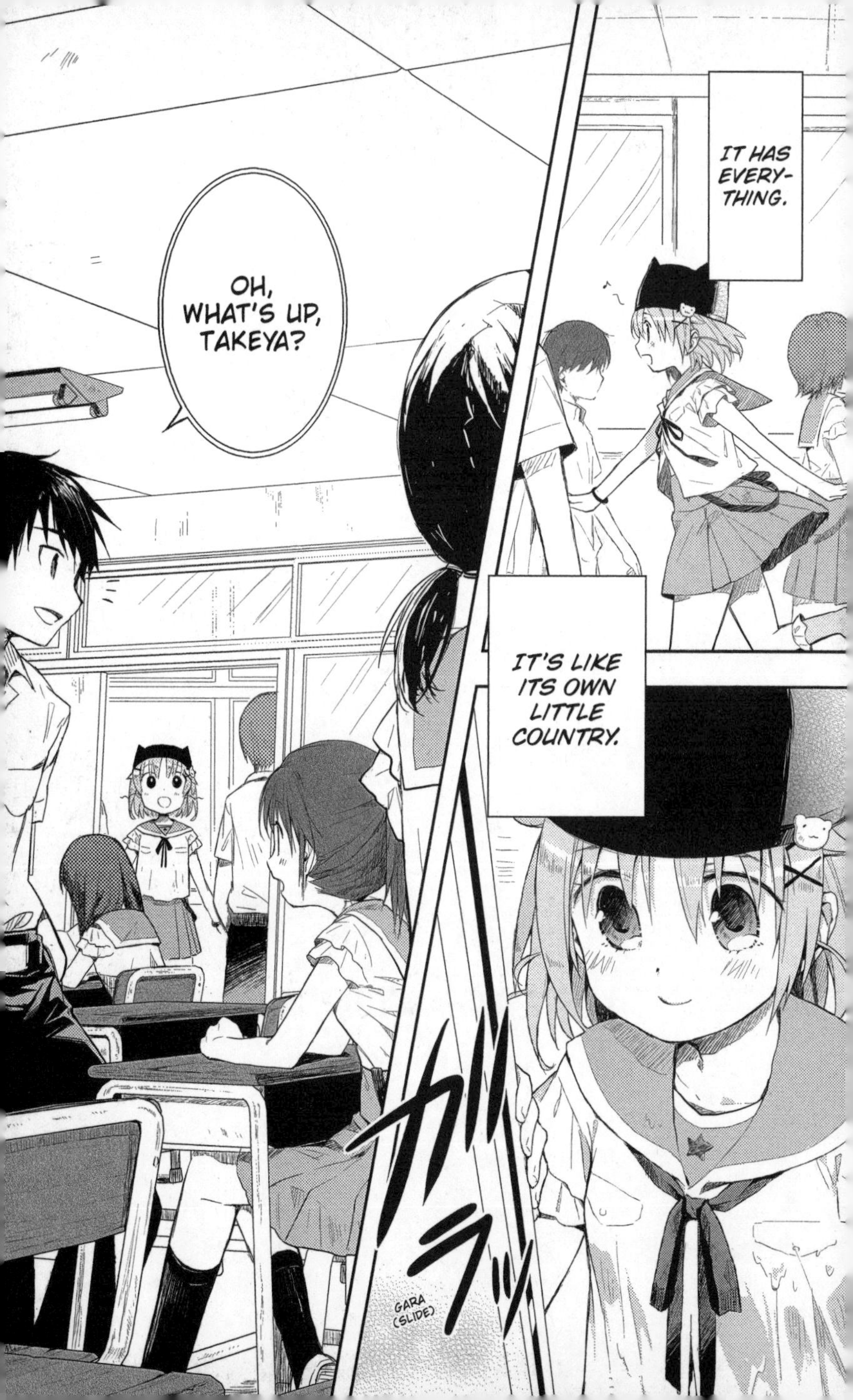
IT HAS EVERY-THING.
IT'S LIKE ITS OWN LITTLE COUNTRY.
OH, WHAT'S UP, TAKEYA?
GARA (SLIDE)

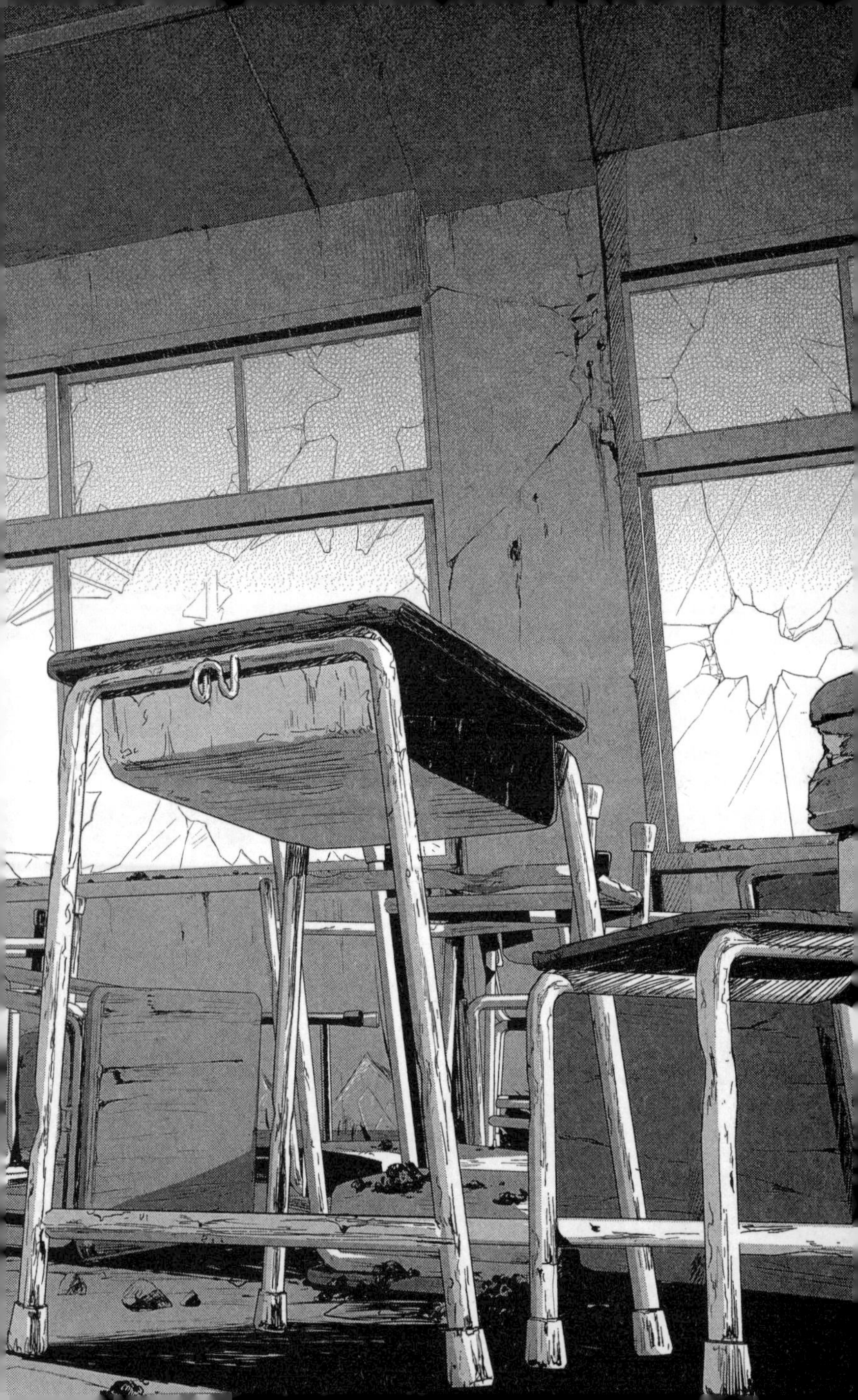

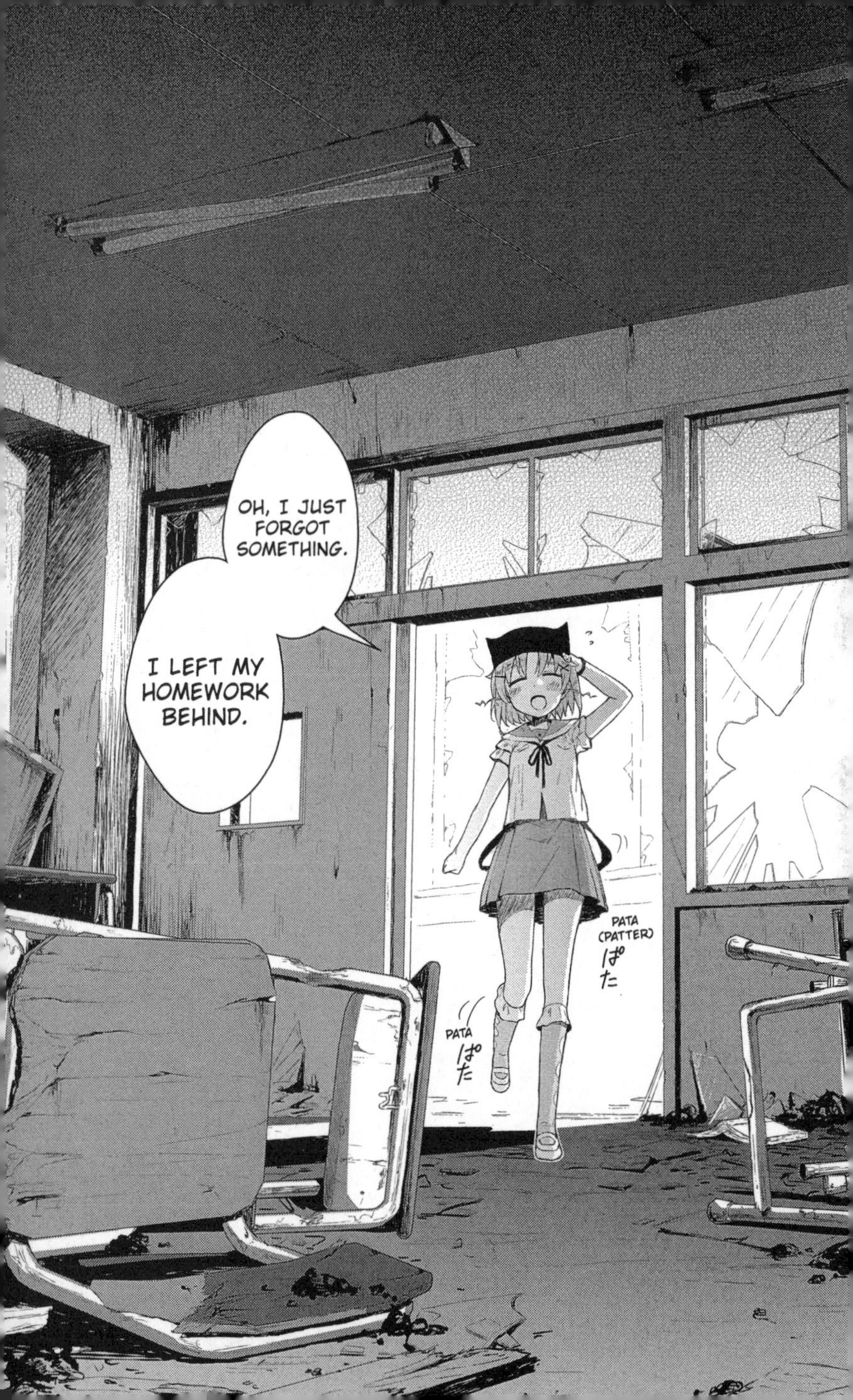
OH, I JUST FORGOT SOMETHING.
I LEFT MY HOMEWORK BEHIND.
PATA (PATTER) ぱた
PATA ぱた

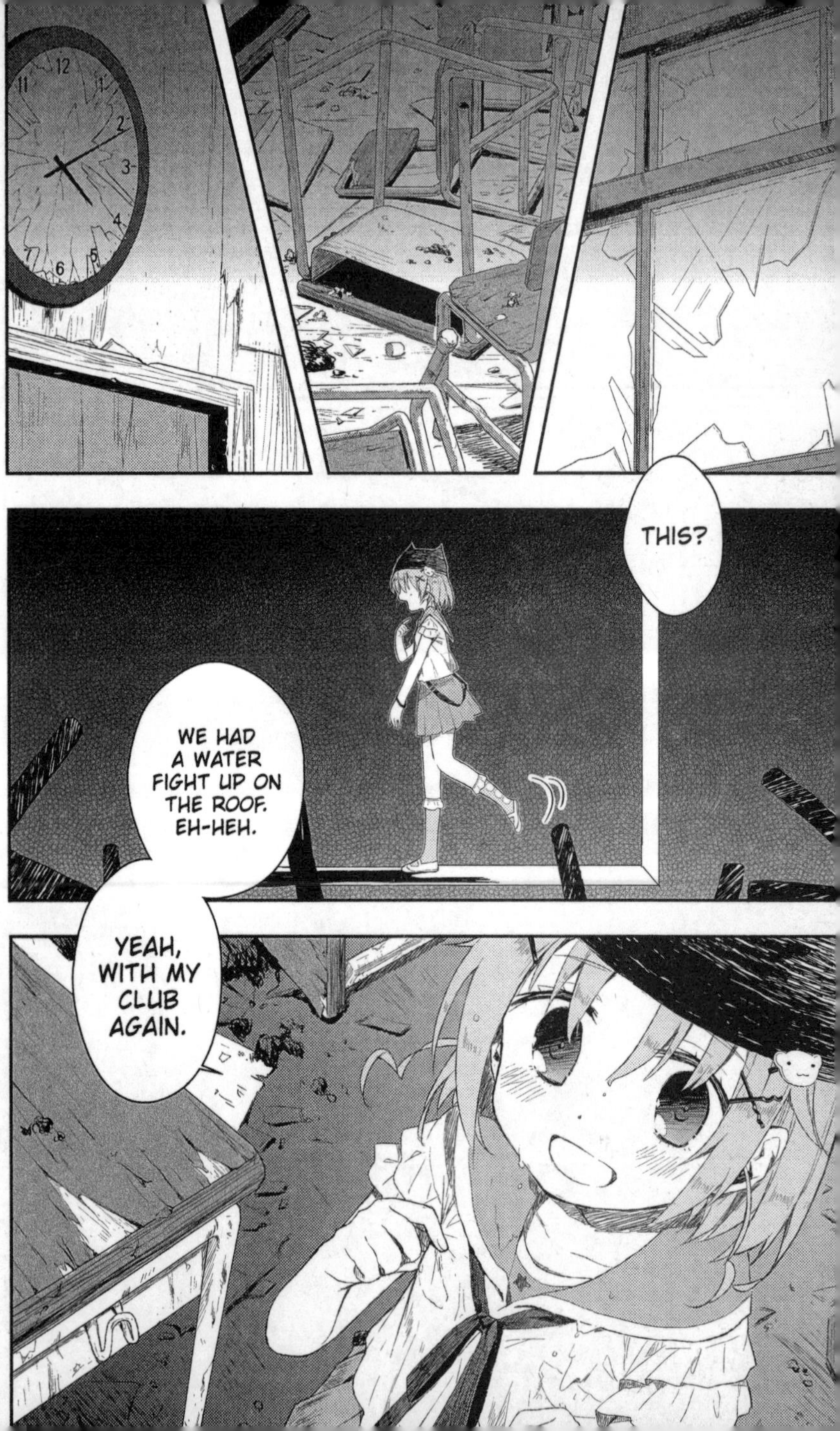
THIS?
WE HAD A WATER FIGHT UP ON THE ROOF. EH-HEH.
YEAH, WITH MY CLUB AGAIN.

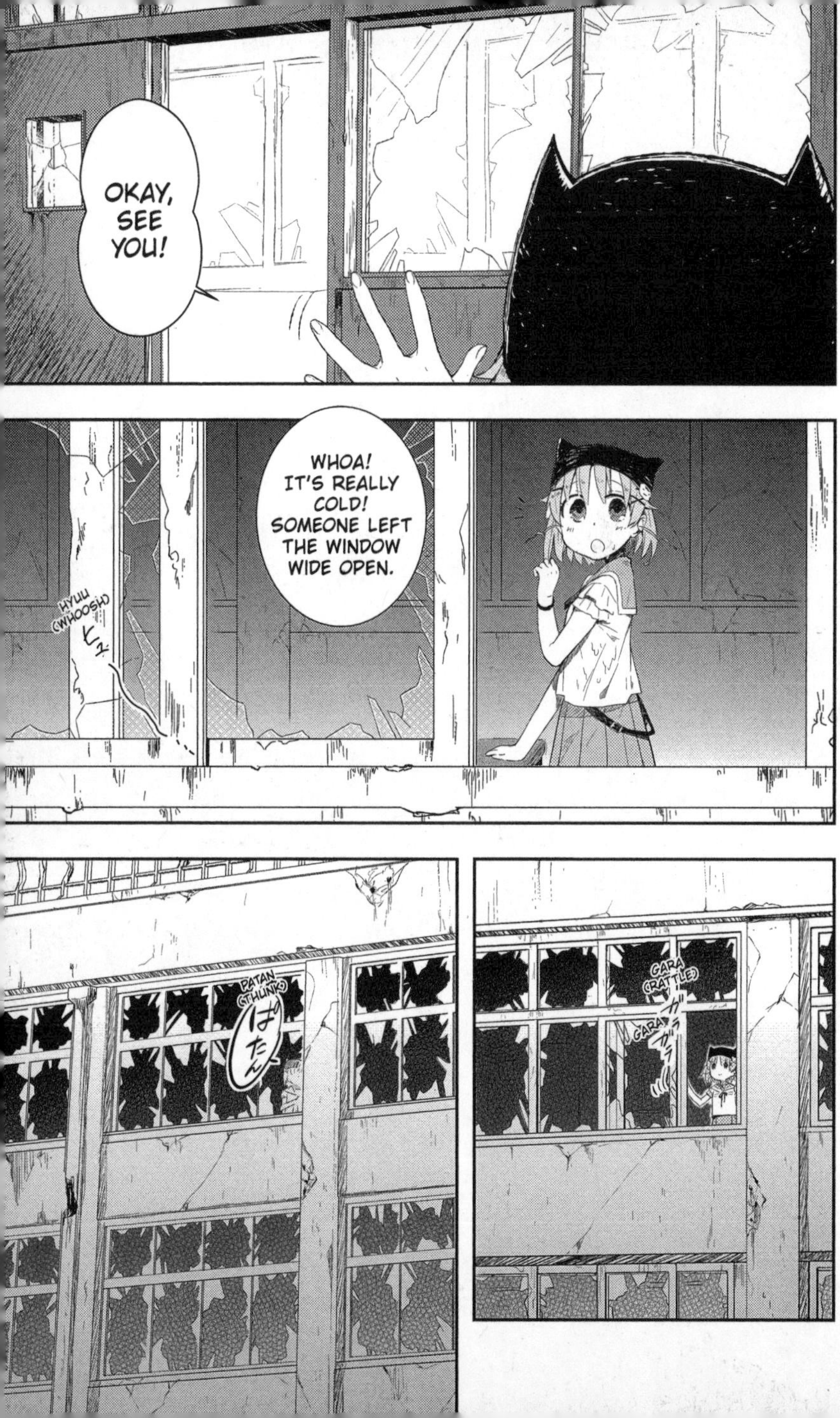
OKAY, SEE YOU!
WHOA! IT'S REALLY COLD! SOMEONE LEFT THE WINDOW WIDE OPEN.
HYUU (WHOOSH)
ヒュ
GARA (RATTLE)
ガラ
GARA
ガラ
PATAN (THUNK)
ぱたん

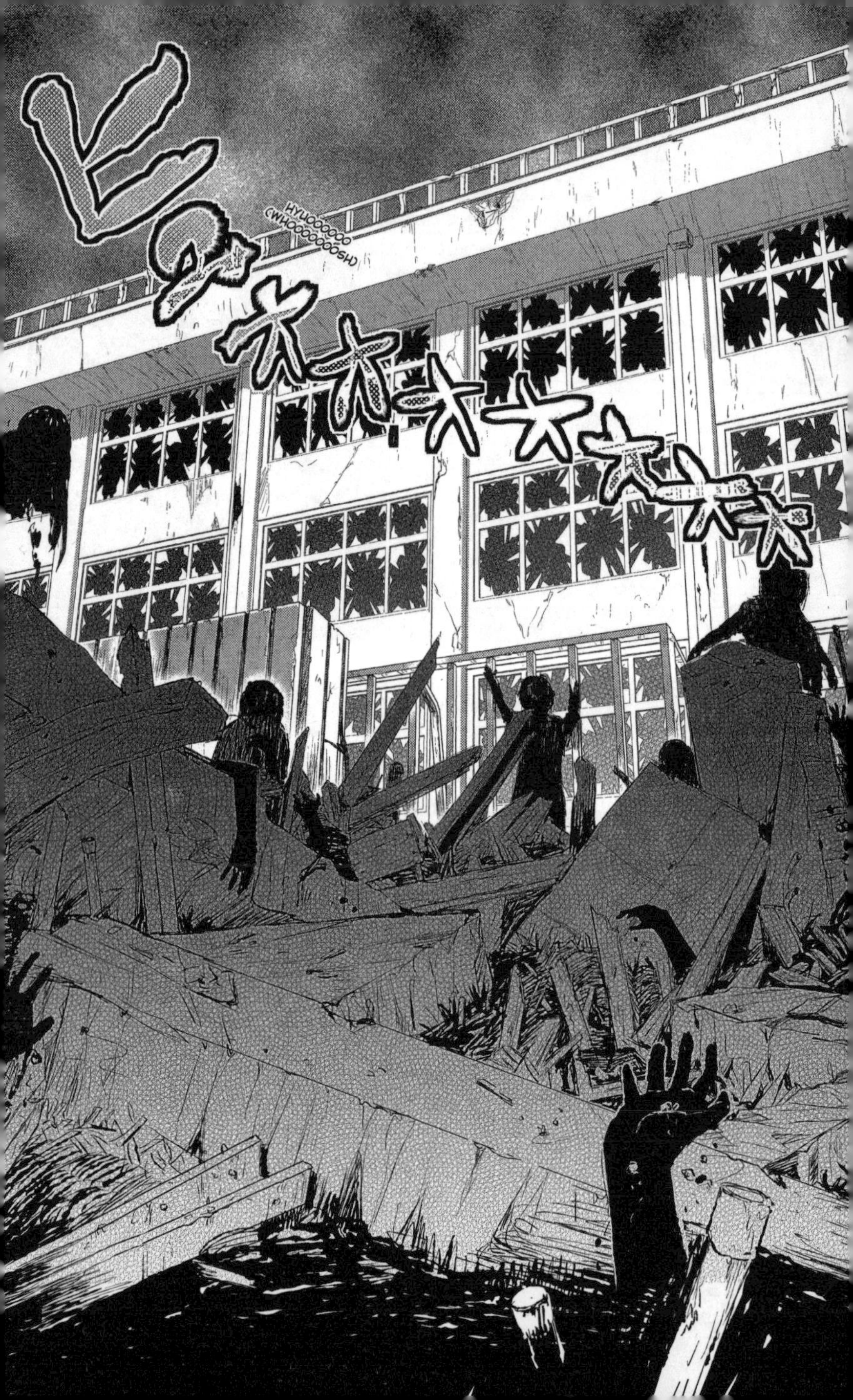
HYUOOOOOOO
(WHOOOOOOOOOSH)

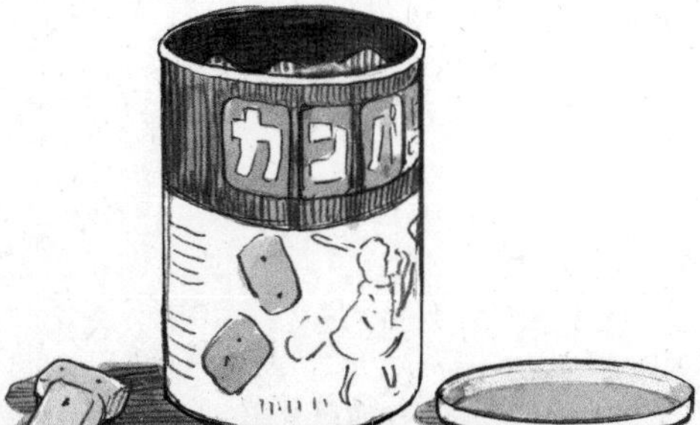
カンパ

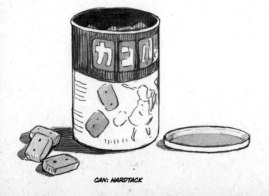

CAN: HARDTACK

SCHOOL-LIVE!

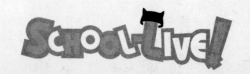

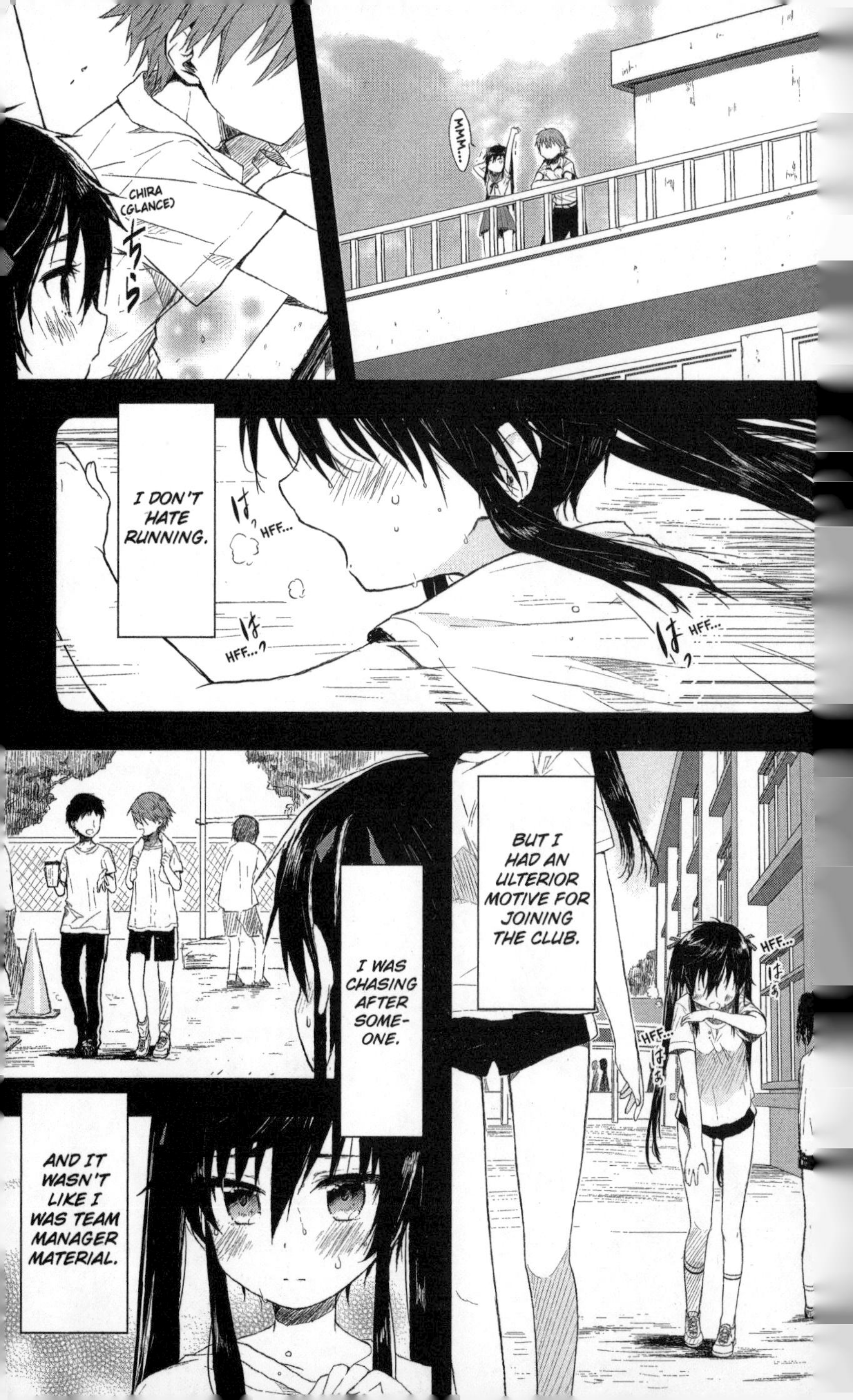
MMM...
CHIRA (GLANCE)
ちら
は HFF...
I DON'T HATE RUNNING.
は HFF...
は HFF...
は HFF...
BUT I HAD AN ULTERIOR MOTIVE FOR JOINING THE CLUB.
HFF... はぁ
HFF... はぁ
I WAS CHASING AFTER SOME-ONE.
AND IT WASN'T LIKE I WAS TEAM MANAGER MATERIAL.

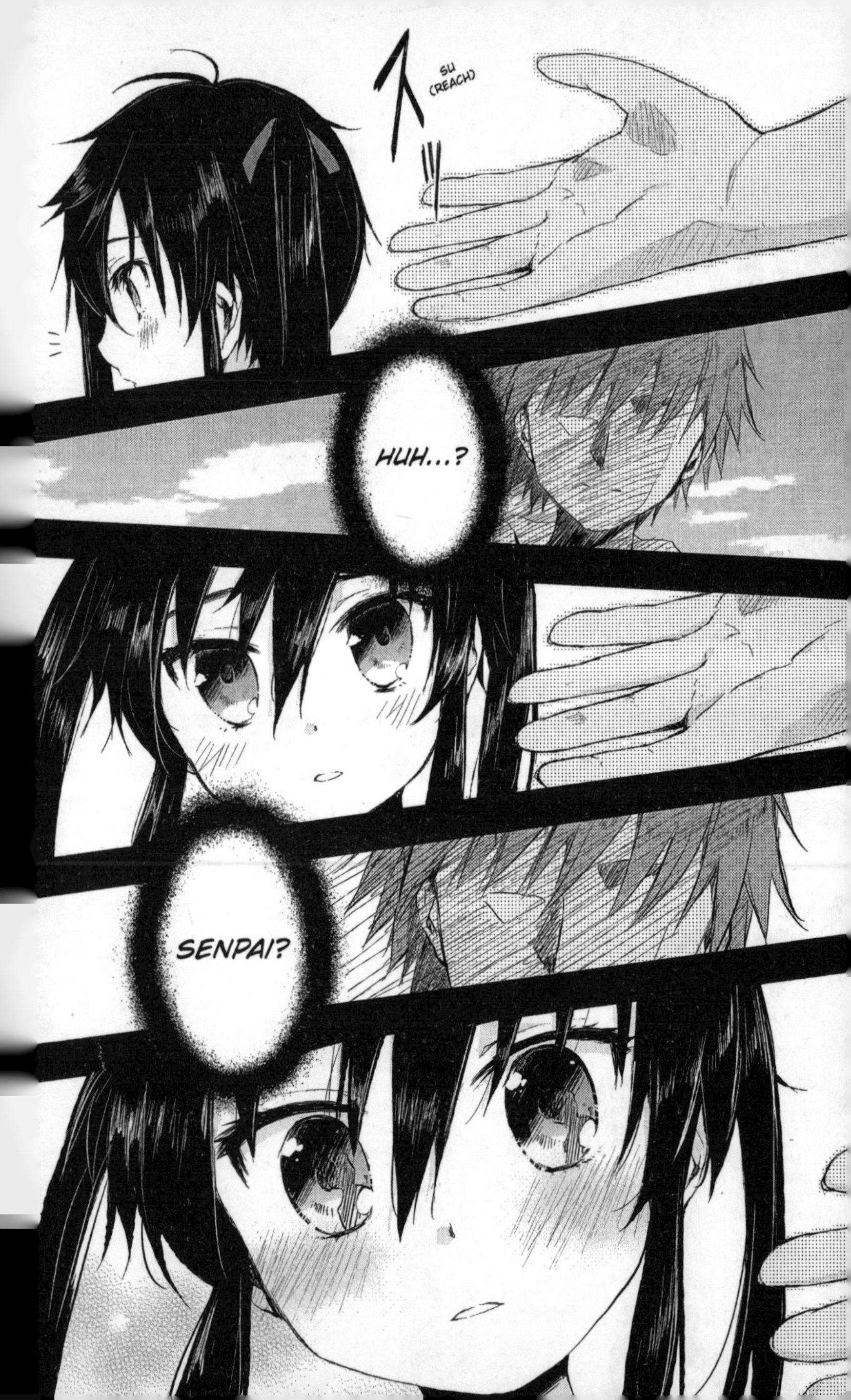
SU (REACH)
HUH...?
SENPAI?

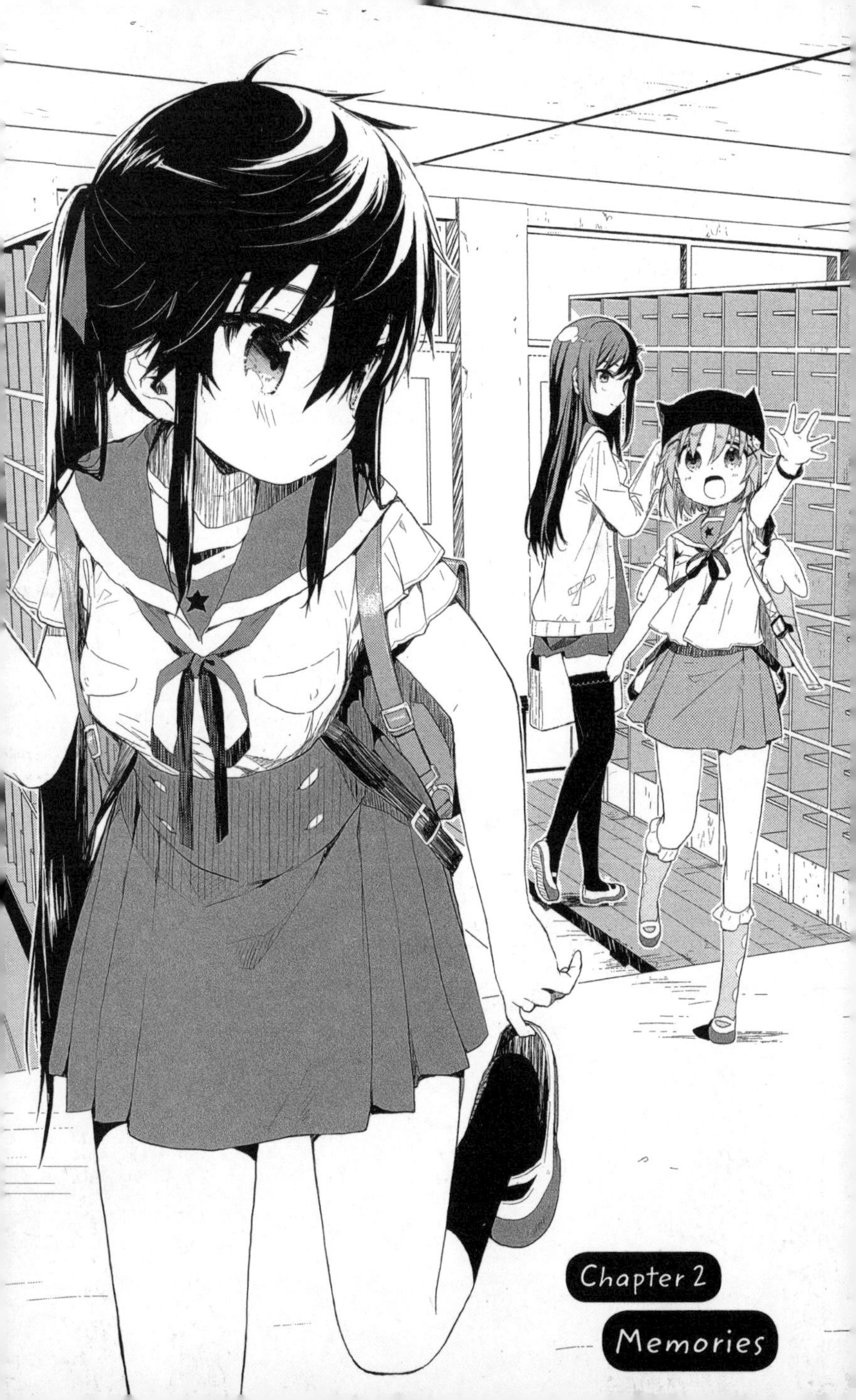
Chapter 2
Memories

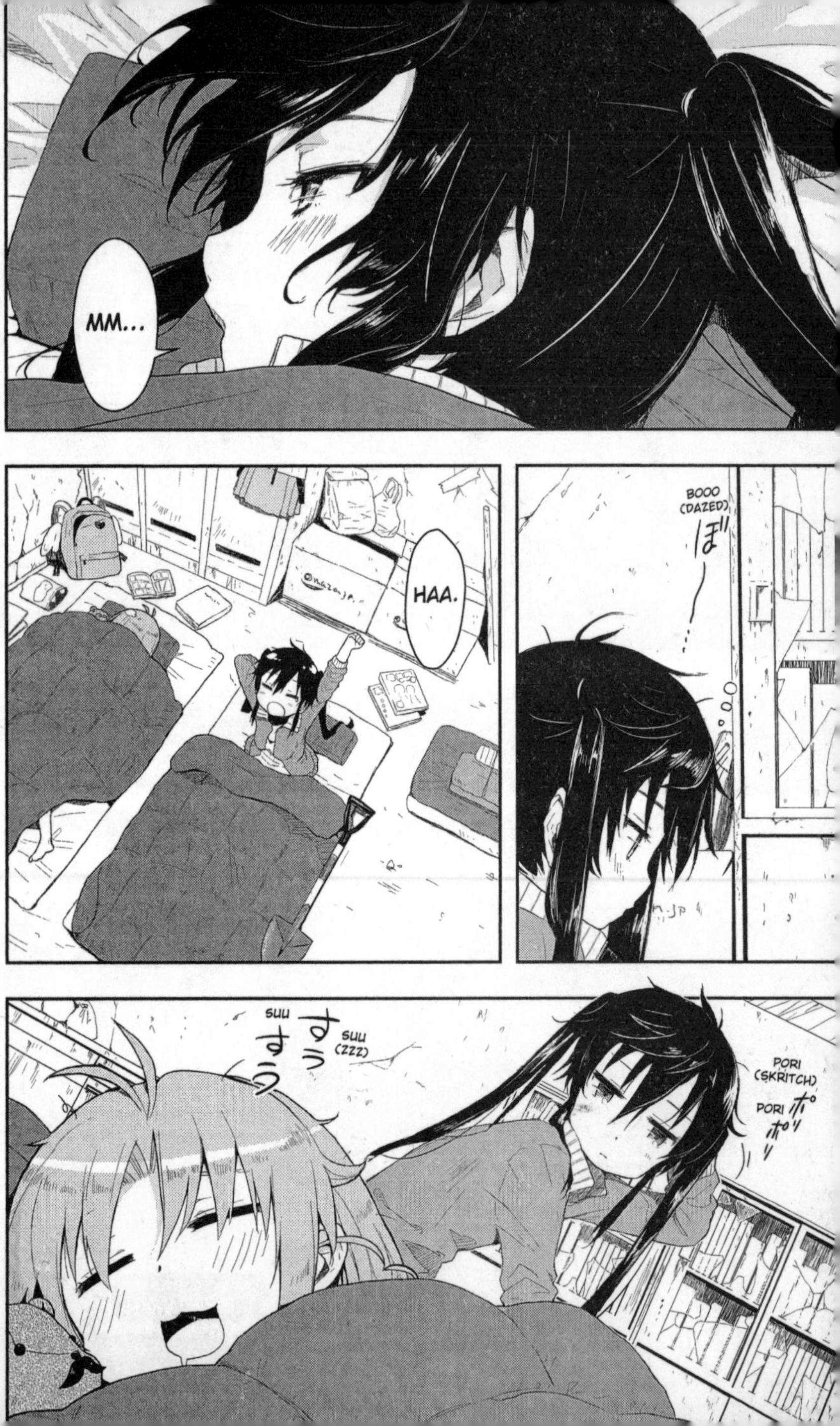
MM...
BOOO (DAZED)
ぼ
HAA.
SUU (ZZZ)
SUU
すぅ
すぅ
PORI (SKRITCH)
PORI
ポリ
ポリ

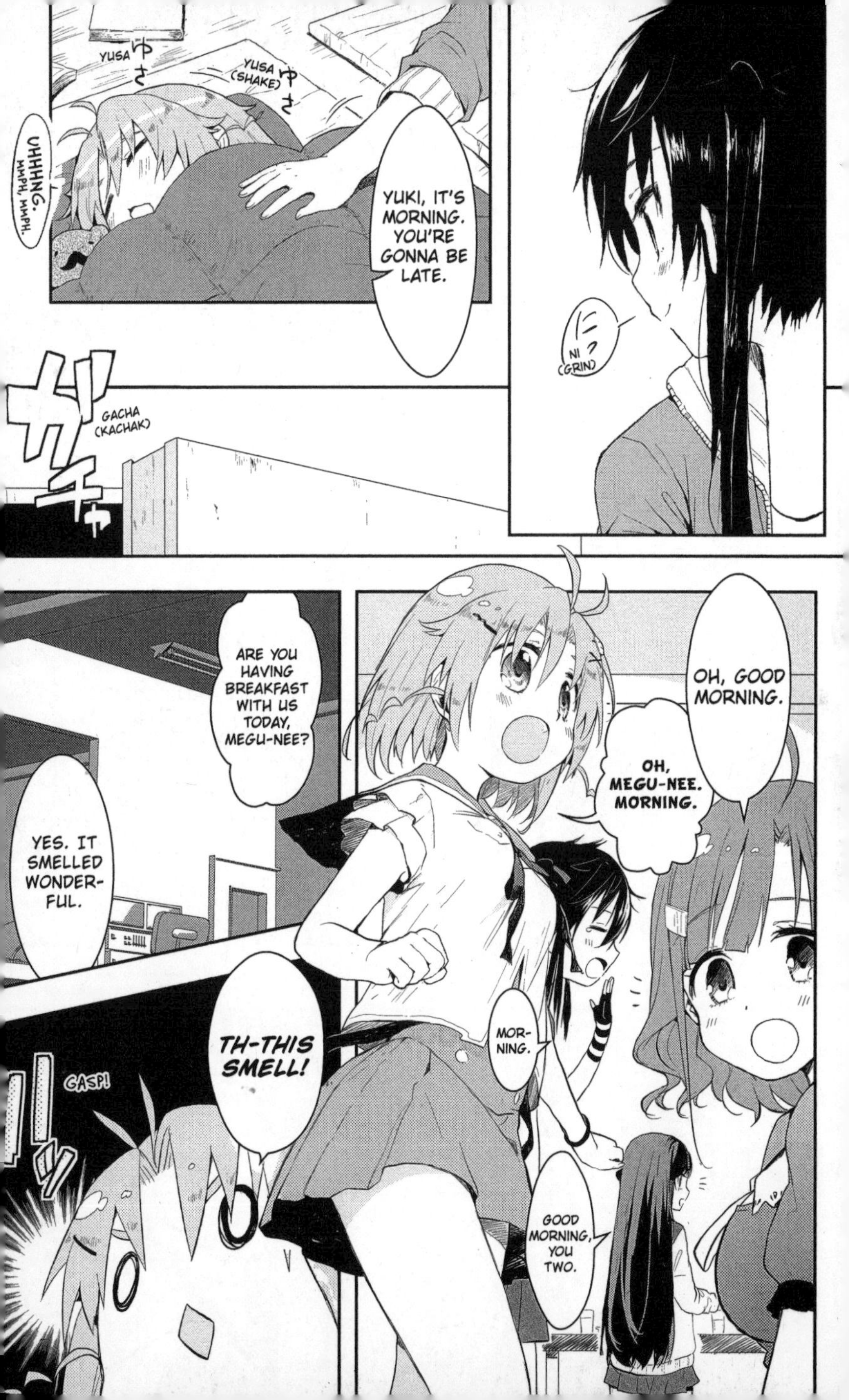
NI (GRIN)
YUSA
YUSA (SHAKE)
YUKI, IT'S MORNING. YOU'RE GONNA BE LATE.
UHHHNG. MMPH, MMPH.
GACHA (KACHAK)
OH, GOOD MORNING.
OH, MEGU-NEE. MORNING.
MOR-NING.
GOOD MORNING, YOU TWO.
ARE YOU HAVING BREAKFAST WITH US TODAY, MEGU-NEE?
YES. IT SMELLED WONDER-FUL.
TH-THIS SMELL!
GASP!

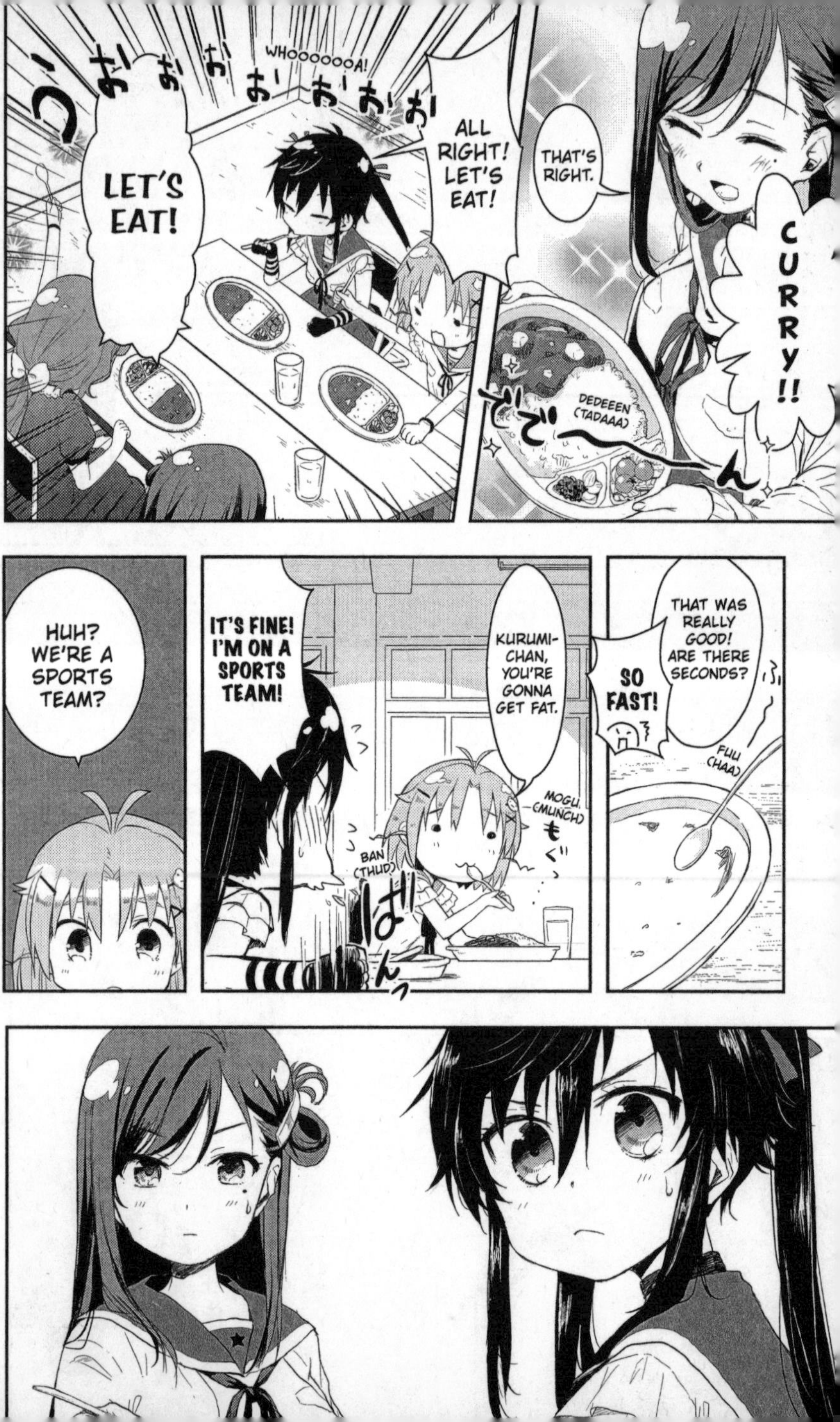
CURRY!!
THAT'S RIGHT.
DEDEEEN (TADAAA)
ALL RIGHT! LET'S EAT!
WHOOOOOOA!
LET'S EAT!
THAT WAS REALLY GOOD! ARE THERE SECONDS?
FUU (HAA)
SO FAST!
KURUMI-CHAN, YOU'RE GONNA GET FAT.
MOGU (MUNCH)
IT'S FINE! I'M ON A SPORTS TEAM!
BAN (THUD)
HUH? WE'RE A SPORTS TEAM?

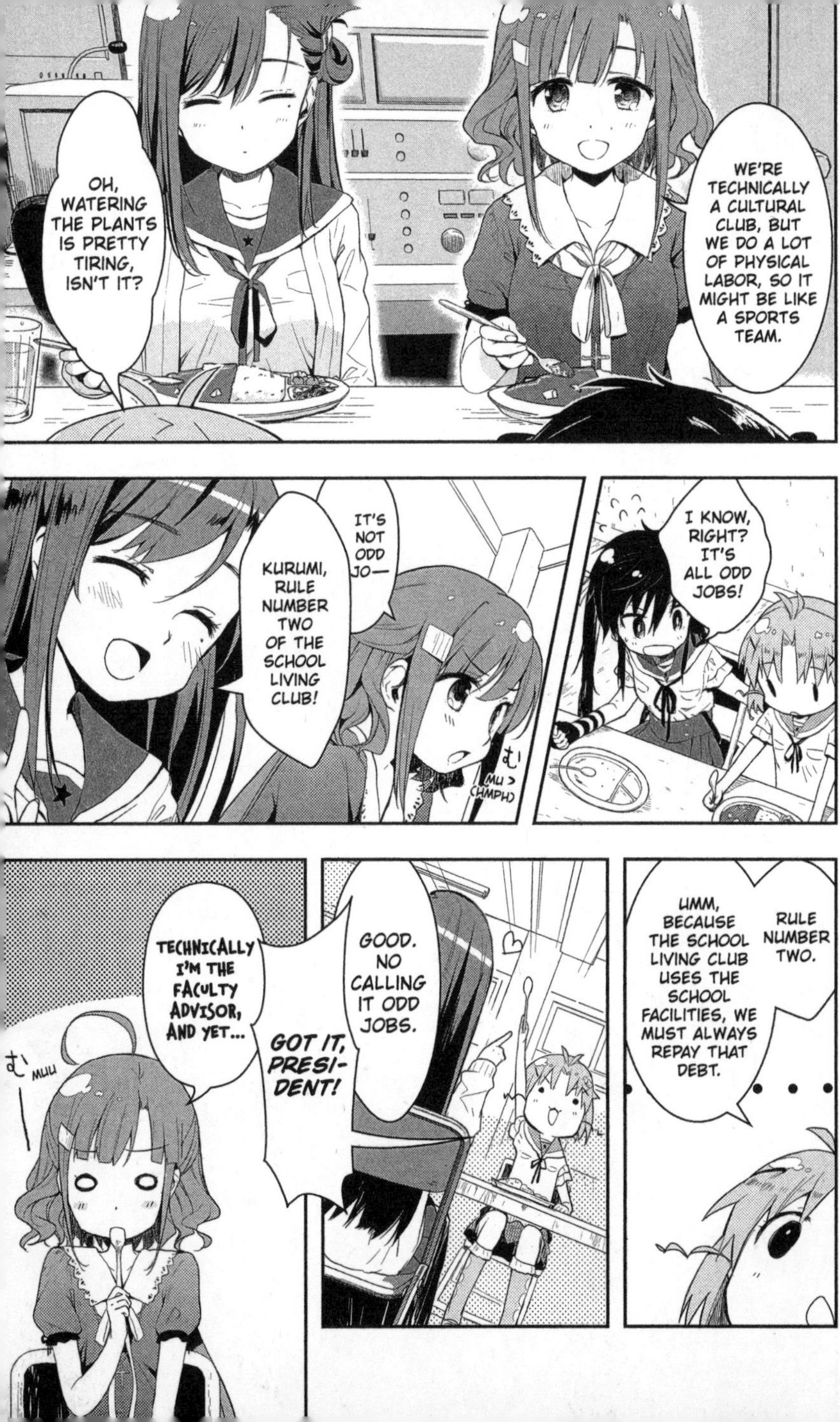
WE'RE TECHNICALLY A CULTURAL CLUB, BUT WE DO A LOT OF PHYSICAL LABOR, SO IT MIGHT BE LIKE A SPORTS TEAM.
OH, WATERING THE PLANTS IS PRETTY TIRING, ISN'T IT?
I KNOW, RIGHT? IT'S ALL ODD JOBS!
IT'S NOT ODD JO—
KURUMI, RULE NUMBER TWO OF THE SCHOOL LIVING CLUB!
む! MU > (HMPH)
RULE NUMBER TWO.
UMM, BECAUSE THE SCHOOL LIVING CLUB USES THE SCHOOL FACILITIES, WE MUST ALWAYS REPAY THAT DEBT.
• • •
GOOD. NO CALLING IT ODD JOBS.
GOT IT, PRESIDENT!
TECHNICALLY I'M THE FACULTY ADVISOR, AND YET...
む MUU

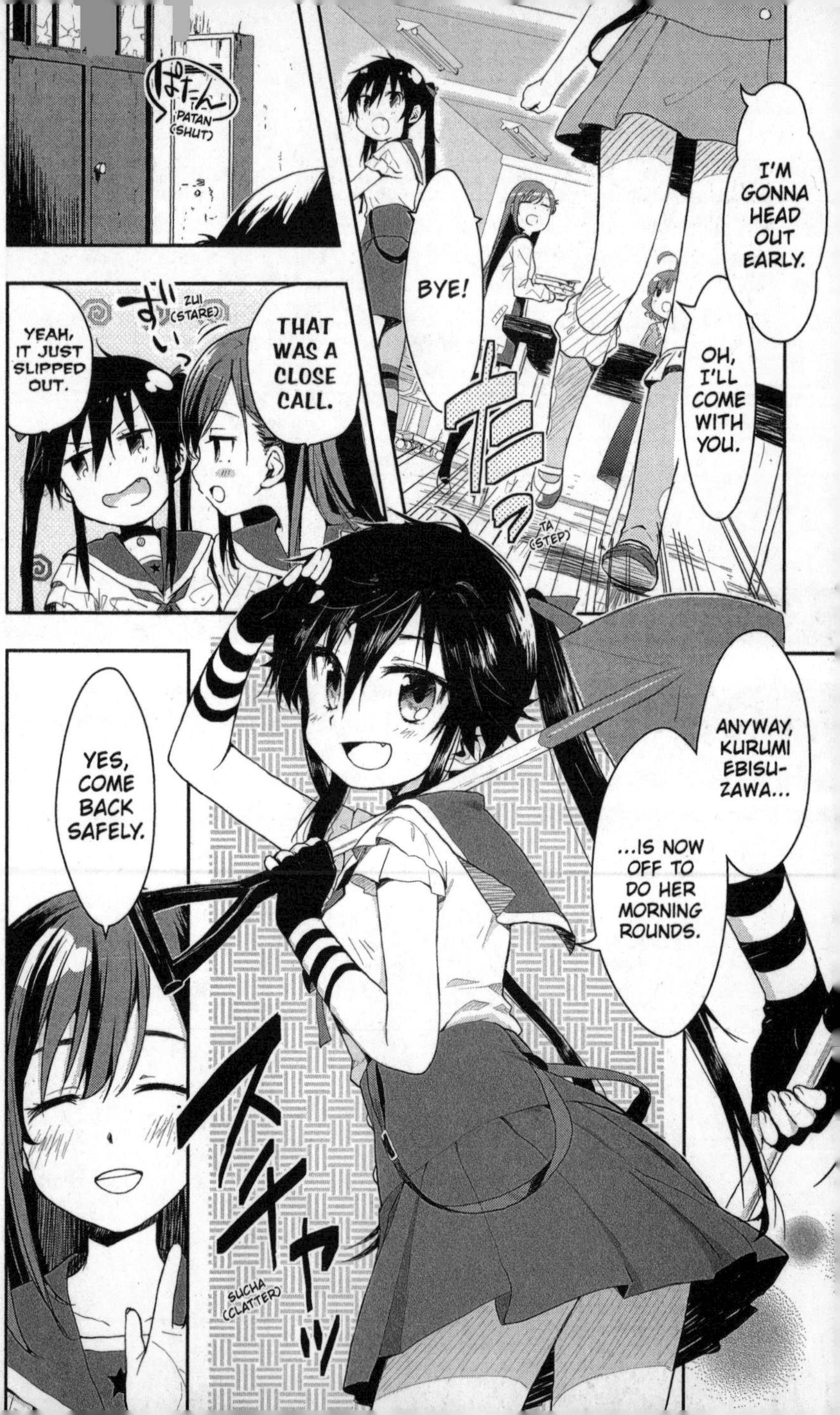
I'M GONNA HEAD OUT EARLY.
OH, I'LL COME WITH YOU.
BYE!
TA (STEP)
ぱたん
PATAN (SHUT)
THAT WAS A CLOSE CALL.
ずい
ZUI (STARE)
YEAH, IT JUST SLIPPED OUT.
ANYWAY, KURUMI EBISU-ZAWA...
...IS NOW OFF TO DO HER MORNING ROUNDS.
SUCHA (CLATTER)
YES, COME BACK SAFELY.

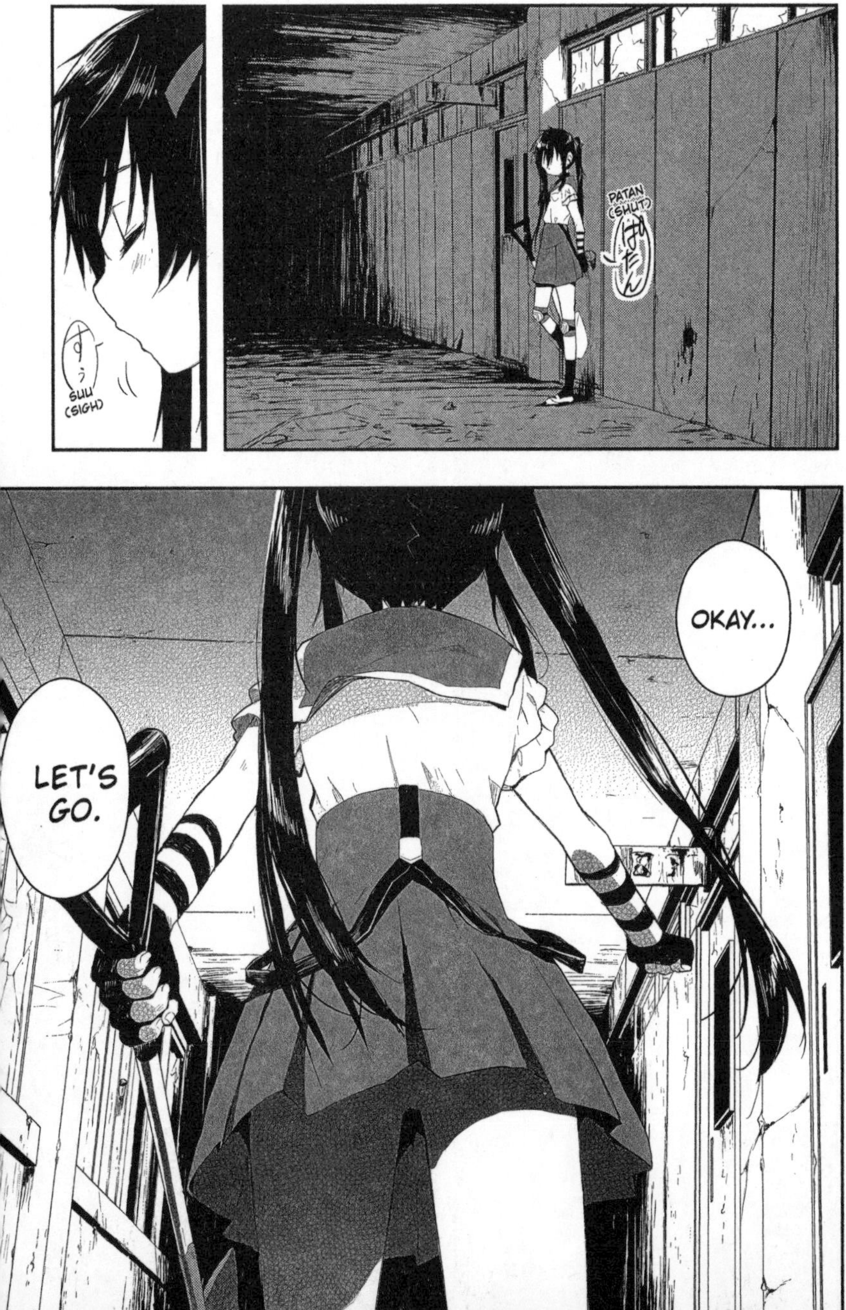
ぱたん
PATAN (SHUT)
すぅ
SUU (SIGH)
OKAY...
LET'S GO.

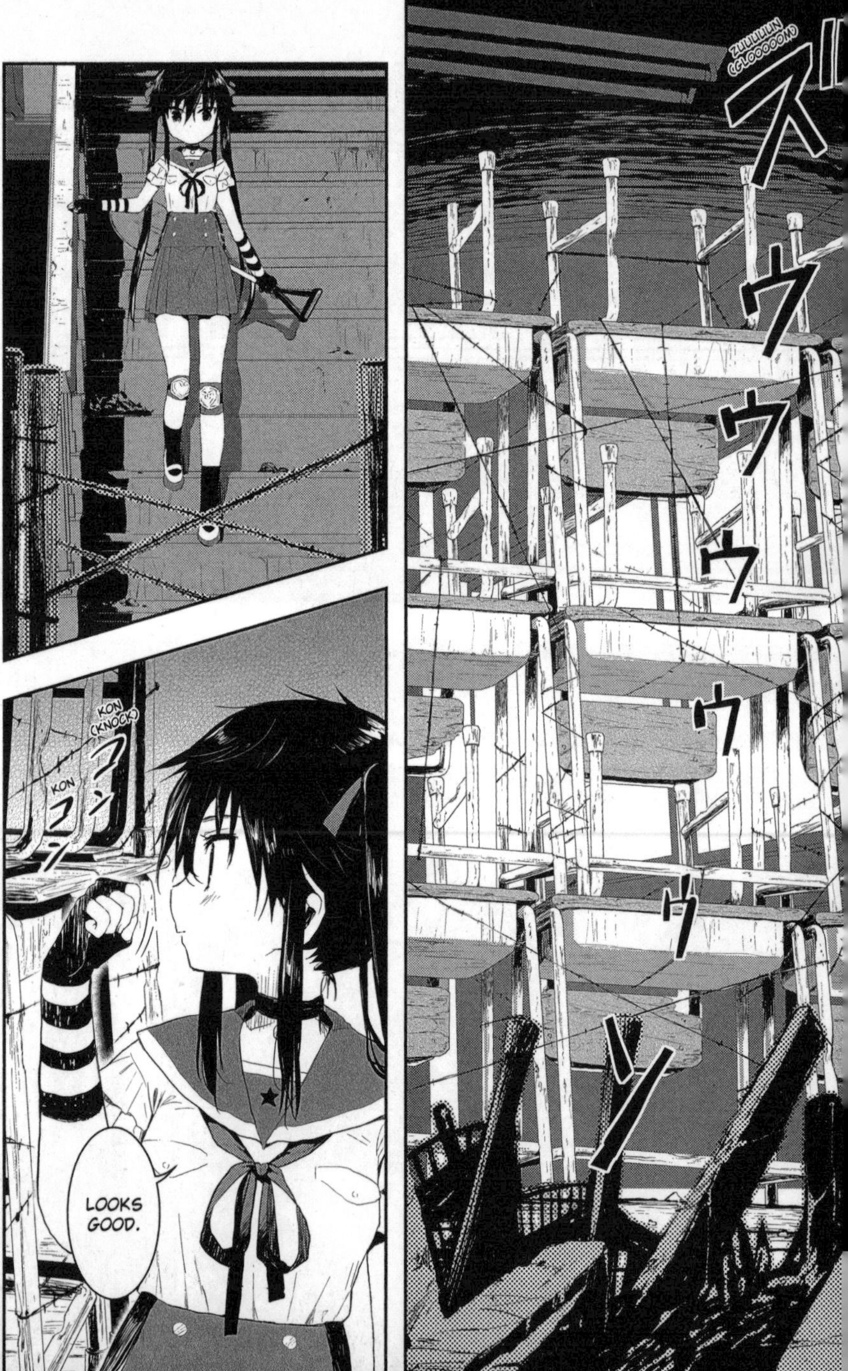
ZUUUUUN (GLOOOOOM)
KON (KNOCK)
KON
LOOKS GOOD.

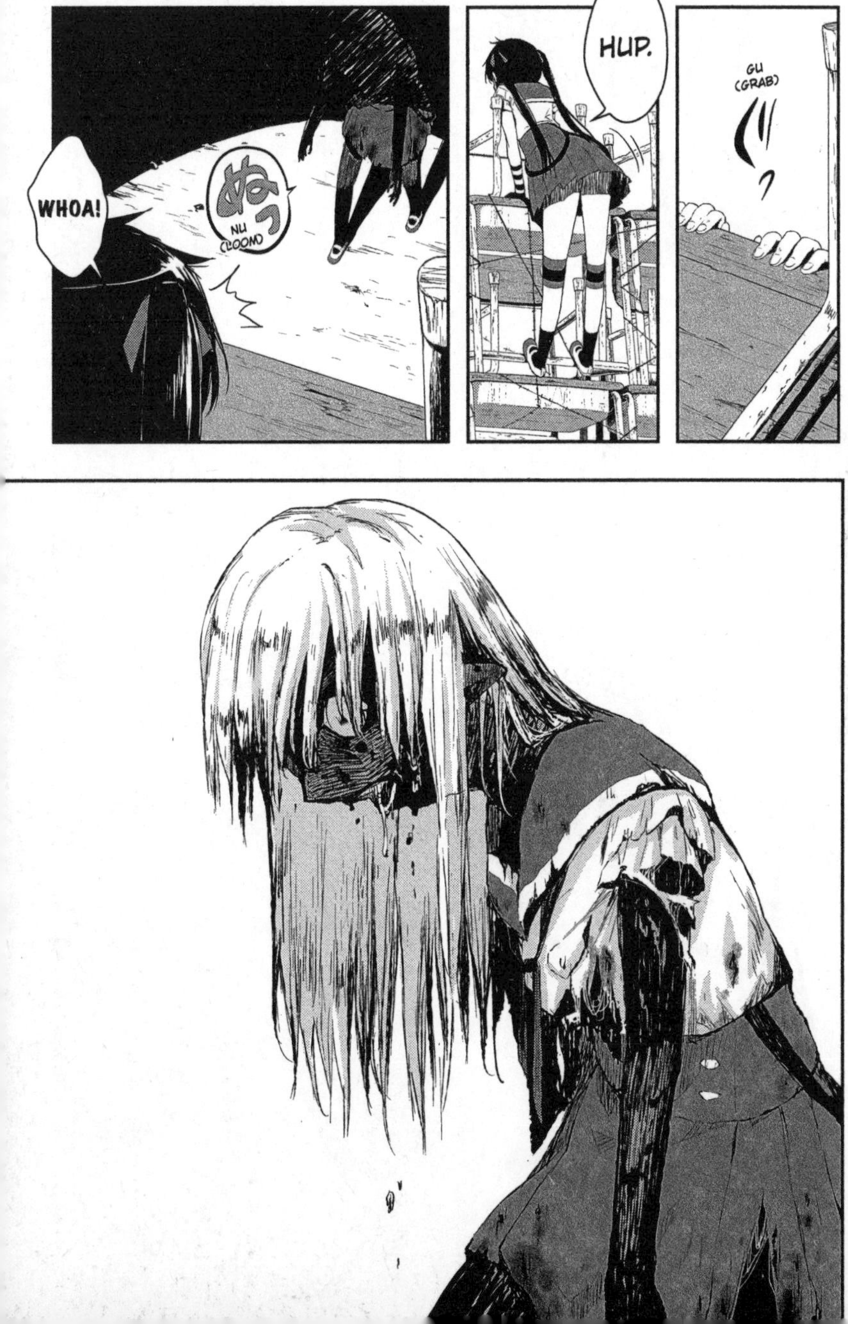
GU (GRAB)
HUP.
ぬっ
NU (LOOM)
WHOA!

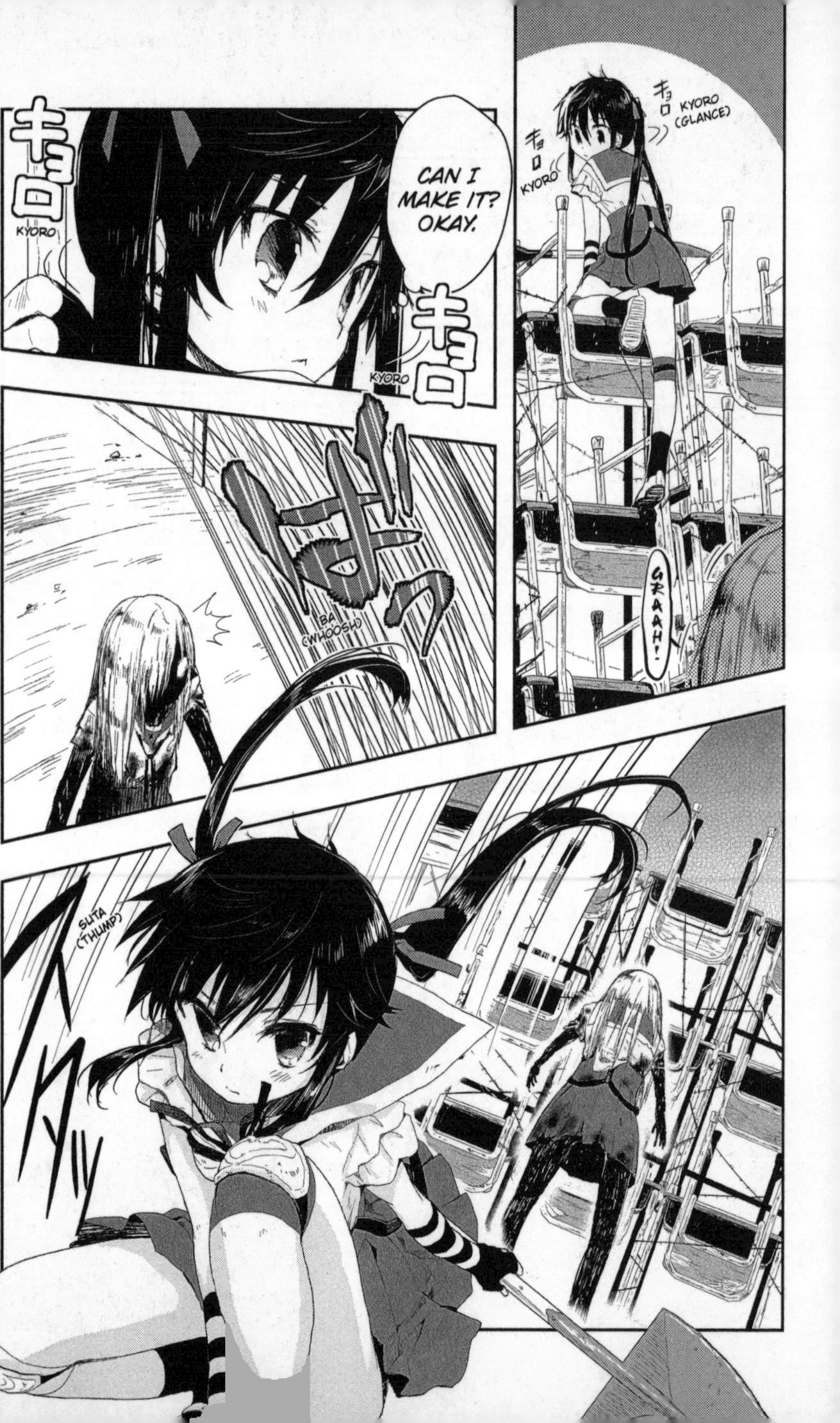
キョロ KYORO (GLANCE)
キョロ KYORO
GRAAAH!
CAN I MAKE IT? OKAY.
キョロ KYORO
キョロ KYORO
ばっ
BA (WHOOSH)
スタッ
SUTA (THUMP)

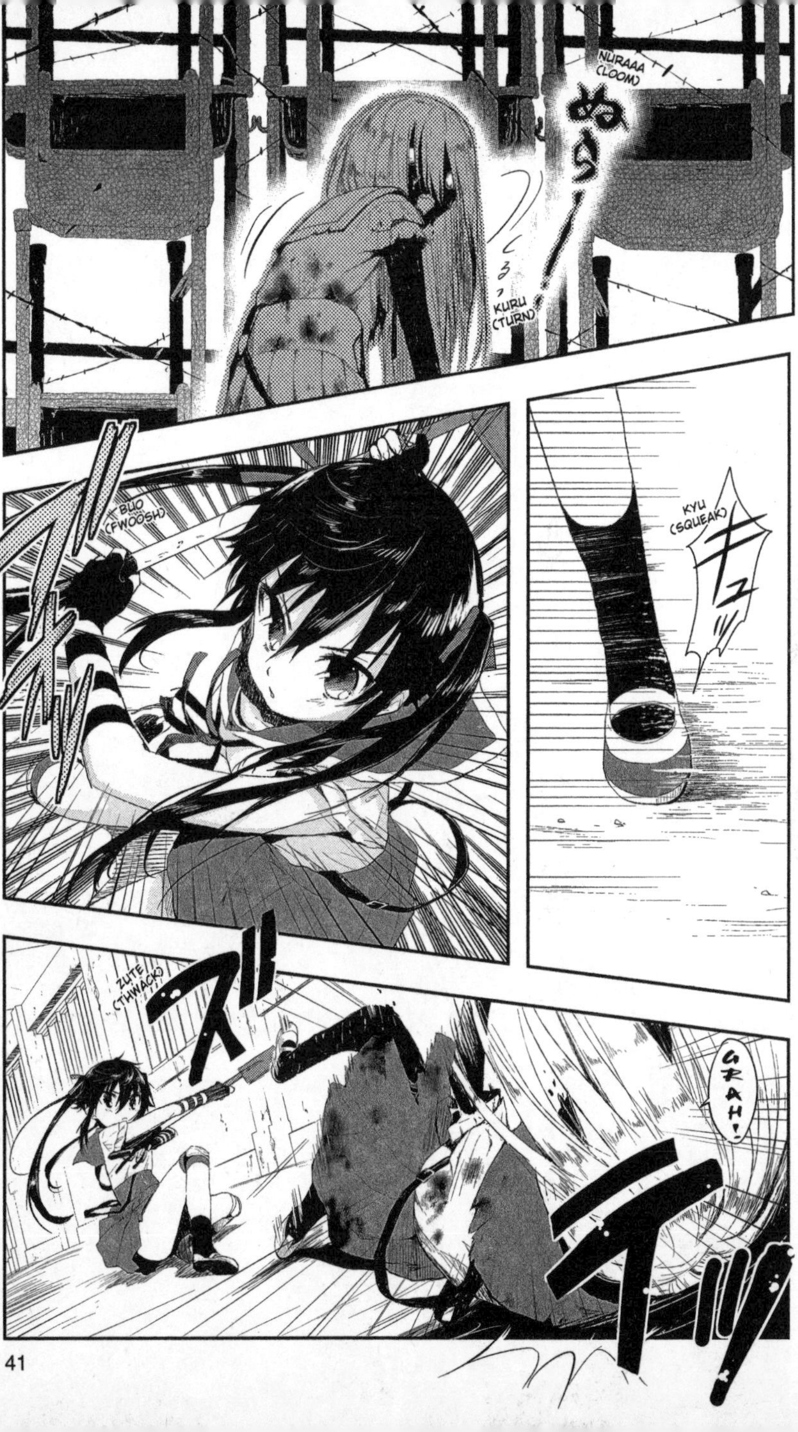
NURAAA (LOOM)
ぬらー
KURU (TURN)
KYU (SQUEAK)
BUO (FWOOSH)
ZUTE (THWACK)
GRAH!

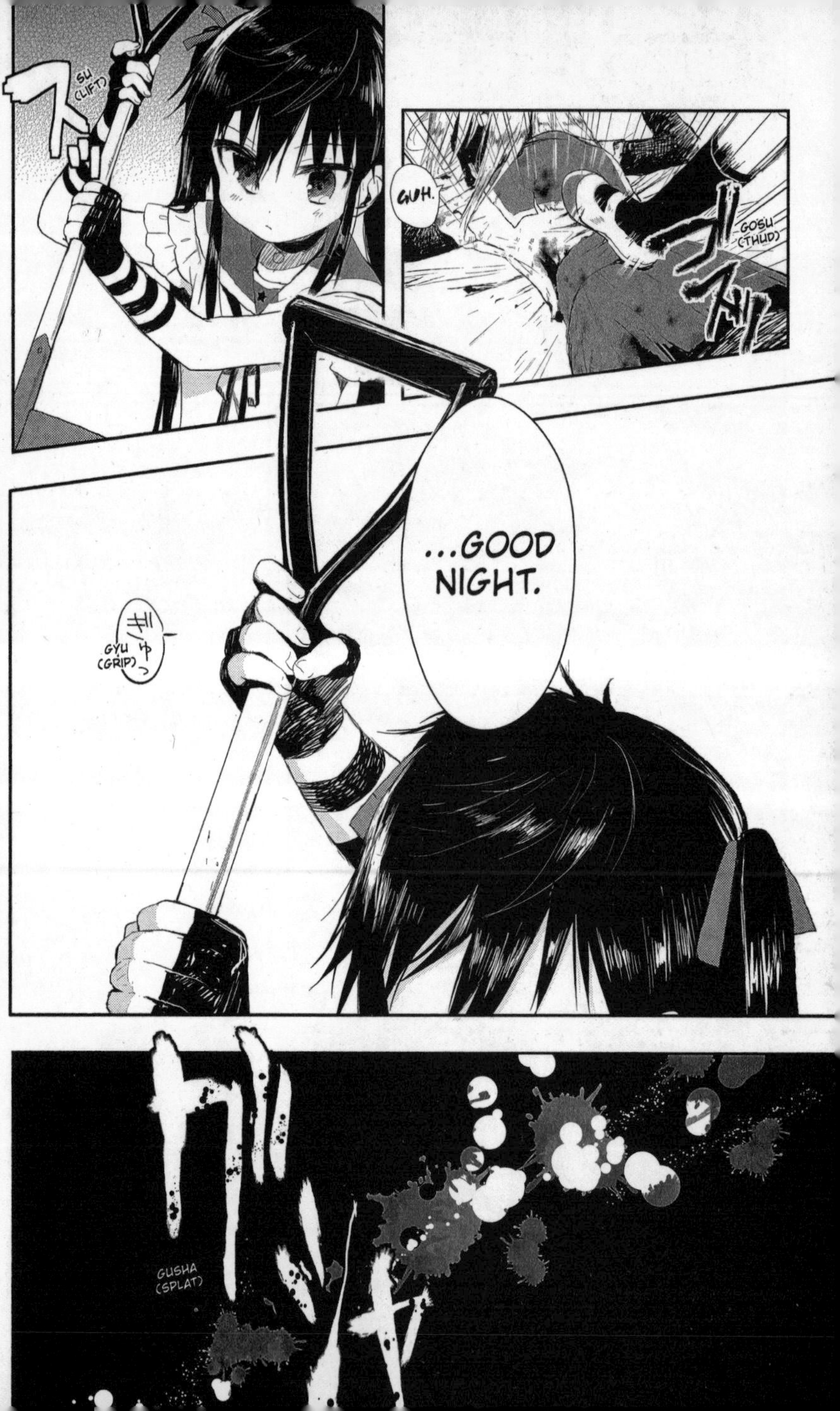
GUH.
GOSU (THUD)
SU (LIFT)
...GOOD NIGHT.
GYU (GRIP)
GUSHA (SPLAT)

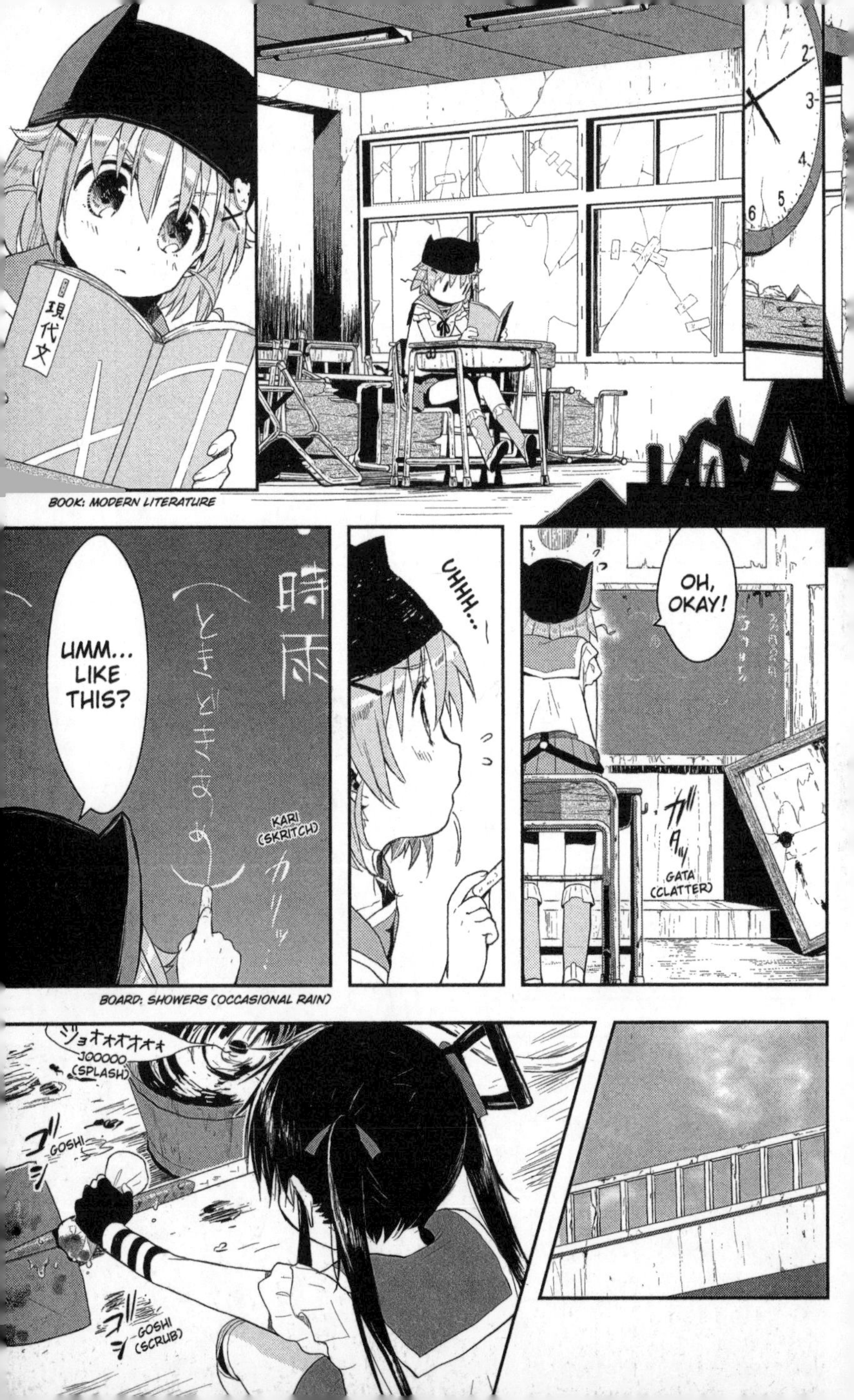
現代文
BOOK: MODERN LITERATURE
OH, OKAY!
ガタッ
GATA (CLATTER)
UHHH...
UMM... LIKE THIS?
時雨
KARI (SKRITCH)
BOARD: SHOWERS (OCCASIONAL RAIN)
ジョオオオオオオ
JOOOOO (SPLASH)
GOSHI
GOSHI (SCRUB)

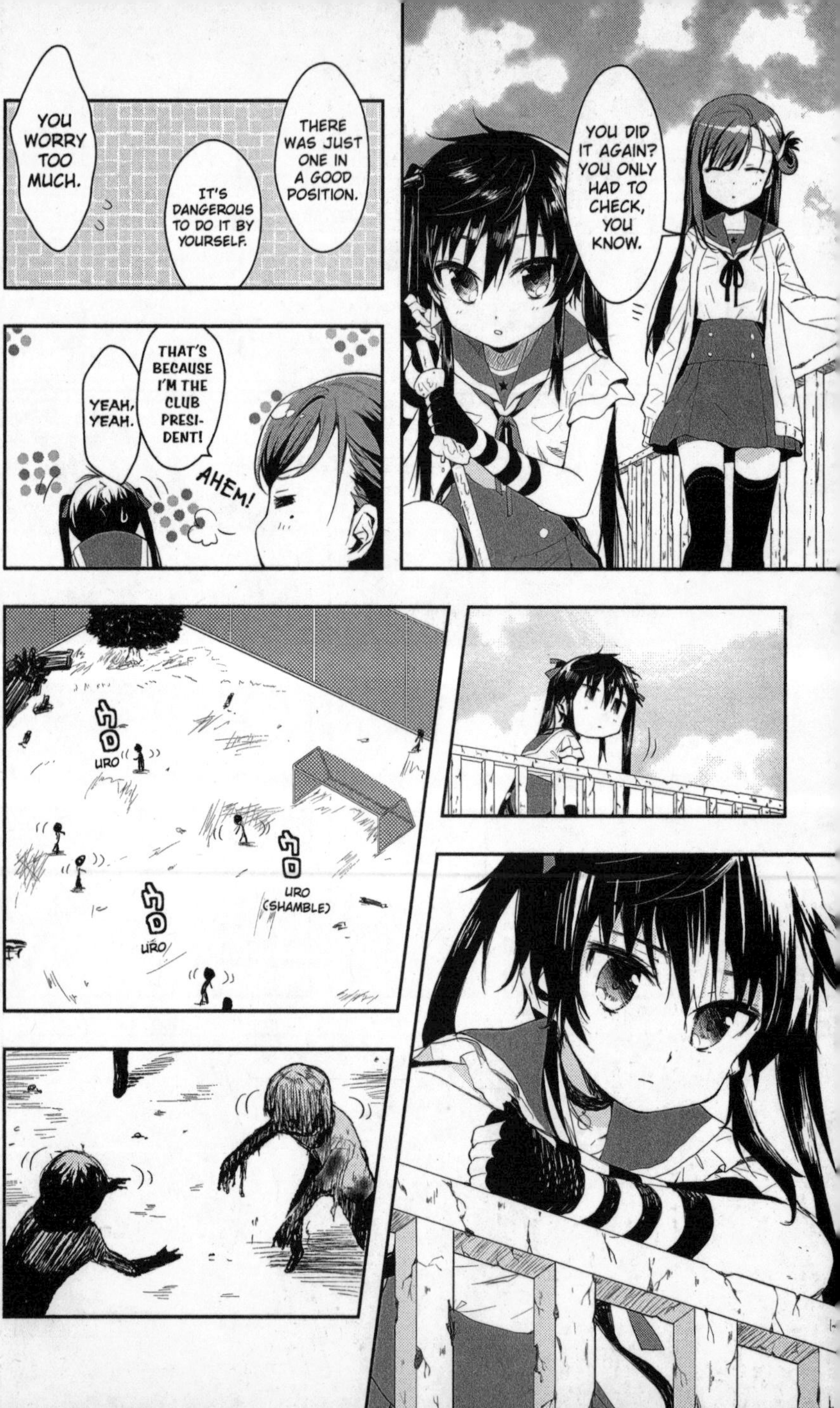
YOU DID IT AGAIN? YOU ONLY HAD TO CHECK, YOU KNOW.
THERE WAS JUST ONE IN A GOOD POSITION.
IT'S DANGEROUS TO DO IT BY YOURSELF.
YOU WORRY TOO MUCH.
THAT'S BECAUSE I'M THE CLUB PRESIDENT!
AHEM!
YEAH, YEAH.
URO
URO (SHAMBLE)
URO

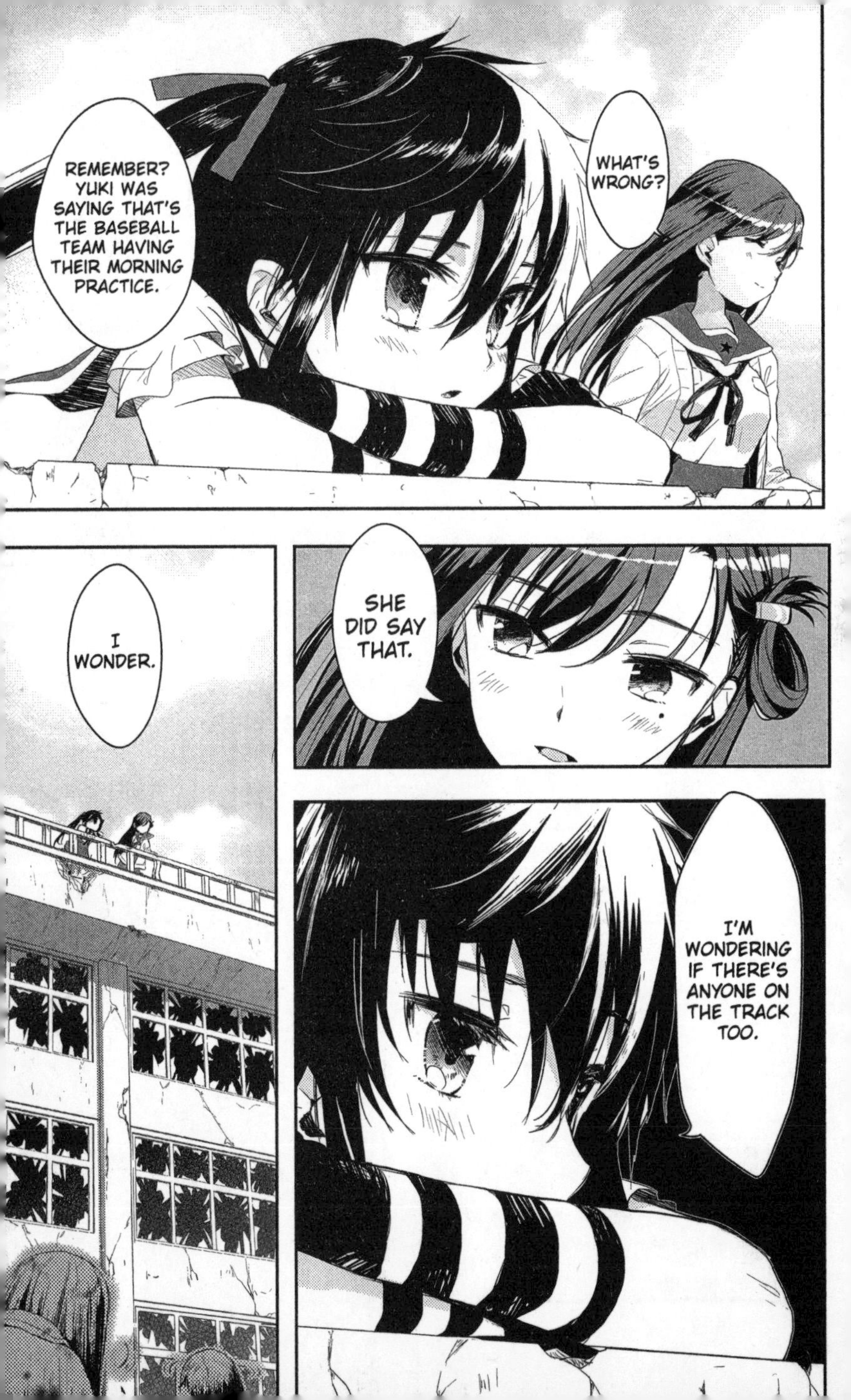
WHAT'S WRONG?
REMEMBER? YUKI WAS SAYING THAT'S THE BASEBALL TEAM HAVING THEIR MORNING PRACTICE.
SHE DID SAY THAT.
I'M WONDERING IF THERE'S ANYONE ON THE TRACK TOO.
I WONDER.

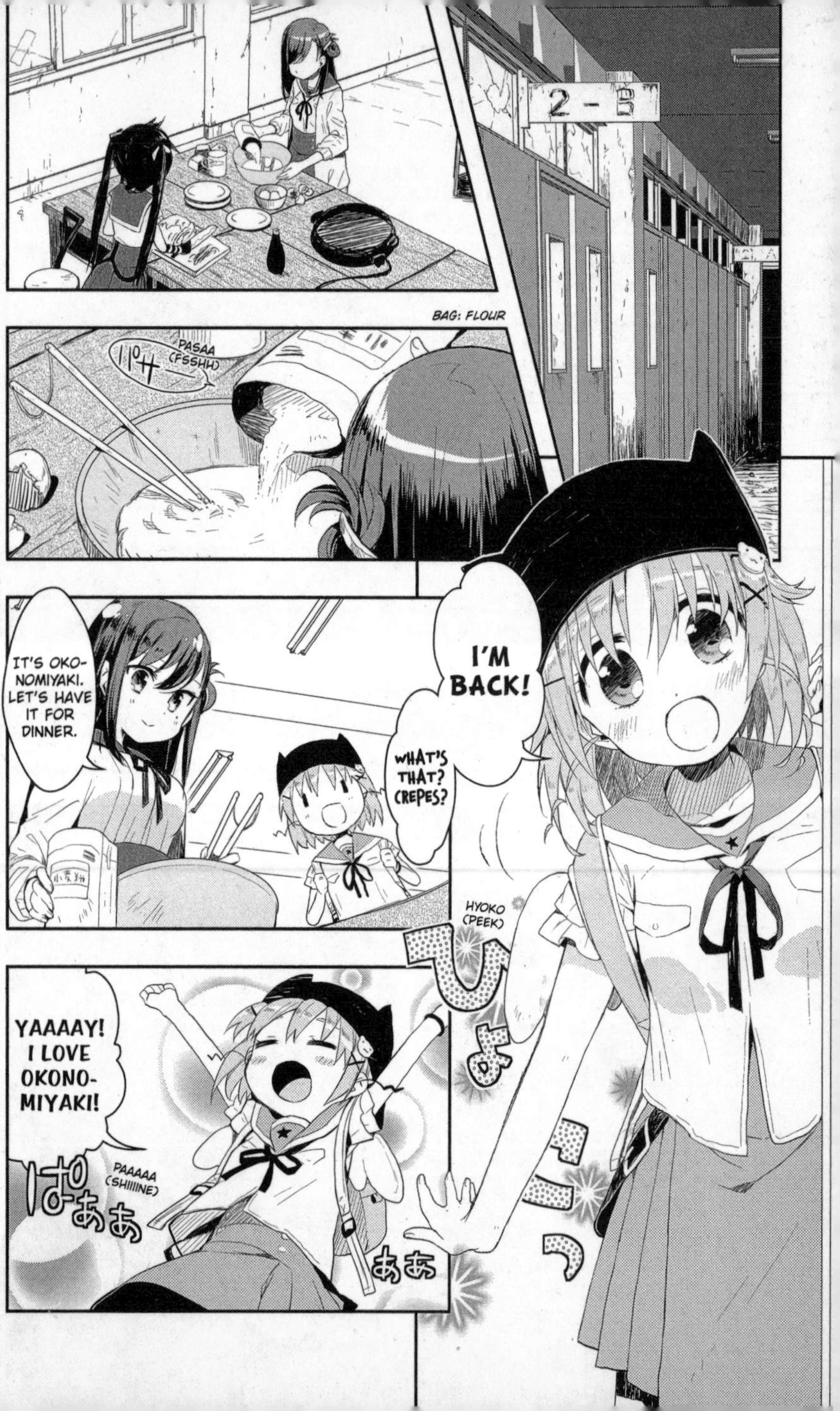
2-B
I'M BACK!
HYOKO (PEEK)
ひょこっ
BAG: FLOUR
PASAA (FSSHH)
パサー
WHAT'S THAT? CREPES?
IT'S OKONOMIYAKI. LET'S HAVE IT FOR DINNER.
小麦粉
YAAAAY! I LOVE OKONOMIYAKI!
PAAAAA (SHIIIINE)
ぱあああああ

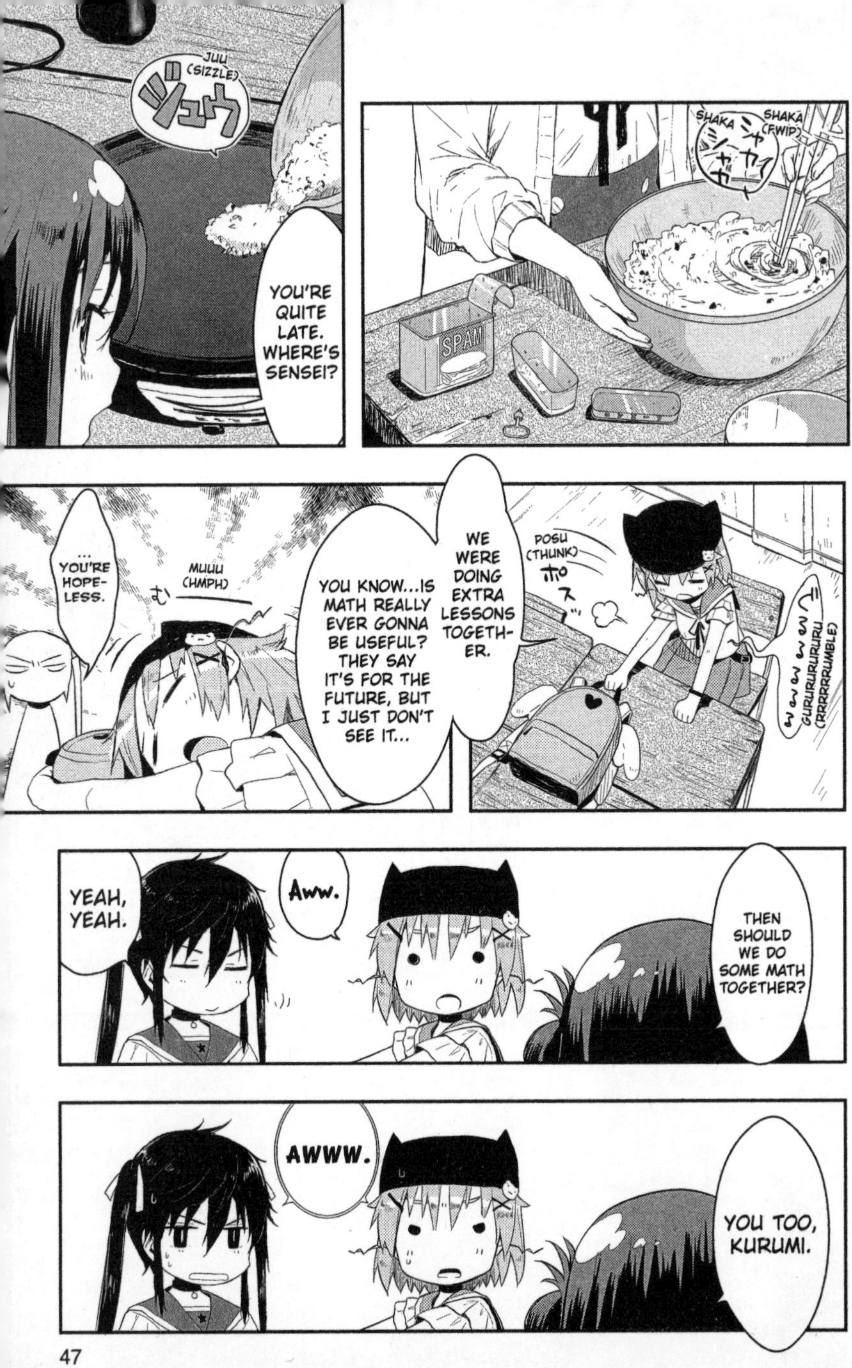

SHAKA SHAKA (FWIP)
シャカシャカ
JUU (SIZZLE)
ジュウ
YOU'RE QUITE LATE. WHERE'S SENSEI?
POSU (THUNK)
ポス
GURURURURU (RRRRRUMBLE)
WE WERE DOING EXTRA LESSONS TOGETHER.
YOU KNOW...IS MATH REALLY EVER GONNA BE USEFUL? THEY SAY IT'S FOR THE FUTURE, BUT I JUST DON'T SEE IT...
MUUU (HMPH)
...YOU'RE HOPELESS.
THEN SHOULD WE DO SOME MATH TOGETHER?
Aww.
YEAH, YEAH.
YOU TOO, KURUMI.
AWWW.

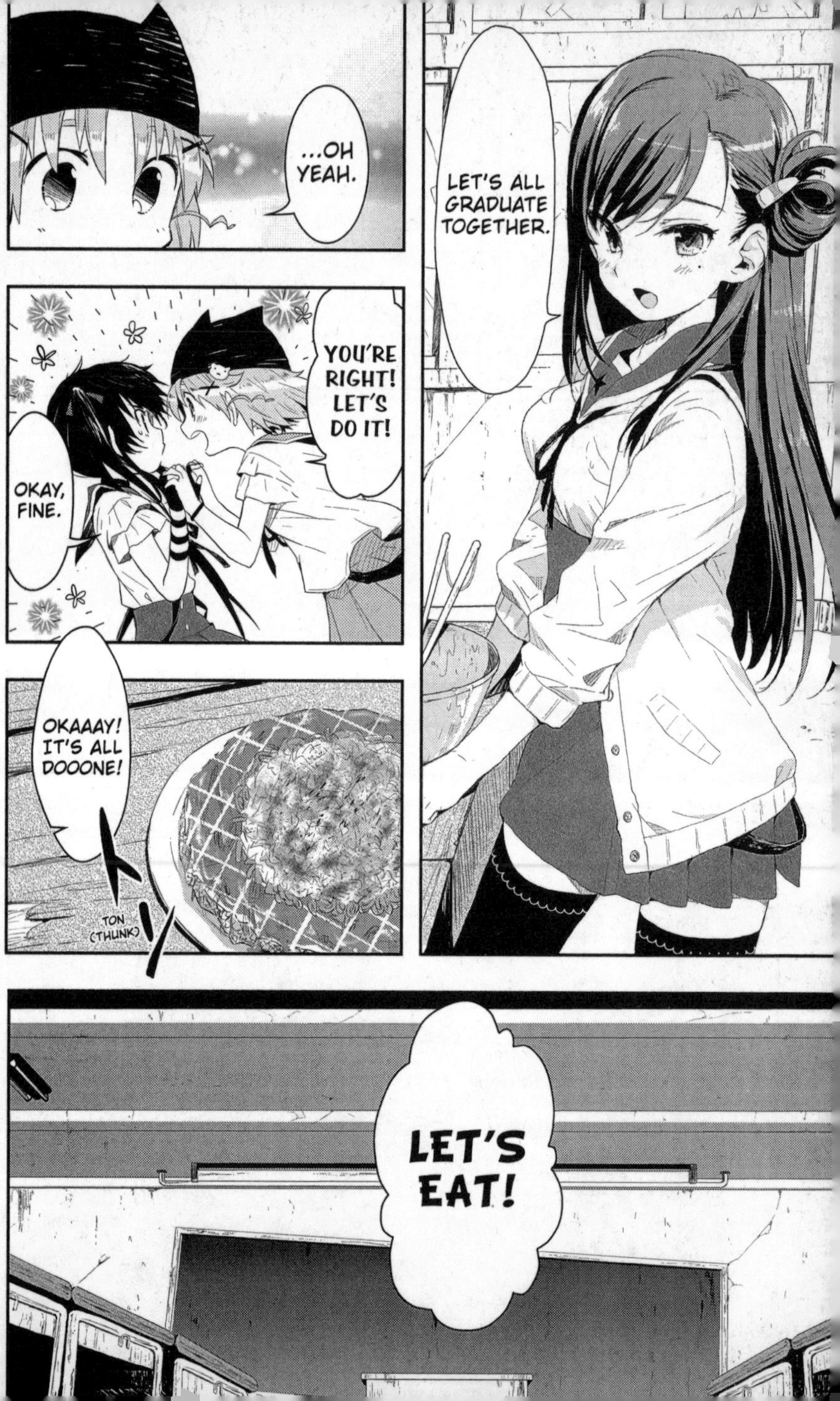
LET'S ALL GRADUATE TOGETHER.
...OH YEAH.
YOU'RE RIGHT! LET'S DO IT!
OKAY, FINE.
OKAAAY! IT'S ALL DOOONE!
TON (THUNK)
LET'S EAT!

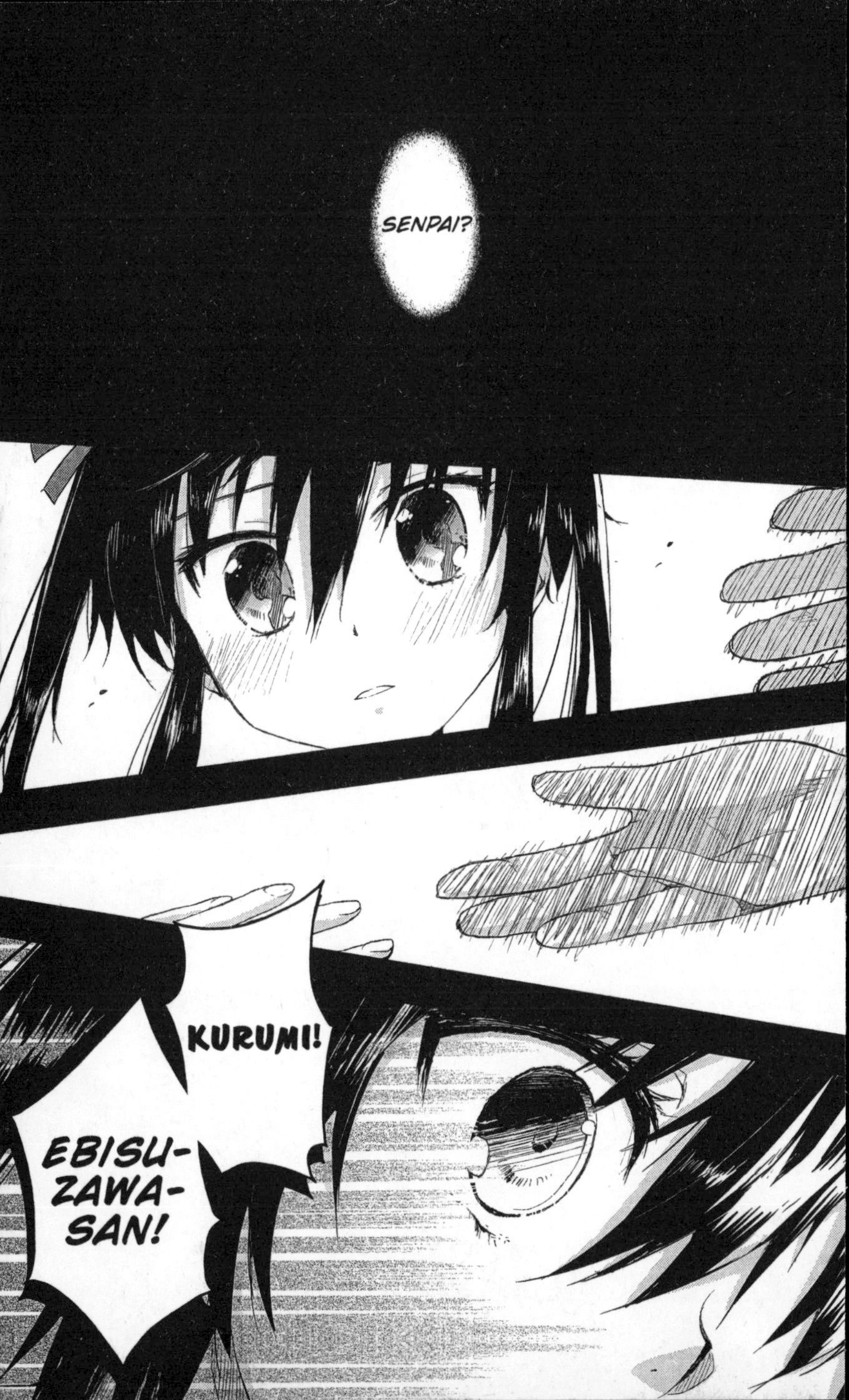
SENPAI?
KURUMI!
EBISU-ZAWA-SAN!

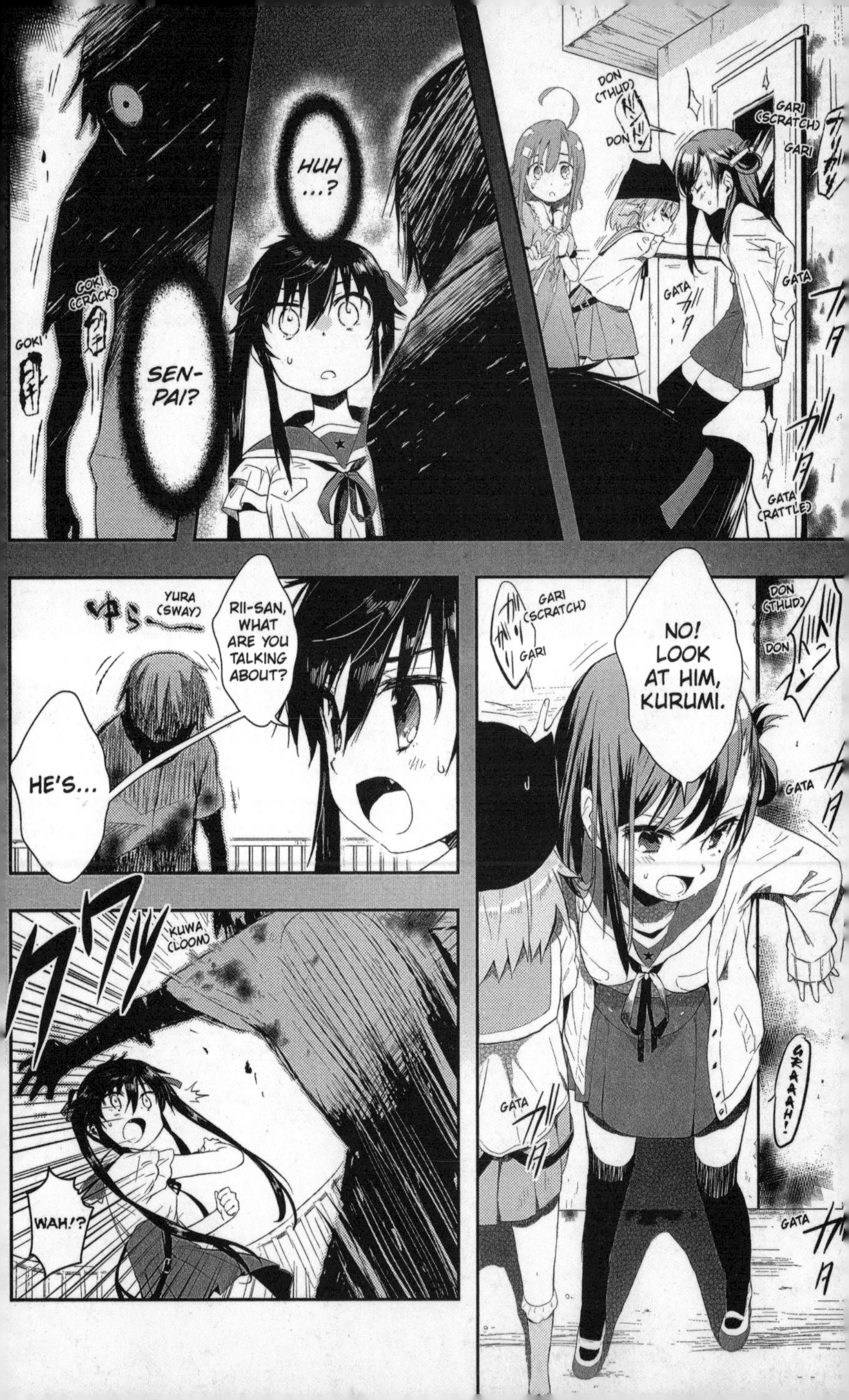

DON (THUD)
DON
GARI (SCRATCH)
GARI
GATA
GATA
GATA (RATTLE)
HUH ...?
GOKI (CRACK)
GOKI
SEN-PAI?
DON (THUD)
DON
GARI (SCRATCH)
GARI
NO! LOOK AT HIM, KURUMI.
GATA
GRAAAAH!
GATA
GATA
YURA (SWAY)
RII-SAN, WHAT ARE YOU TALKING ABOUT?
HE'S...
KUWA (LOOM)
WAH!?

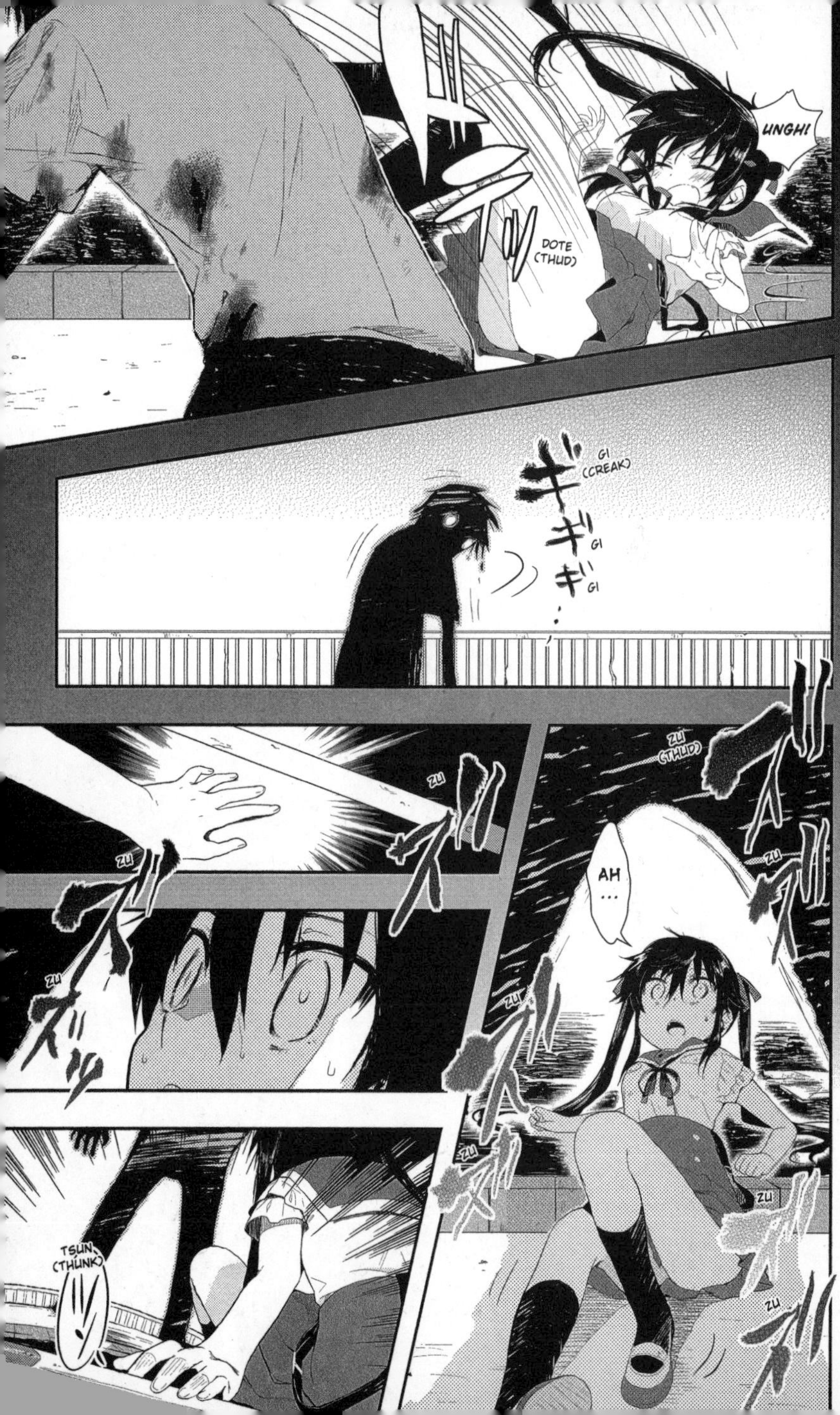
UNGH!
DOTE (THUD)
GI (CREAK)
GI
GI
ZU (THUD)
ZU
AH…
ZU
ZU
ZU
ZU
ZU
ZU
ZU
ZU
TSUN (THUNK)

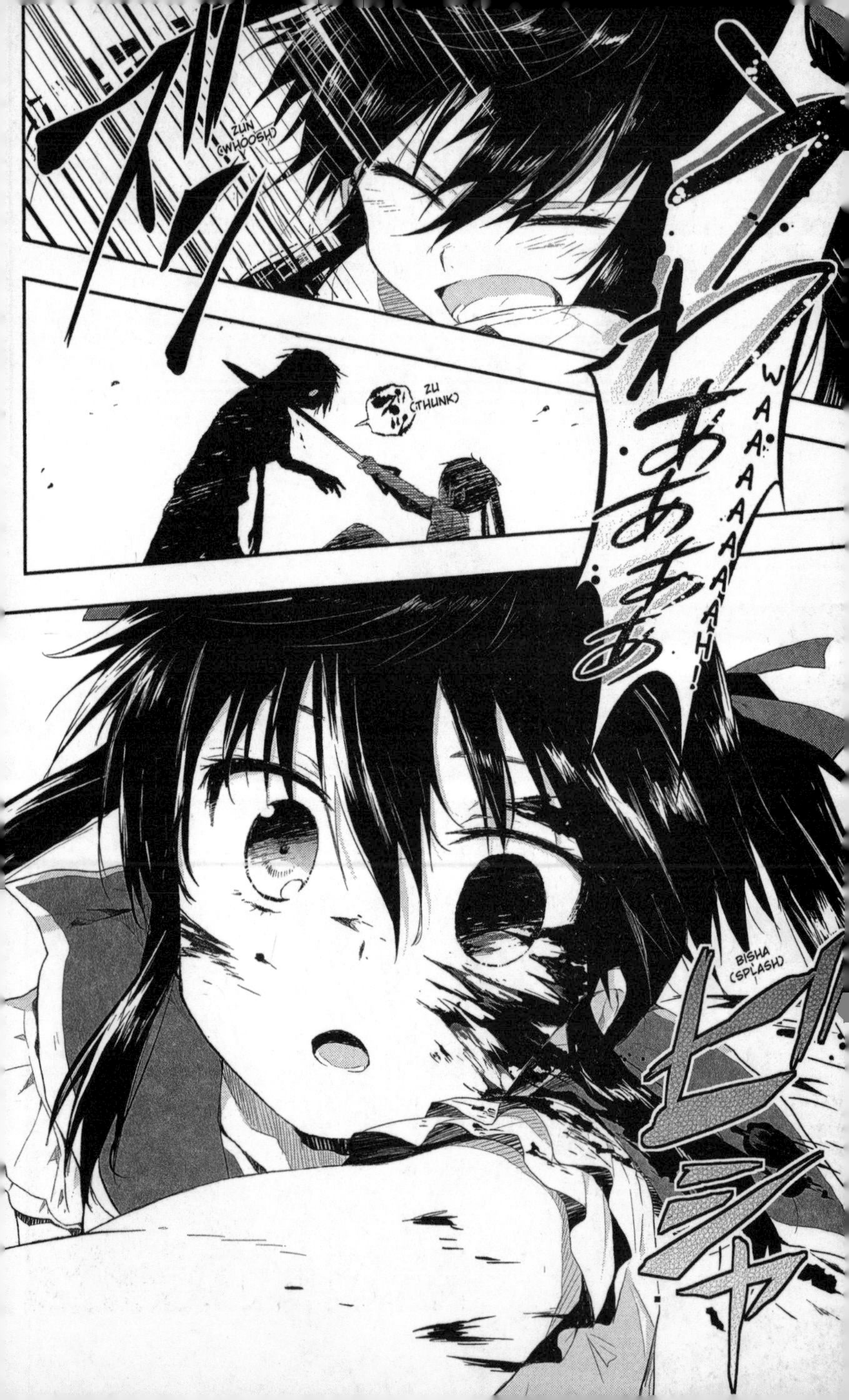
WAAAAAAAAH!
ZUN (WHOOSH)
ZU (THUNK)
BISHA (SPLASH)

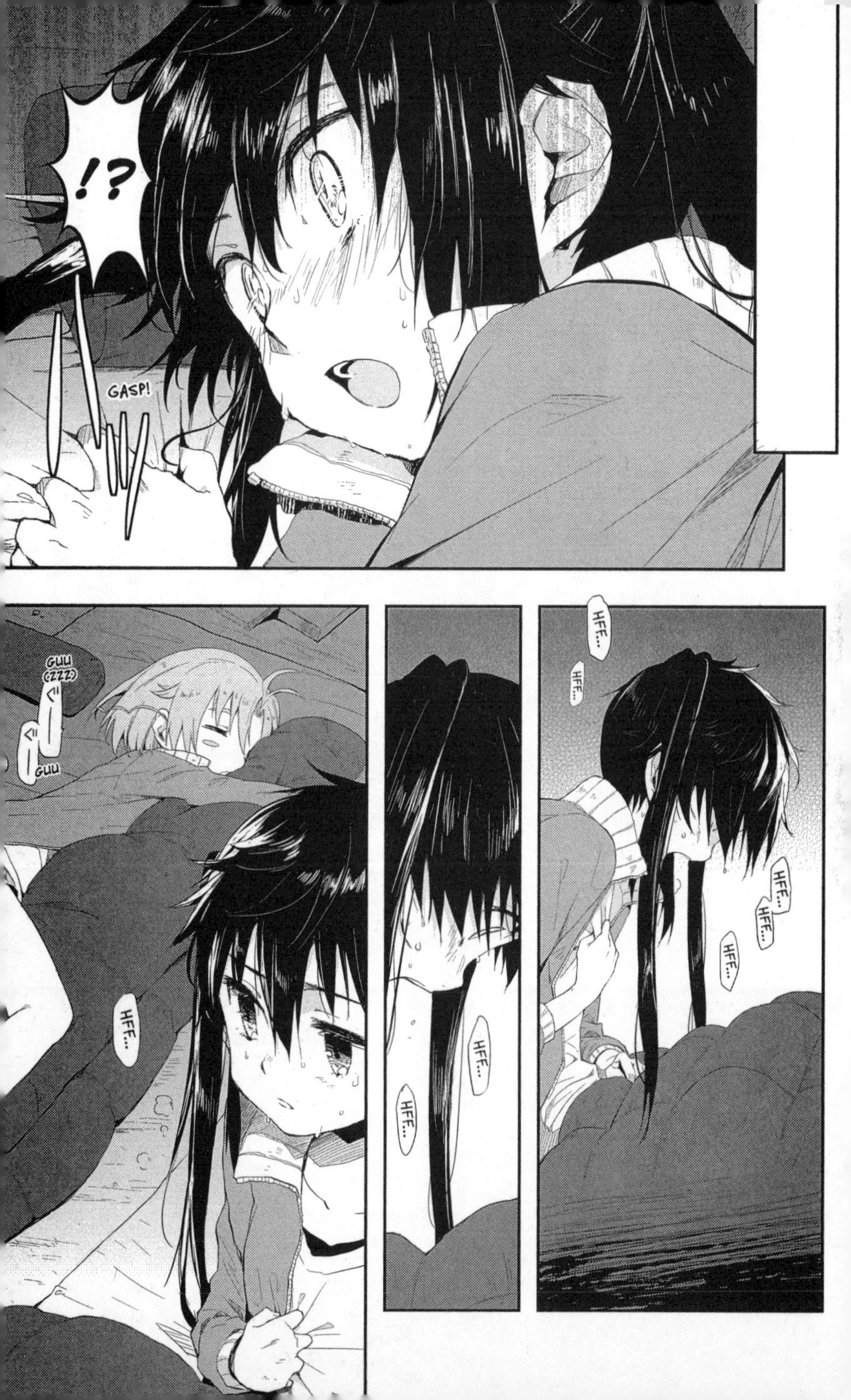
!?
GASP!
HFF...
HFF...
HFF...
HFF...
HFF...
HFF...
HFF...
GUU (ZZZ)
GUU
HFF...

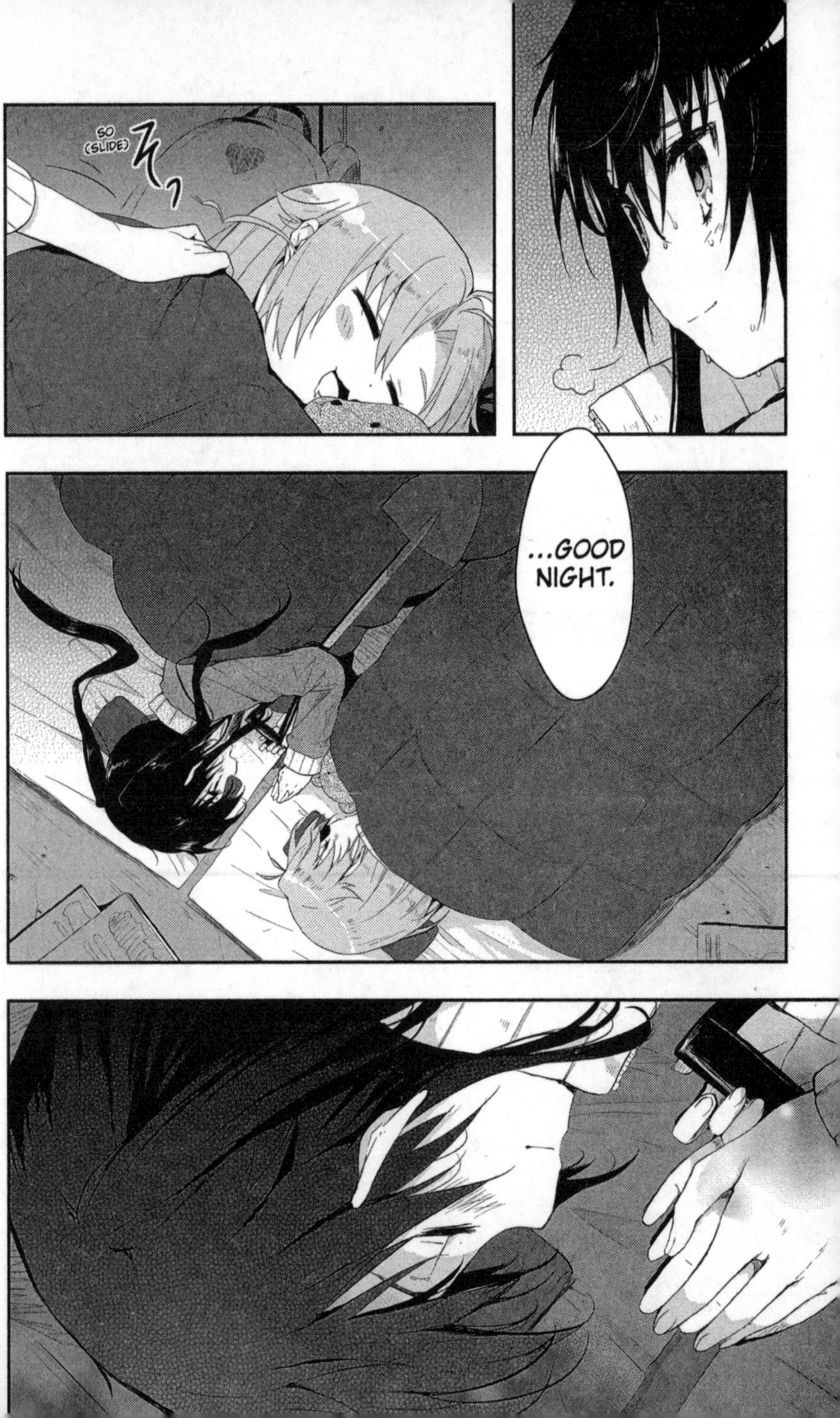
SO (SLIDE)
...GOOD NIGHT.

SCHOOL-LIVE!

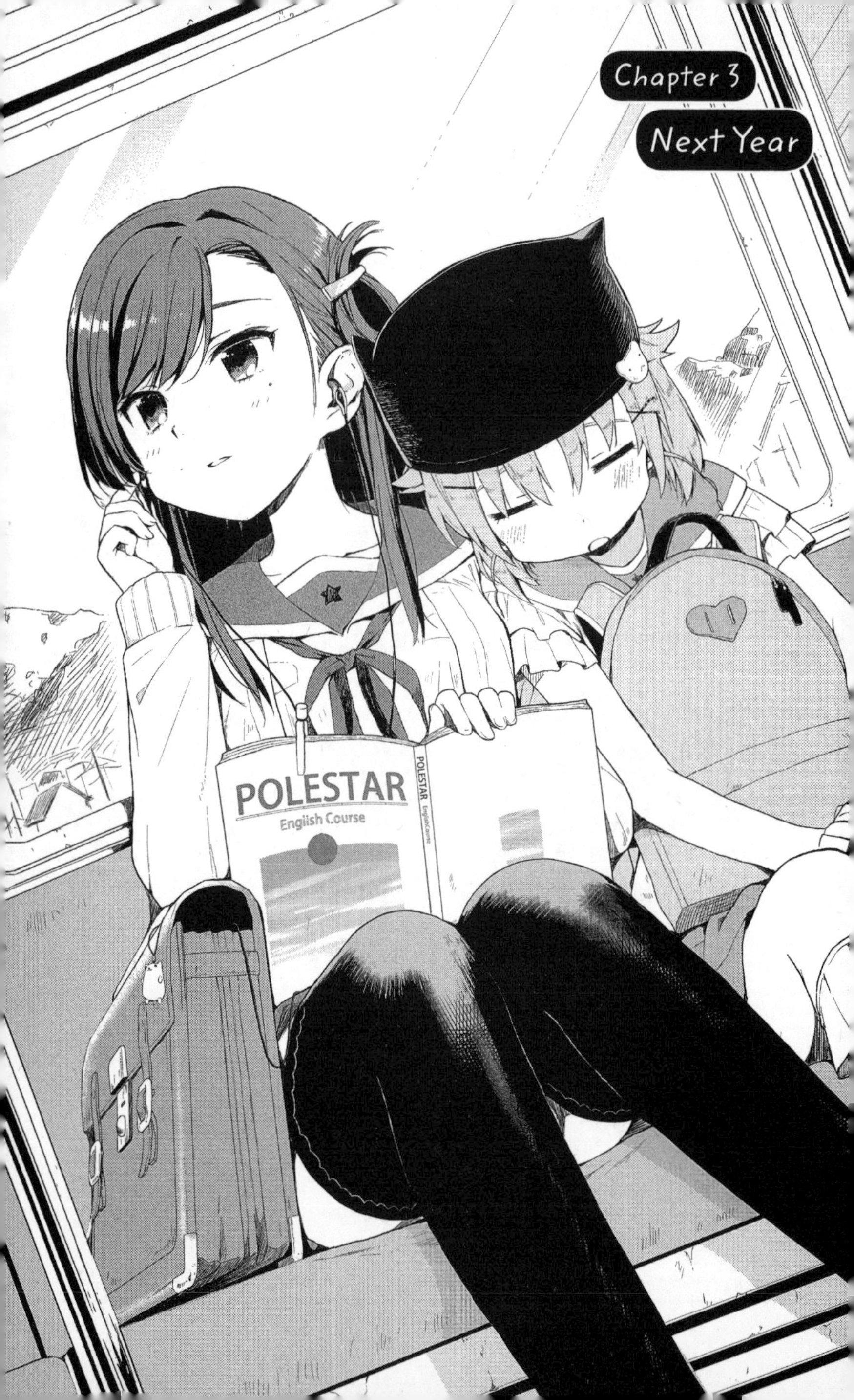
Chapter 3
Next Year
POLESTAR
English Course
POLESTAR English Course

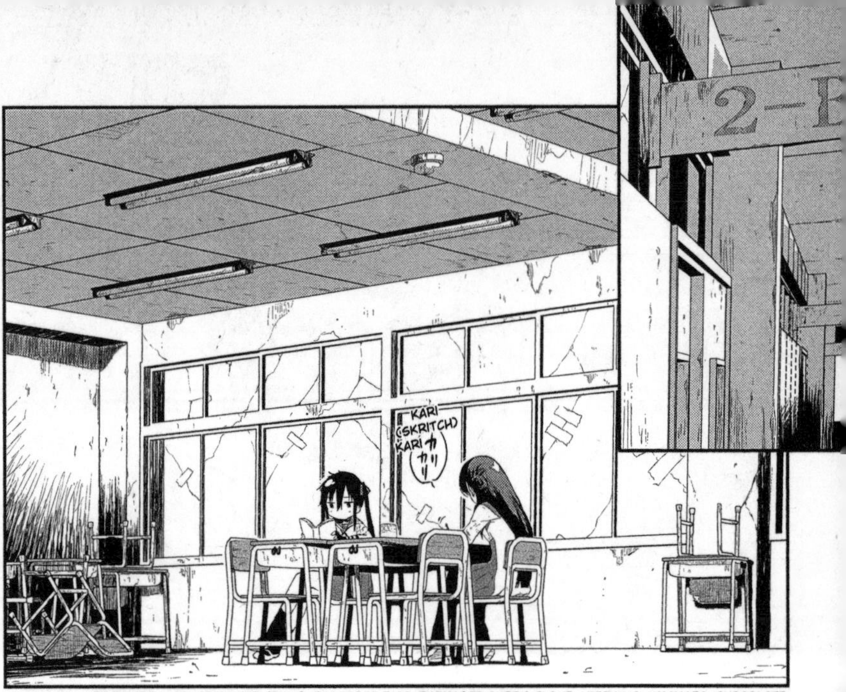
2-B
KARI (SKRITCH) KARI
カリカリ

BOOK: 10/4: SOLAR POWER (RAIN), PACKAGED RICE, PACKAGED CURRY, FLOUR, VITAMINS, UMAKABO, CHOCOLATE, UNIFORMS, HARDTACK 10/5: SOLAR POWER (CLOUDY) [LEFT PAGE] ONIONS HAVE SPROUTED. BRINGING THEM!!

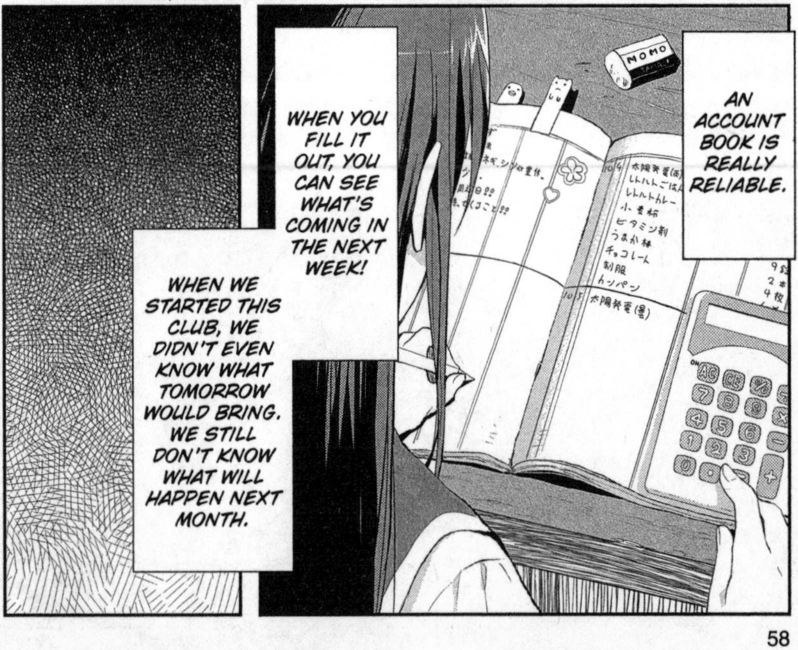
AN ACCOUNT BOOK IS REALLY RELIABLE.
WHEN YOU FILL IT OUT, YOU CAN SEE WHAT'S COMING IN THE NEXT WEEK!
MOMO
WHEN WE STARTED THIS CLUB, WE DIDN'T EVEN KNOW WHAT TOMORROW WOULD BRING. WE STILL DON'T KNOW WHAT WILL HAPPEN NEXT MONTH.

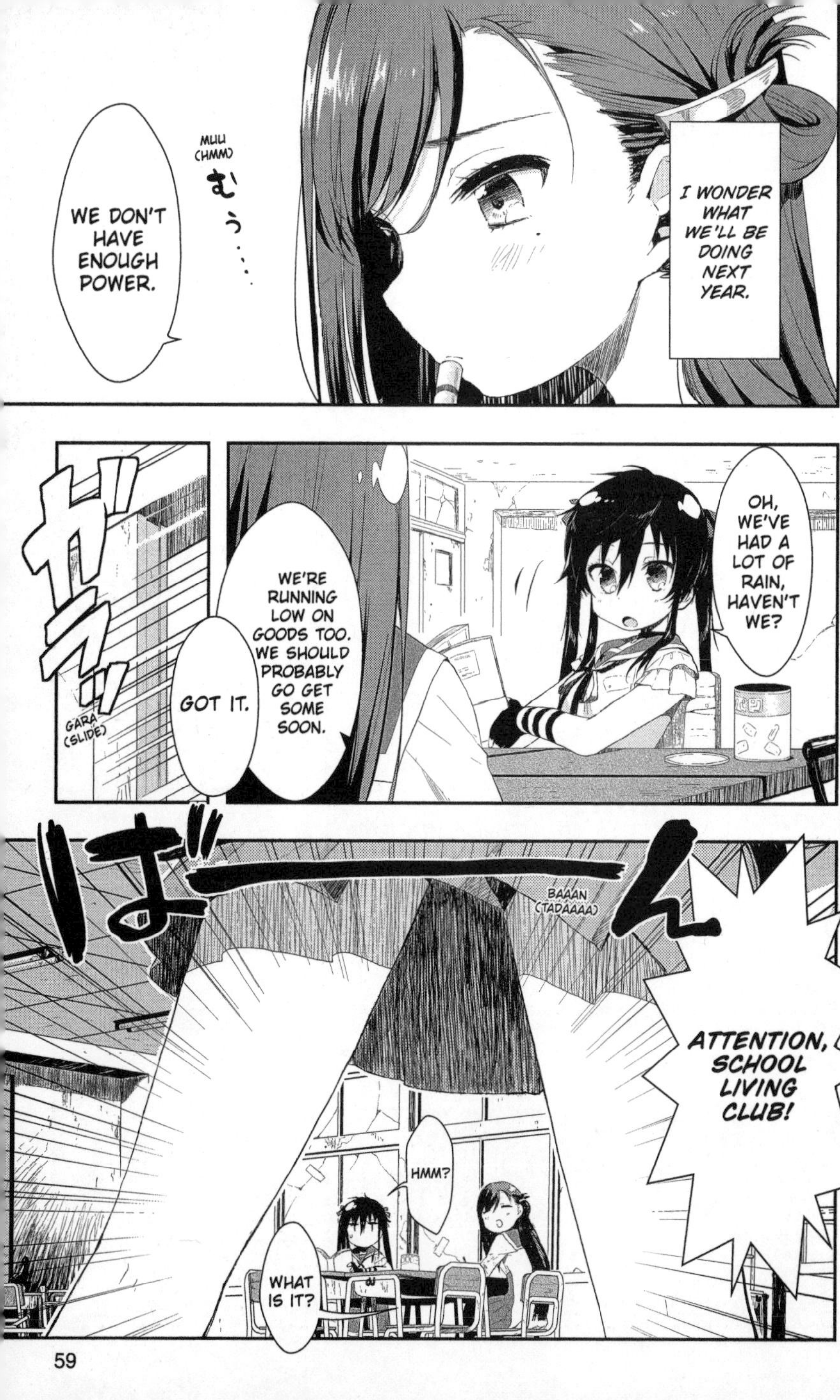
I WONDER WHAT WE'LL BE DOING NEXT YEAR.
MUU (HMM)
むう…
WE DON'T HAVE ENOUGH POWER.
OH, WE'VE HAD A LOT OF RAIN, HAVEN'T WE?
WE'RE RUNNING LOW ON GOODS TOO. WE SHOULD PROBABLY GO GET SOME SOON.
GOT IT.
ガラッ
GARA (SLIDE)
ばーーーん
BAAAN (TADAAAA)
ATTENTION, SCHOOL LIVING CLUB!
HMM?
WHAT IS IT?

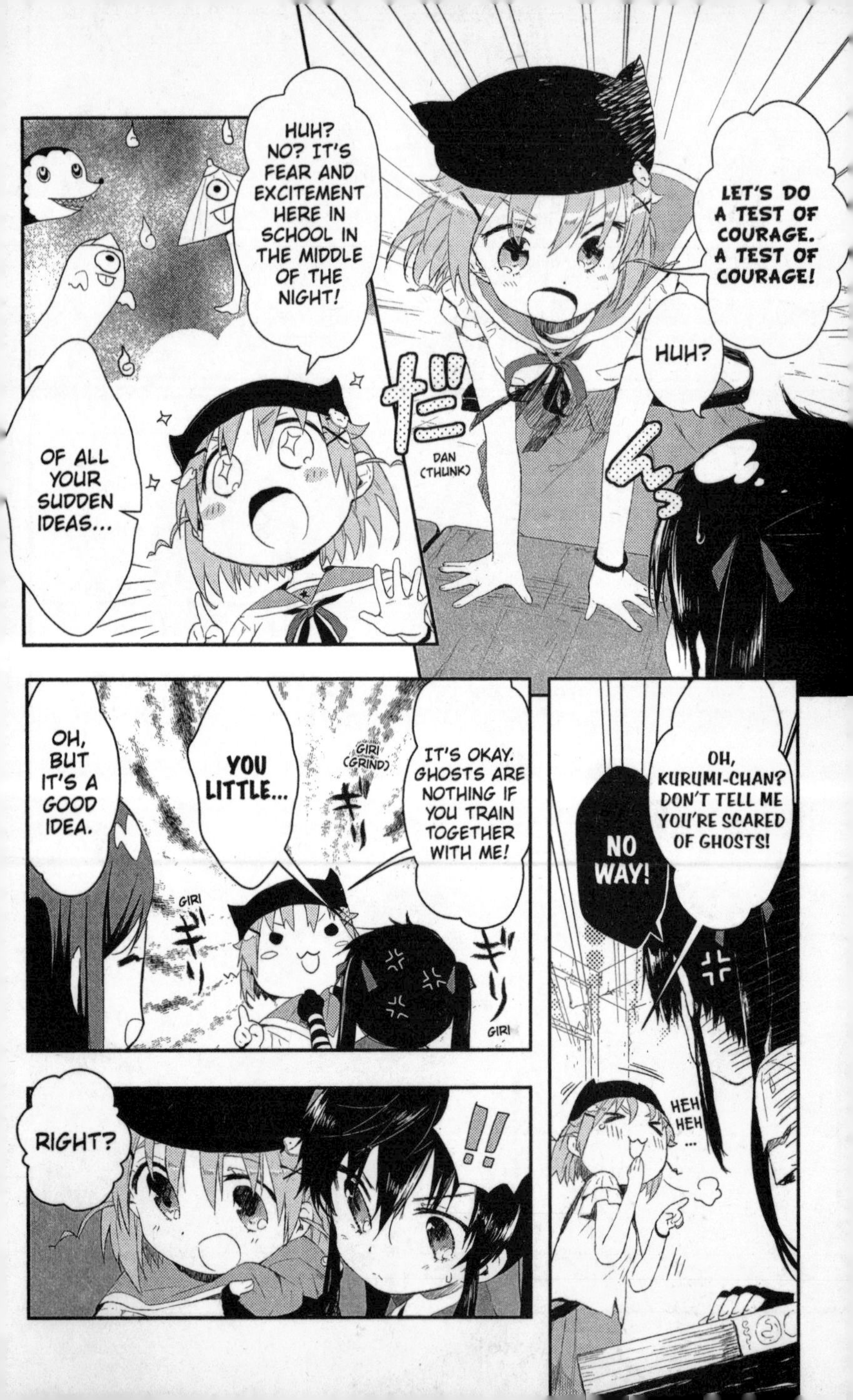
LET'S DO A TEST OF COURAGE. A TEST OF COURAGE!
HUH?
DAN (THUNK)
HUH? NO? IT'S FEAR AND EXCITEMENT HERE IN SCHOOL IN THE MIDDLE OF THE NIGHT!
OF ALL YOUR SUDDEN IDEAS...
OH, KURUMI-CHAN? DON'T TELL ME YOU'RE SCARED OF GHOSTS!
NO WAY!
HEH HEH ...
IT'S OKAY. GHOSTS ARE NOTHING IF YOU TRAIN TOGETHER WITH ME!
GIRI (GRIND)
YOU LITTLE...
OH, BUT IT'S A GOOD IDEA.
GIRI
GIRI
!!
RIGHT?

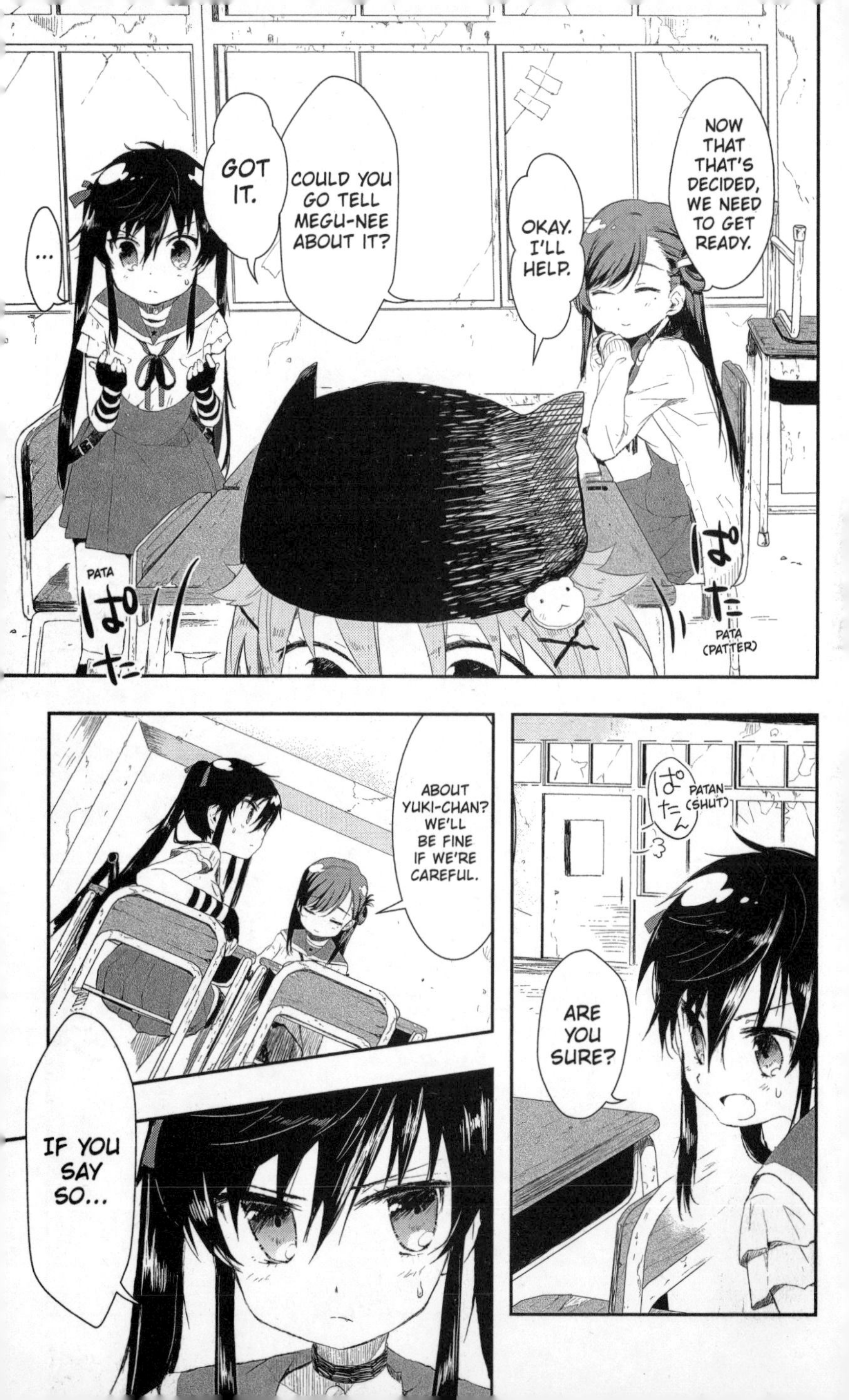
NOW THAT THAT'S DECIDED, WE NEED TO GET READY.
OKAY. I'LL HELP.
COULD YOU GO TELL MEGU-NEE ABOUT IT?
GOT IT.
...
ぱた
PATA (PATTER)
PATA
ぱた
ぱたん
PATAN (SHUT)
ARE YOU SURE?
ABOUT YUKI-CHAN? WE'LL BE FINE IF WE'RE CAREFUL.
IF YOU SAY SO...

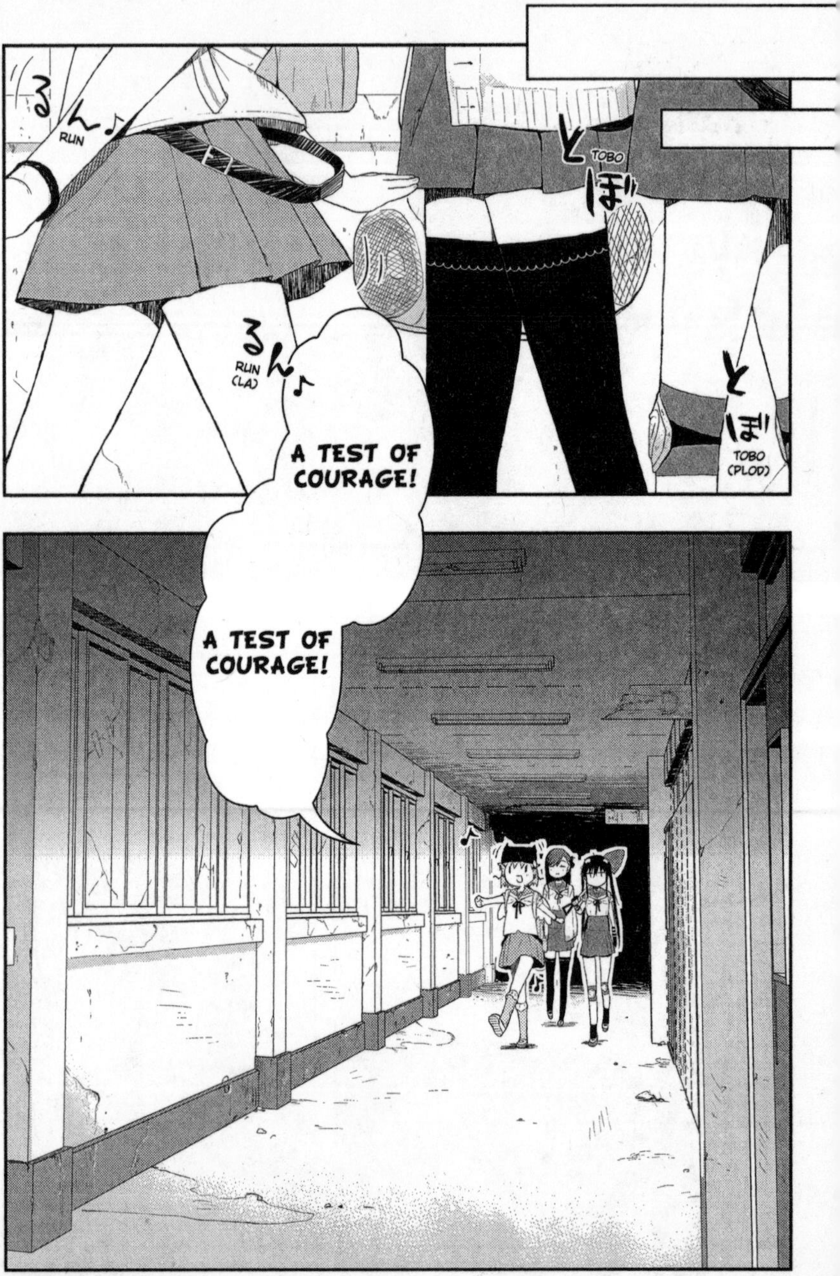
とぼ
TOBO
とぼ
TOBO (PLOD)
るん♪
RUN
るん♪
RUN (LA)
A TEST OF COURAGE!
A TEST OF COURAGE!

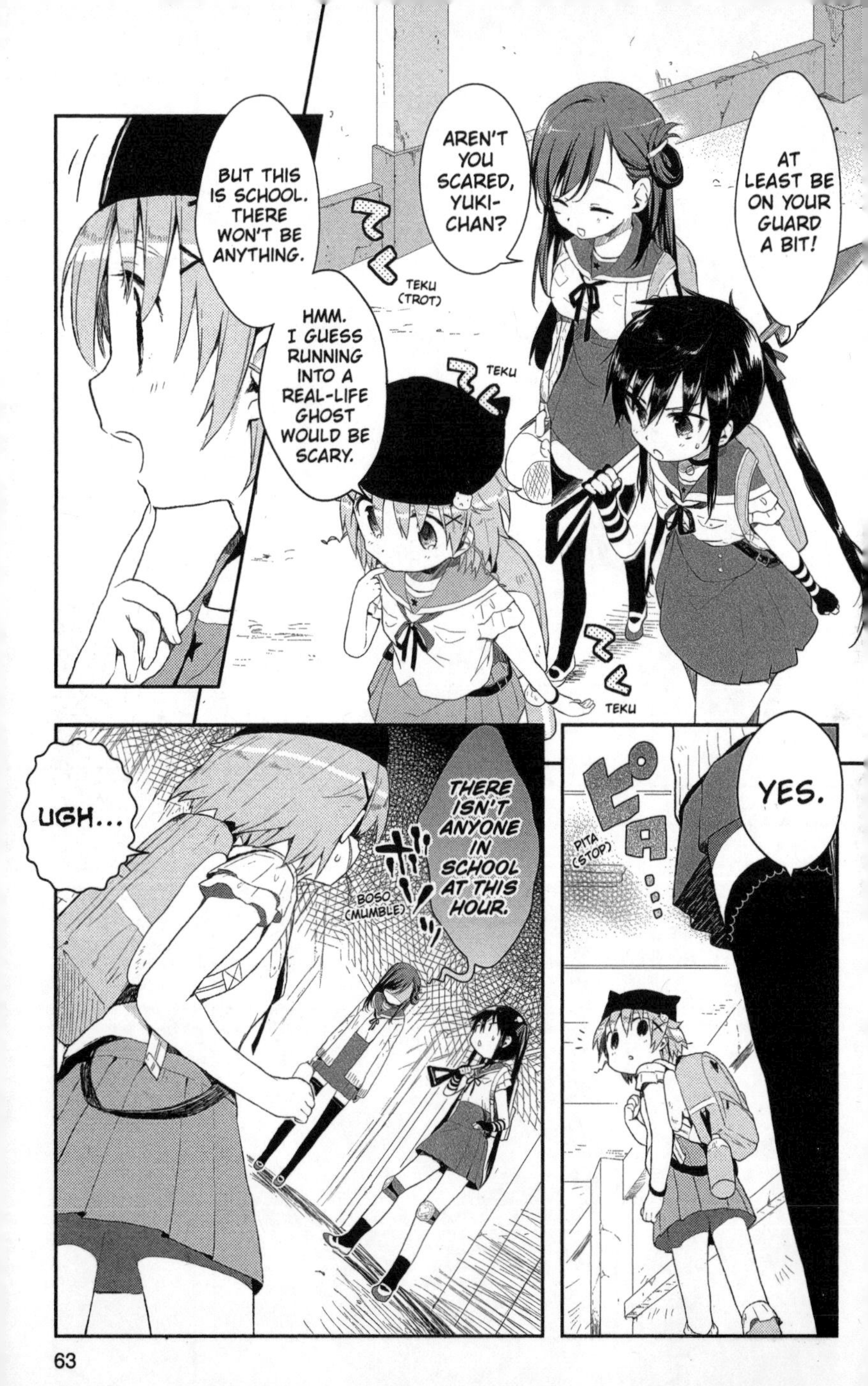
AT LEAST BE ON YOUR GUARD A BIT!
AREN'T YOU SCARED, YUKI-CHAN?
TEKU (TROT)
HMM. I GUESS RUNNING INTO A REAL-LIFE GHOST WOULD BE SCARY.
TEKU
TEKU
BUT THIS IS SCHOOL. THERE WON'T BE ANYTHING.
YES.
PITA (STOP)
THERE ISN'T ANYONE IN SCHOOL AT THIS HOUR.
BOSO (MUMBLE)
UGH...

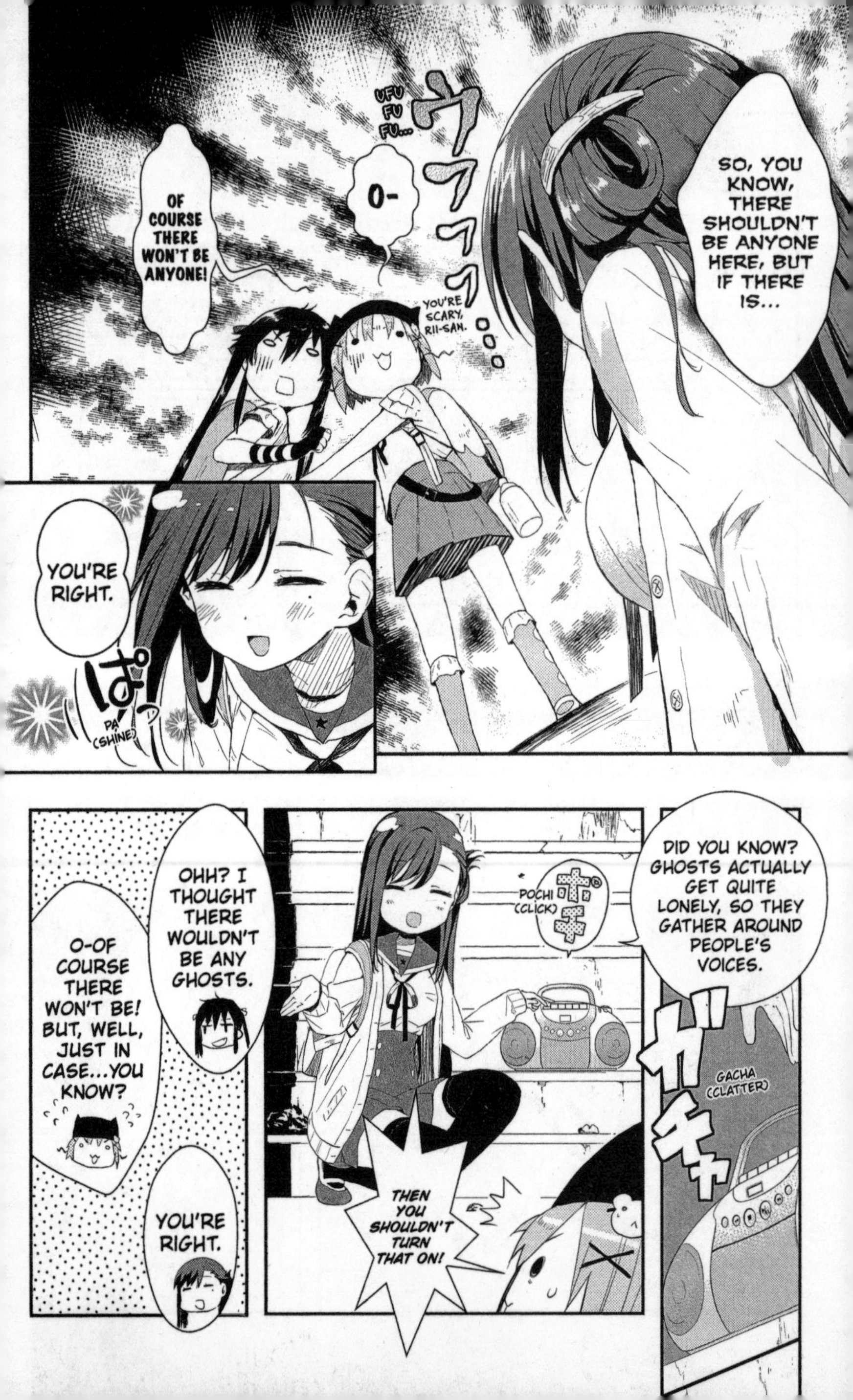
SO, YOU KNOW, THERE SHOULDN'T BE ANYONE HERE, BUT IF THERE IS...
UFU FU FU...
O-
YOU'RE SCARY, RII-SAN.
OF COURSE THERE WON'T BE ANYONE!
YOU'RE RIGHT.
PA (SHINE)
DID YOU KNOW? GHOSTS ACTUALLY GET QUITE LONELY, SO THEY GATHER AROUND PEOPLE'S VOICES.
GACHA (CLATTER)
POCHI (CLICK)
OHH? I THOUGHT THERE WOULDN'T BE ANY GHOSTS.
THEN YOU SHOULDN'T TURN THAT ON!
O-OF COURSE THERE WON'T BE! BUT, WELL, JUST IN CASE...YOU KNOW?
YOU'RE RIGHT.

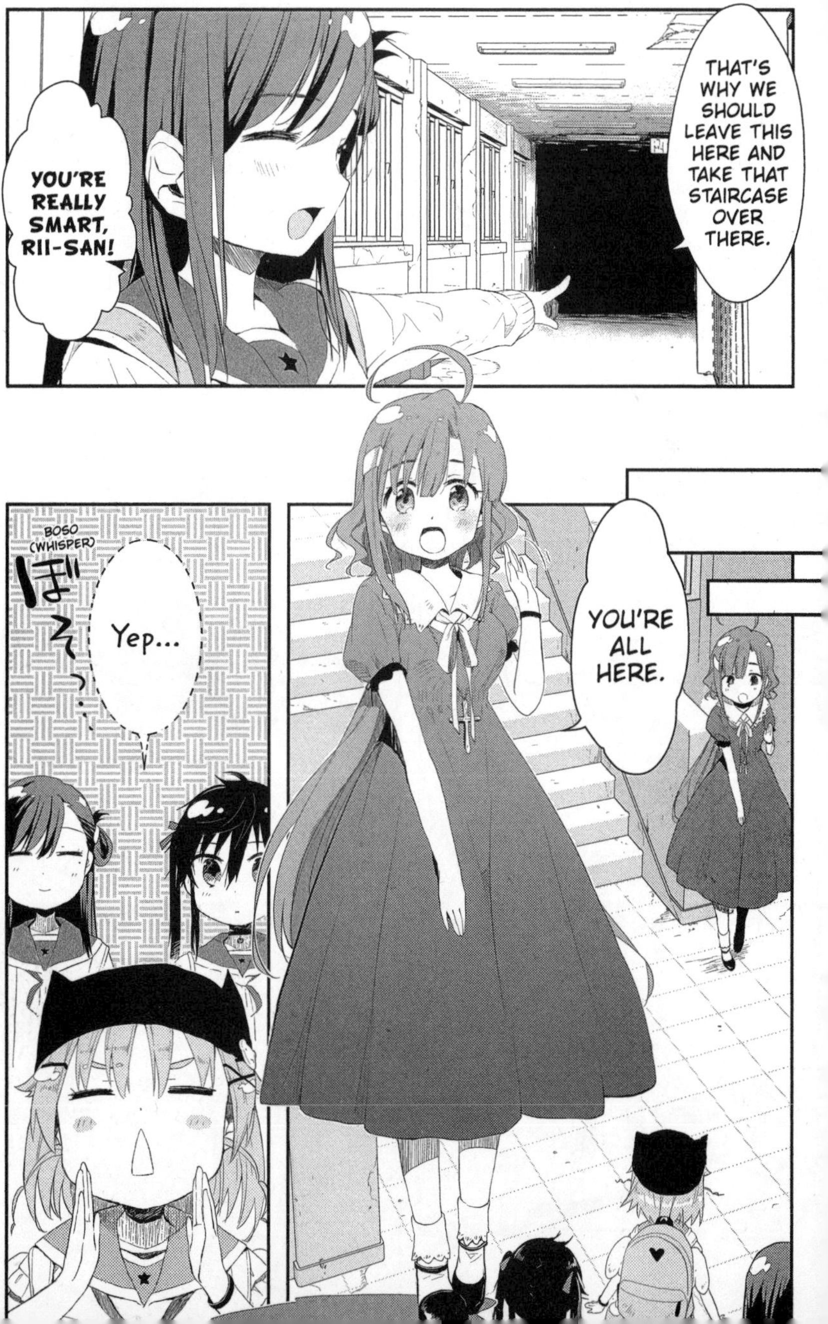
THAT'S WHY WE SHOULD LEAVE THIS HERE AND TAKE THAT STAIRCASE OVER THERE.
YOU'RE REALLY SMART, RII-SAN!
YOU'RE ALL HERE.
BOSO (WHISPER)
ぼそっ
Yep...

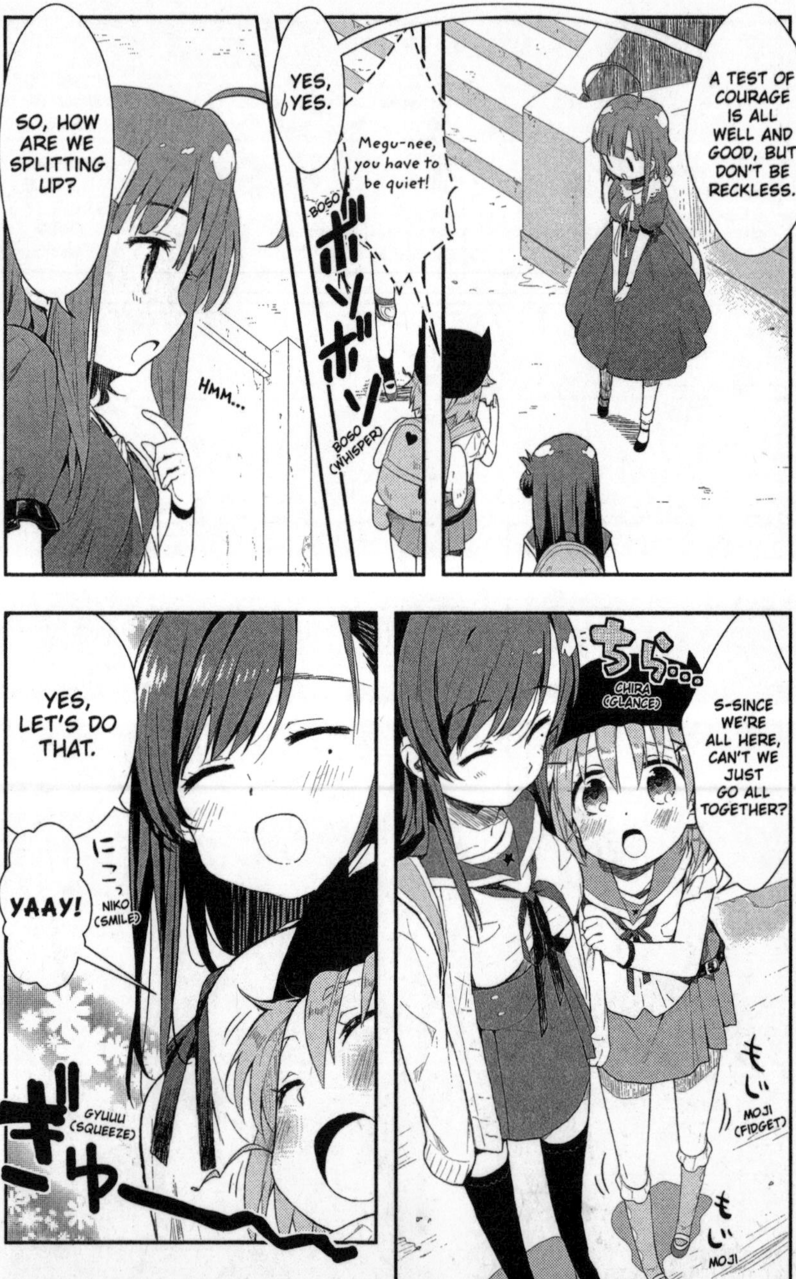
A TEST OF COURAGE IS ALL WELL AND GOOD, BUT DON'T BE RECKLESS.
YES, YES.
Megu-nee, you have to be quiet!
BOSO
ボソボソ
BOSO (WHISPER)
SO, HOW ARE WE SPLITTING UP?
HMM...
ちら…
CHIRA (GLANCE)
S-SINCE WE'RE ALL HERE, CAN'T WE JUST GO ALL TOGETHER?
もじ
MOJI (FIDGET)
もじ
MOJI
YES, LET'S DO THAT.
にこっ
NIKO (SMILE)
YAAY!
ぎゅ～
GYUUU (SQUEEZE)

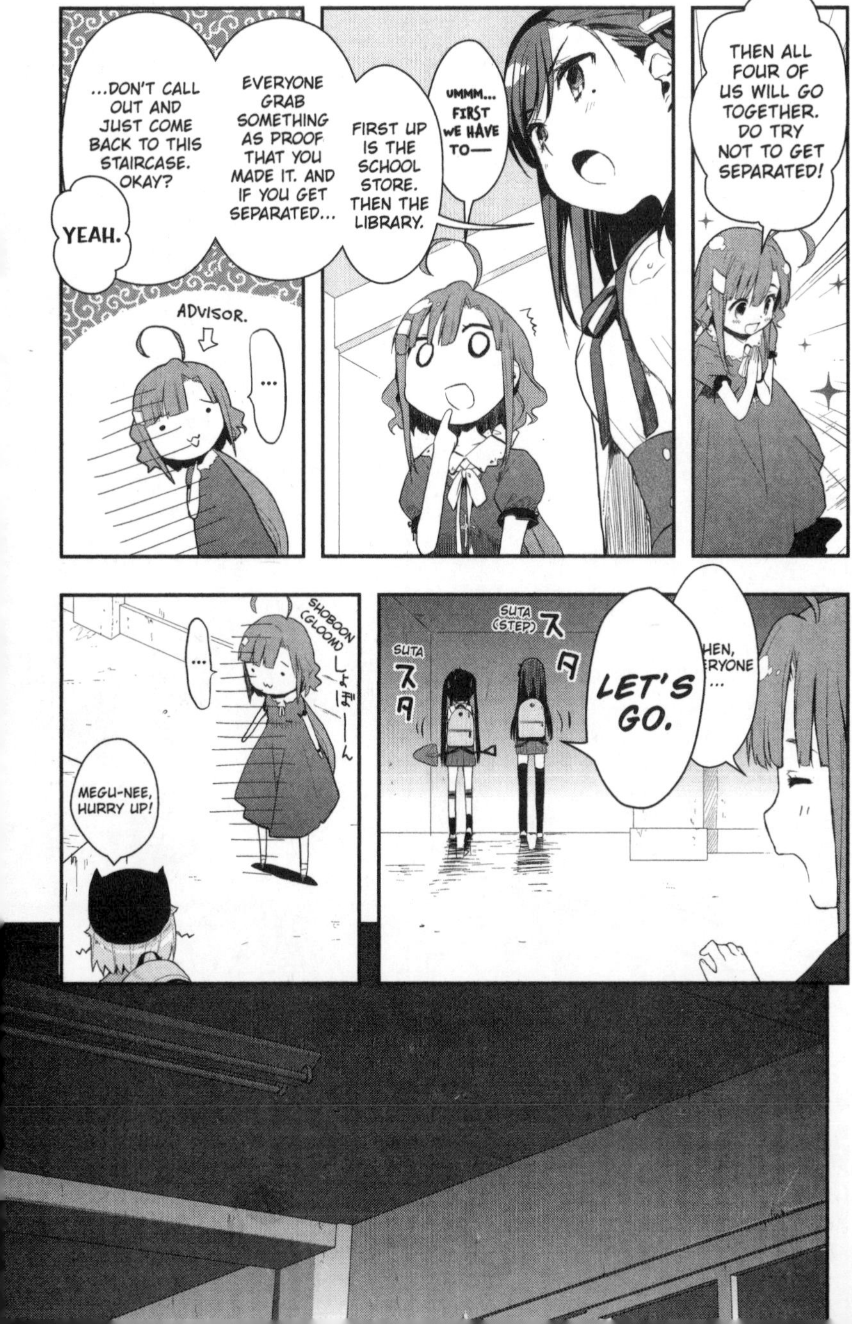
THEN ALL FOUR OF US WILL GO TOGETHER. DO TRY NOT TO GET SEPARATED!
UMMM... FIRST WE HAVE TO—
FIRST UP IS THE SCHOOL STORE. THEN THE LIBRARY.
EVERYONE GRAB SOMETHING AS PROOF THAT YOU MADE IT. AND IF YOU GET SEPARATED...
...DON'T CALL OUT AND JUST COME BACK TO THIS STAIRCASE. OKAY?
YEAH.
ADVISOR.
...
HEN, ERYONE ...
LET'S GO.
SUTA (STEP) スタ
SUTA スタ
...
SHOBOON (GLOOM) しょぼーん
MEGU-NEE, HURRY UP!

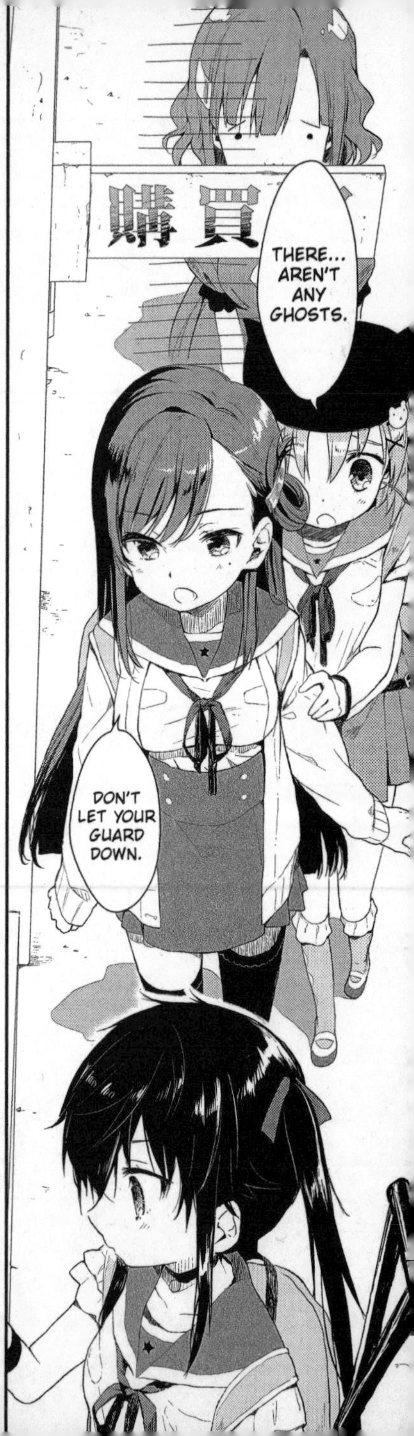
THERE... AREN'T ANY GHOSTS.
DON'T LET YOUR GUARD DOWN.

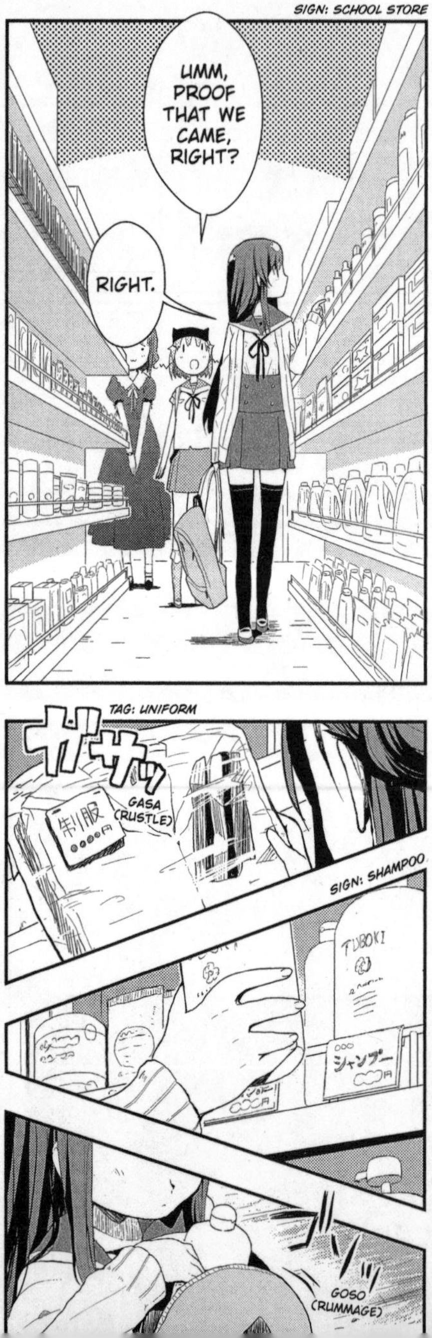
SIGN: SCHOOL STORE
UMM, PROOF THAT WE CAME, RIGHT?
RIGHT.
TAG: UNIFORM
ガサッ
GASA (RUSTLE)
制服
○○○○円
SIGN: SHAMPOO
TUBOKI
○○○
シャンプー
○○○円
GOSO (RUMMAGE)

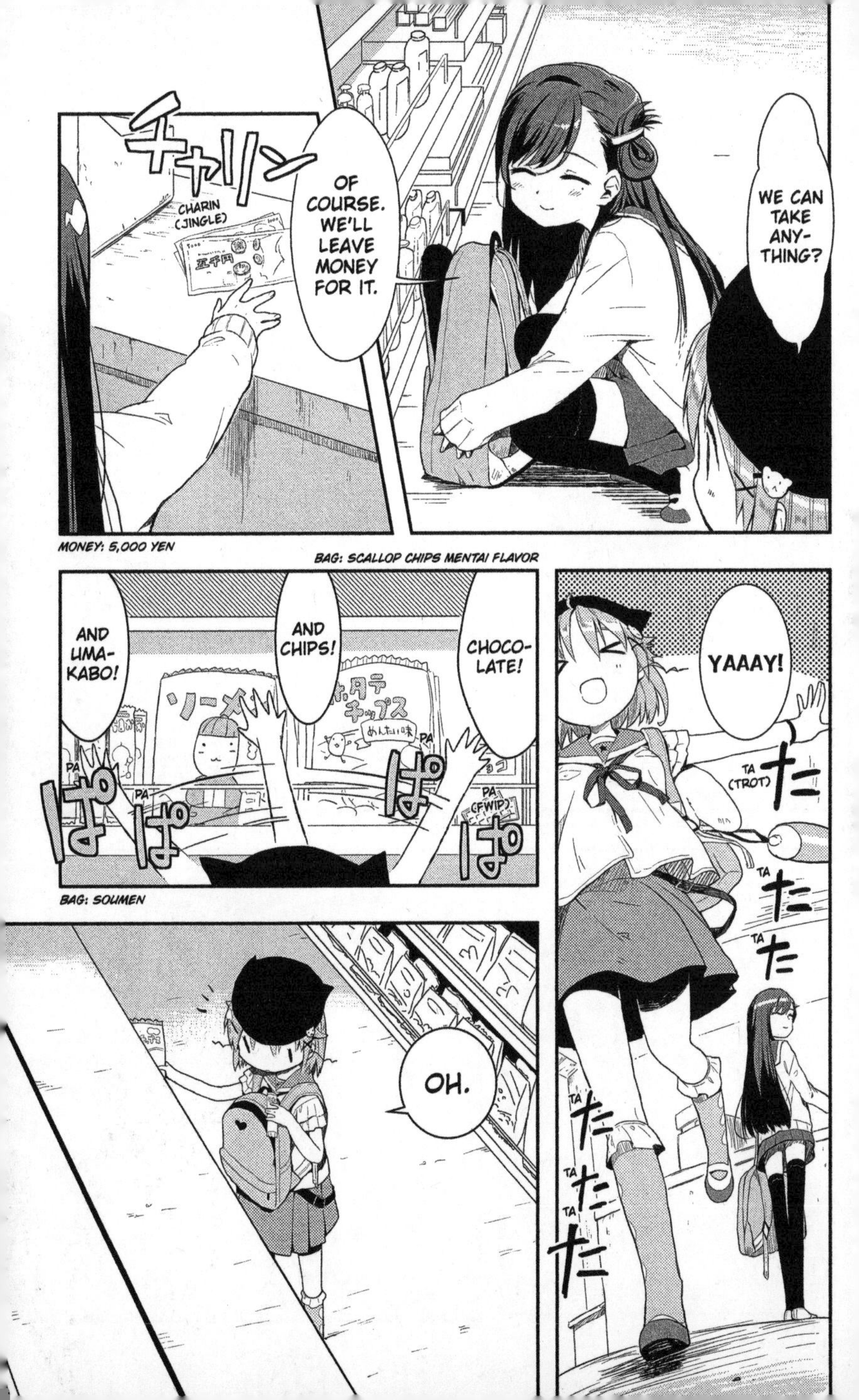
WE CAN TAKE ANYTHING?
OF COURSE. WE'LL LEAVE MONEY FOR IT.
チャリン
CHARIN (JINGLE)
MONEY: 5,000 YEN
BAG: SCALLOP CHIPS MENTAI FLAVOR
YAAAY!
TA (TROT) た
TA た
TA た
TA た
TA た
TA た
CHOCO-LATE!
AND CHIPS!
AND UMA-KABO!
PA (FWIP) ぱ
PA ぱ
PA ぱ
PA ぱ
BAG: SOUMEN
OH.

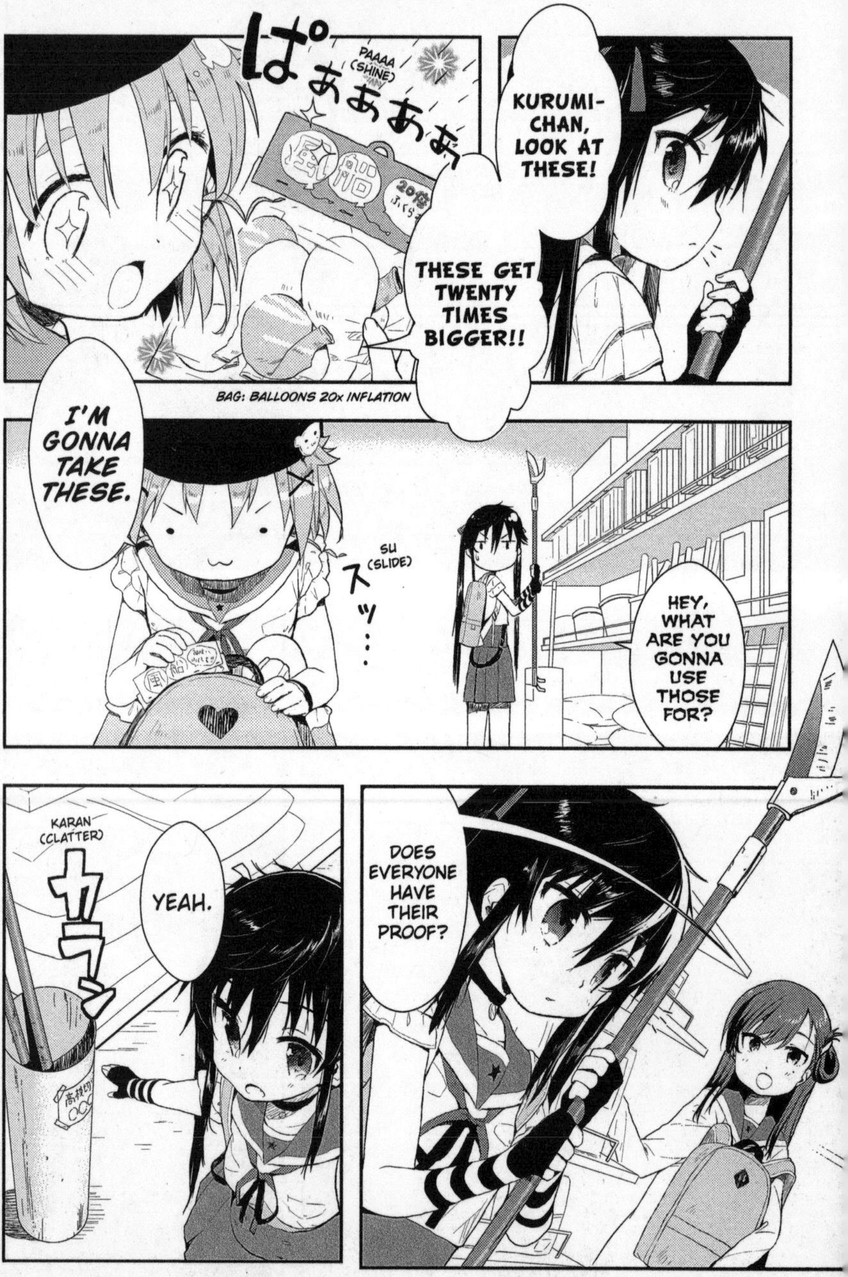
KURUMI-CHAN, LOOK AT THESE!
THESE GET TWENTY TIMES BIGGER!!
PAAAA (SHINE)
BAG: BALLOONS 20x INFLATION
HEY, WHAT ARE YOU GONNA USE THOSE FOR?
SU (SLIDE)
I'M GONNA TAKE THESE.
DOES EVERYONE HAVE THEIR PROOF?
YEAH.
KARAN (CLATTER)

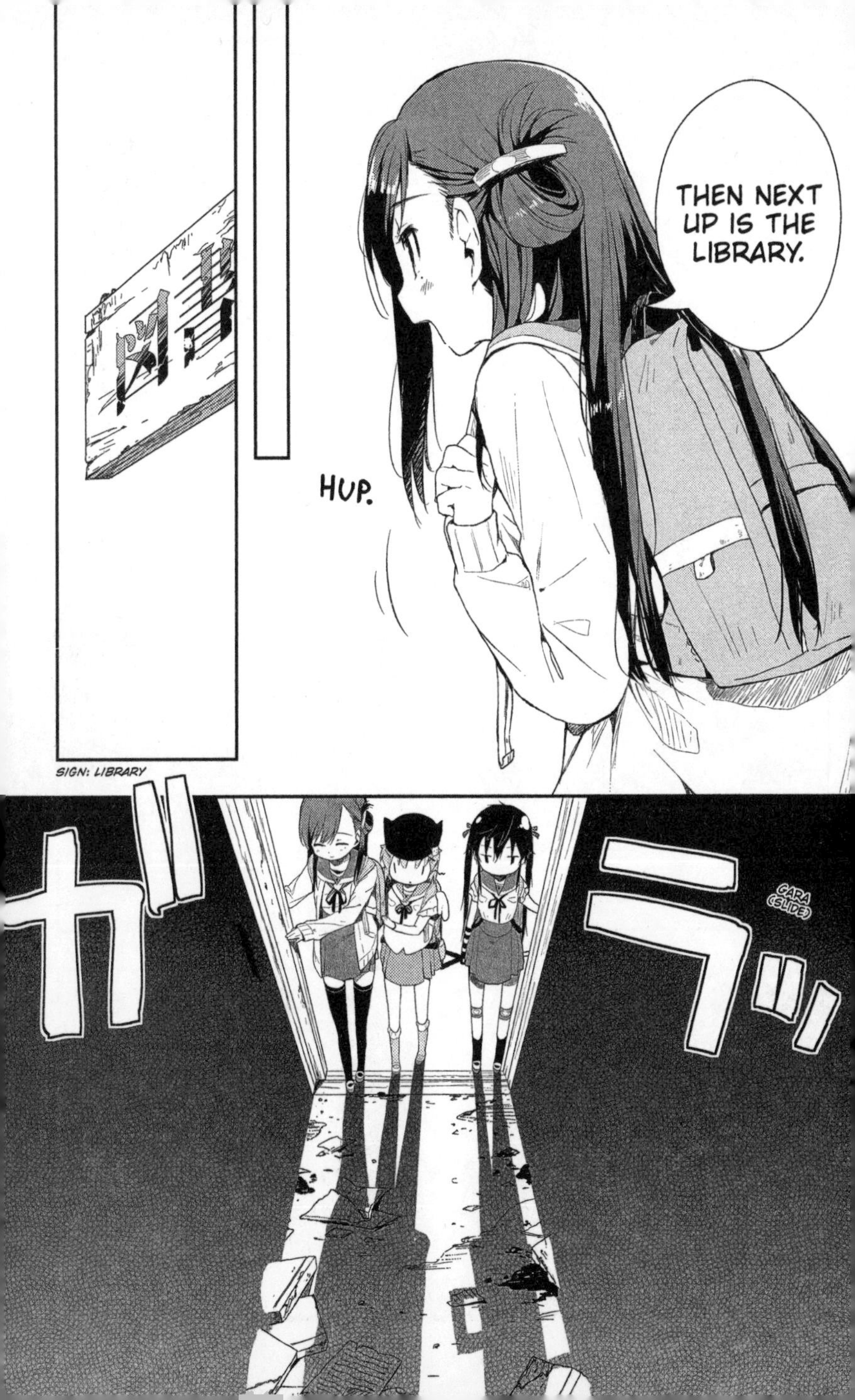
THEN NEXT UP IS THE LIBRARY.
HUP.
SIGN: LIBRARY
ガラッ
GARA (SLIDE)

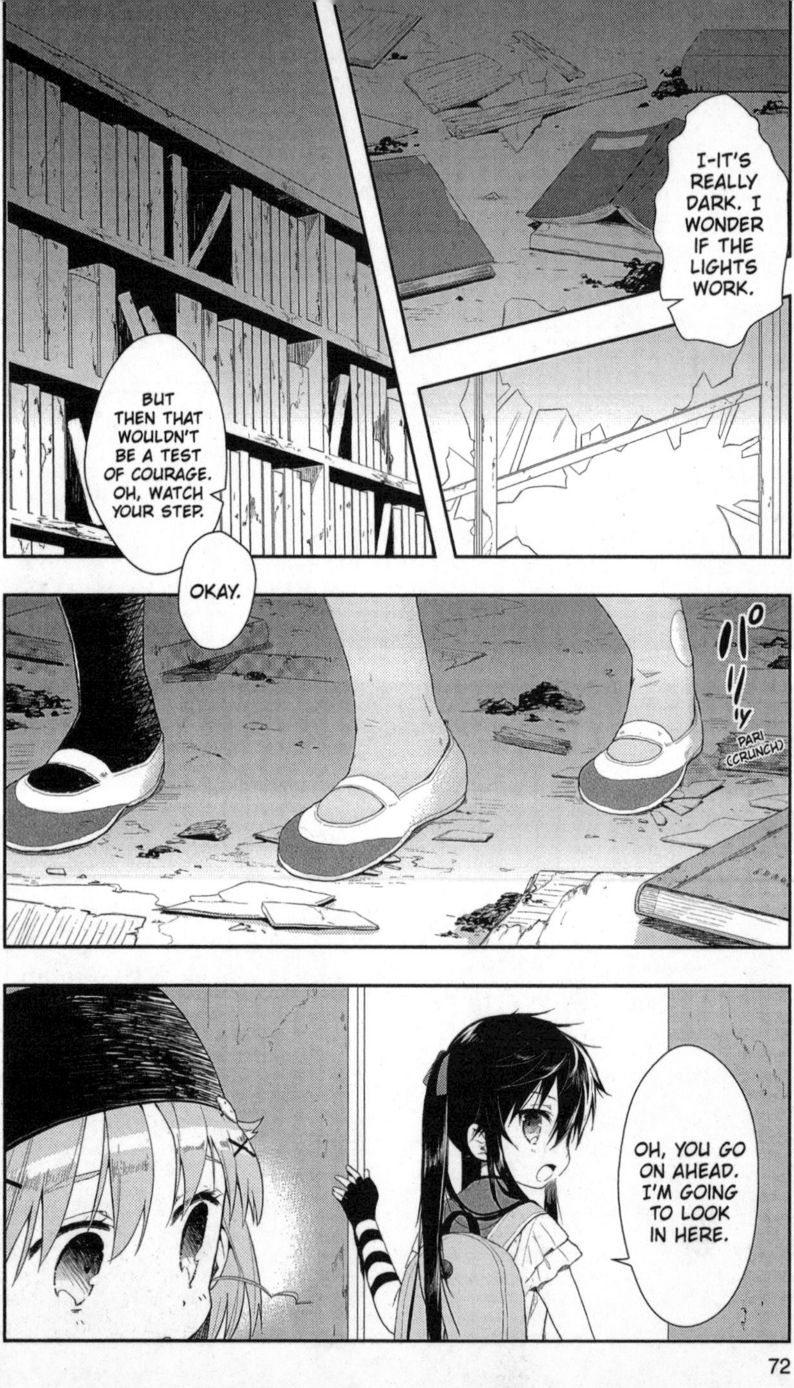
I-IT'S REALLY DARK. I WONDER IF THE LIGHTS WORK.
BUT THEN THAT WOULDN'T BE A TEST OF COURAGE. OH, WATCH YOUR STEP.
OKAY.
パリッ
PARI (CRUNCH)
OH, YOU GO ON AHEAD. I'M GOING TO LOOK IN HERE.

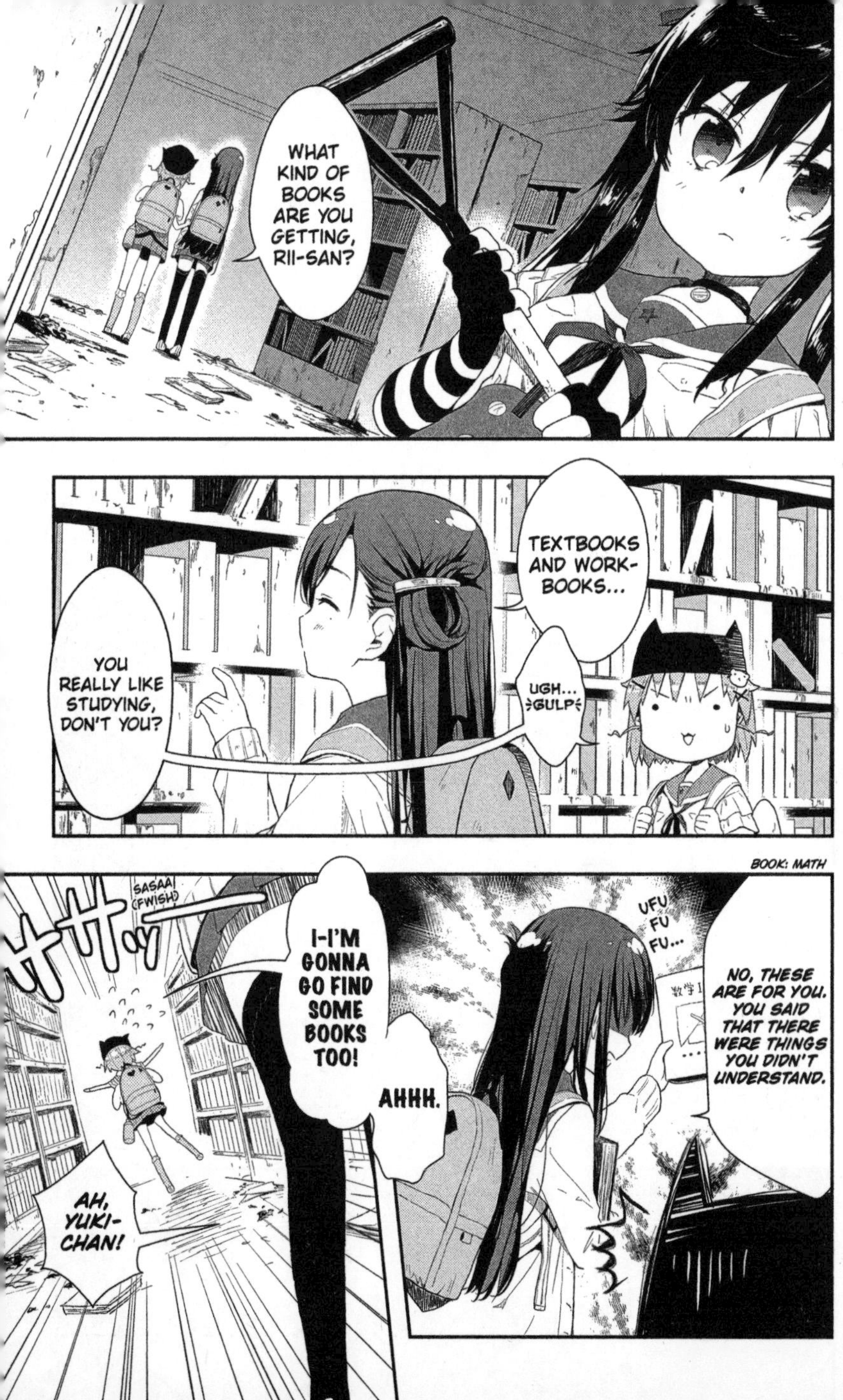
WHAT KIND OF BOOKS ARE YOU GETTING, RII-SAN?
TEXTBOOKS AND WORK-BOOKS...
UGH... GULP
YOU REALLY LIKE STUDYING, DON'T YOU?
BOOK: MATH
UFU FU FU...
NO, THESE ARE FOR YOU. YOU SAID THAT THERE WERE THINGS YOU DIDN'T UNDERSTAND.
AHHH.
I-I'M GONNA GO FIND SOME BOOKS TOO!
SASAA (FWISH)
AH, YUKI-CHAN!

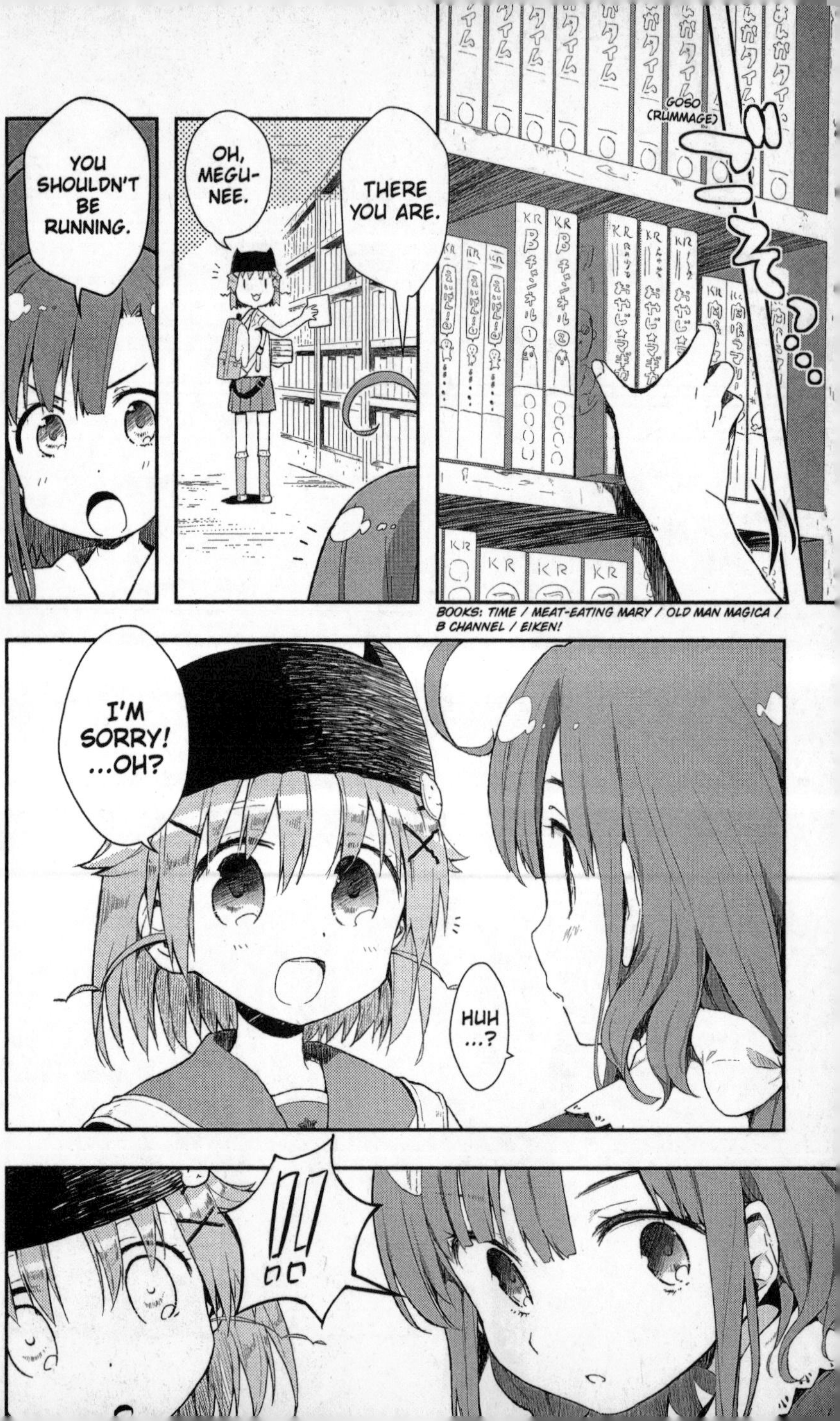
GOSO (RUMMAGE)
THERE YOU ARE.
OH, MEGU-NEE.
YOU SHOULDN'T BE RUNNING.
I'M SORRY! ...OH?
HUH ...?
!!

BOOKS: TIME / MEAT-EATING MARY / OLD MAN MAGICA / B CHANNEL / EIKEN!

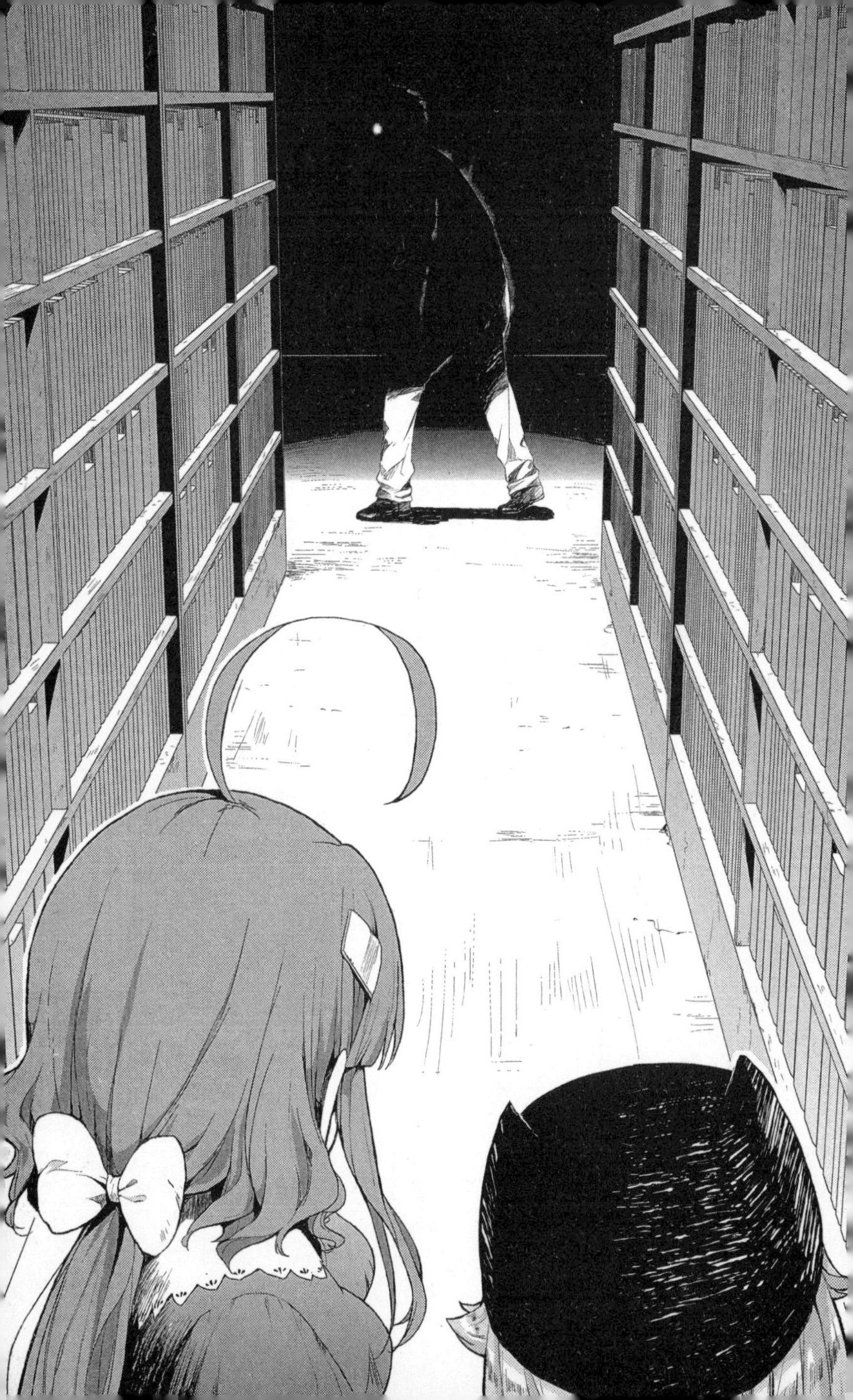

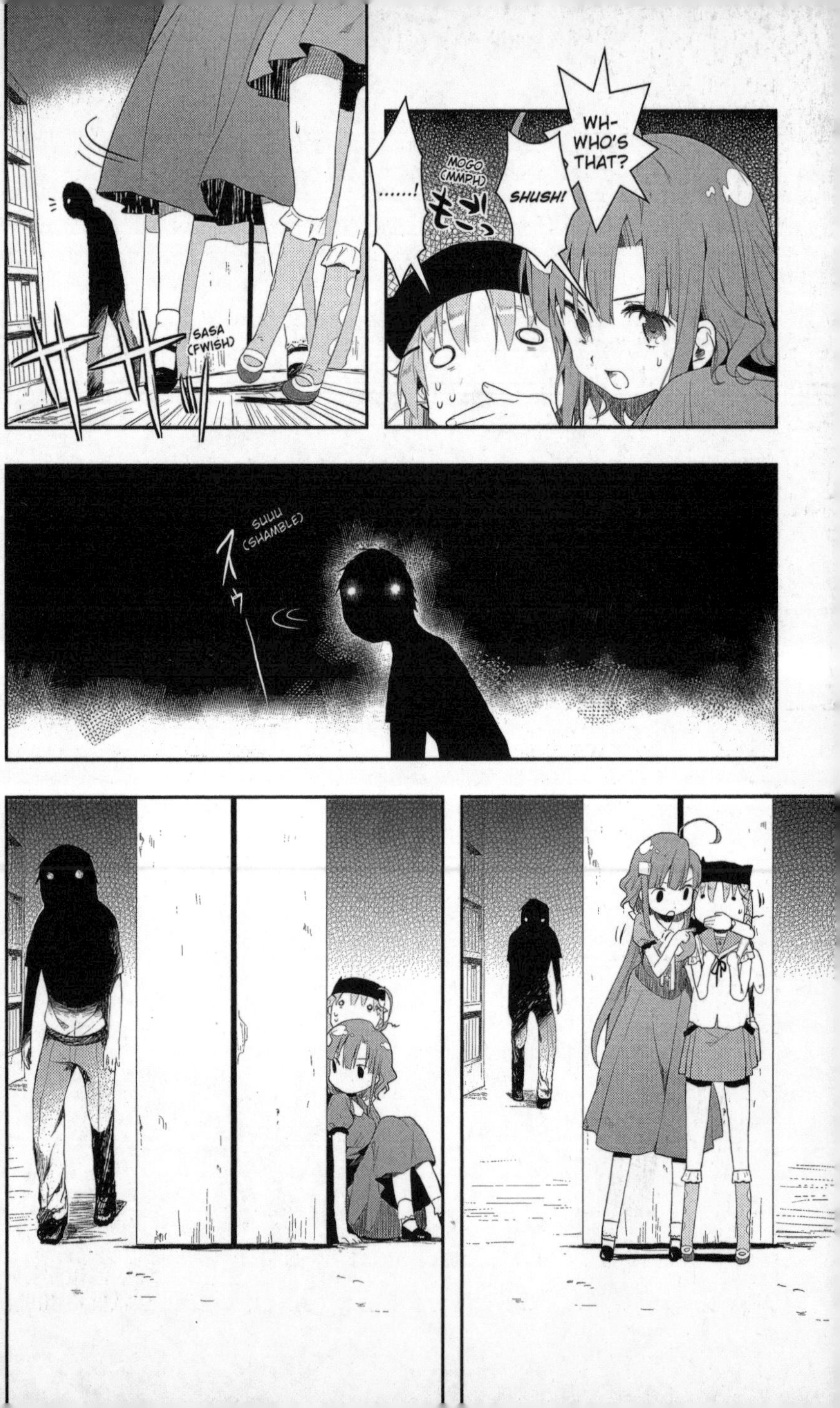
WH- WHO'S THAT?
SHUSH!
MOGO (MMPH)
......!
SASA (FWISH)
SUUU (SHAMBLE)

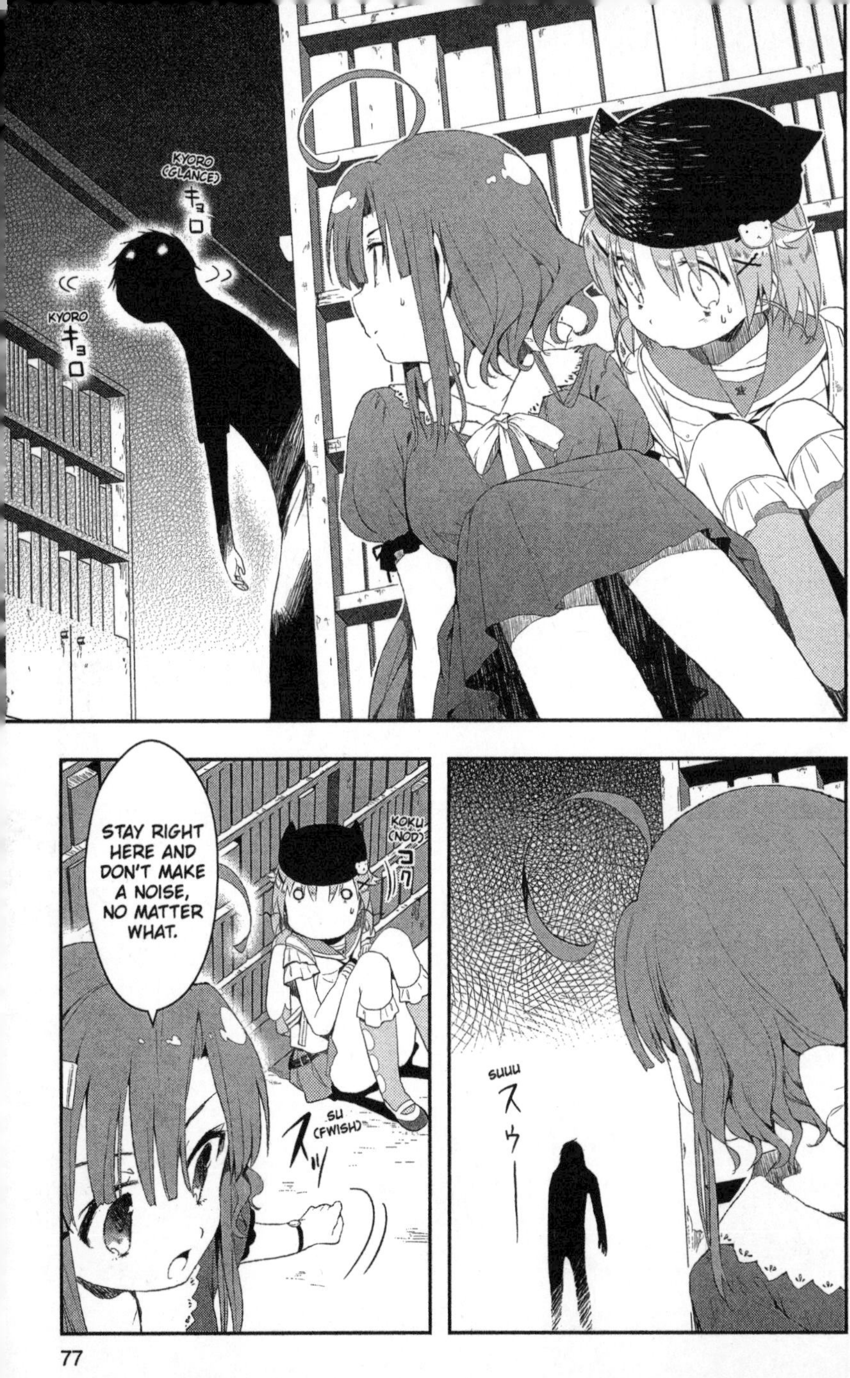
KYORO (GLANCE)
キョロ
KYORO
キョロ
SUUU
スウーー
KOKU (NOD)
コク
STAY RIGHT HERE AND DON'T MAKE A NOISE, NO MATTER WHAT.
SU (FWISH)
スッ

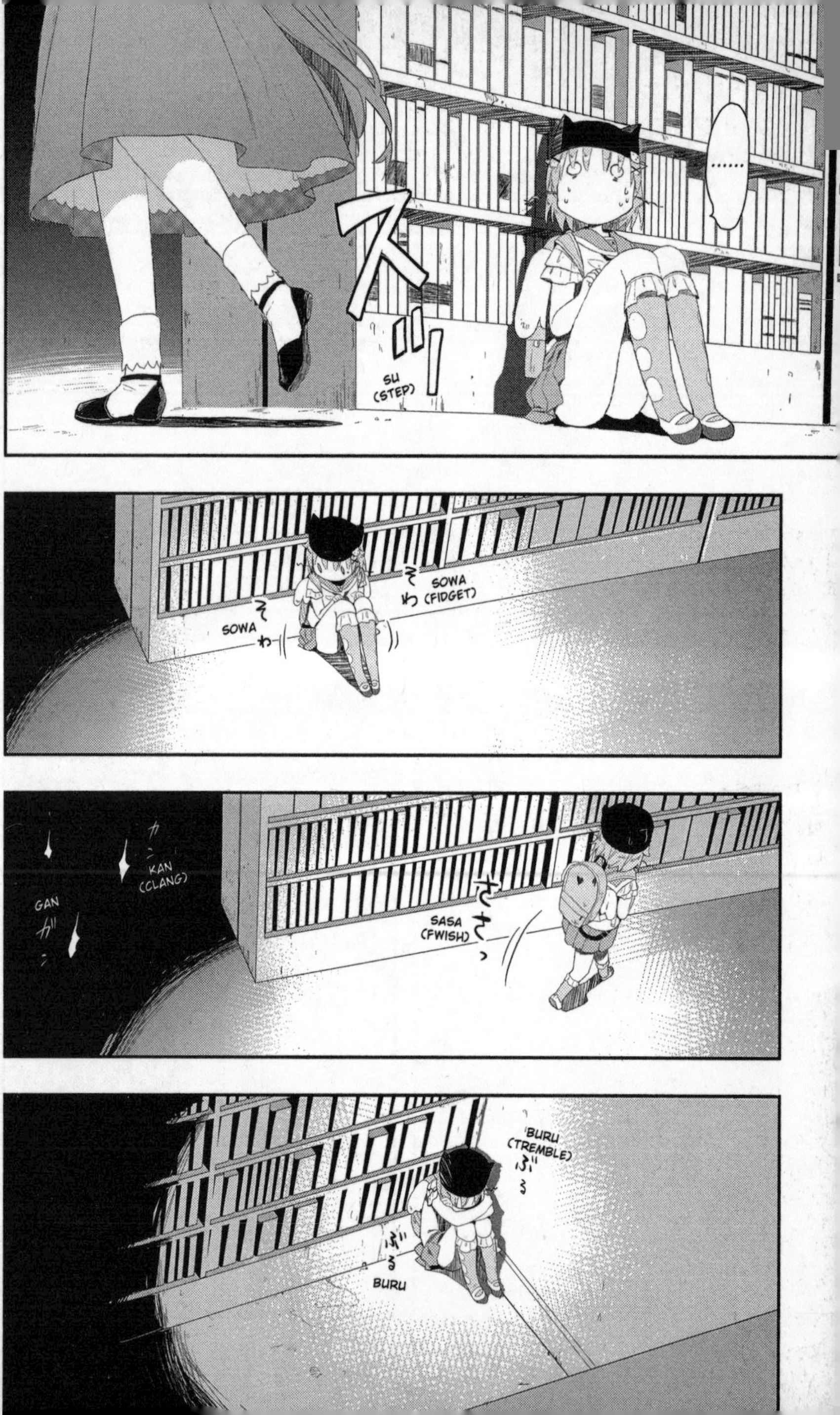

......
ス
SU (STEP)
SOWA (FIDGET)
SOWA
KAN (CLANG)
GAN
SASA (FWISH)
BURU (TREMBLE)
BURU

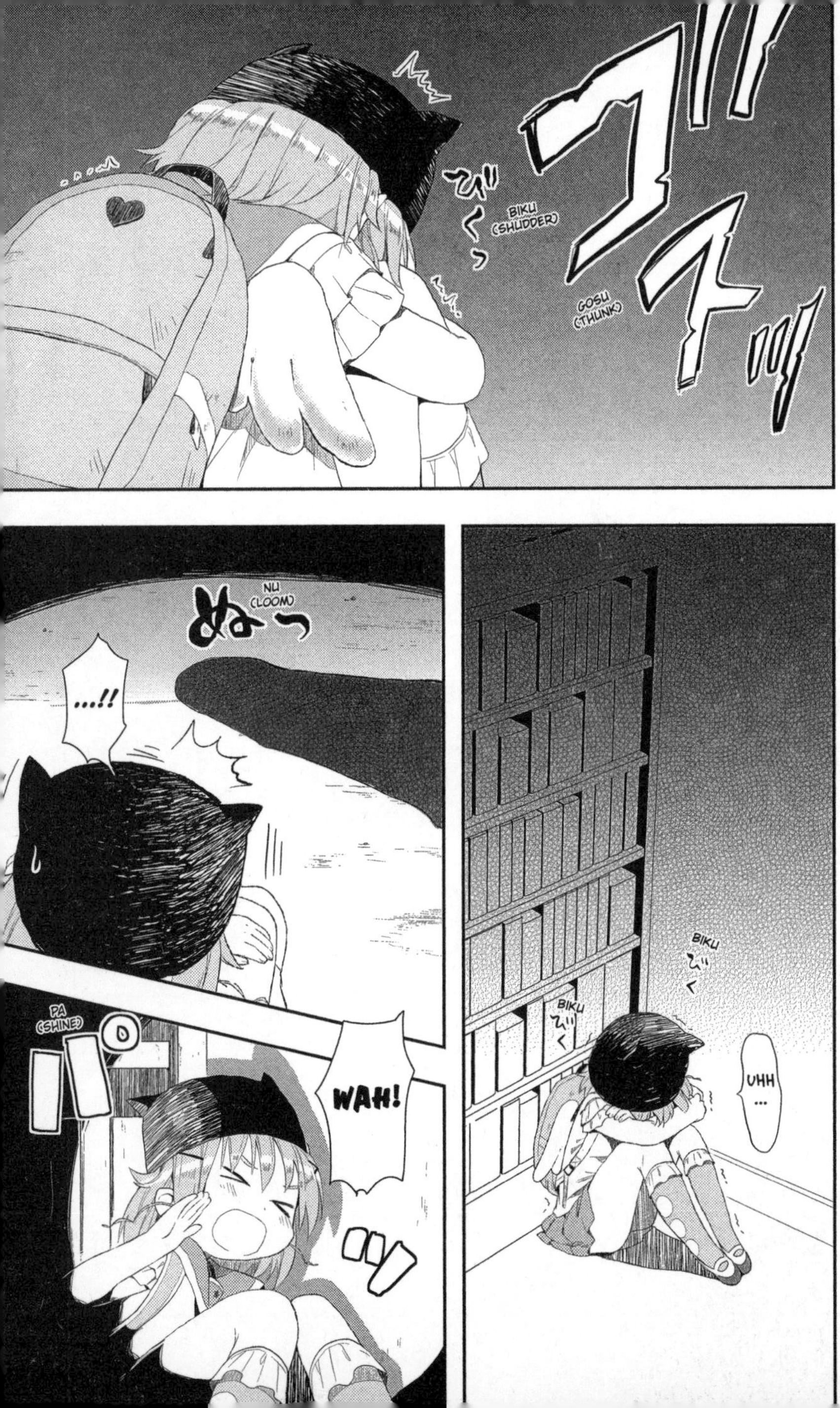
GOSU (THUNK)
BIKU (SHUDDER)
BIKU
BIKU
UHH ...
NU (LOOM)
...!!
PA (SHINE)
WAH!

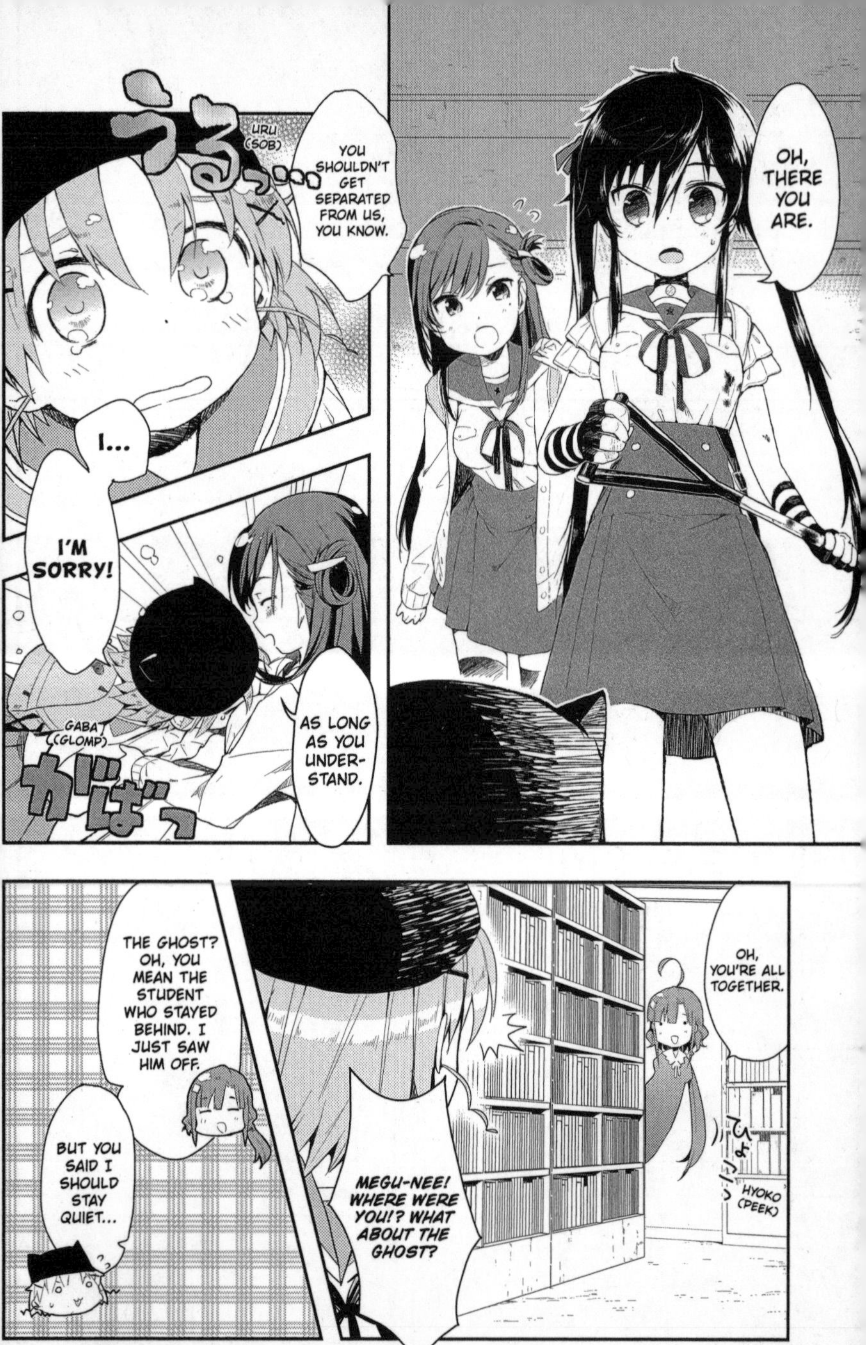
OH, THERE YOU ARE.
うるっ…
URU (SOB)
YOU SHOULDN'T GET SEPARATED FROM US, YOU KNOW.
I...
I'M SORRY!
がばっ
GABA (GLOMP)
AS LONG AS YOU UNDER-STAND.
OH, YOU'RE ALL TOGETHER.
ひょこっ
HYOKO (PEEK)
MEGU-NEE! WHERE WERE YOU!? WHAT ABOUT THE GHOST?
THE GHOST? OH, YOU MEAN THE STUDENT WHO STAYED BEHIND. I JUST SAW HIM OFF.
BUT YOU SAID I SHOULD STAY QUIET...

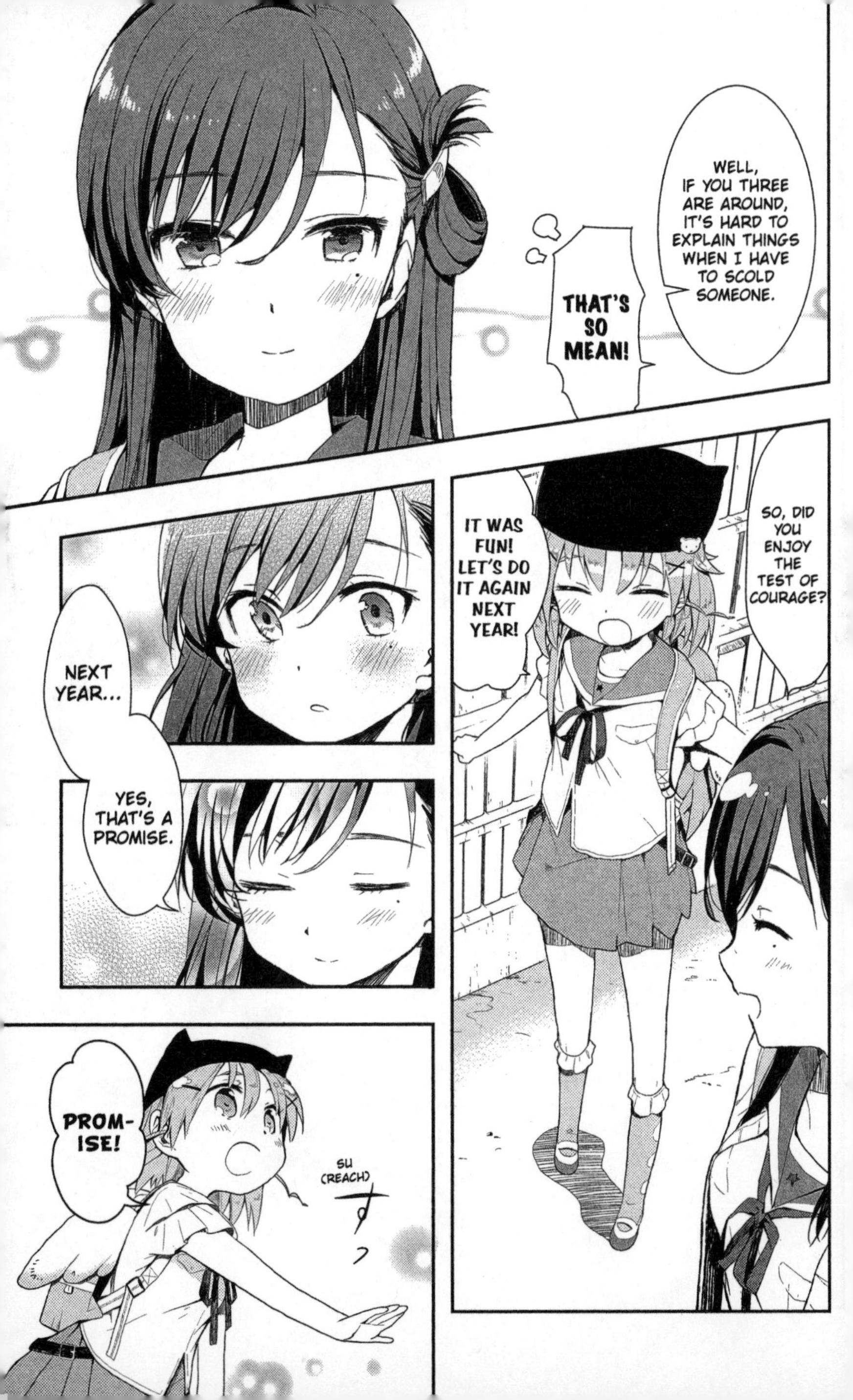

WELL, IF YOU THREE ARE AROUND, IT'S HARD TO EXPLAIN THINGS WHEN I HAVE TO SCOLD SOMEONE.
THAT'S SO MEAN!
SO, DID YOU ENJOY THE TEST OF COURAGE?
IT WAS FUN! LET'S DO IT AGAIN NEXT YEAR!
NEXT YEAR...
YES, THAT'S A PROMISE.
PROM-ISE!
SU (REACH)

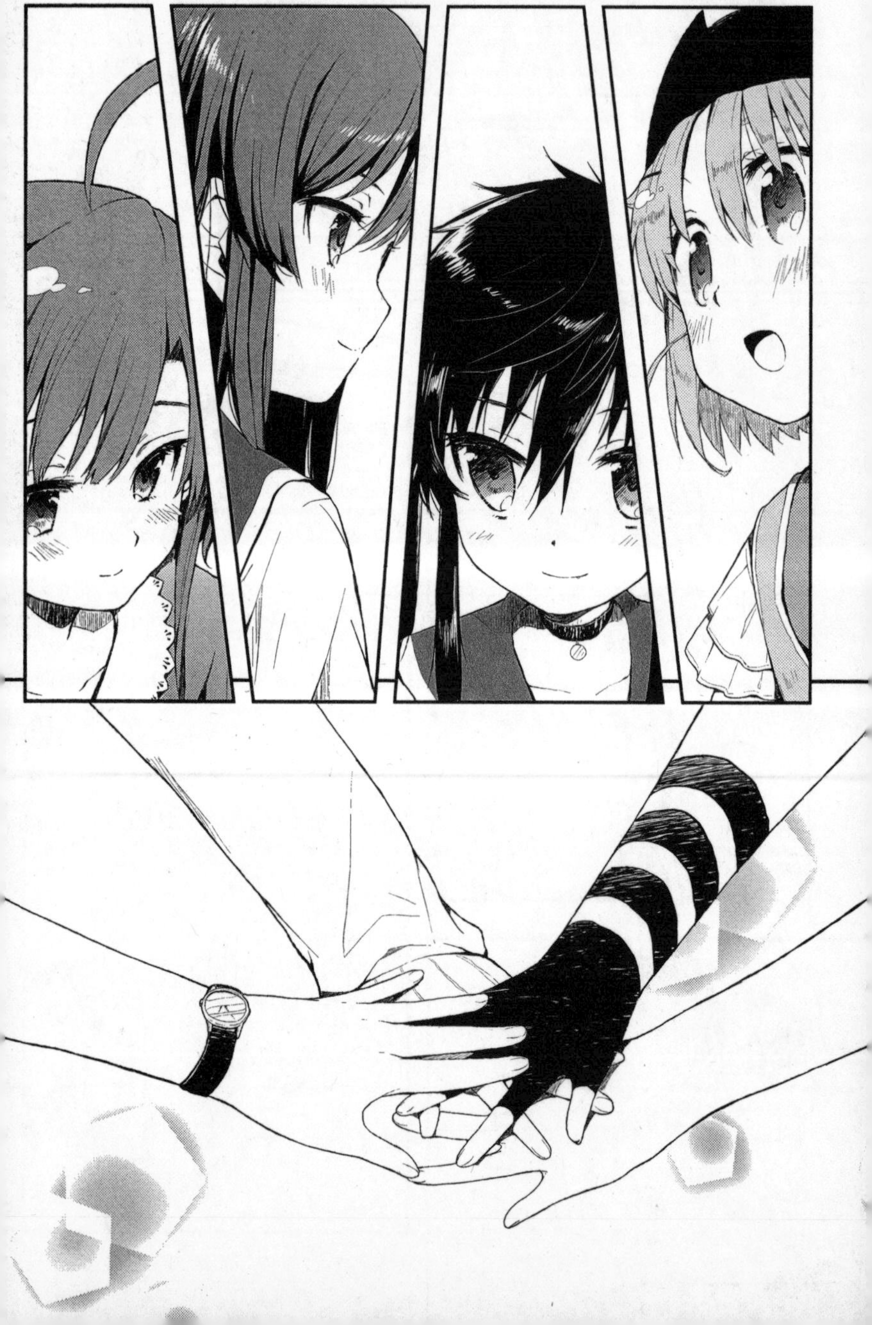

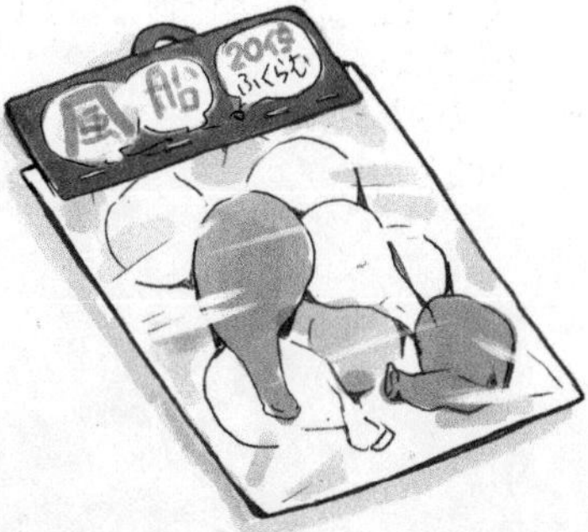
風船
ふくらむ

BAG: BALLOONS 20x INFLATION

SCHOOL-LIVE!

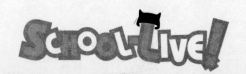

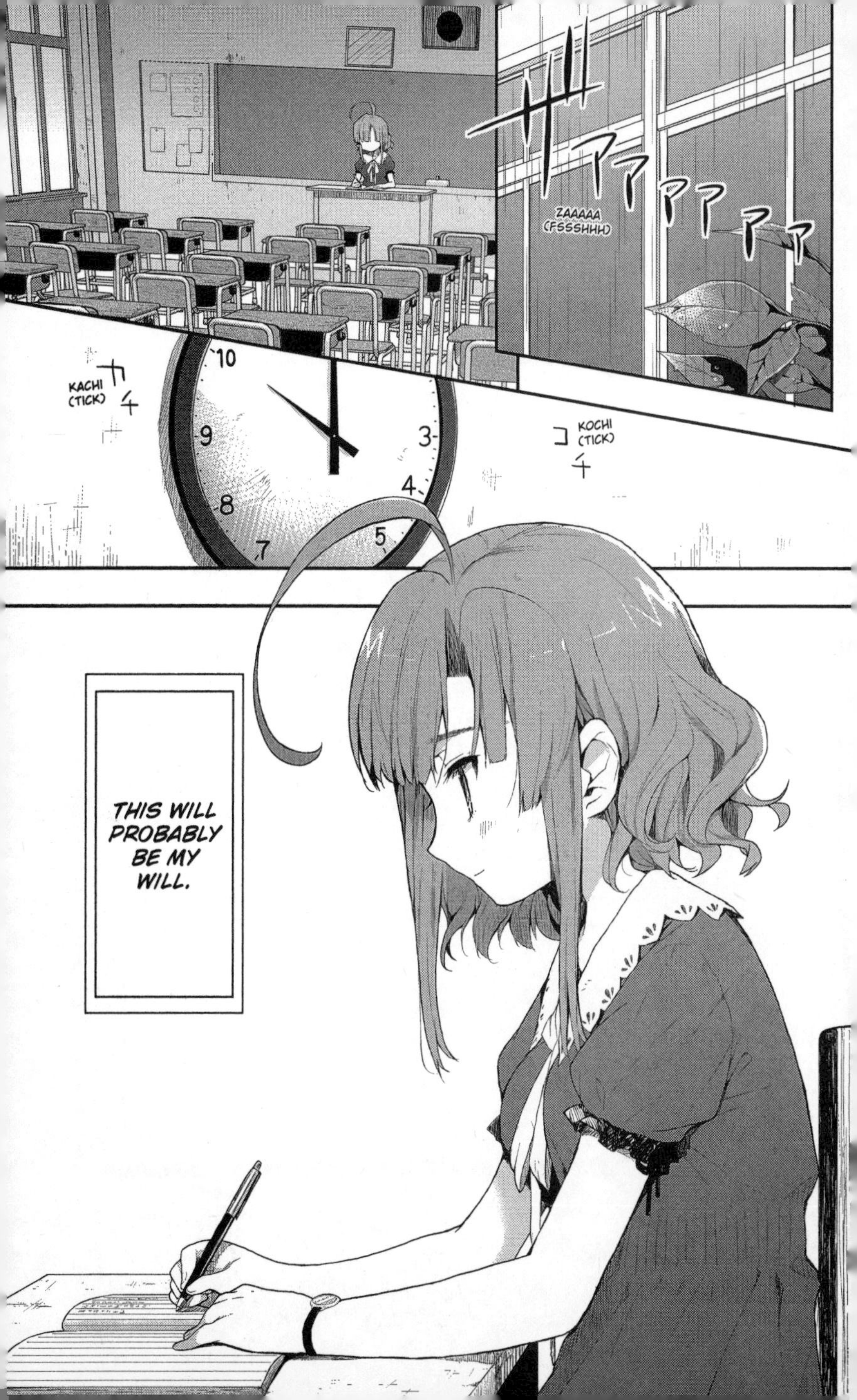

ザァァァァァ
ZAAAAAA (FSSSHHH)
カチ
KACHI (TICK)
コチ
KOCHI (TICK)
THIS WILL PROBABLY BE MY WILL.

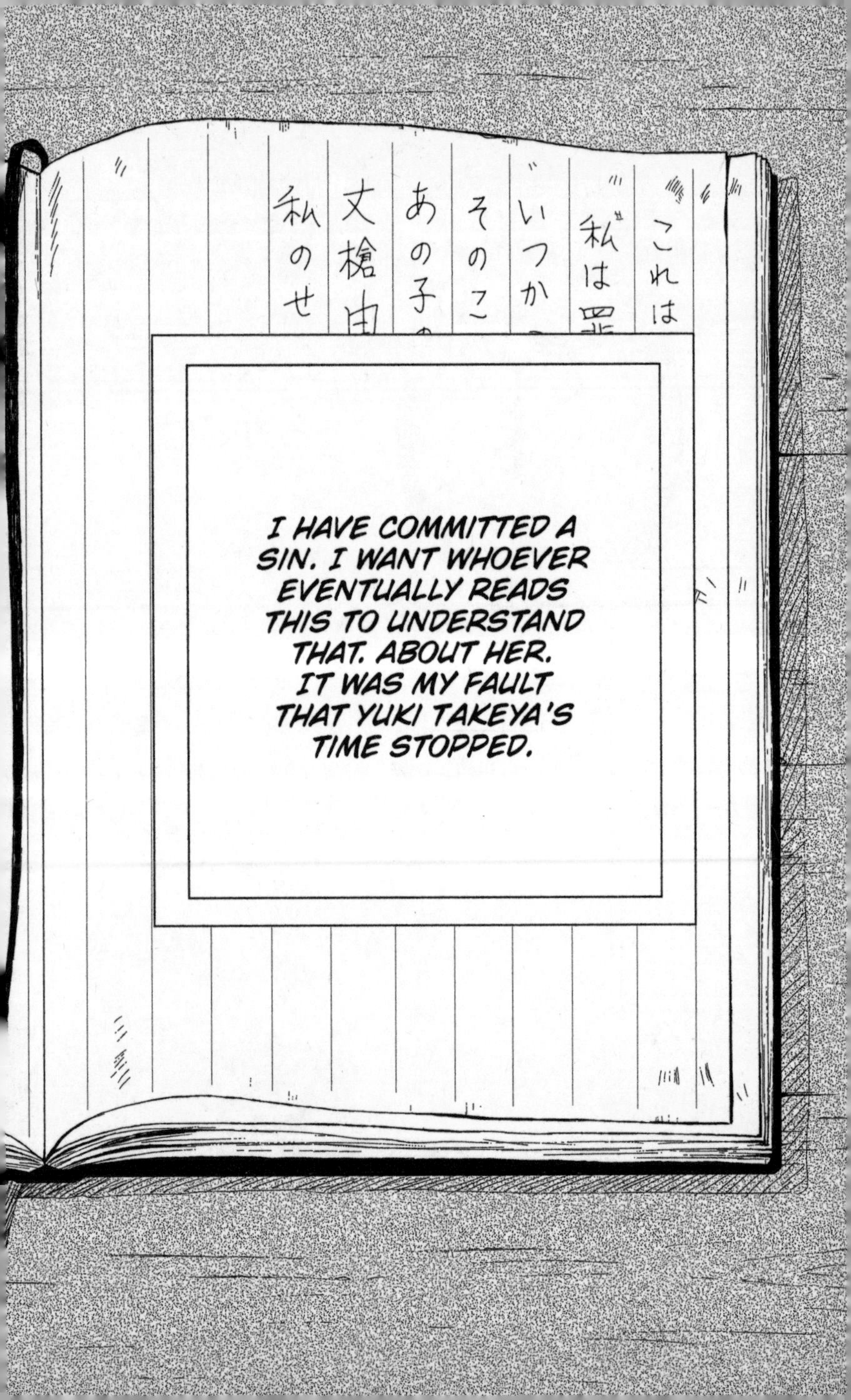

これは
"私は罪
"いつか
そのこ
あの子の
丈槍由
私のせ
I HAVE COMMITTED A SIN. I WANT WHOEVER EVENTUALLY READS THIS TO UNDERSTAND THAT. ABOUT HER. IT WAS MY FAULT THAT YUKI TAKEYA'S TIME STOPPED.

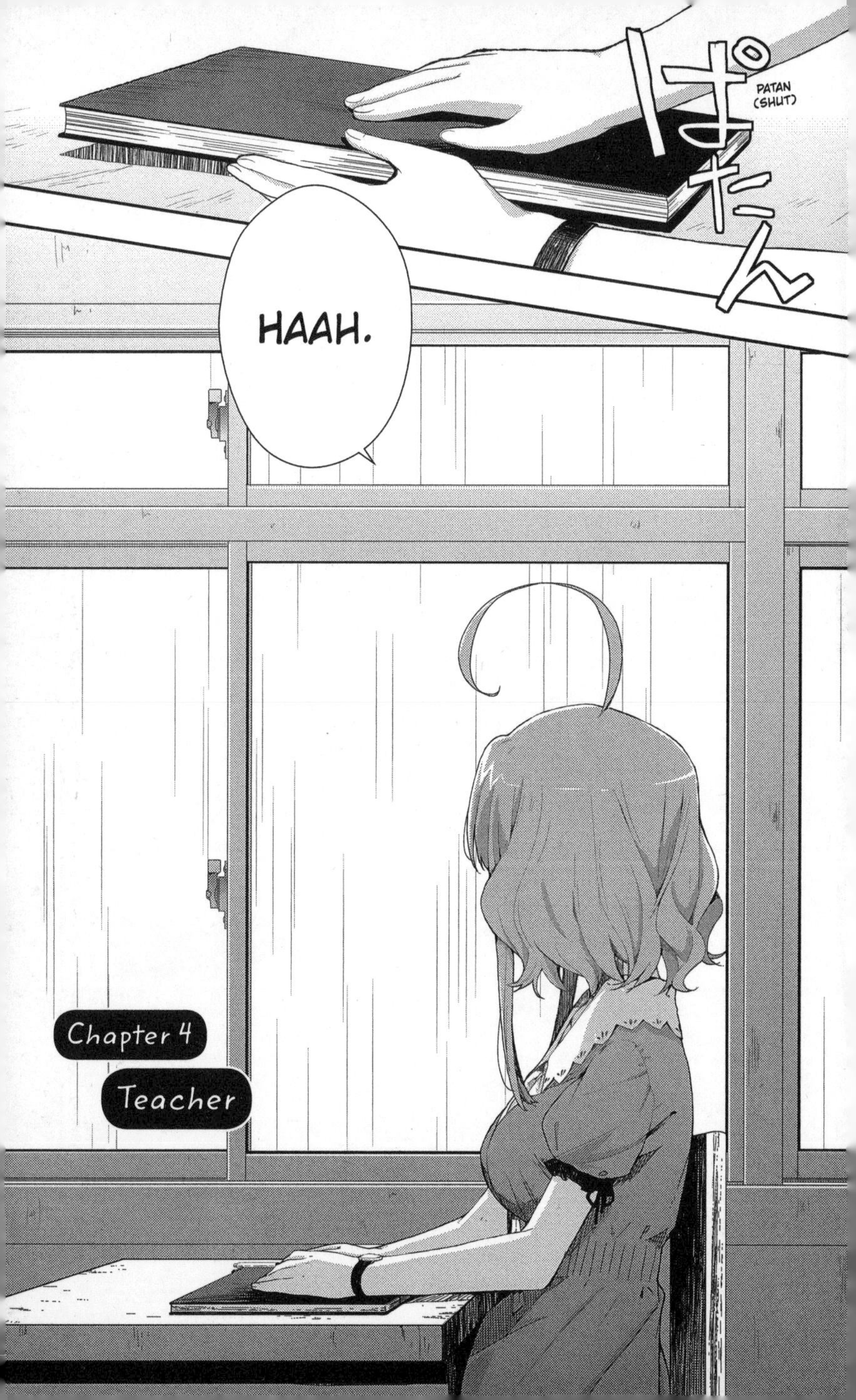
ぱたーん
PATAN (SHUT)
HAAH.
Chapter 4
Teacher

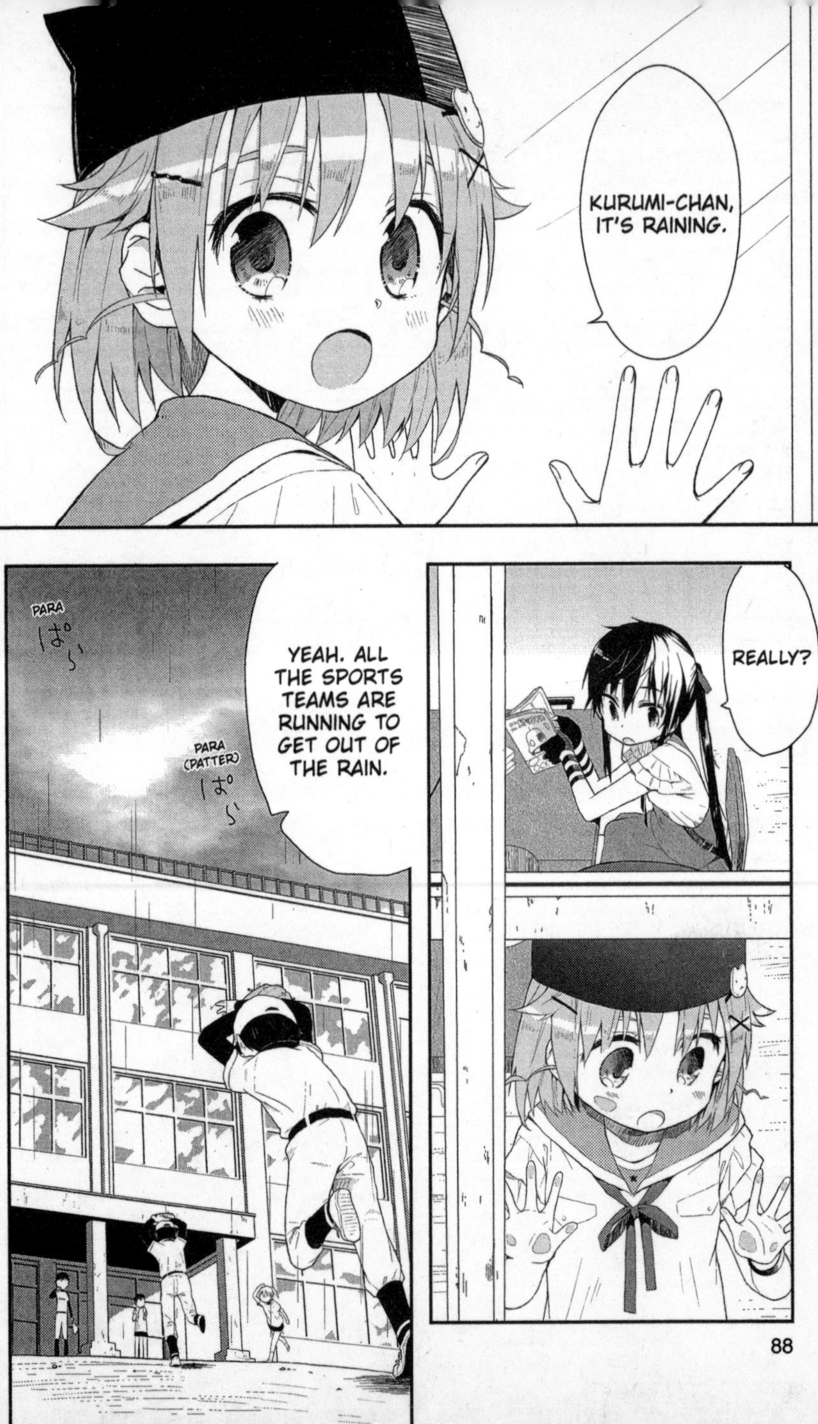
KURUMI-CHAN, IT'S RAINING.
REALLY?
YEAH. ALL THE SPORTS TEAMS ARE RUNNING TO GET OUT OF THE RAIN.
PARA
ぱら
PARA (PATTER)
ぱら

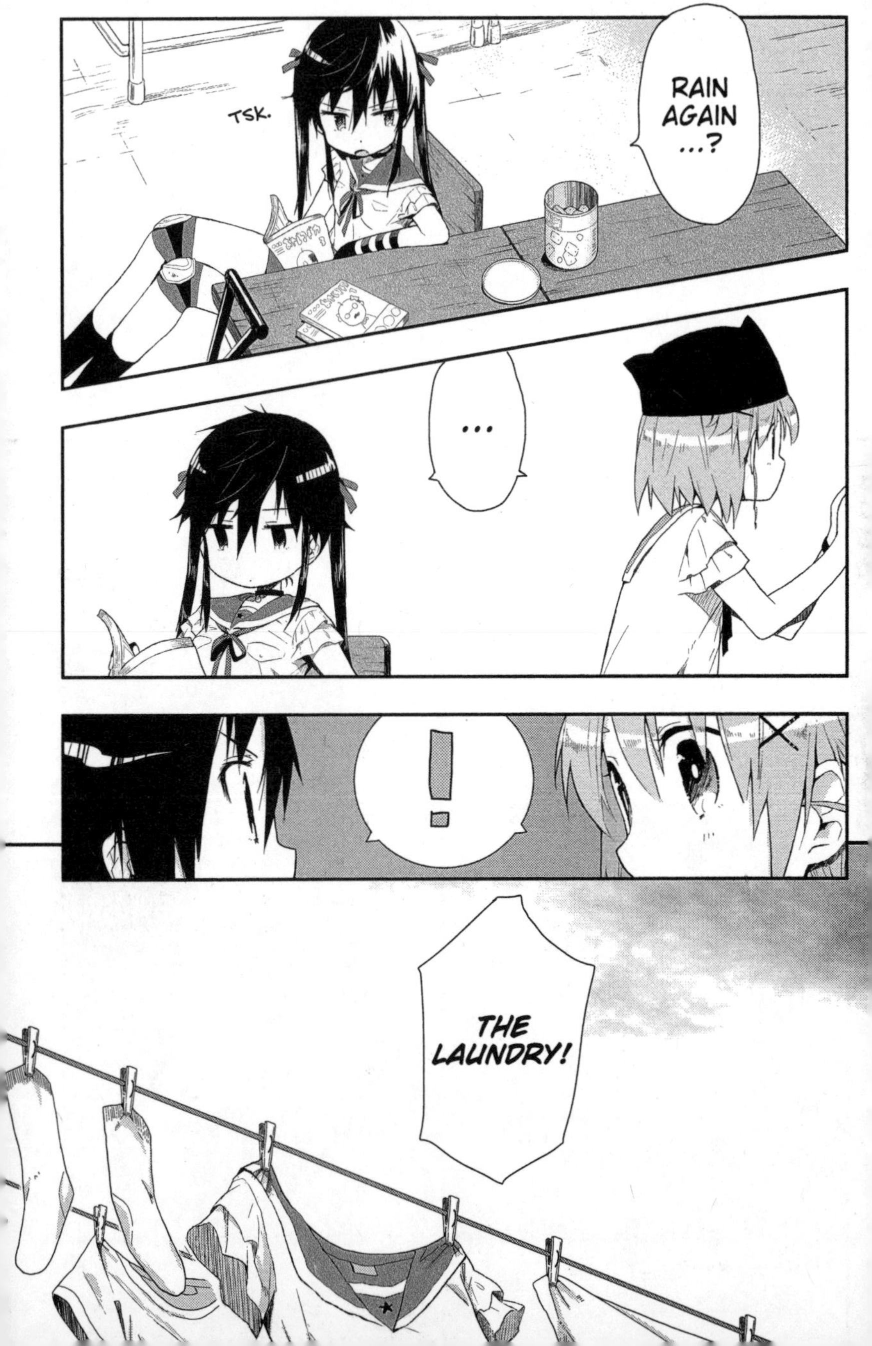
RAIN AGAIN ...?
TSK.
...
!
THE LAUNDRY!

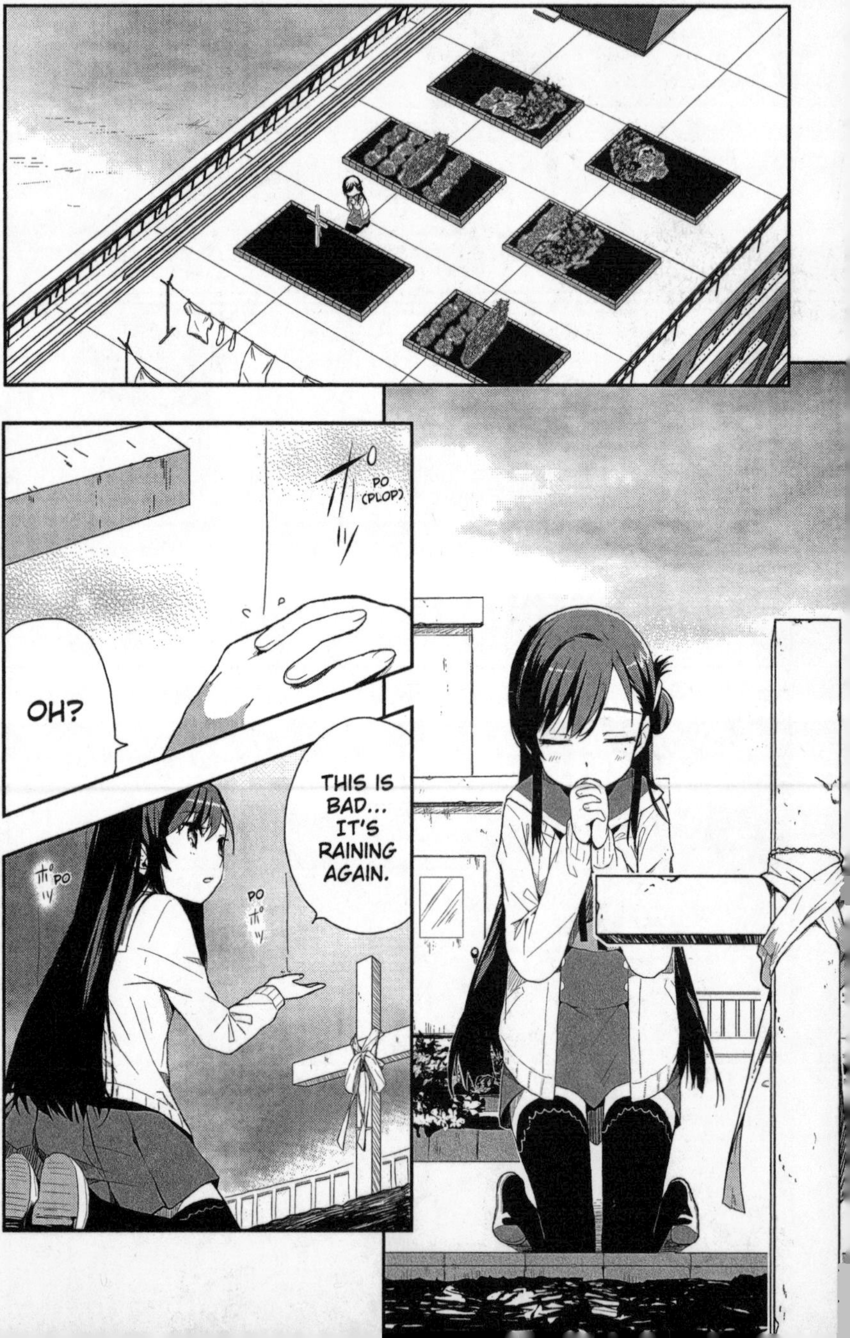
PO (PLOP)
OH?
THIS IS BAD... IT'S RAINING AGAIN.
PO ポッ
ポッ PO

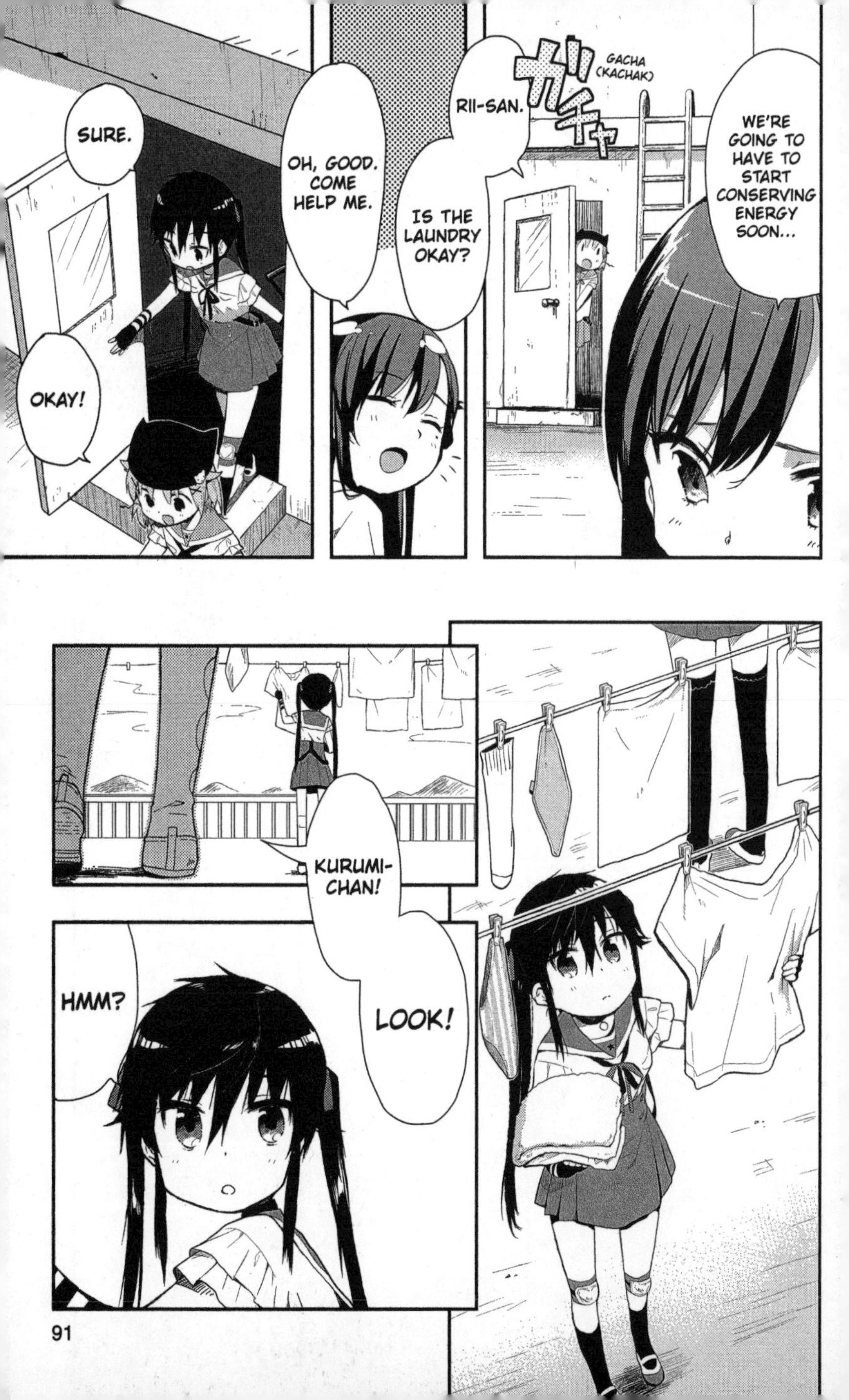
WE'RE GOING TO HAVE TO START CONSERVING ENERGY SOON...
GACHA (KACHAK)
RII-SAN.
IS THE LAUNDRY OKAY?
OH, GOOD. COME HELP ME.
SURE.
OKAY!
KURUMI-CHAN!
LOOK!
HMM?

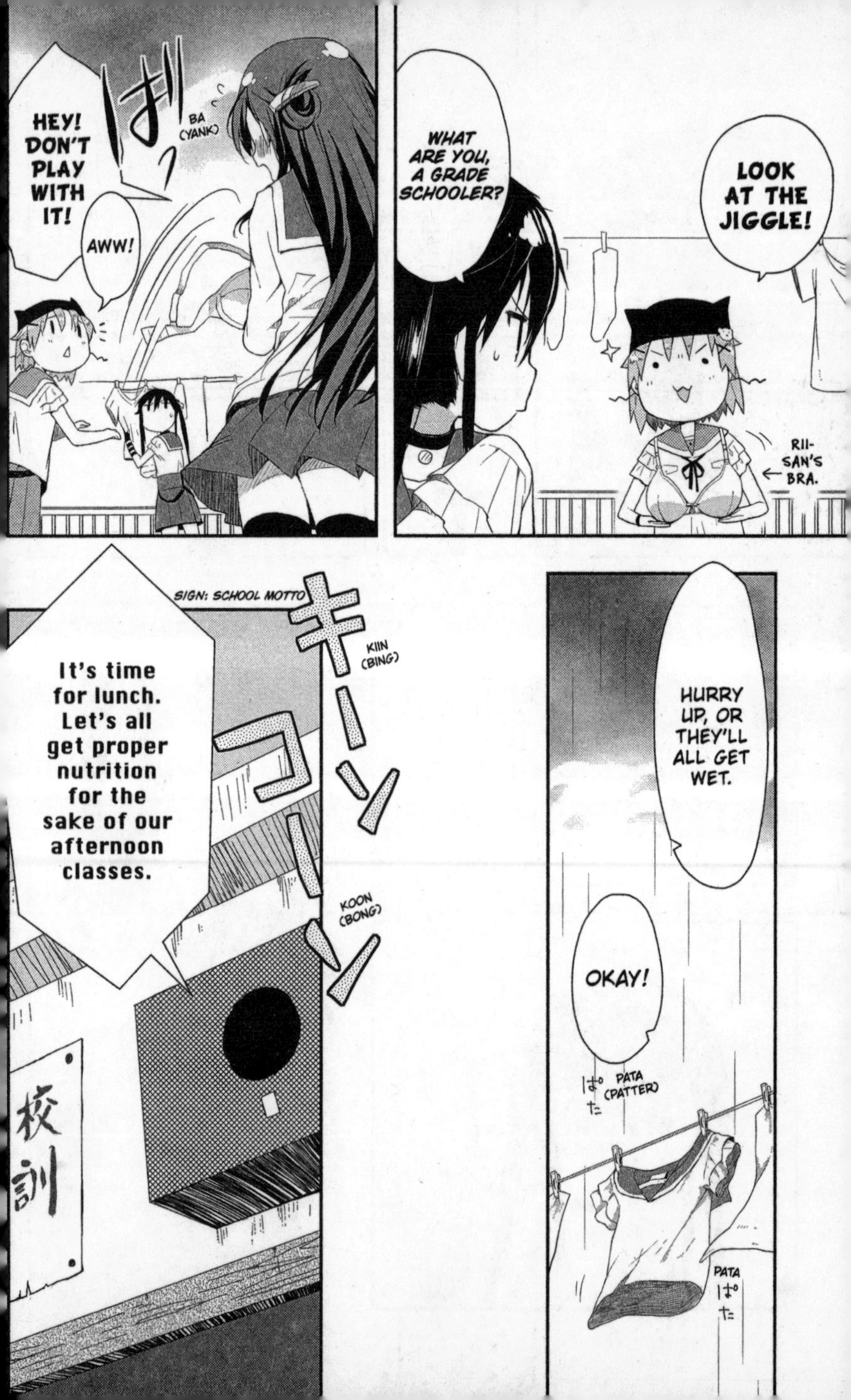
LOOK AT THE JIGGLE!
WHAT ARE YOU, A GRADE SCHOOLER?
RII-SAN'S BRA.
BA (YANK)
HEY! DON'T PLAY WITH IT!
AWW!
HURRY UP, OR THEY'LL ALL GET WET.
OKAY!
ぱた PATA (PATTER)
PATA ぱた
キーンコーン
KIIN (BING)
KOON (BONG)
SIGN: SCHOOL MOTTO
It's time for lunch. Let's all get proper nutrition for the sake of our afternoon classes.
校訓

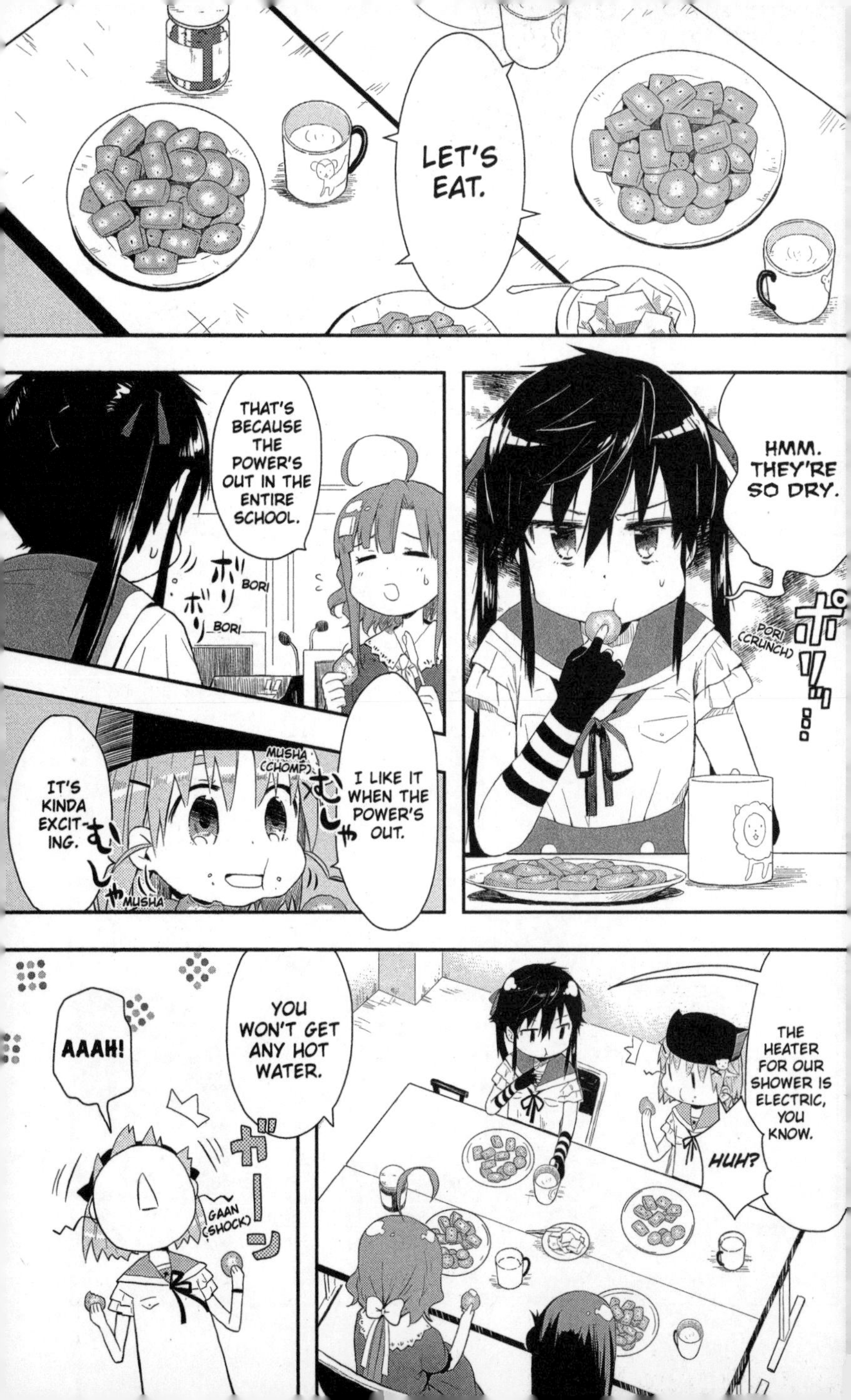
LET'S EAT.
HMM. THEY'RE SO DRY.
PORI (CRUNCH)
THAT'S BECAUSE THE POWER'S OUT IN THE ENTIRE SCHOOL.
BORI
BORI
MUSHA (CHOMP)
I LIKE IT WHEN THE POWER'S OUT.
IT'S KINDA EXCIT-ING.
MUSHA
THE HEATER FOR OUR SHOWER IS ELECTRIC, YOU KNOW.
HUH?
YOU WON'T GET ANY HOT WATER.
GAAN (SHOCK)
AAAH!

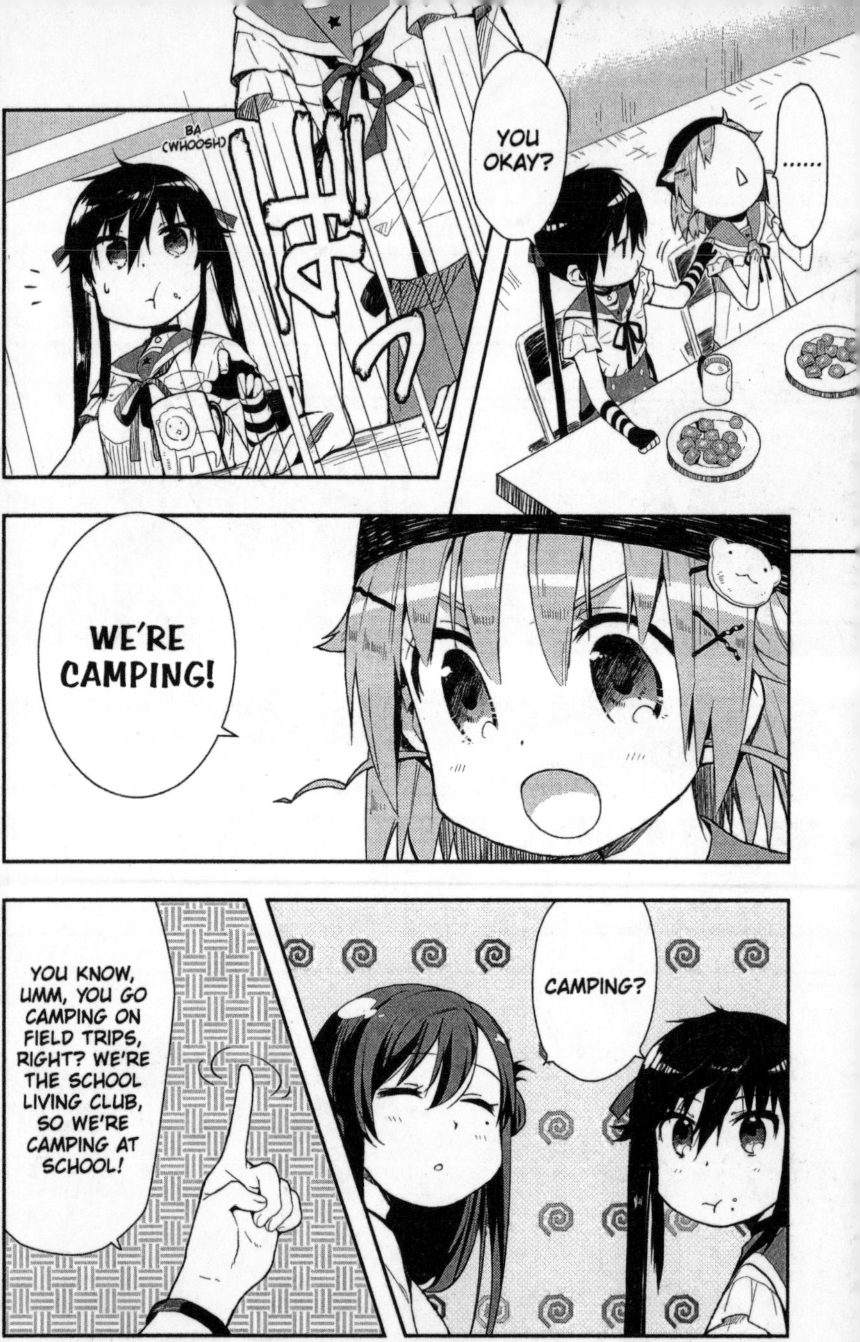
YOU OKAY?
......
BA (WHOOSH)
WE'RE CAMPING!
CAMPING?
YOU KNOW, UMM, YOU GO CAMPING ON FIELD TRIPS, RIGHT? WE'RE THE SCHOOL LIVING CLUB, SO WE'RE CAMPING AT SCHOOL!

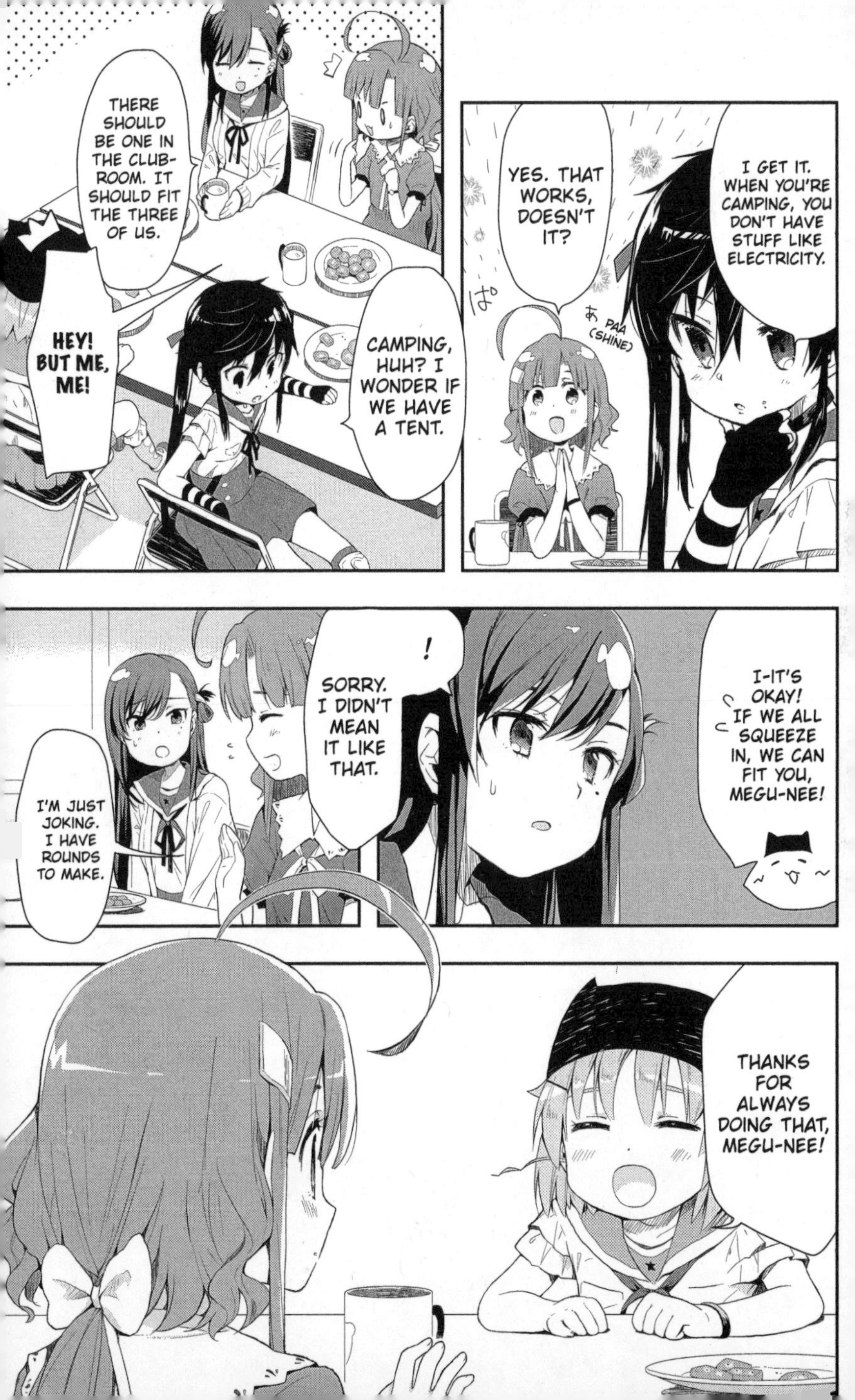

I GET IT. WHEN YOU'RE CAMPING, YOU DON'T HAVE STUFF LIKE ELECTRICITY.
YES. THAT WORKS, DOESN'T IT?
ぱ
あ PAA (SHINE)
CAMPING, HUH? I WONDER IF WE HAVE A TENT.
THERE SHOULD BE ONE IN THE CLUB-ROOM. IT SHOULD FIT THE THREE OF US.
HEY! BUT ME, ME!
I-IT'S OKAY! IF WE ALL SQUEEZE IN, WE CAN FIT YOU, MEGU-NEE!
!
SORRY. I DIDN'T MEAN IT LIKE THAT.
I'M JUST JOKING. I HAVE ROUNDS TO MAKE.
THANKS FOR ALWAYS DOING THAT, MEGU-NEE!

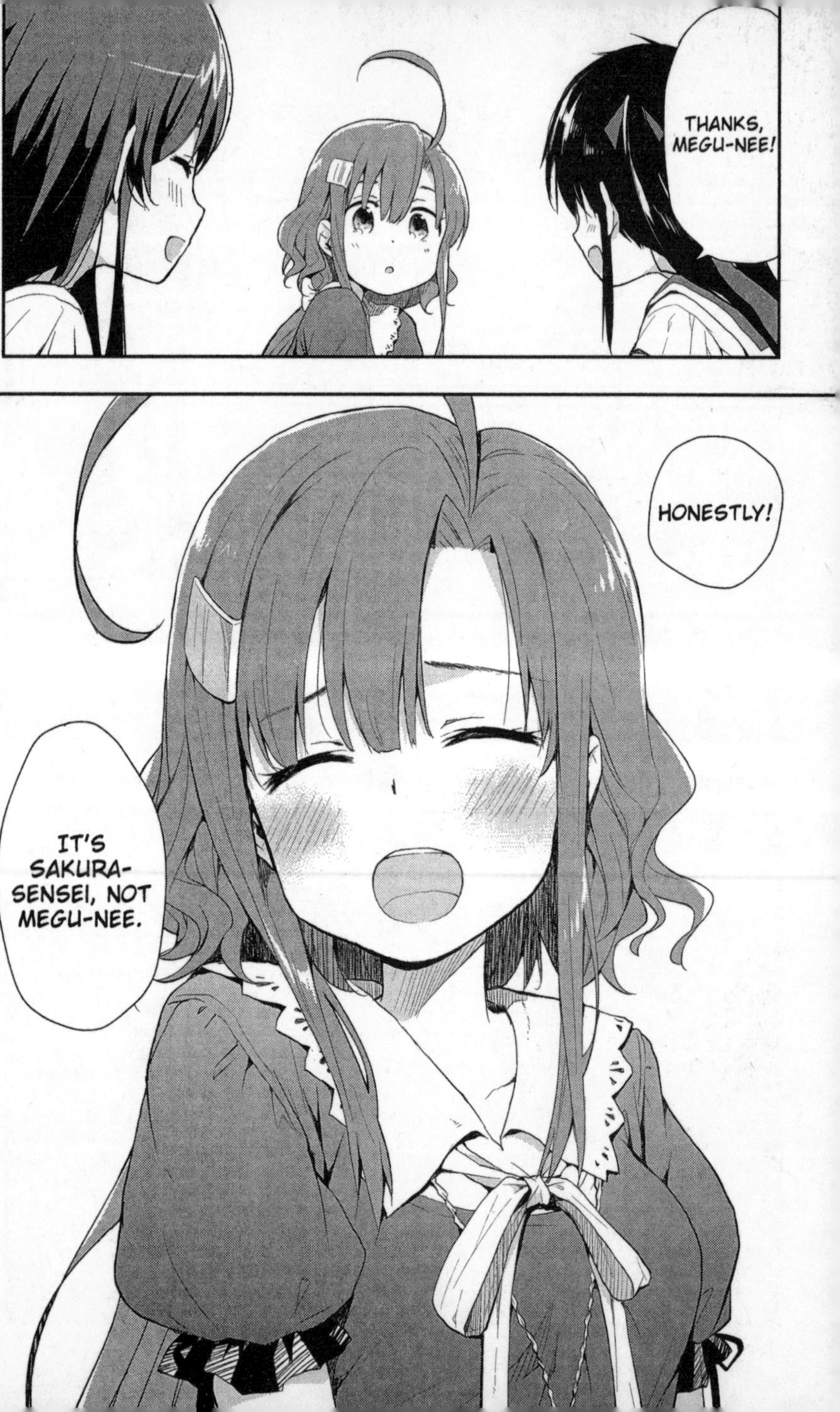
THANKS, MEGU-NEE!
HONESTLY!
IT'S SAKURA-SENSEI, NOT MEGU-NEE.

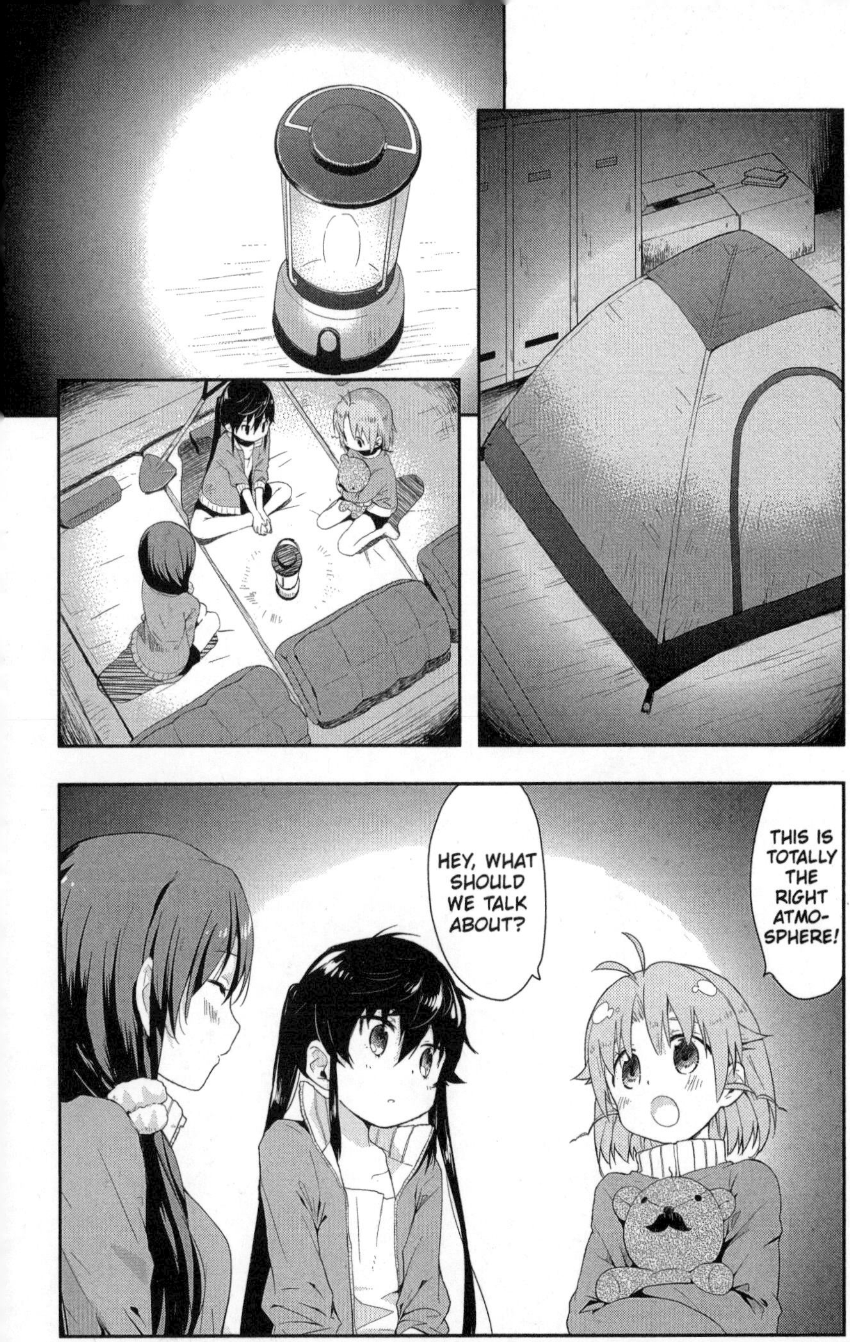
THIS IS TOTALLY THE RIGHT ATMO-SPHERE!
HEY, WHAT SHOULD WE TALK ABOUT?

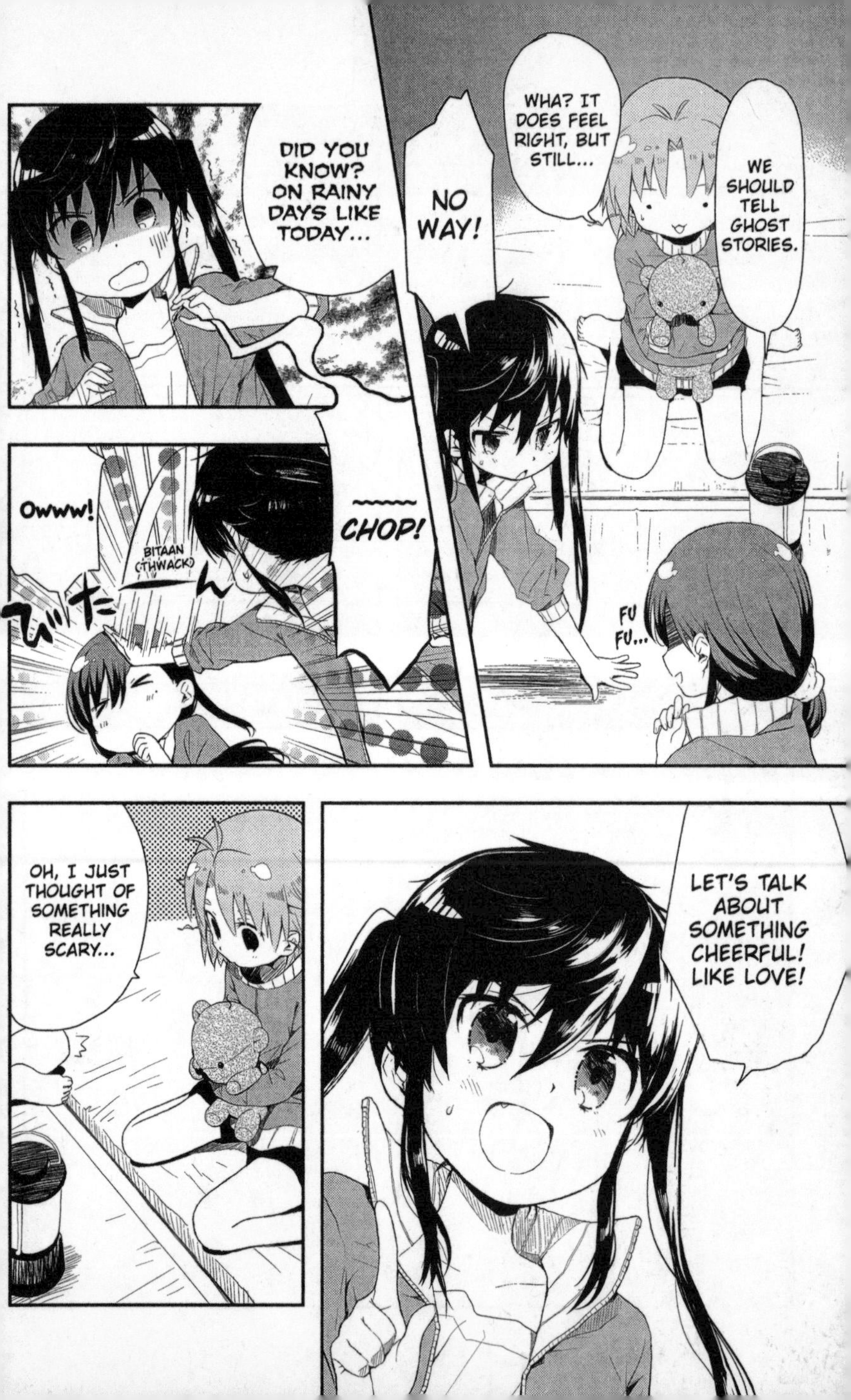
WE SHOULD TELL GHOST STORIES.
WHA? IT DOES FEEL RIGHT, BUT STILL...
NO WAY!
FU FU...
DID YOU KNOW? ON RAINY DAYS LIKE TODAY...
CHOP!
BITAAN (THWACK)
Owww!
LET'S TALK ABOUT SOMETHING CHEERFUL! LIKE LOVE!
OH, I JUST THOUGHT OF SOMETHING REALLY SCARY...

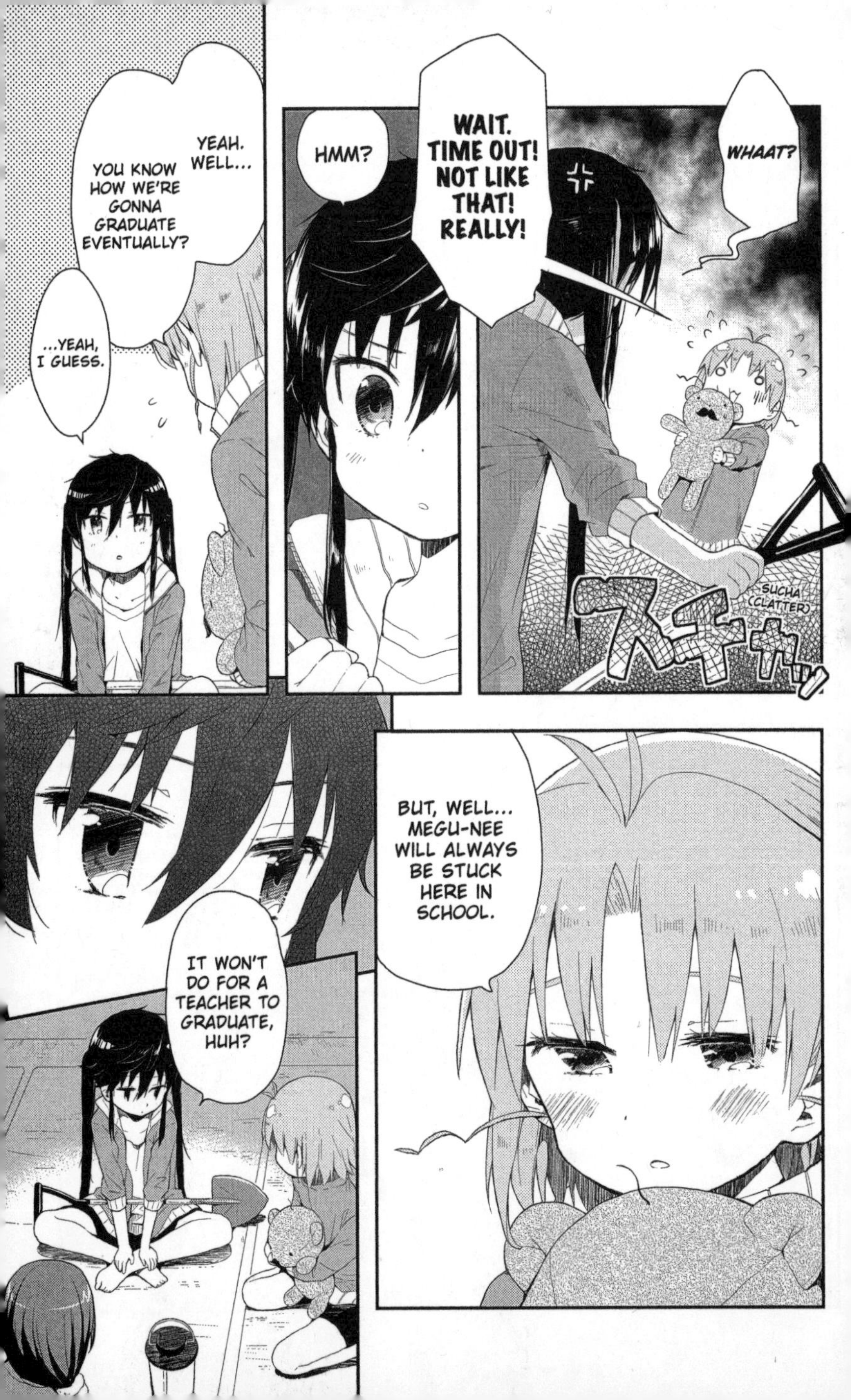
WHAAT?
WAIT. TIME OUT! NOT LIKE THAT! REALLY!
SUCHA (CLATTER)
HMM?
YEAH. WELL... YOU KNOW HOW WE'RE GONNA GRADUATE EVENTUALLY?
...YEAH, I GUESS.
BUT, WELL... MEGU-NEE WILL ALWAYS BE STUCK HERE IN SCHOOL.
IT WON'T DO FOR A TEACHER TO GRADUATE, HUH?

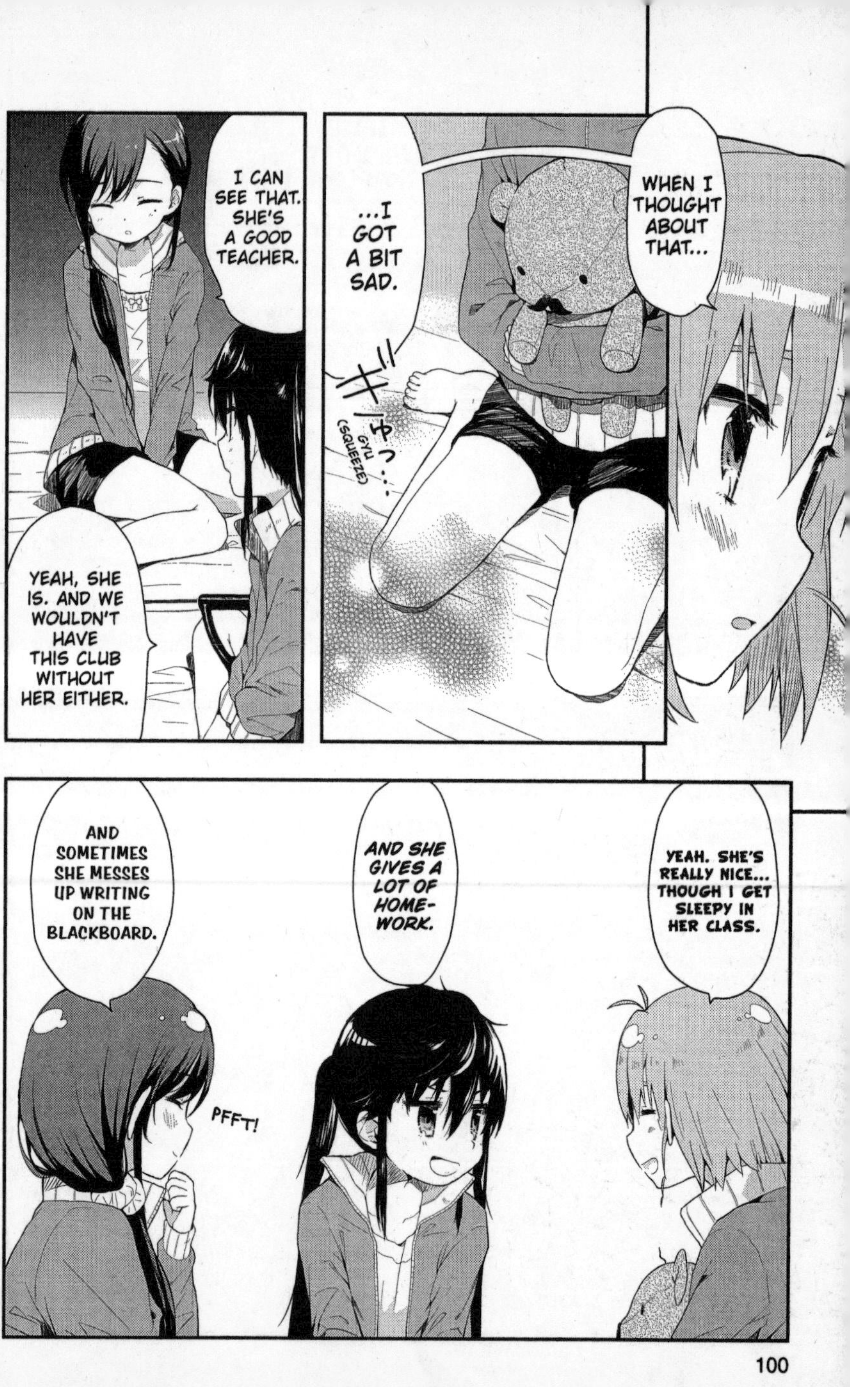
WHEN I THOUGHT ABOUT THAT...
...I GOT A BIT SAD.
GYU (SQUEEZE)
I CAN SEE THAT. SHE'S A GOOD TEACHER.
YEAH, SHE IS. AND WE WOULDN'T HAVE THIS CLUB WITHOUT HER EITHER.
YEAH. SHE'S REALLY NICE... THOUGH I GET SLEEPY IN HER CLASS.
AND SHE GIVES A LOT OF HOME-WORK.
AND SOMETIMES SHE MESSES UP WRITING ON THE BLACKBOARD.
PFFT!

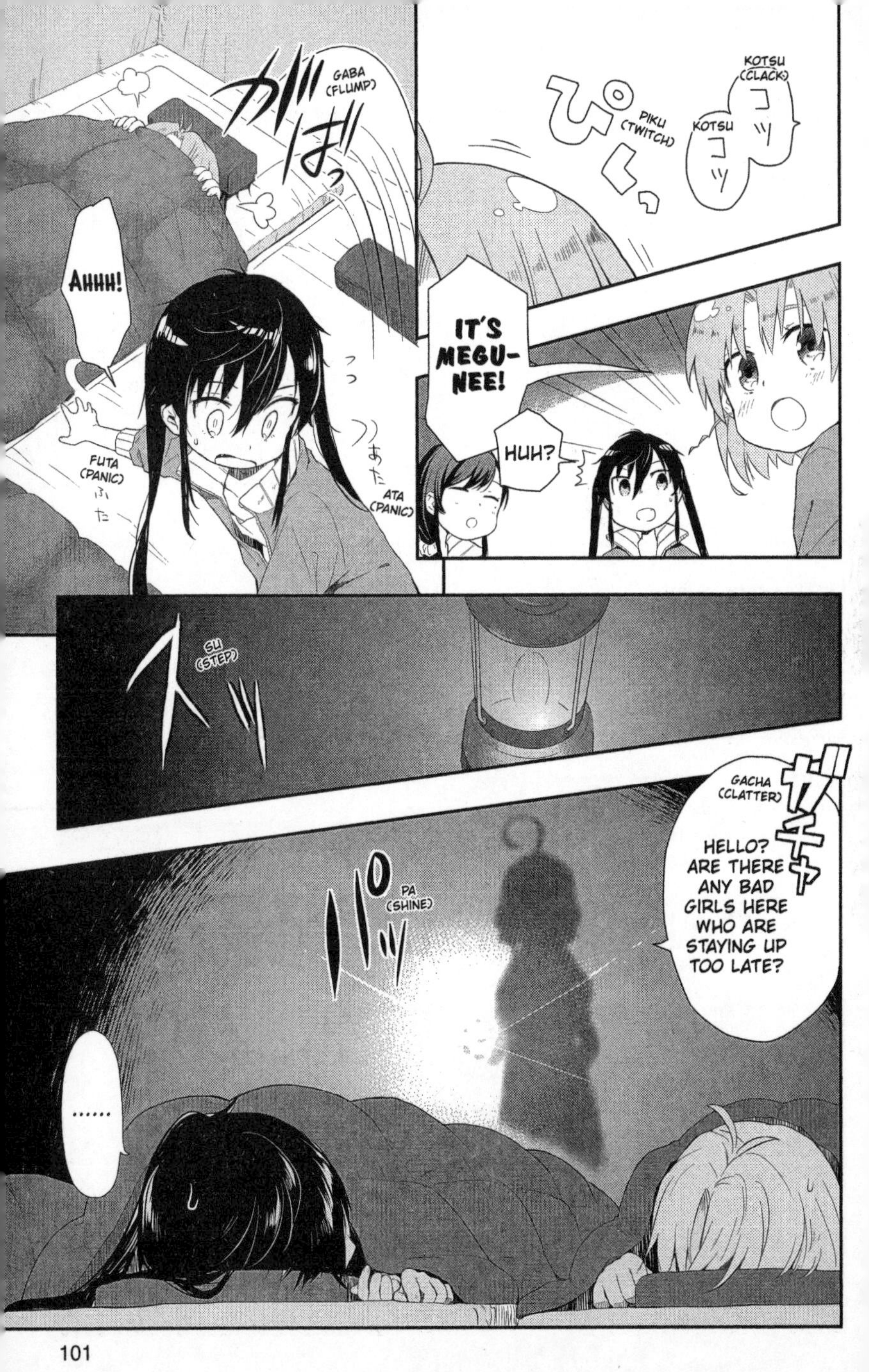
KOTSU (CLACK)
KOTSU
PIKU (TWITCH)
IT'S MEGU-NEE!
HUH?
GABA (FLUMP)
AHHH!
ATA (PANIC)
FUTA (PANIC)
SU (STEP)
GACHA (CLATTER)
HELLO? ARE THERE ANY BAD GIRLS HERE WHO ARE STAYING UP TOO LATE?
PA (SHINE)
......

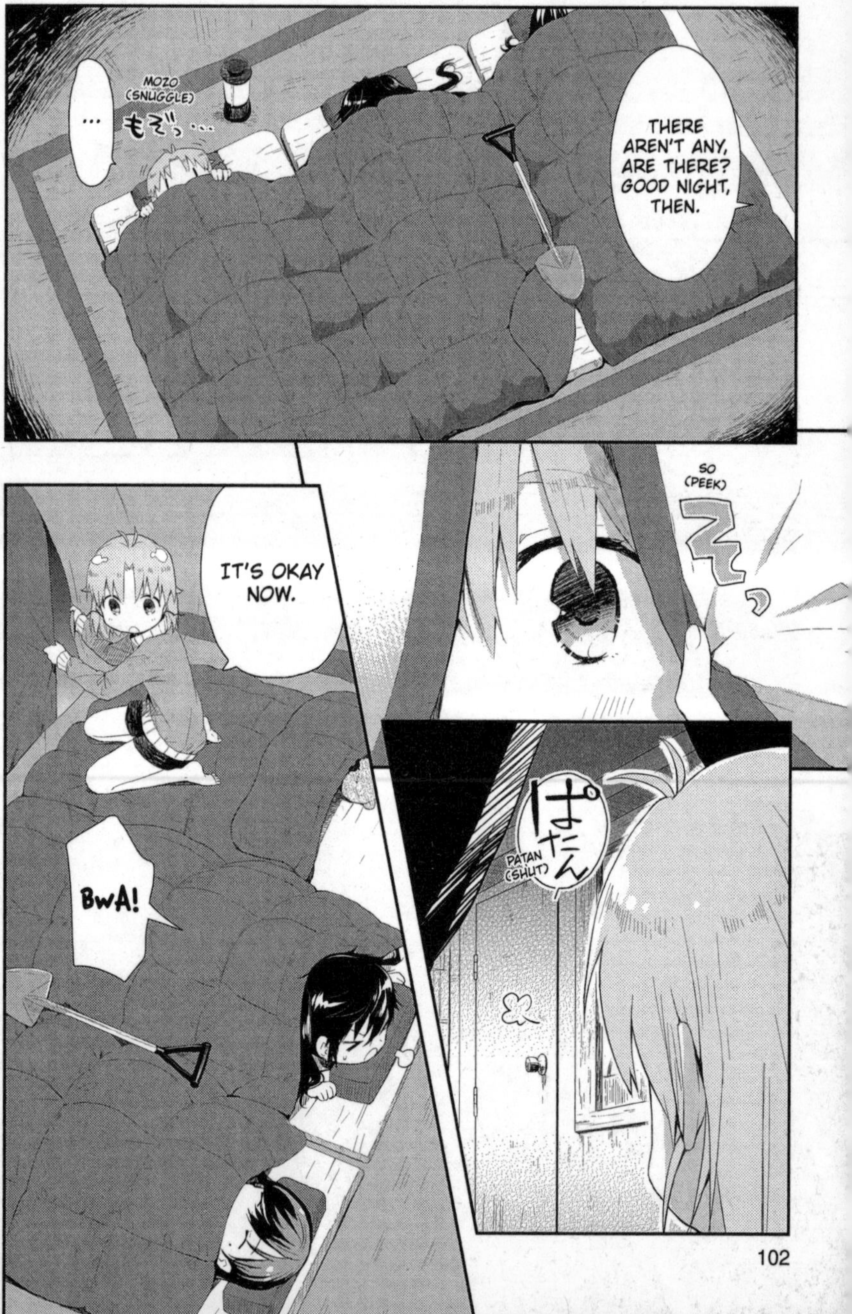
THERE AREN'T ANY, ARE THERE? GOOD NIGHT, THEN.
もぞっ...
MOZO (SNUGGLE)
...
そっ
SO (PEEK)
ぱたん
PATAN (SHUT)
IT'S OKAY NOW.
BWA!

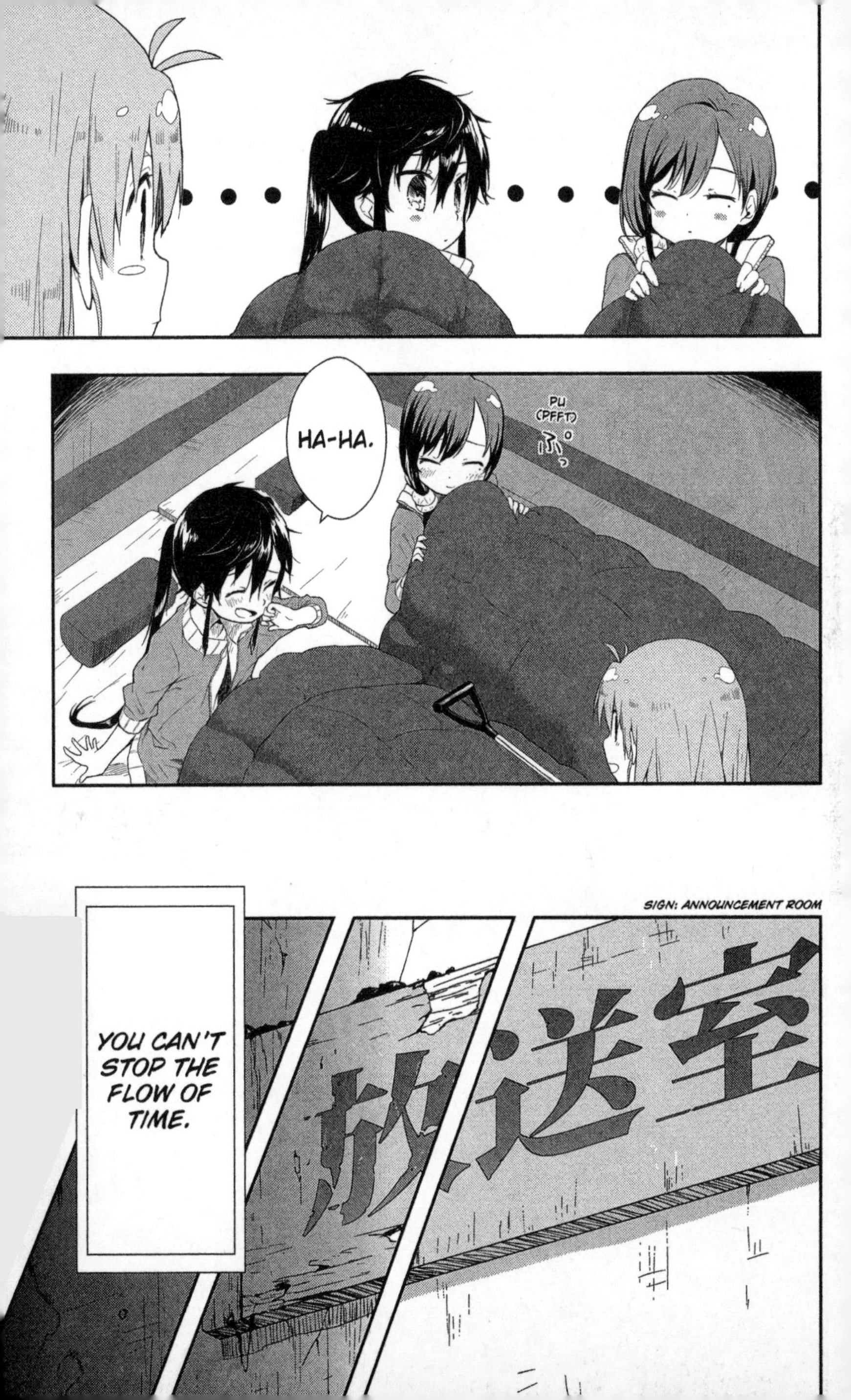
PU (PFFT)
ふっ
HA-HA.
SIGN: ANNOUNCEMENT ROOM
放送室
YOU CAN'T STOP THE FLOW OF TIME.

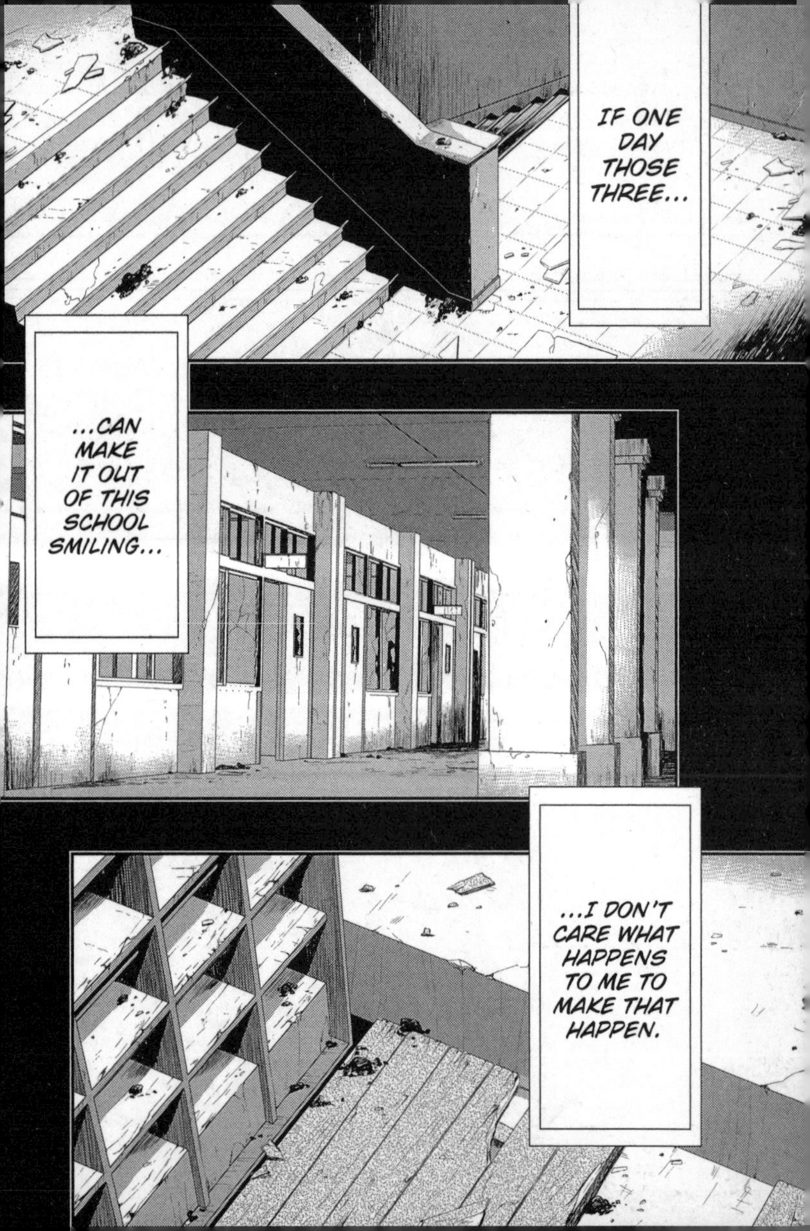
IF ONE DAY THOSE THREE...
...CAN MAKE IT OUT OF THIS SCHOOL SMILING...
...I DON'T CARE WHAT HAPPENS TO ME TO MAKE THAT HAPPEN.

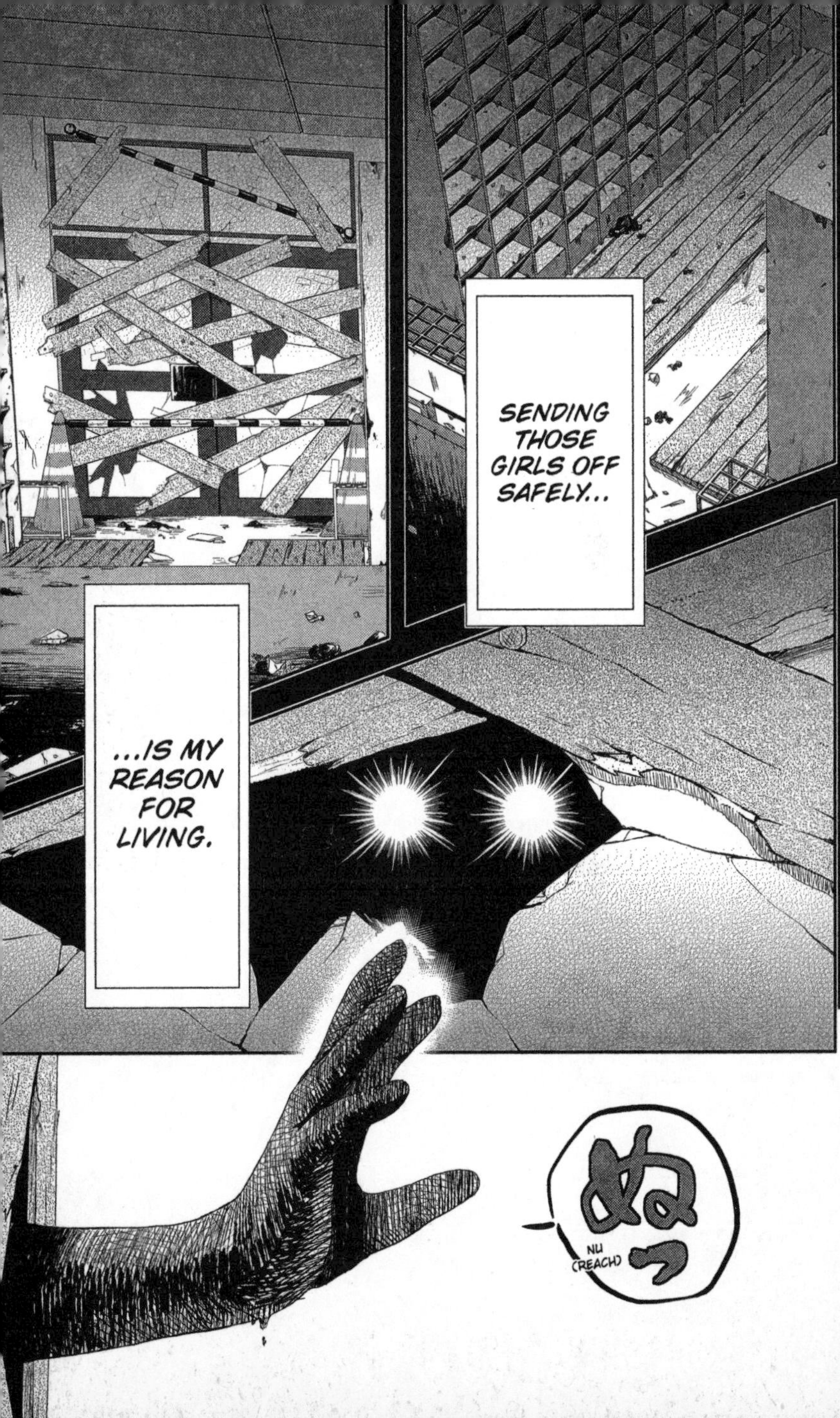
SENDING THOSE GIRLS OFF SAFELY...
...IS MY REASON FOR LIVING.
ぬっ
NU (REACH)

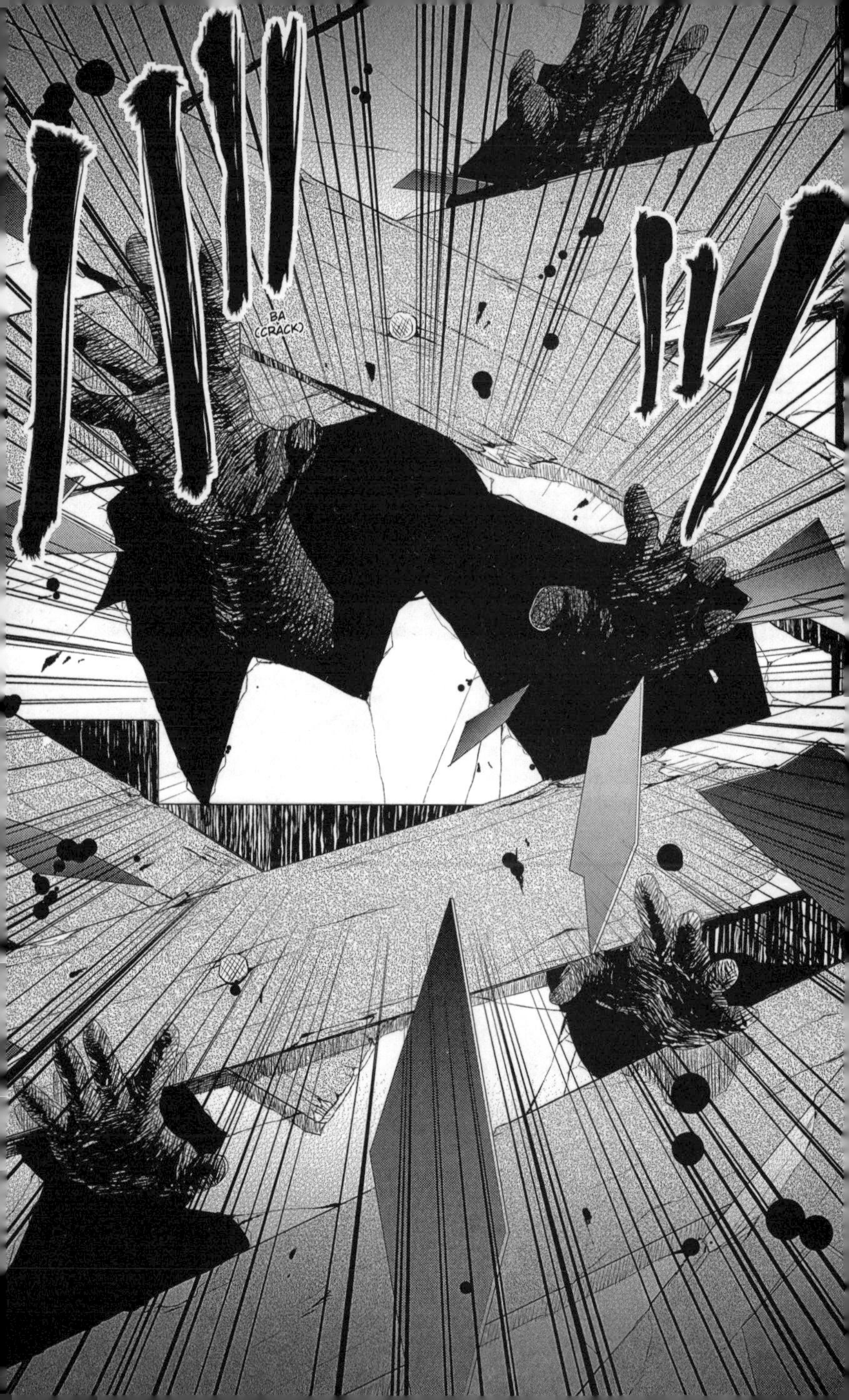
BA
(CRACK)

SCHOOL-LIVE!

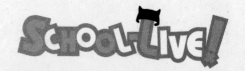

SIGN: MEGURIGA—
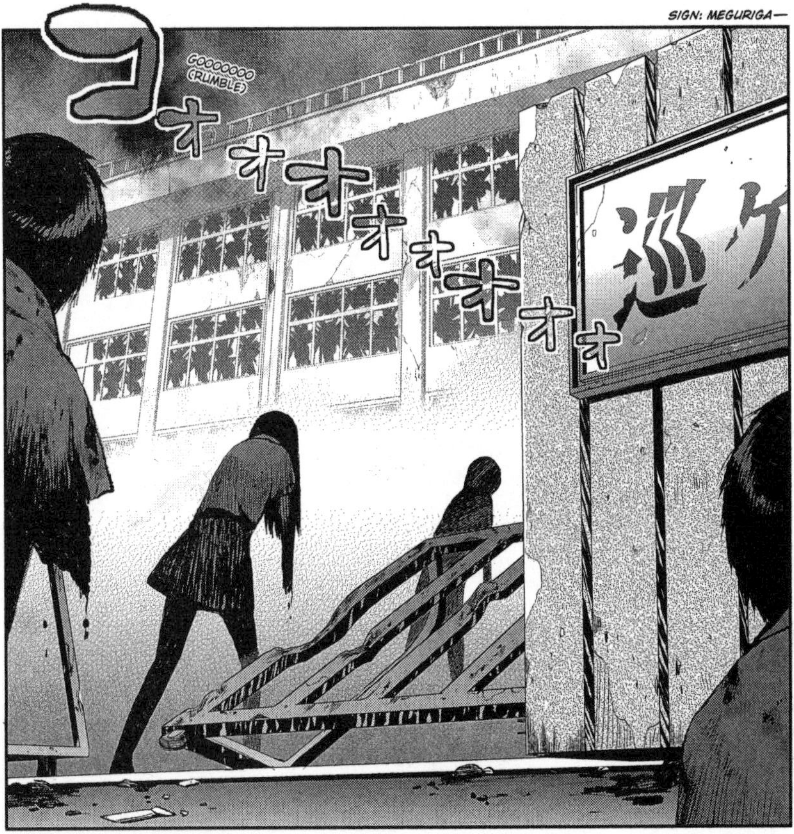
GOOOOOOOO
(RUMBLE)
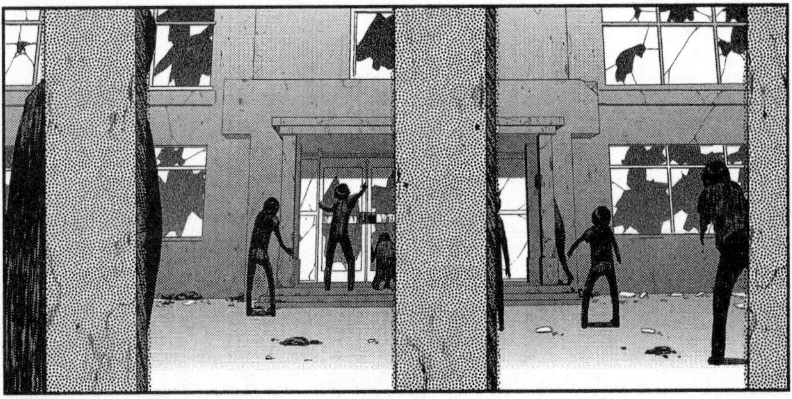

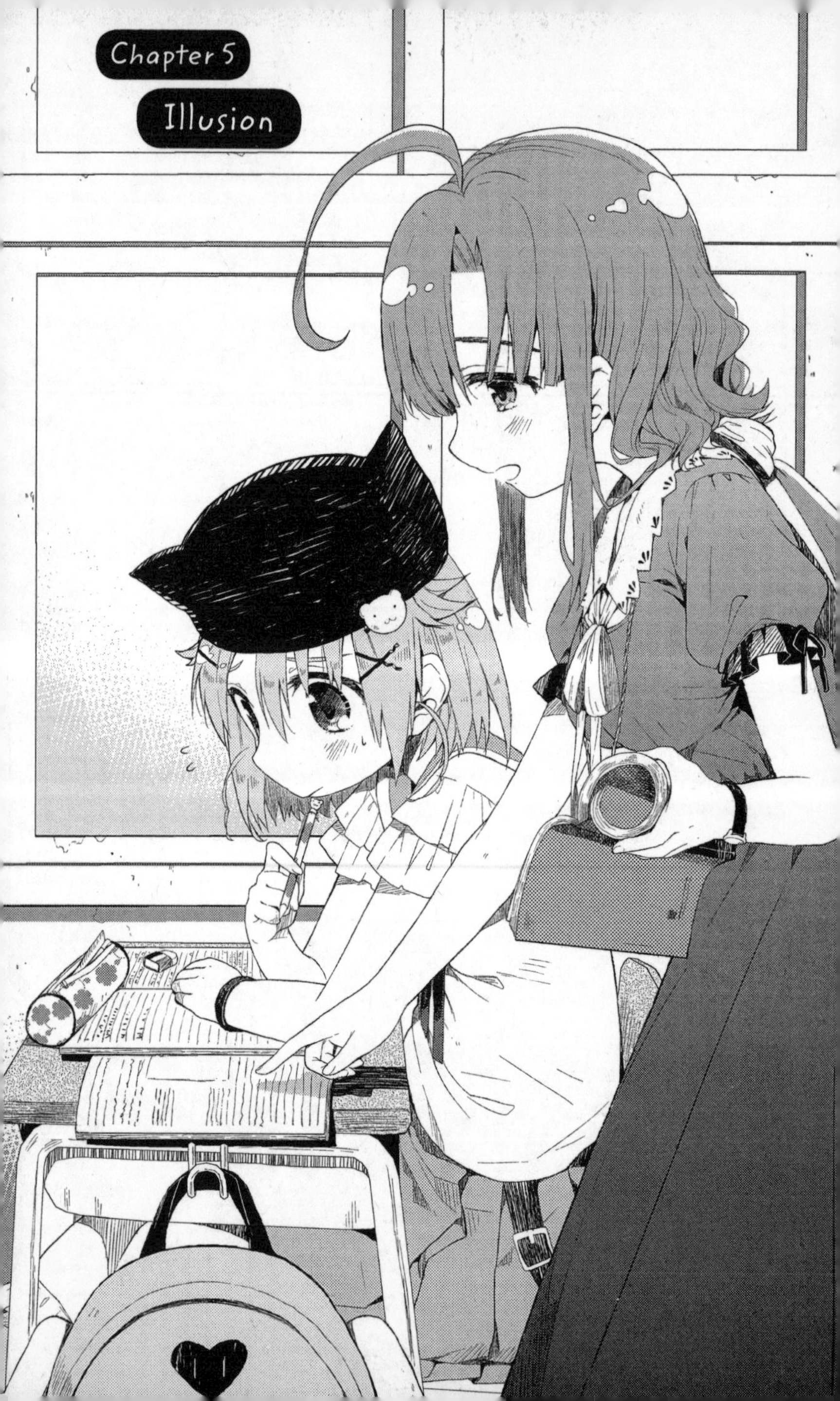
Chapter 5
Illusion

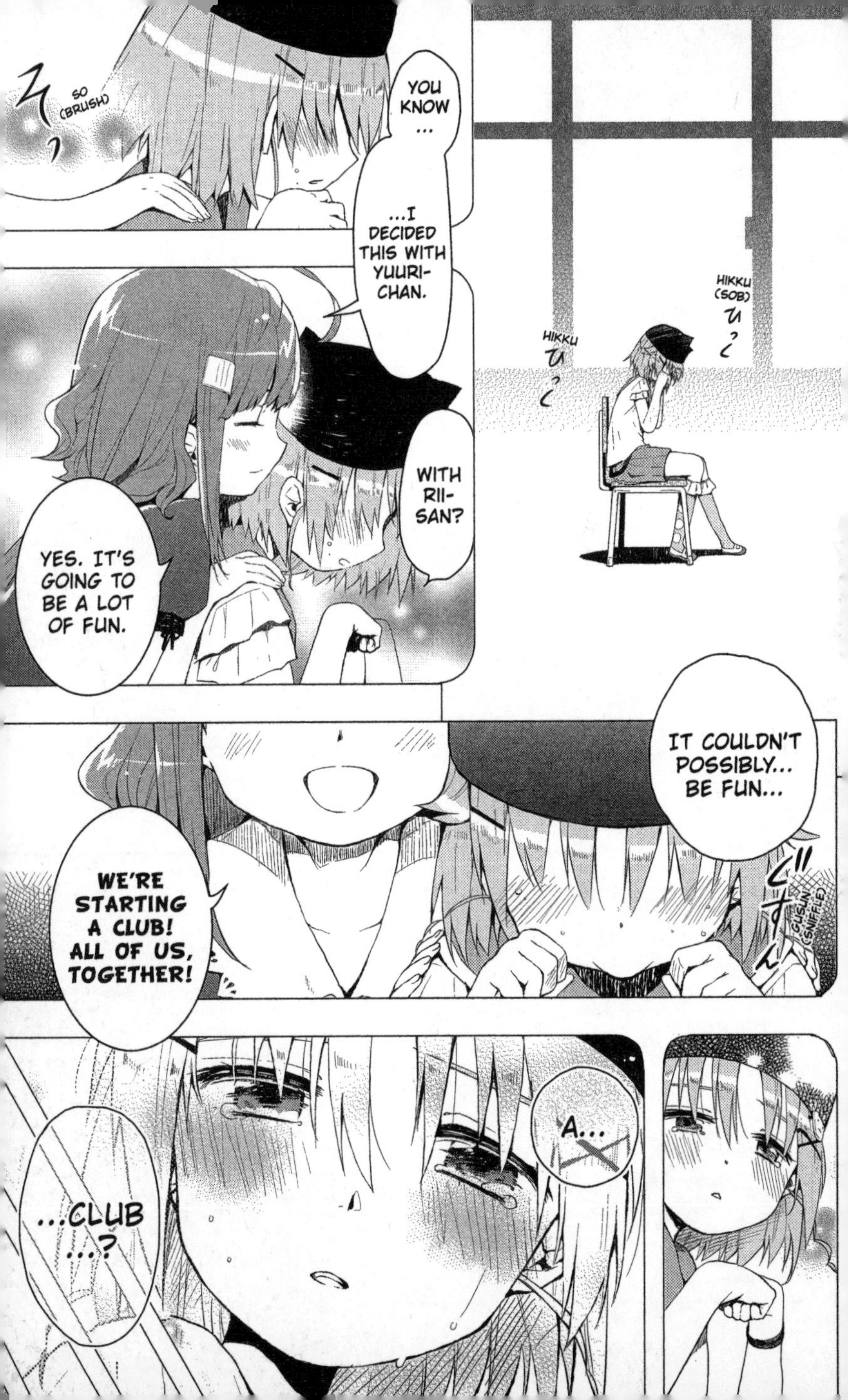
HIKKU (SOB)
HIKKU
SO (BRUSH)
YOU KNOW ...
...I DECIDED THIS WITH YUURI-CHAN.
WITH RII-SAN?
YES. IT'S GOING TO BE A LOT OF FUN.
IT COULDN'T POSSIBLY... BE FUN...
GUSUN (SNIFFLE)
WE'RE STARTING A CLUB! ALL OF US, TOGETHER!
A...
...CLUB ...?

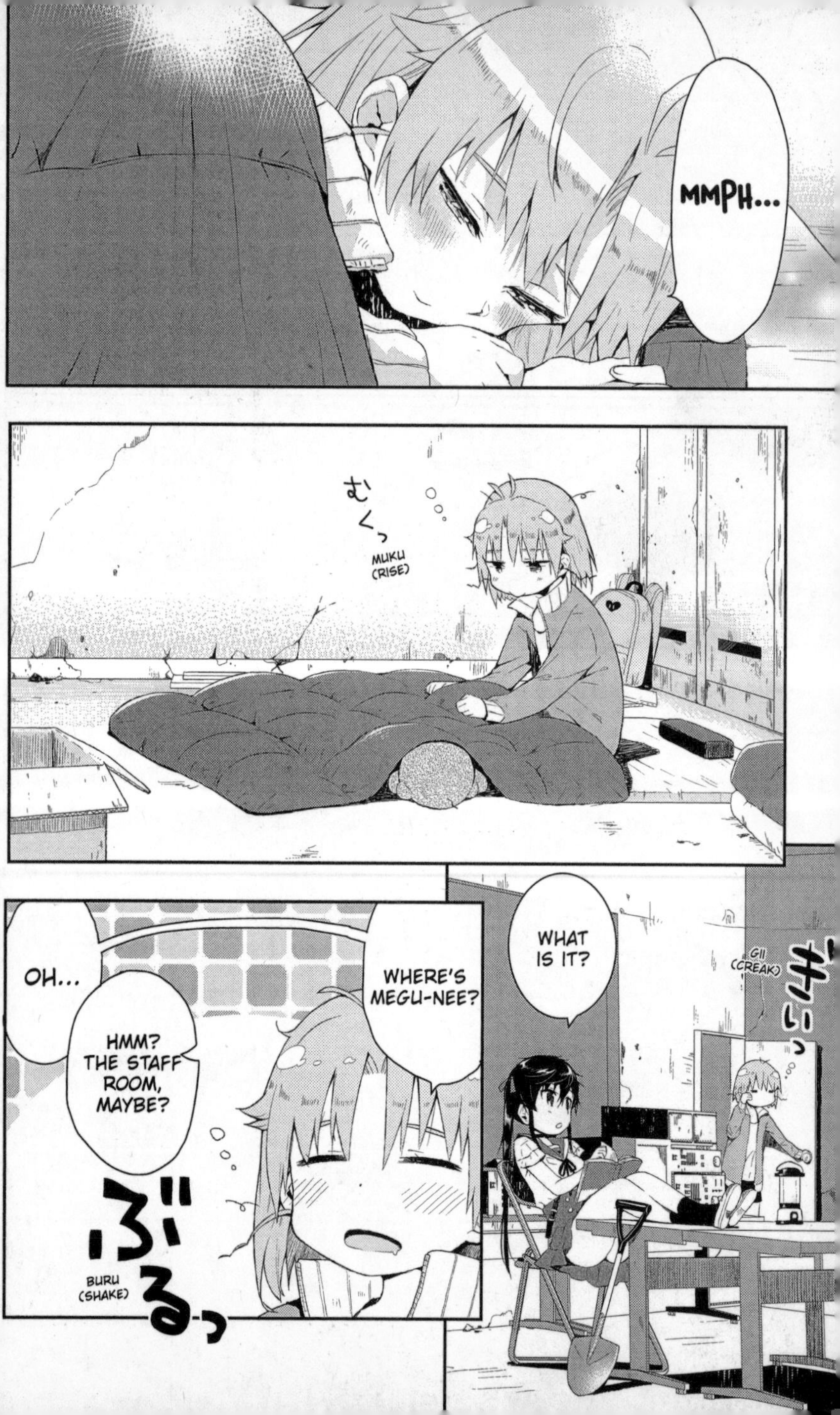
MMPH...
むくっ
MUKU (RISE)
ぎぃっ
GII (CREAK)
WHAT IS IT?
WHERE'S MEGU-NEE?
OH...
HMM? THE STAFF ROOM, MAYBE?
ぶるっ
BURU (SHAKE)

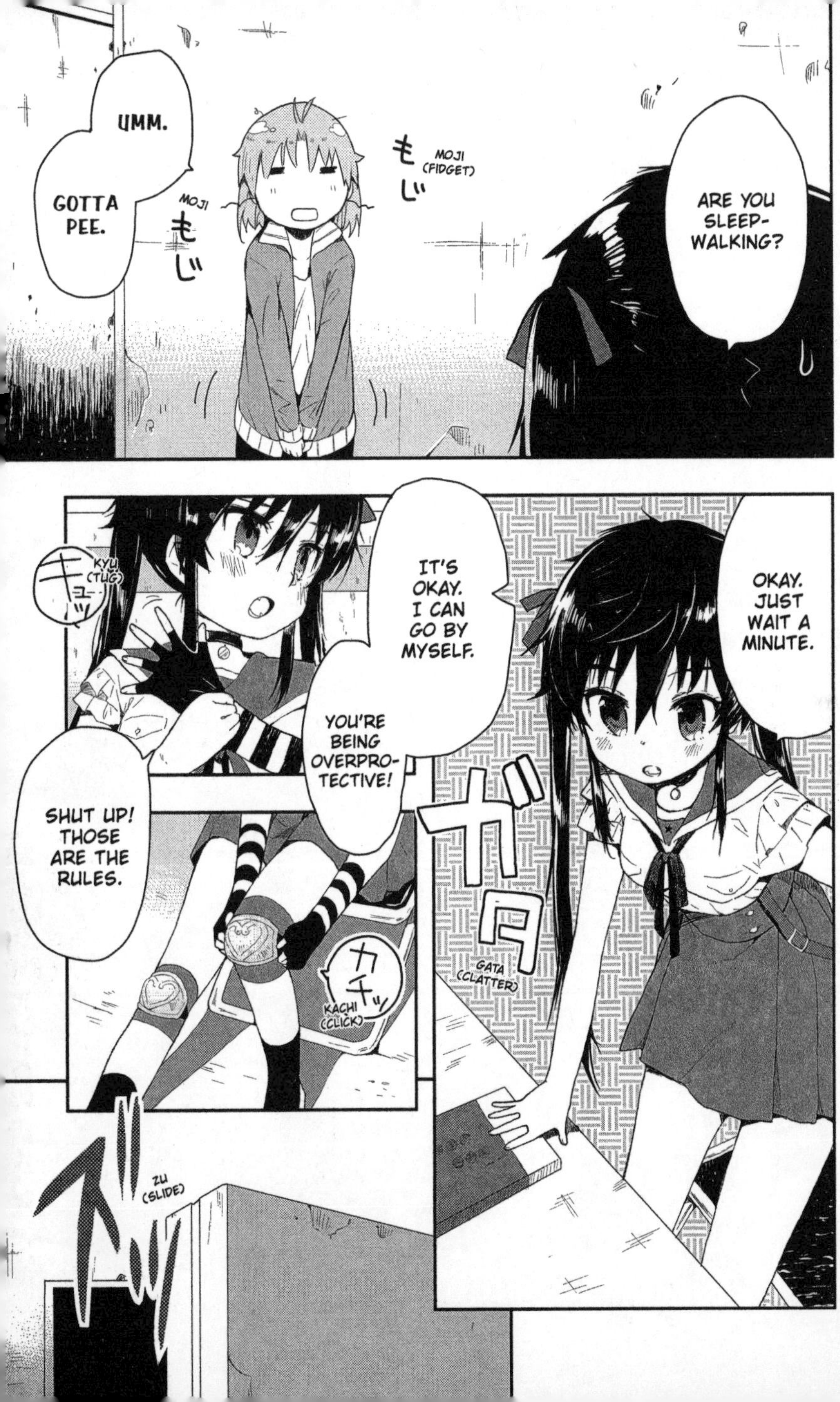
ARE YOU SLEEP-WALKING?
MOJI (FIDGET)
MOJI
UMM.
GOTTA PEE.
OKAY. JUST WAIT A MINUTE.
GATA (CLATTER)
IT'S OKAY. I CAN GO BY MYSELF.
KYU (TUG)
YOU'RE BEING OVERPROTECTIVE!
SHUT UP! THOSE ARE THE RULES.
KACHI (CLICK)
ZU (SLIDE)

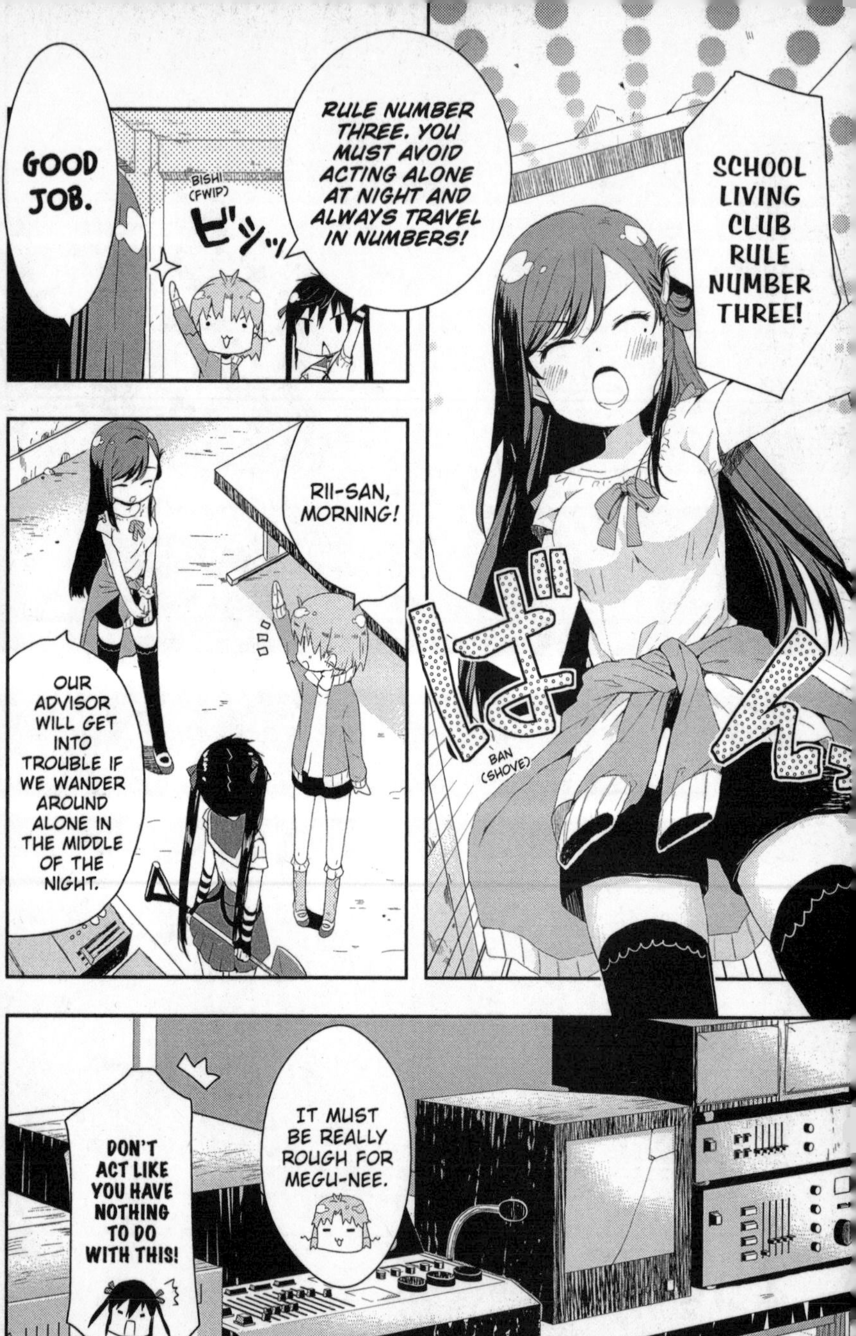
SCHOOL LIVING CLUB RULE NUMBER THREE!
ばん
BAN (SHOVE)
RULE NUMBER THREE. YOU MUST AVOID ACTING ALONE AT NIGHT AND ALWAYS TRAVEL IN NUMBERS!
ビシッ
BISHI (FWIP)
GOOD JOB.
RII-SAN, MORNING!
OUR ADVISOR WILL GET INTO TROUBLE IF WE WANDER AROUND ALONE IN THE MIDDLE OF THE NIGHT.
IT MUST BE REALLY ROUGH FOR MEGU-NEE.
DON'T ACT LIKE YOU HAVE NOTHING TO DO WITH THIS!

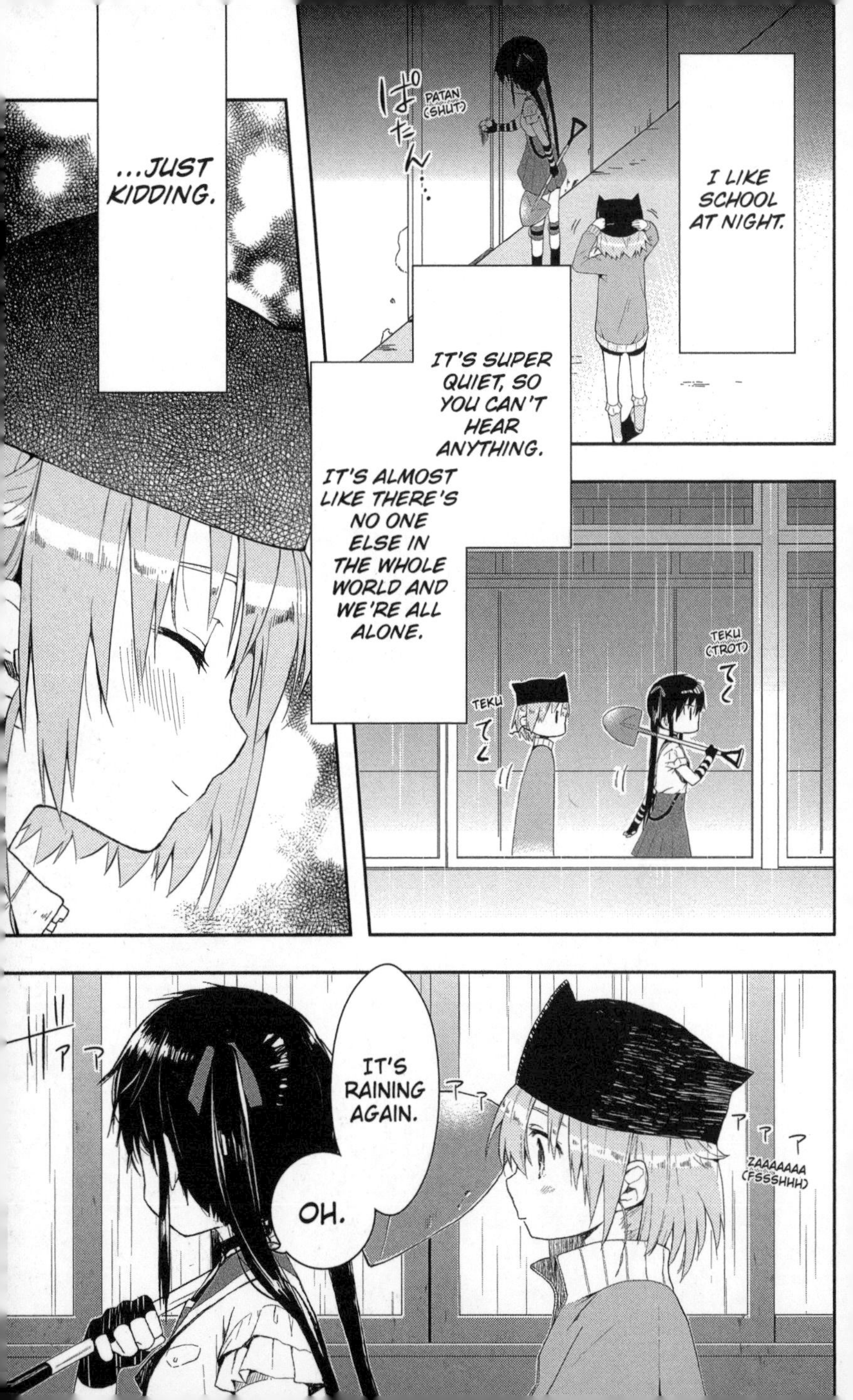
I LIKE SCHOOL AT NIGHT.
ぱたん…
PATAN (SHUT)
IT'S SUPER QUIET, SO YOU CAN'T HEAR ANYTHING.
IT'S ALMOST LIKE THERE'S NO ONE ELSE IN THE WHOLE WORLD AND WE'RE ALL ALONE.
TEKU (TROT)
てく
TEKU
てく
...JUST KIDDING.
ZAAAAAAA (FSSSHHH)
IT'S RAINING AGAIN.
OH.

SIGN: GIRLS' BATHROOM

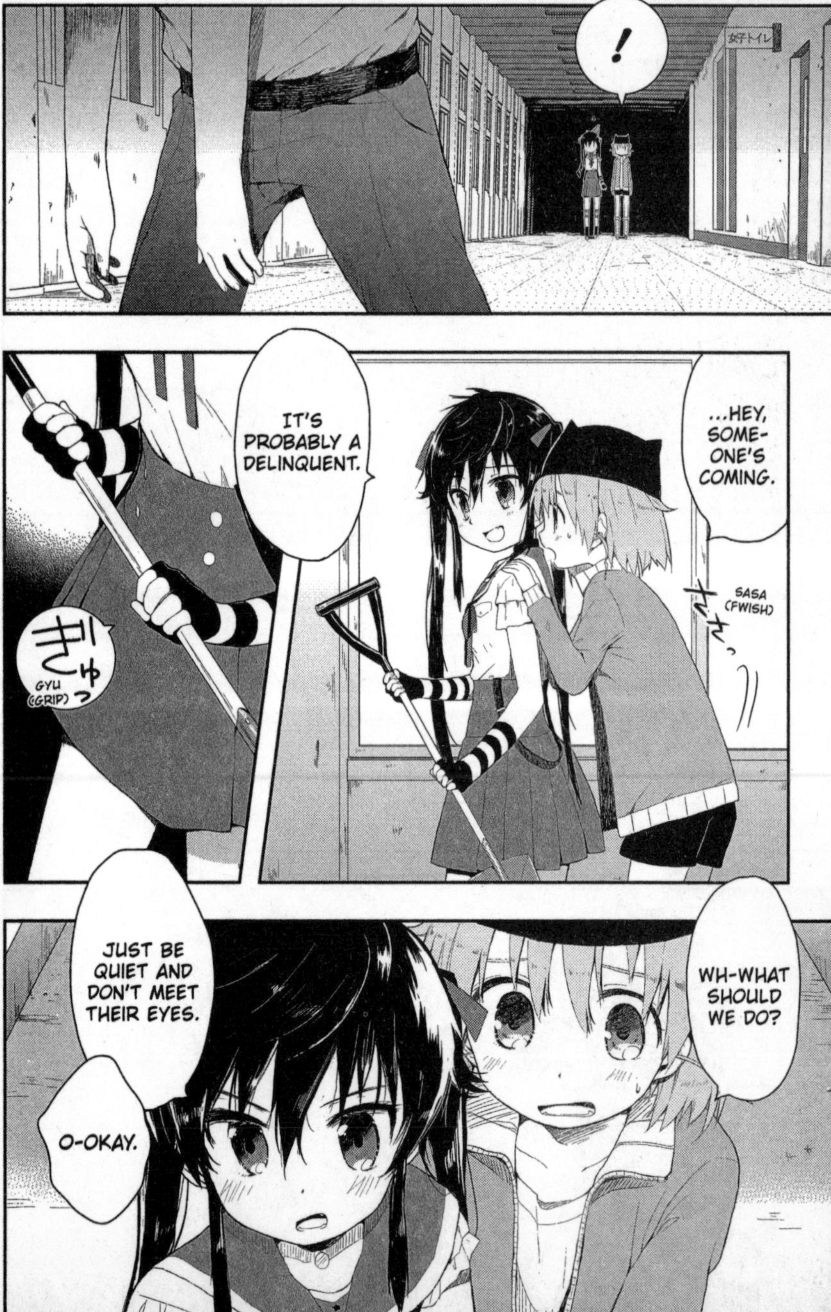
!
女子トイレ
...HEY, SOMEONE'S COMING.
ささっ
SASA (FWISH)
IT'S PROBABLY A DELINQUENT.
ぎゅっ
GYU (GRIP)
WH-WHAT SHOULD WE DO?
JUST BE QUIET AND DON'T MEET THEIR EYES.
O-OKAY.

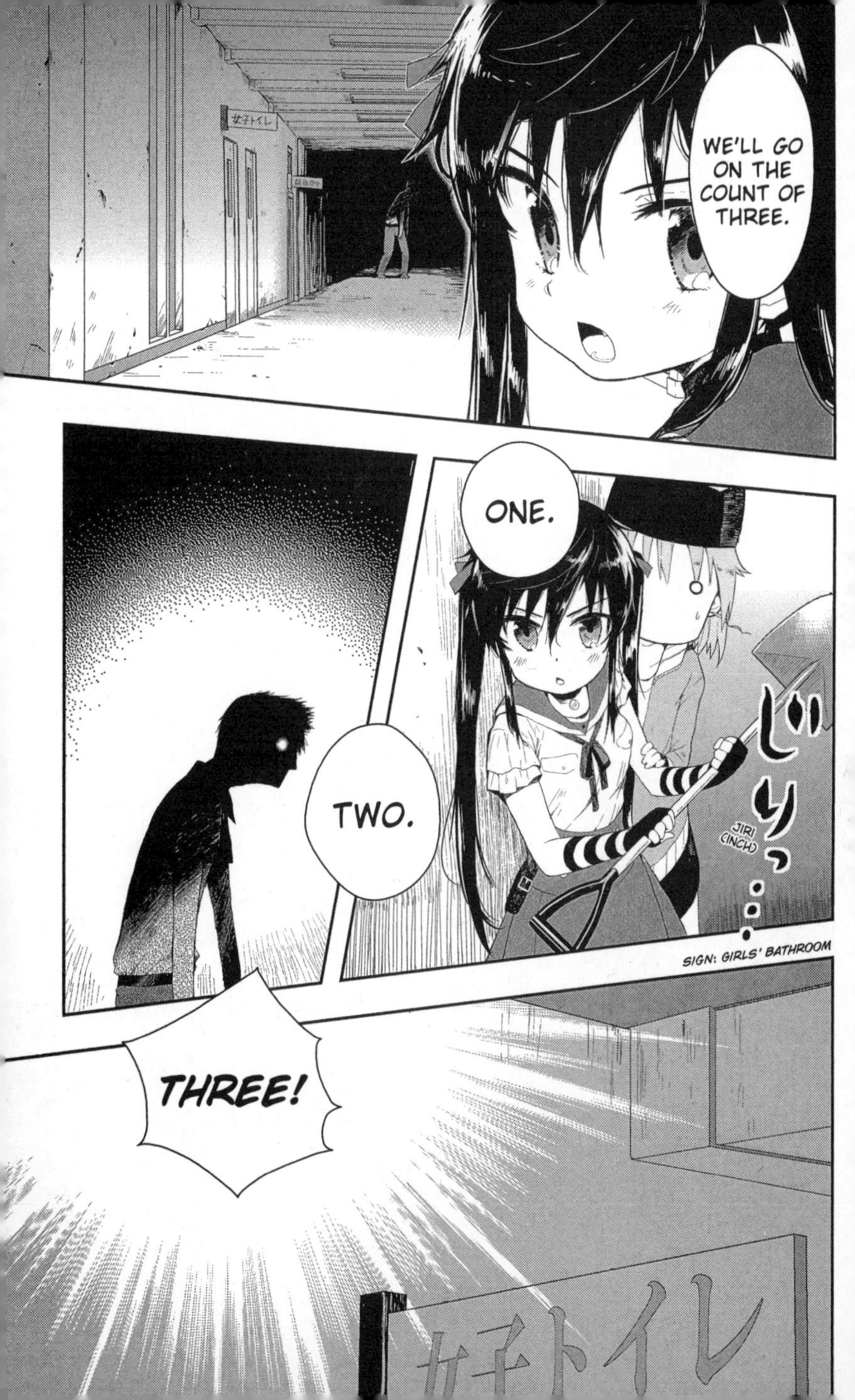
WE'LL GO ON THE COUNT OF THREE.
女子トイレ
ONE.
じりっ…
JIRI (INCH)
TWO.
THREE!
女子トイレ
SIGN: GIRLS' BATHROOM

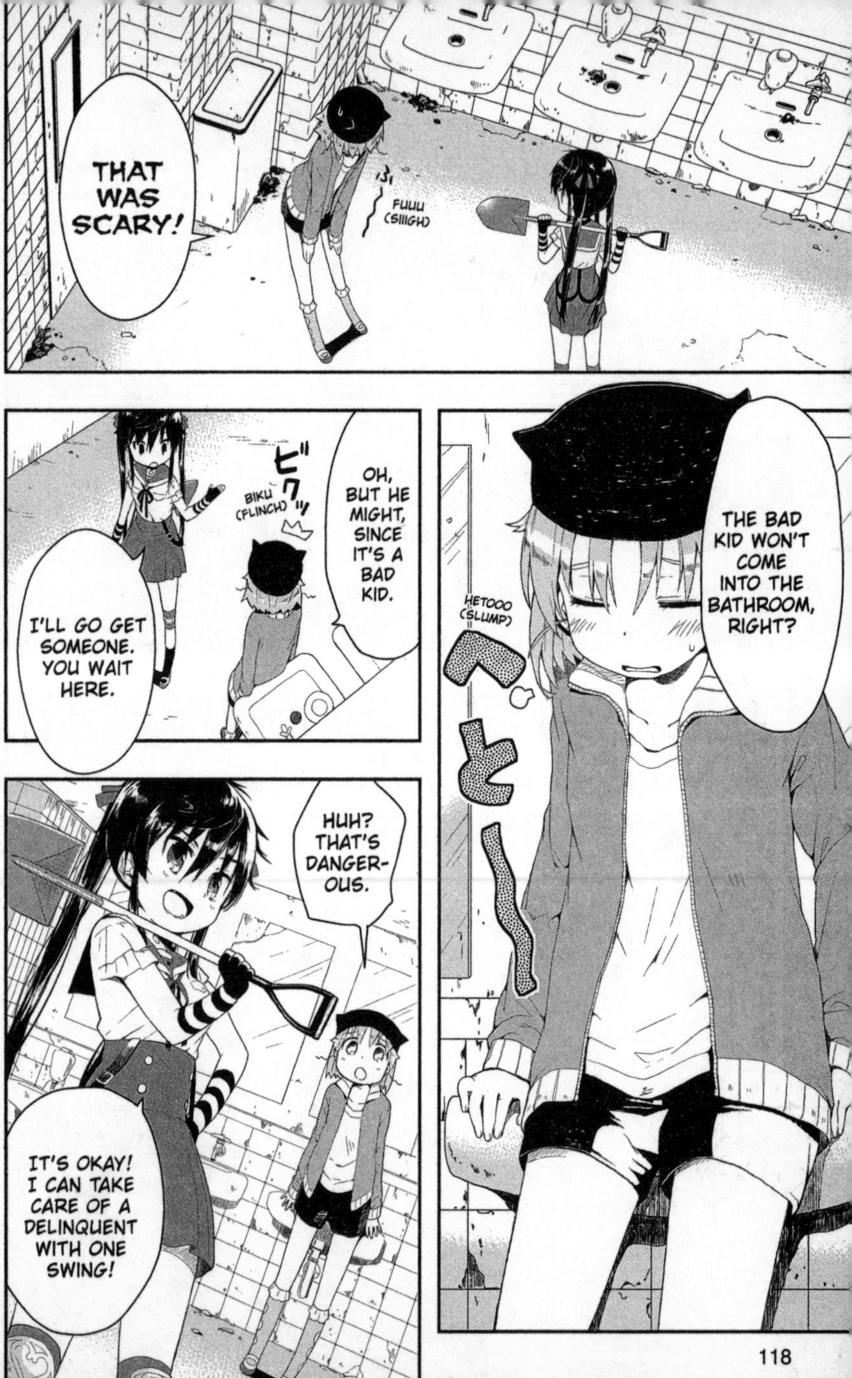
THAT WAS SCARY!
FUUU (SIIIGH)
THE BAD KID WON'T COME INTO THE BATHROOM, RIGHT?
HETOOO (SLUMP)
OH, BUT HE MIGHT, SINCE IT'S A BAD KID.
BIKU (FLINCH)
I'LL GO GET SOMEONE. YOU WAIT HERE.
HUH? THAT'S DANGER-OUS.
IT'S OKAY! I CAN TAKE CARE OF A DELINQUENT WITH ONE SWING!

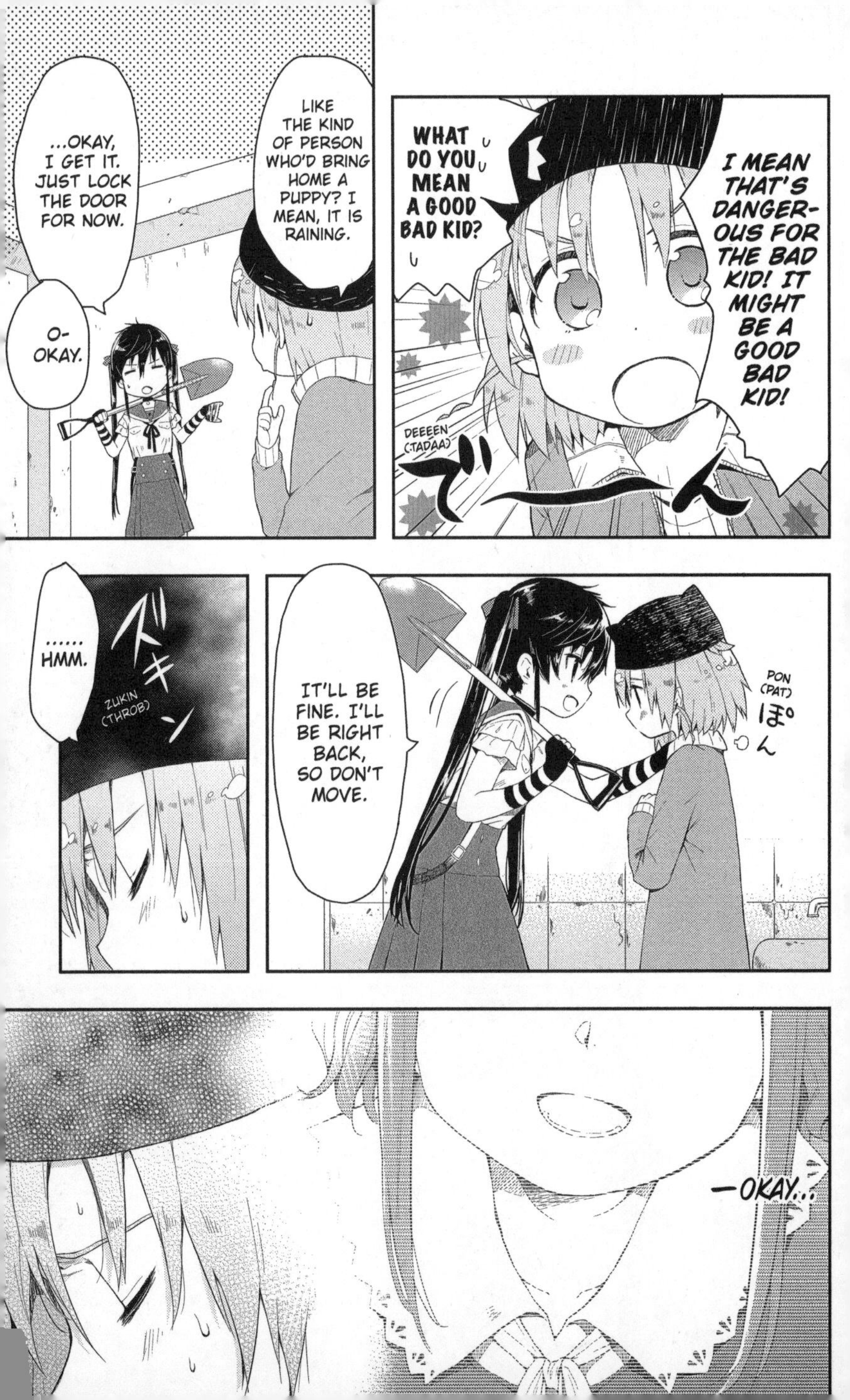
I MEAN THAT'S DANGEROUS FOR THE BAD KID! IT MIGHT BE A GOOD BAD KID!
DEEEEN (TADAA)
WHAT DO YOU MEAN A GOOD BAD KID?
LIKE THE KIND OF PERSON WHO'D BRING HOME A PUPPY? I MEAN, IT IS RAINING.
...OKAY, I GET IT. JUST LOCK THE DOOR FOR NOW.
O-OKAY.
PON (PAT)
ぽん
IT'LL BE FINE. I'LL BE RIGHT BACK, SO DON'T MOVE.
ズキン
ZUKIN (THROB)
...... HMM.
—OKAY...

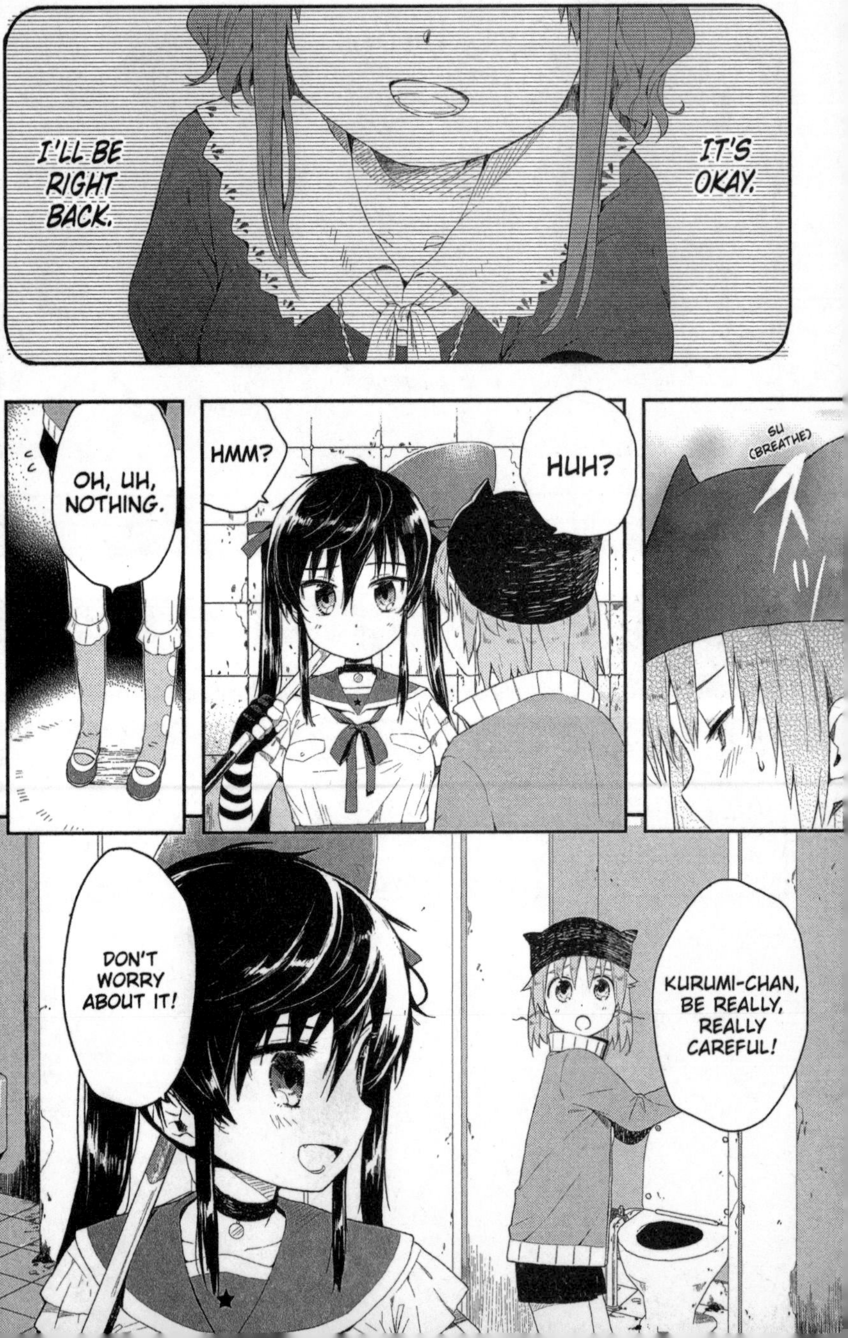
IT'S OKAY.
I'LL BE RIGHT BACK.
SU (BREATHE)
HUH?
HMM?
OH, UH, NOTHING.
KURUMI-CHAN, BE REALLY, REALLY CAREFUL!
DON'T WORRY ABOUT IT!

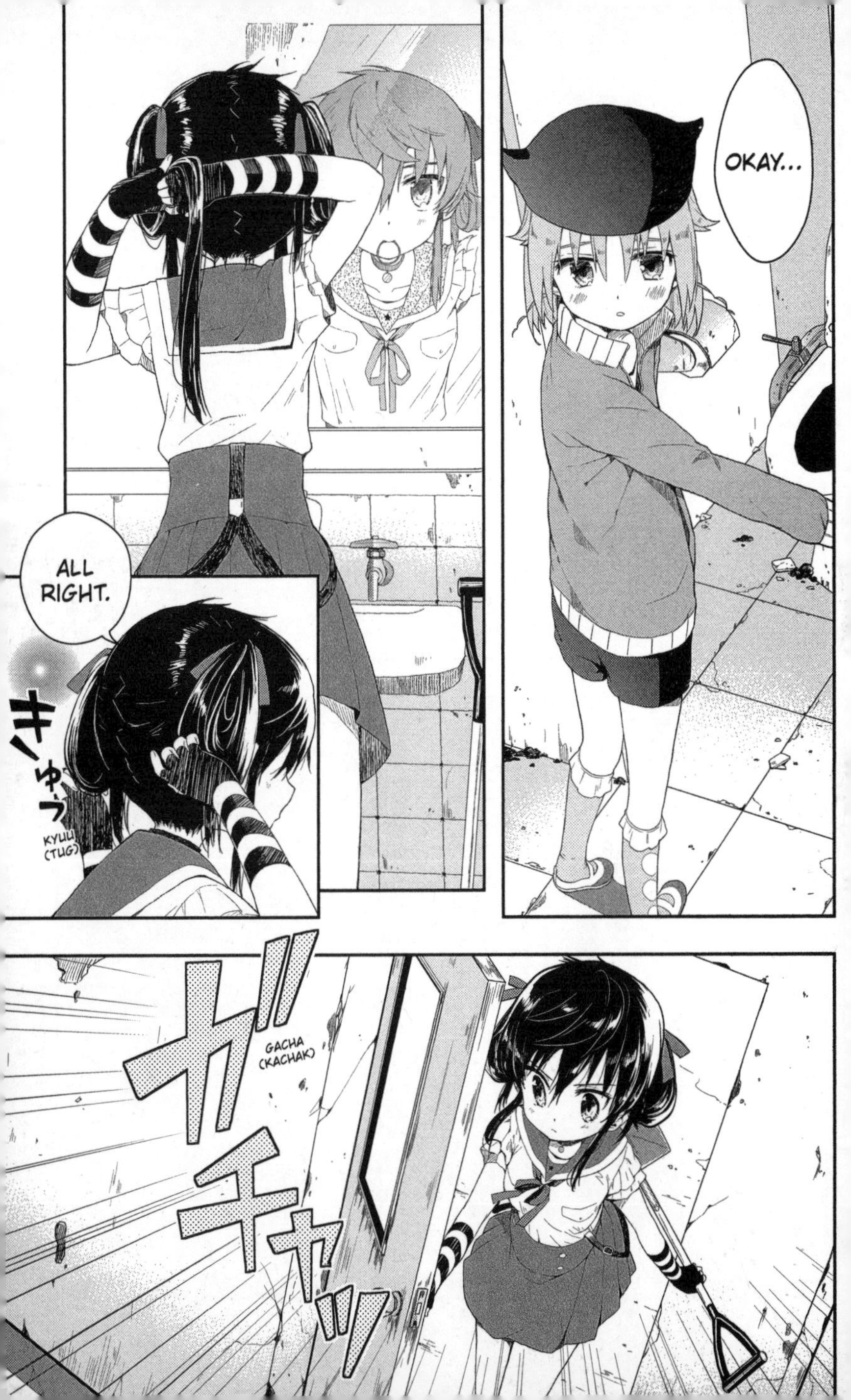
OKAY...
ALL RIGHT.
KYUU (TUG)
GACHA (KACHAK)

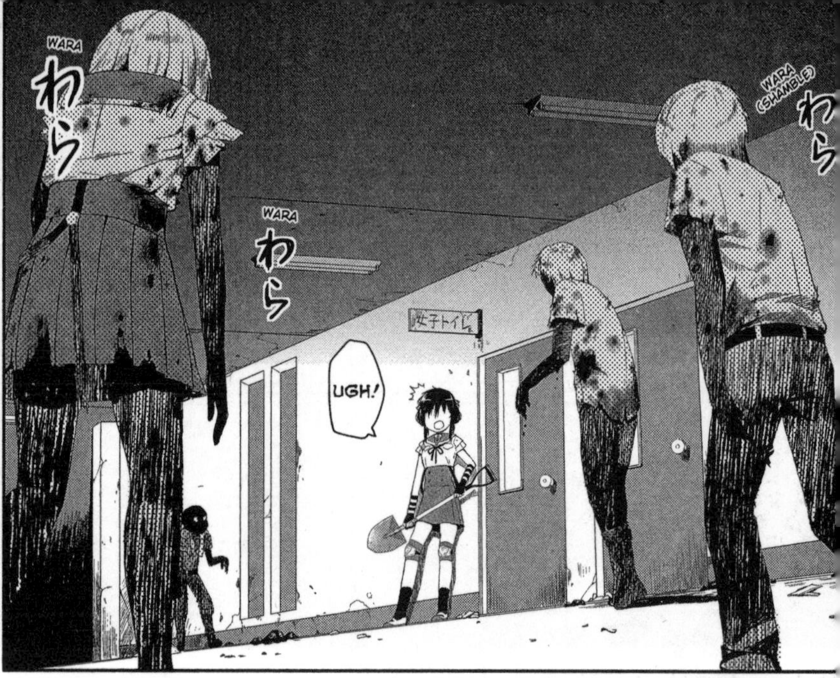
WARA (SHAMBLE)
わら
WARA
わら
WARA
わら
女子トイレ
UGH!

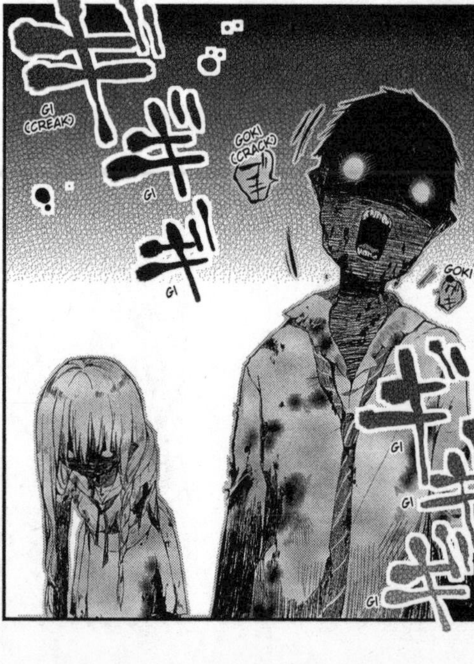
GOKI (CRACK)
ギギギ
GI (CREAK)
GI
GI
GOKI
ギギギ
GI
GI
GI

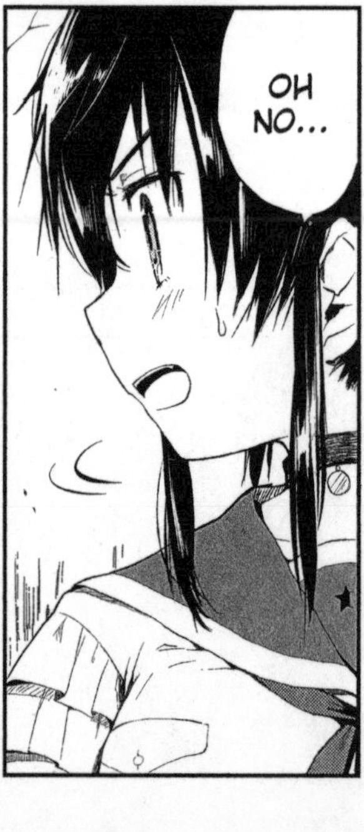
OH NO...

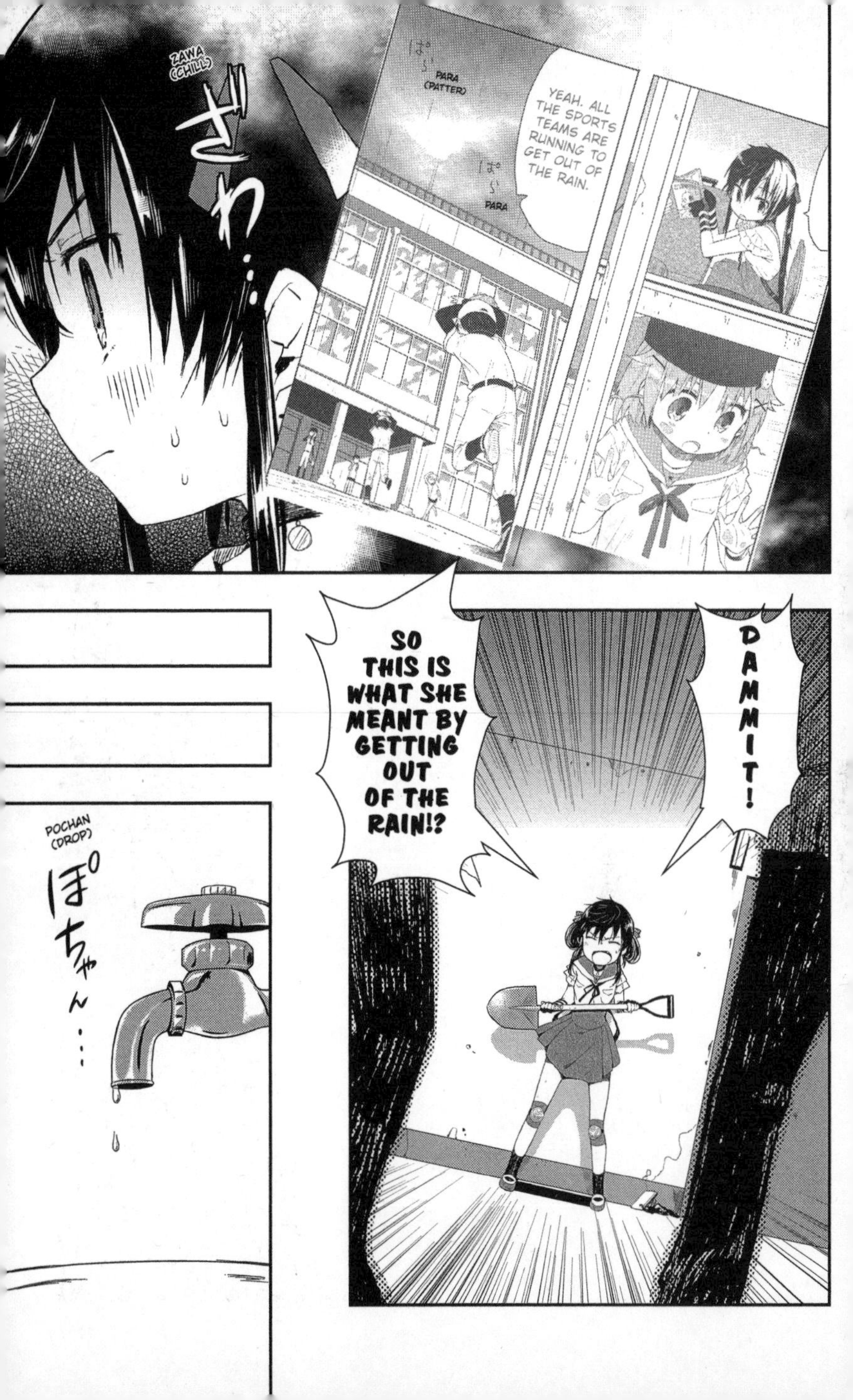

YEAH. ALL THE SPORTS TEAMS ARE RUNNING TO GET OUT OF THE RAIN.
ぱら
PARA (PATTER)
ぱら
PARA
ZAWA (CHILL)
ざわ…
DAMMIT!
SO THIS IS WHAT SHE MEANT BY GETTING OUT OF THE RAIN!?
POCHAN (DROP)
ぽちゃん…

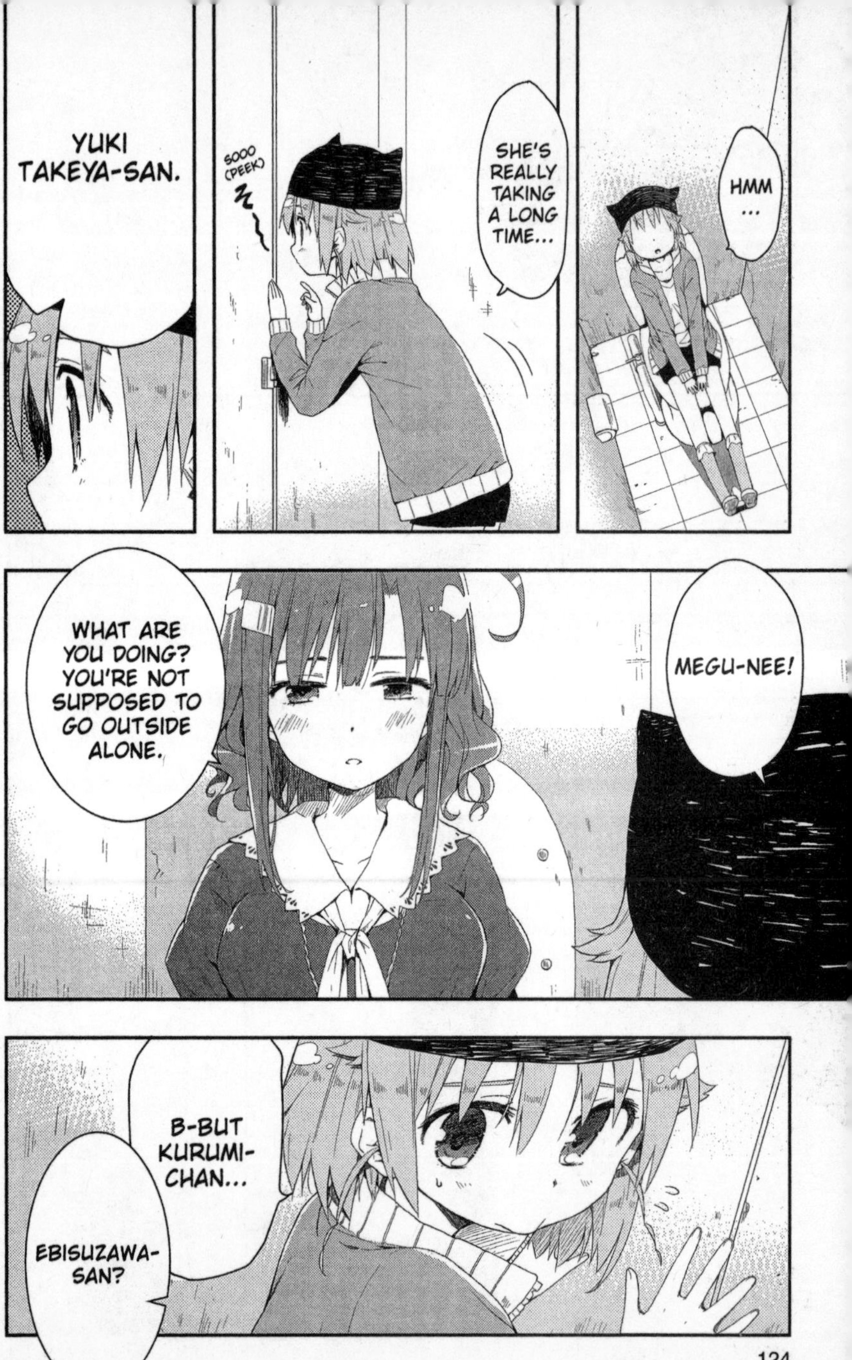
HMM ...
SHE'S REALLY TAKING A LONG TIME...
SOOO (PEEK)
YUKI TAKEYA-SAN.
MEGU-NEE!
WHAT ARE YOU DOING? YOU'RE NOT SUPPOSED TO GO OUTSIDE ALONE.
B-BUT KURUMI-CHAN...
EBISUZAWA-SAN?

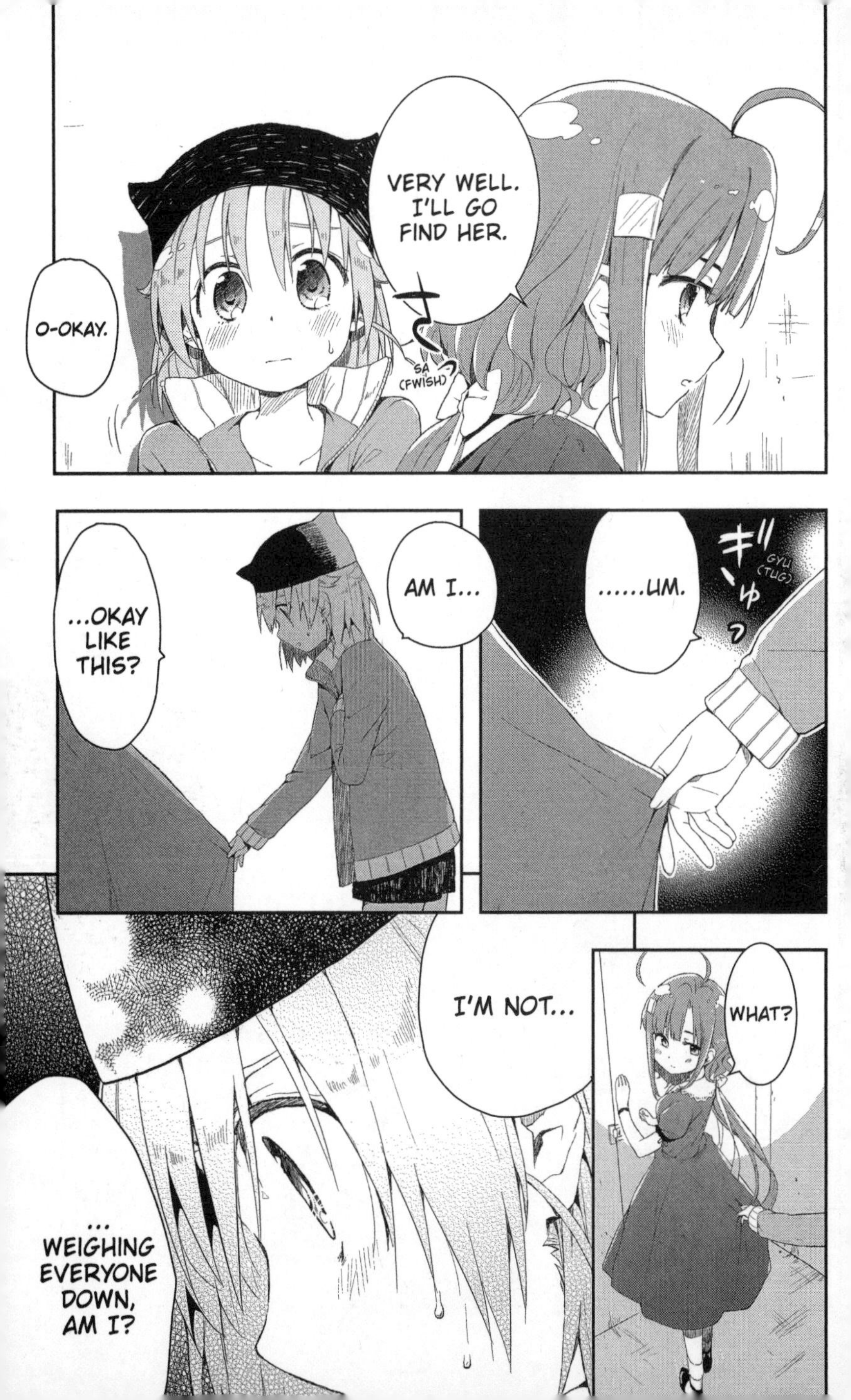

VERY WELL. I'LL GO FIND HER.
SA (FWISH)
O-OKAY.
GYU (TUG)
......UM.
AM I...
...OKAY LIKE THIS?
WHAT?
I'M NOT...
...WEIGHING EVERYONE DOWN, AM I?

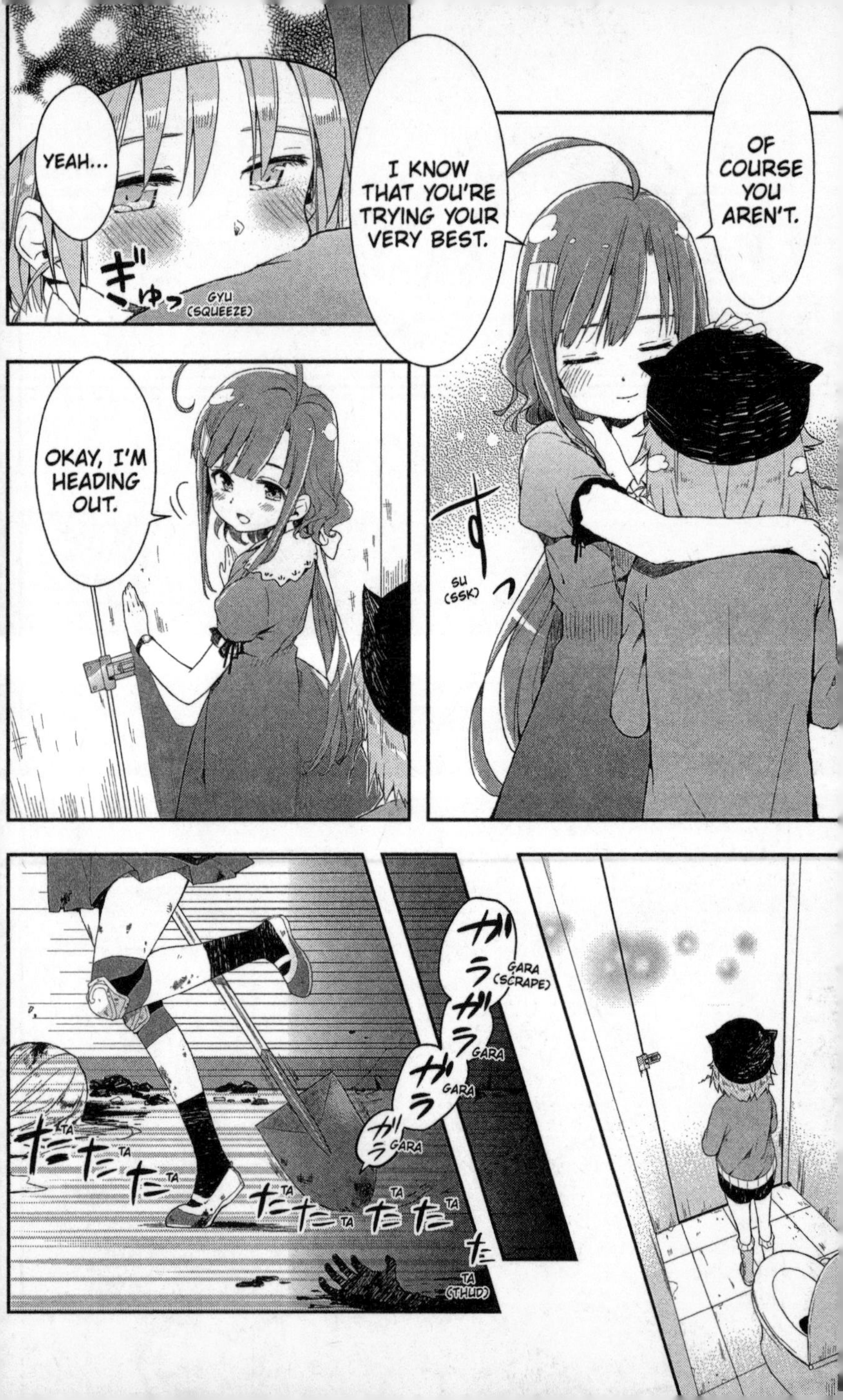
OF COURSE YOU AREN'T.
I KNOW THAT YOU'RE TRYING YOUR VERY BEST.
すっ
SU (SSK)
YEAH...
ギュっ
GYU (SQUEEZE)
OKAY, I'M HEADING OUT.
ガラ
GARA (SCRAPE)
ガラ
GARA
ガラ
GARA
ガラ
GARA
た
TA (THUD)
たたたたたたたた
TA TA TA TA TA TA TA TA

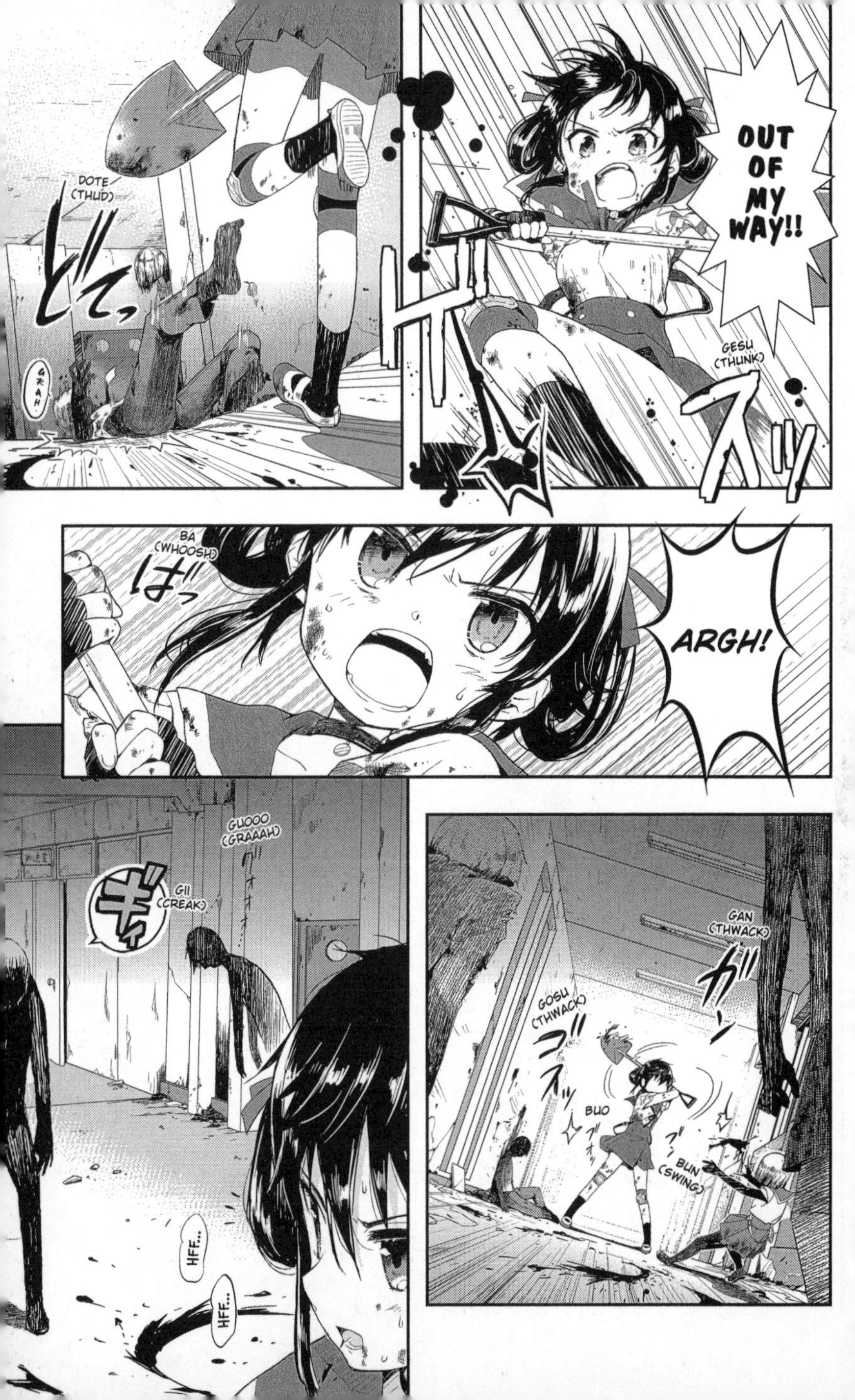
OUT OF MY WAY!!
GESU (THUNK)
DOTE (THUD)
GRAH
ARGH!
BA (WHOOSH)
GAN (THWACK)
GOSU (THWACK)
BUO
BUN (SWING)
GUOOO (GRAAAH)
GII (CREAK)
HFF...
HFF...

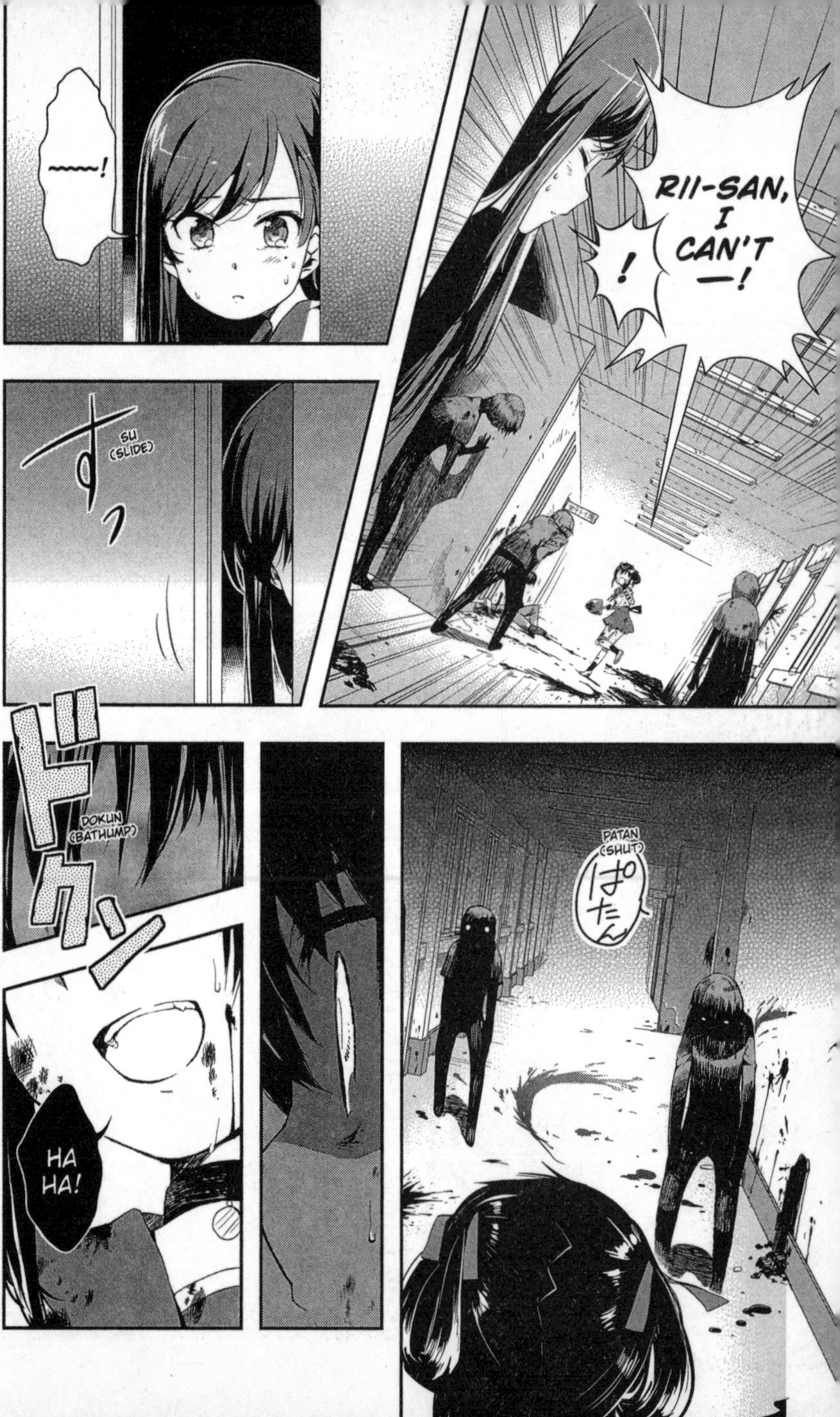
RII-SAN, I CAN'T —!
!
——!
SU (SLIDE)
すっ
PATAN (SHUT)
ぱたん
DOKUN (BATHUMP)
ドクン
HA HA!

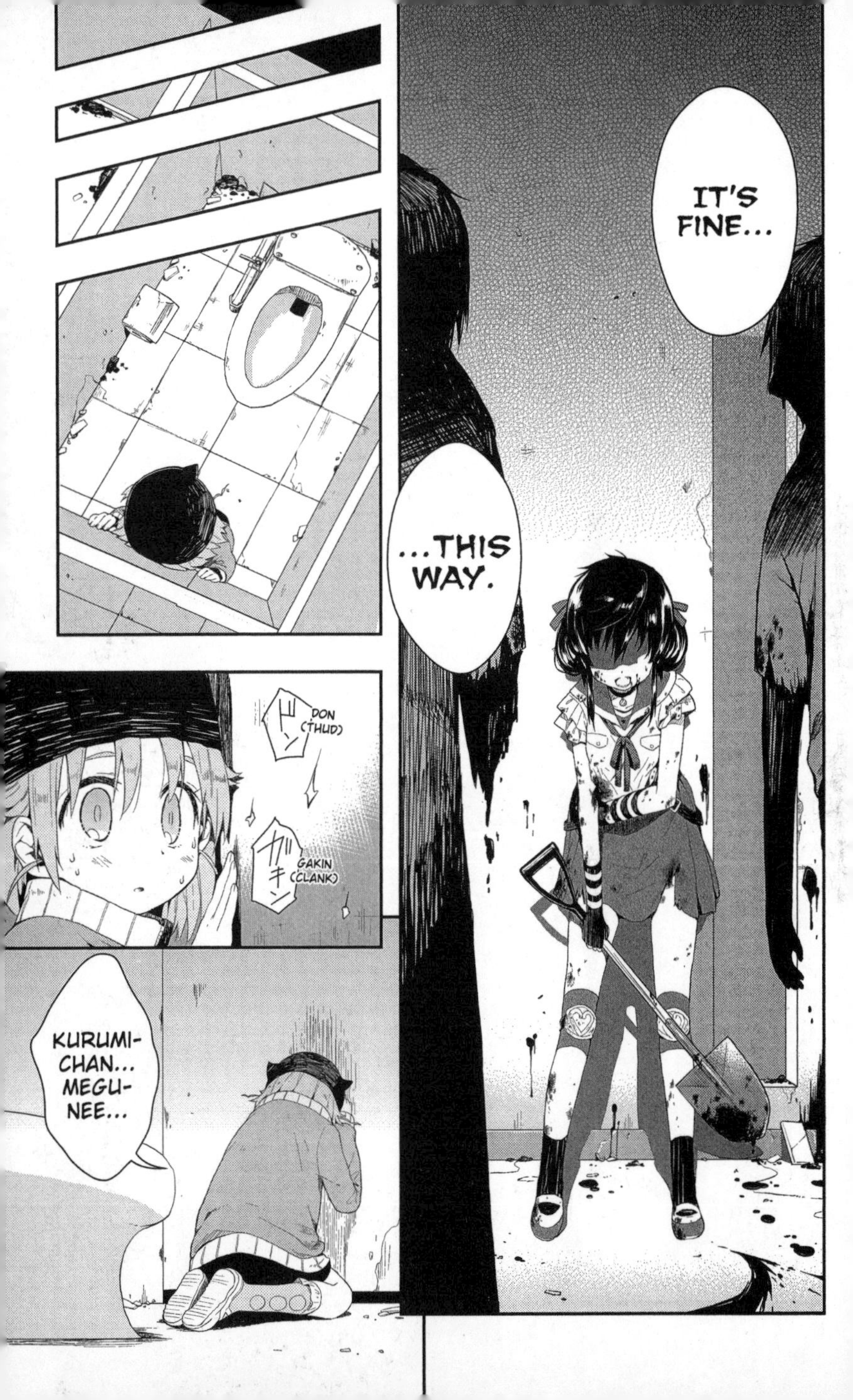
IT'S FINE...
...THIS WAY.
DON (THUD)
GAKIN (CLANK)
KURUMI-CHAN... MEGU-NEE...

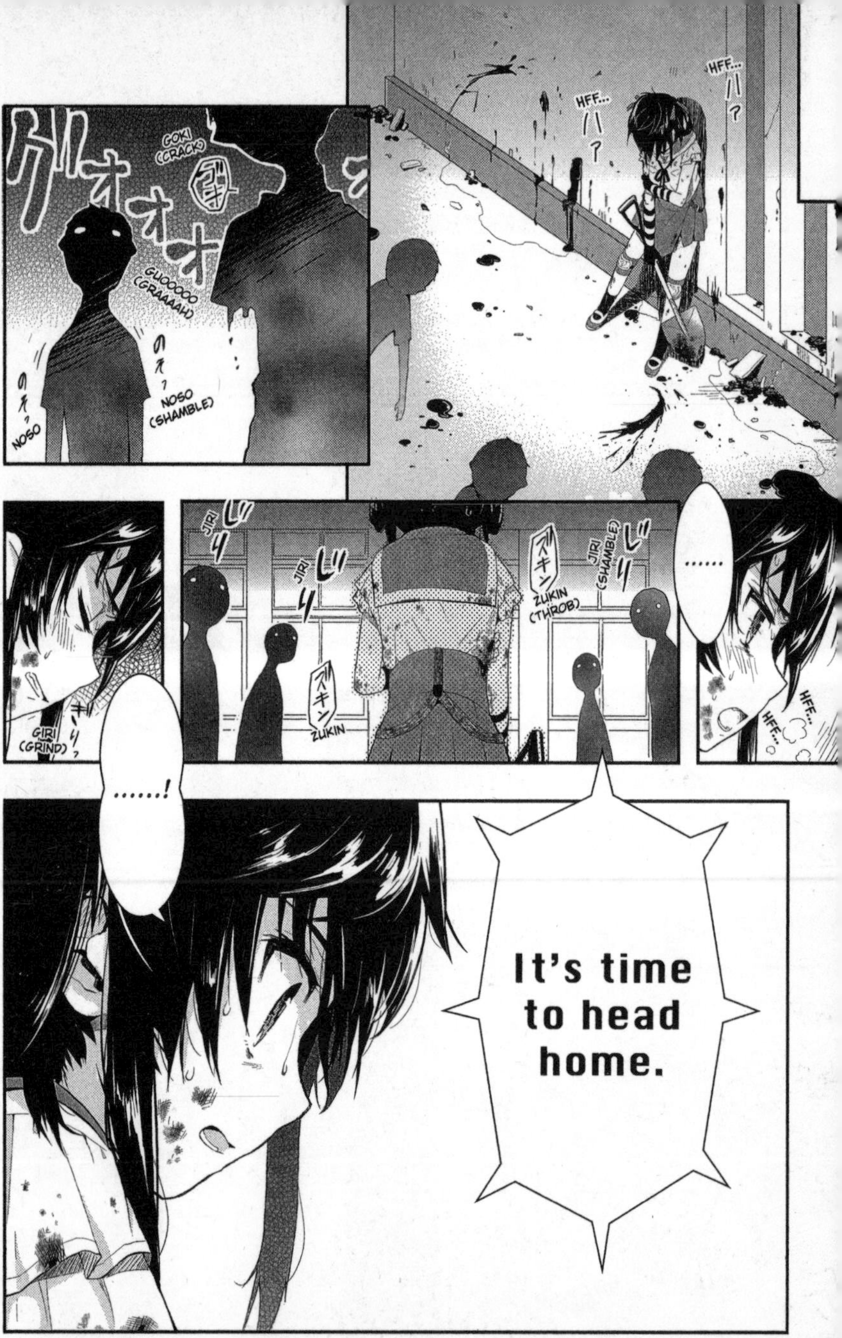

HFF... ハァ
HFF... ハァ
GOKI (CRACK)
GUOOOOO (GRAAAAH)
NOSO (SHAMBLE)
NOSO
......
HFF... HFF...
JIRI (SHAMBLE)
ZUKIN (THROB)
JIRI
JIRI
ZUKIN
GIRI (GRIND)
......!
It's time to head home.

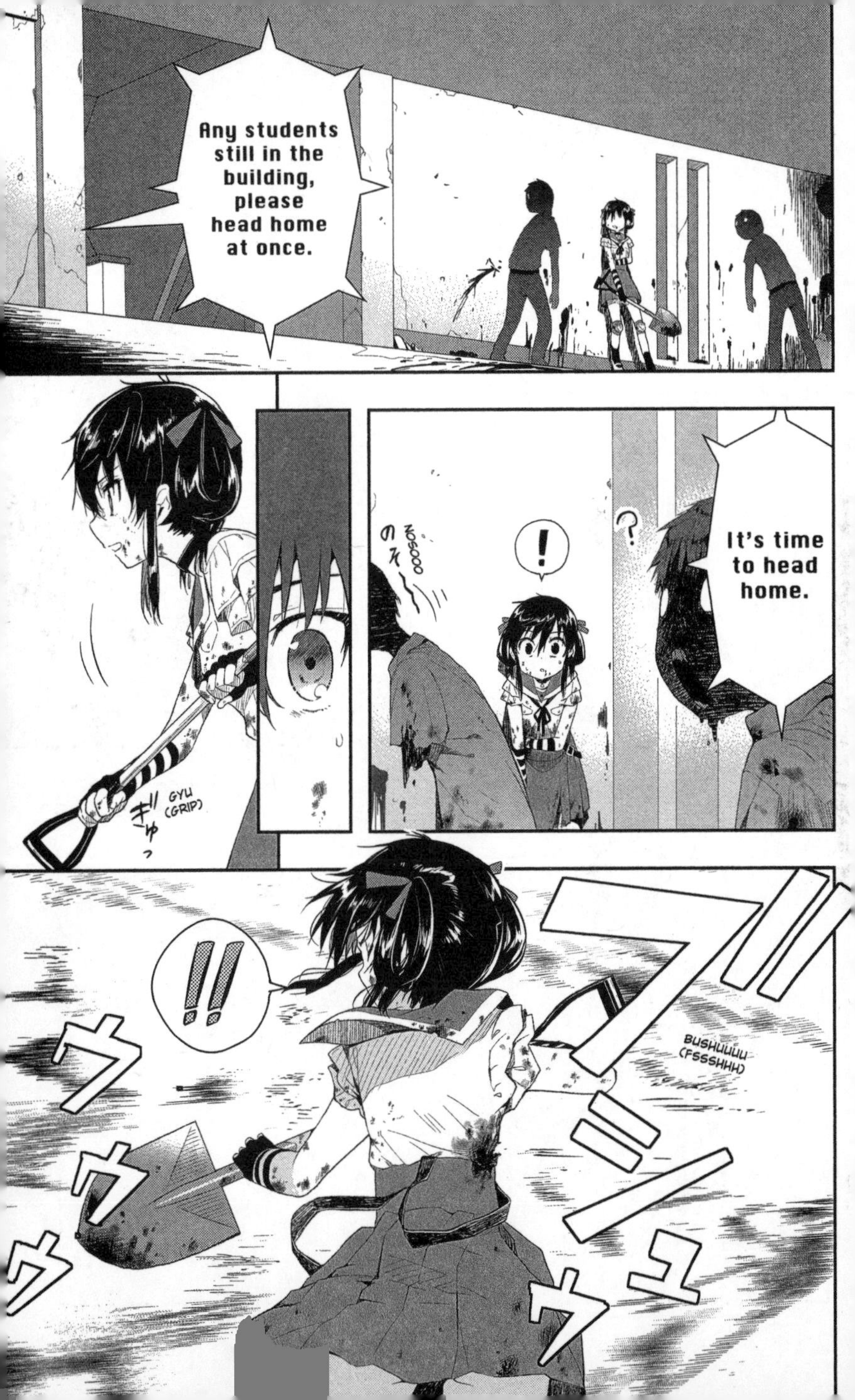
Any students still in the building, please head home at once.
It's time to head home.
?
!
のそ~
NOSOOO
ぎゅっ
GYU (GRIP)
!!
ブシュウ
ウウウ
BUSHUUUU (FSSSHHH)

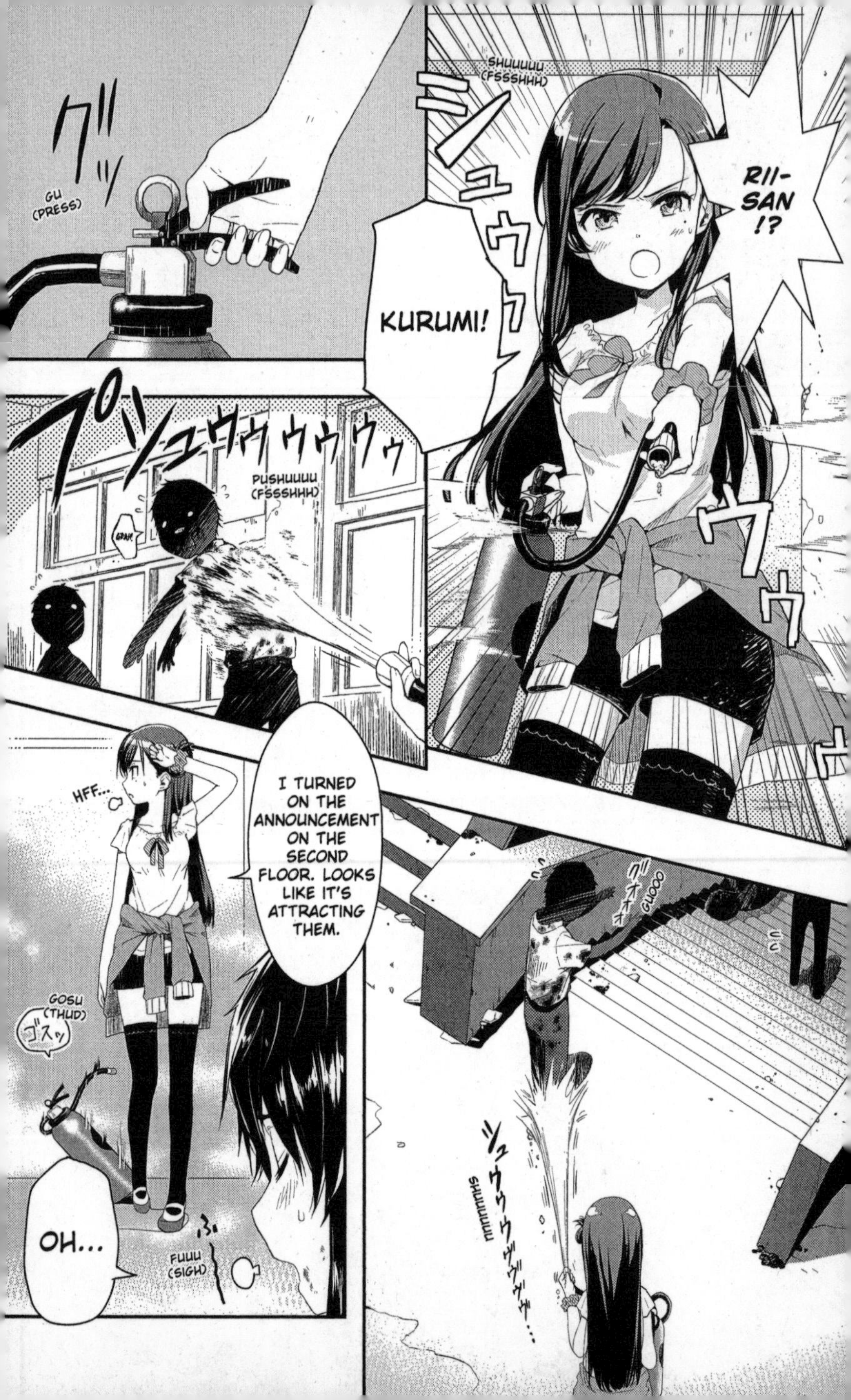

SHUUUUUU (FSSSHHH)
RII-SAN!?
KURUMI!
GU (PRESS)
PUSHUUUU (FSSSHHH)
GRAH!
GUOOO
SHUUUUU
HFF...
I TURNED ON THE ANNOUNCEMENT ON THE SECOND FLOOR. LOOKS LIKE IT'S ATTRACTING THEM.
GOSU (THUD)
OH...
FUUU (SIGH)

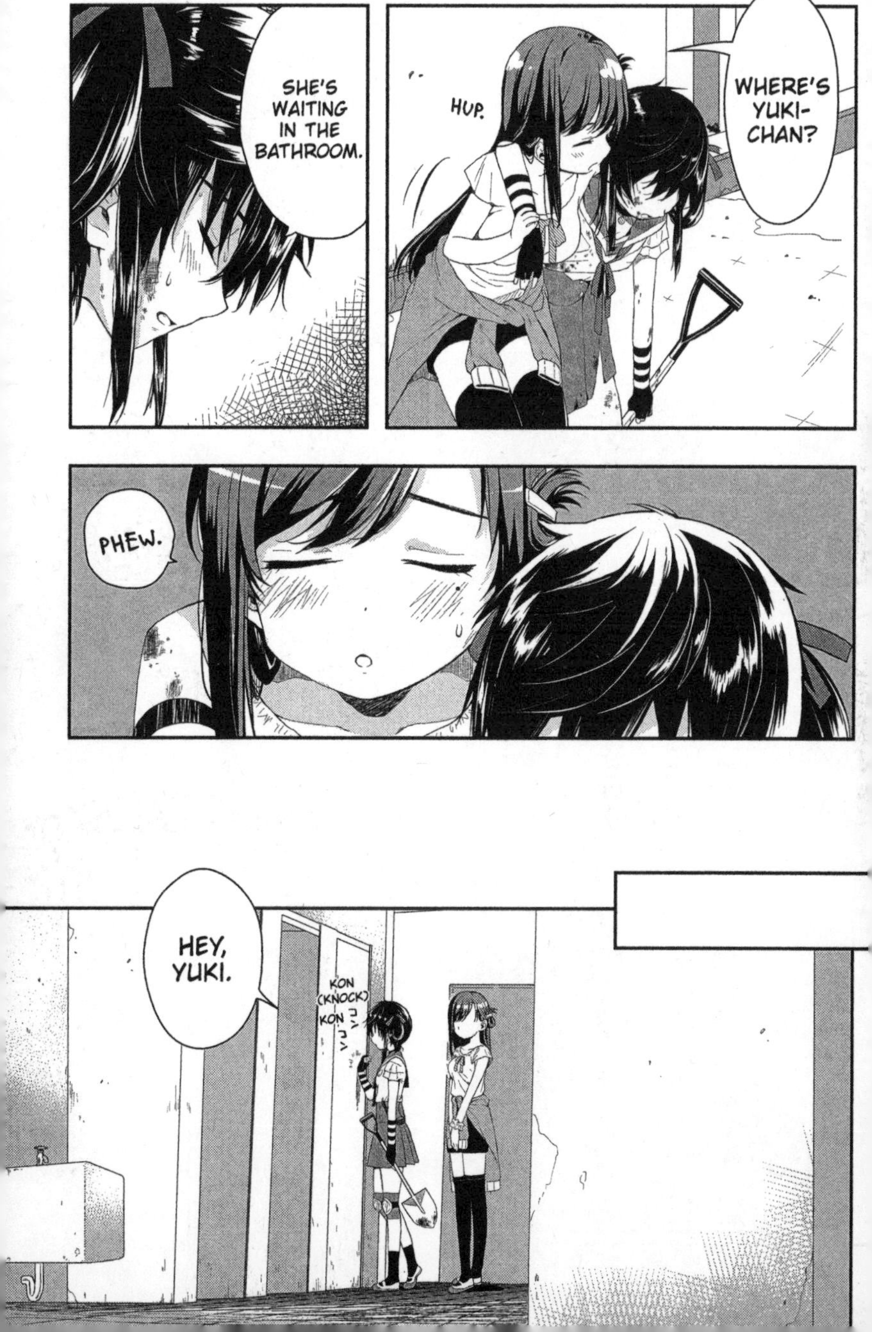
WHERE'S YUKI-CHAN?
HUP.
SHE'S WAITING IN THE BATHROOM.
PHEW.
HEY, YUKI.
KON (KNOCK) KON

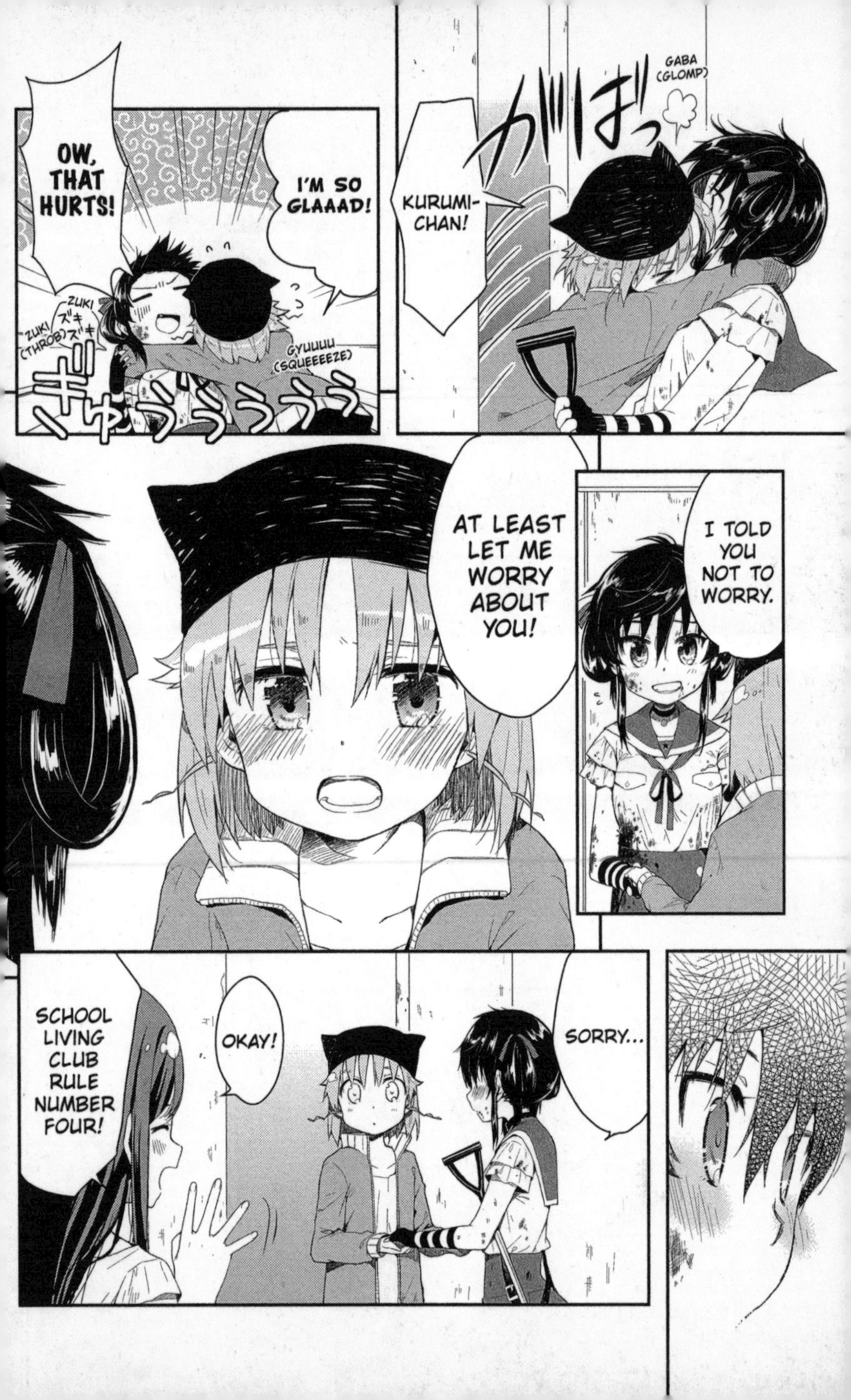
GABA (GLOMP)
がばっ
KURUMI-CHAN!
I'M SO GLAAAD!
OW, THAT HURTS!
GYUUUU (SQUEEEEZE)
ぎゅうううううう
ZUKI ズキ
ZUKI (THROB) ズキ
I TOLD YOU NOT TO WORRY.
AT LEAST LET ME WORRY ABOUT YOU!
SORRY...
OKAY!
SCHOOL LIVING CLUB RULE NUMBER FOUR!

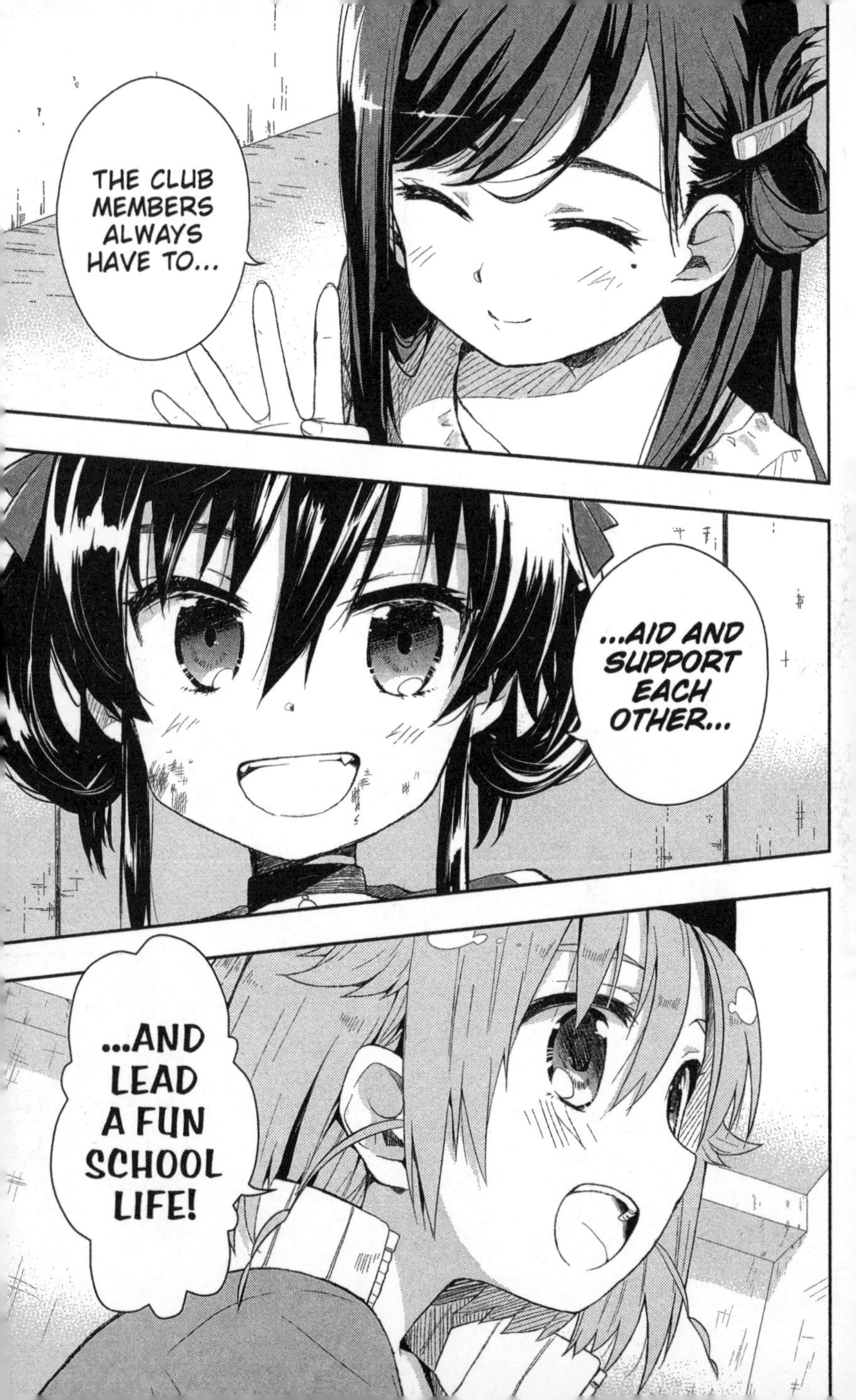
THE CLUB MEMBERS ALWAYS HAVE TO...
...AID AND SUPPORT EACH OTHER...
...AND LEAD A FUN SCHOOL LIFE!

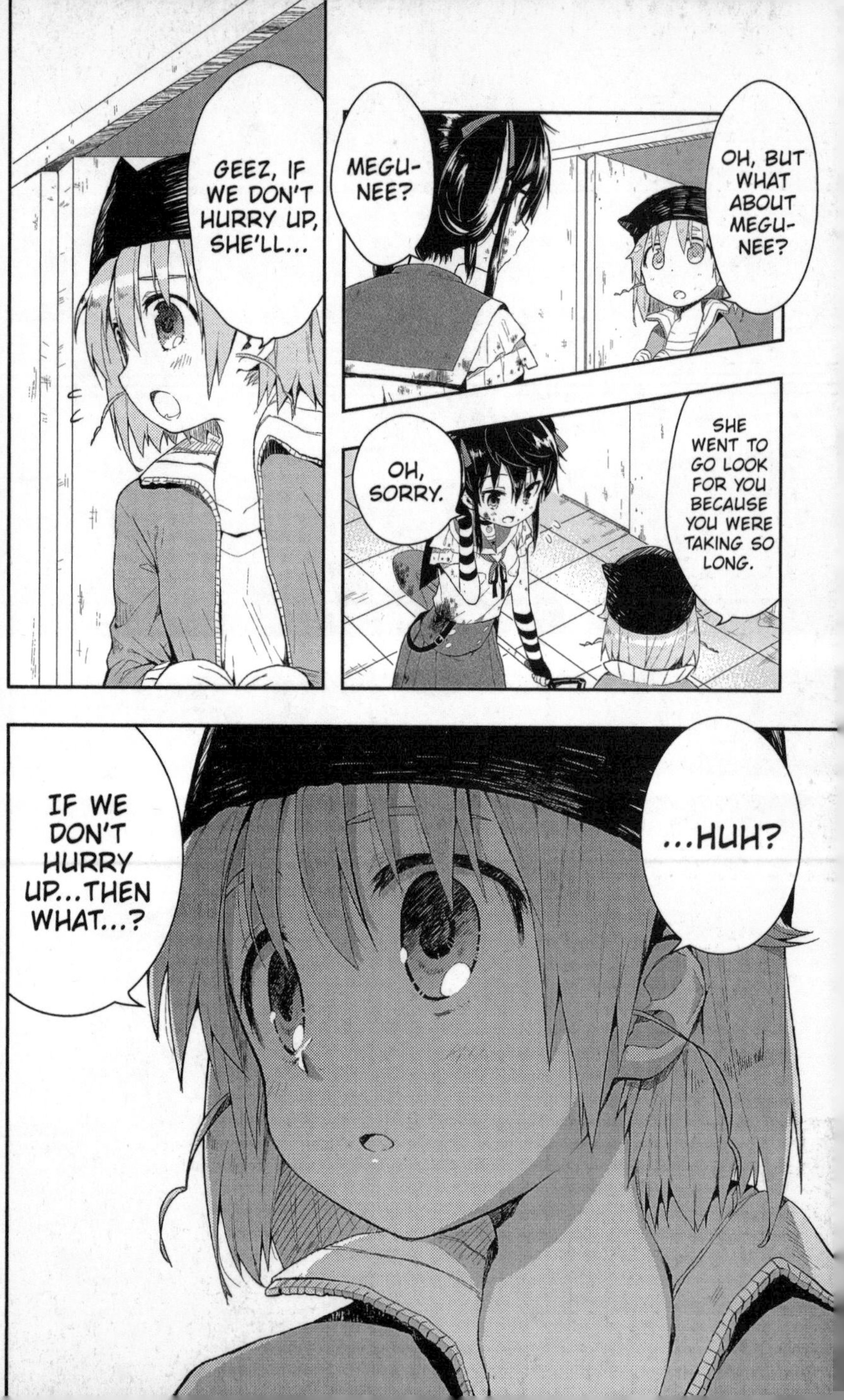
OH, BUT WHAT ABOUT MEGU-NEE?
MEGU-NEE?
SHE WENT TO GO LOOK FOR YOU BECAUSE YOU WERE TAKING SO LONG.
OH, SORRY.
GEEZ, IF WE DON'T HURRY UP, SHE'LL...
...HUH?
IF WE DON'T HURRY UP...THEN WHAT...?

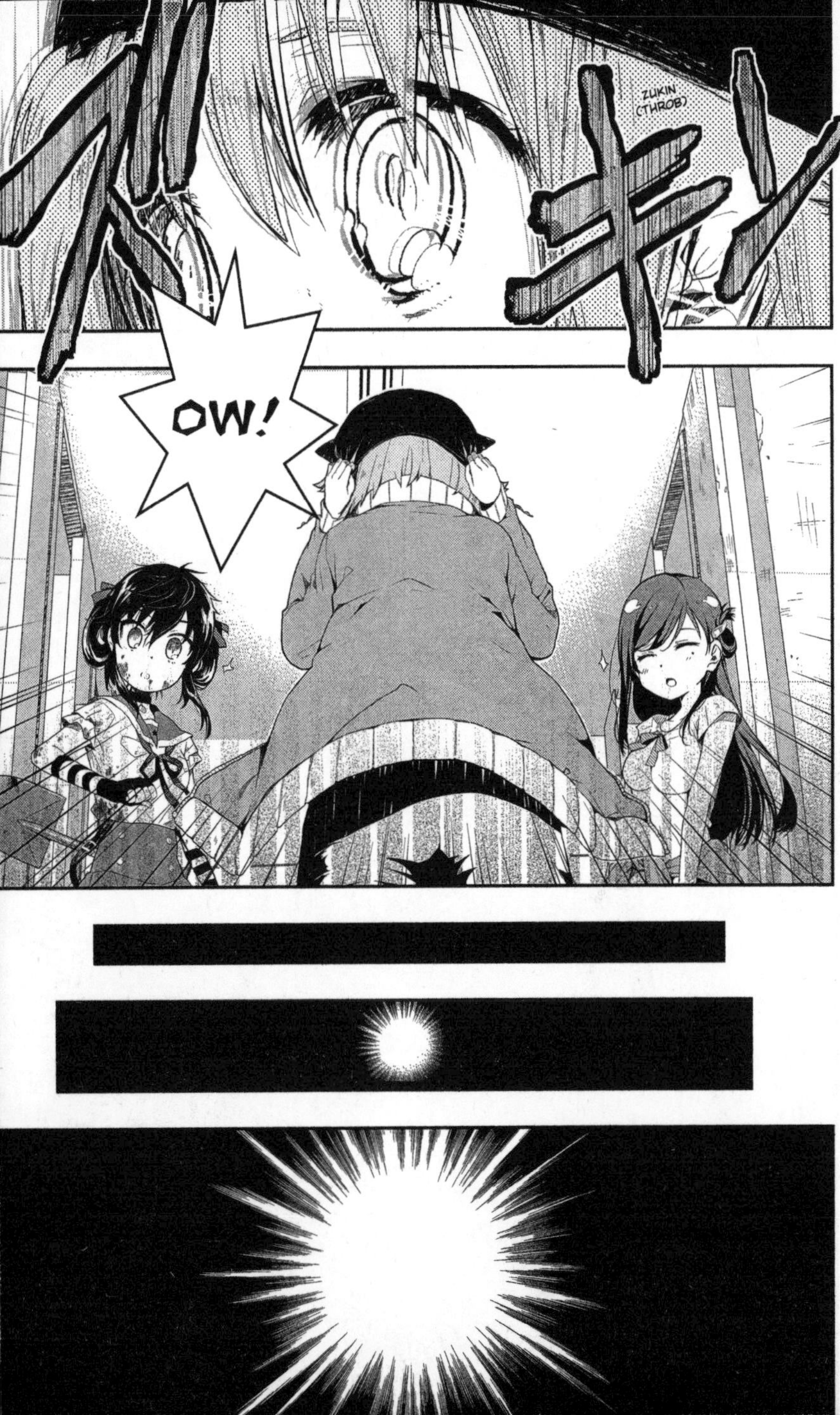
ZUKIN
(THROB)
OW!

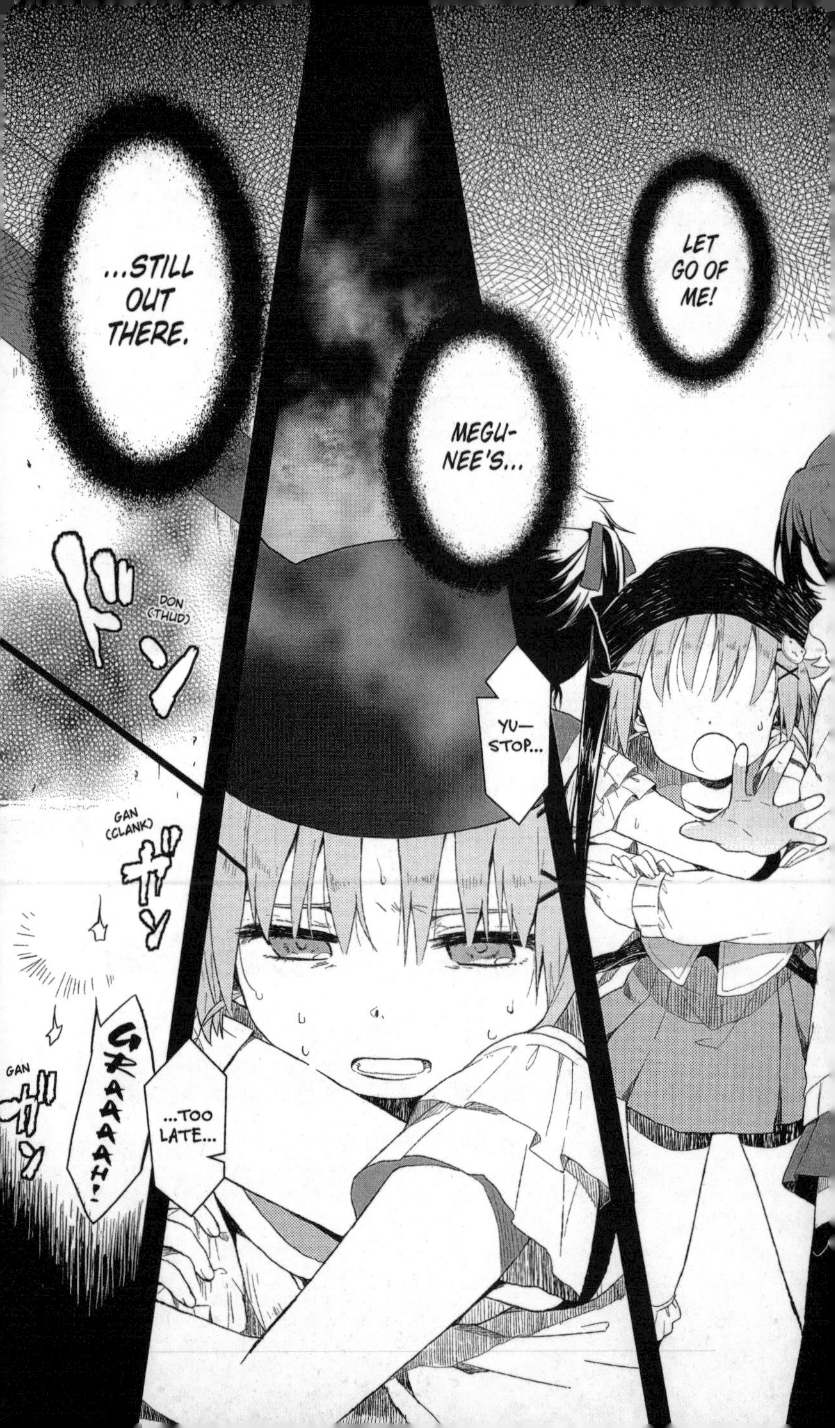
LET GO OF ME!
YU— STOP...
MEGU-NEE'S...
...TOO LATE...
...STILL OUT THERE.
DON (THUD)
GAN (CLANK)
GRAAAAAH!
GAN

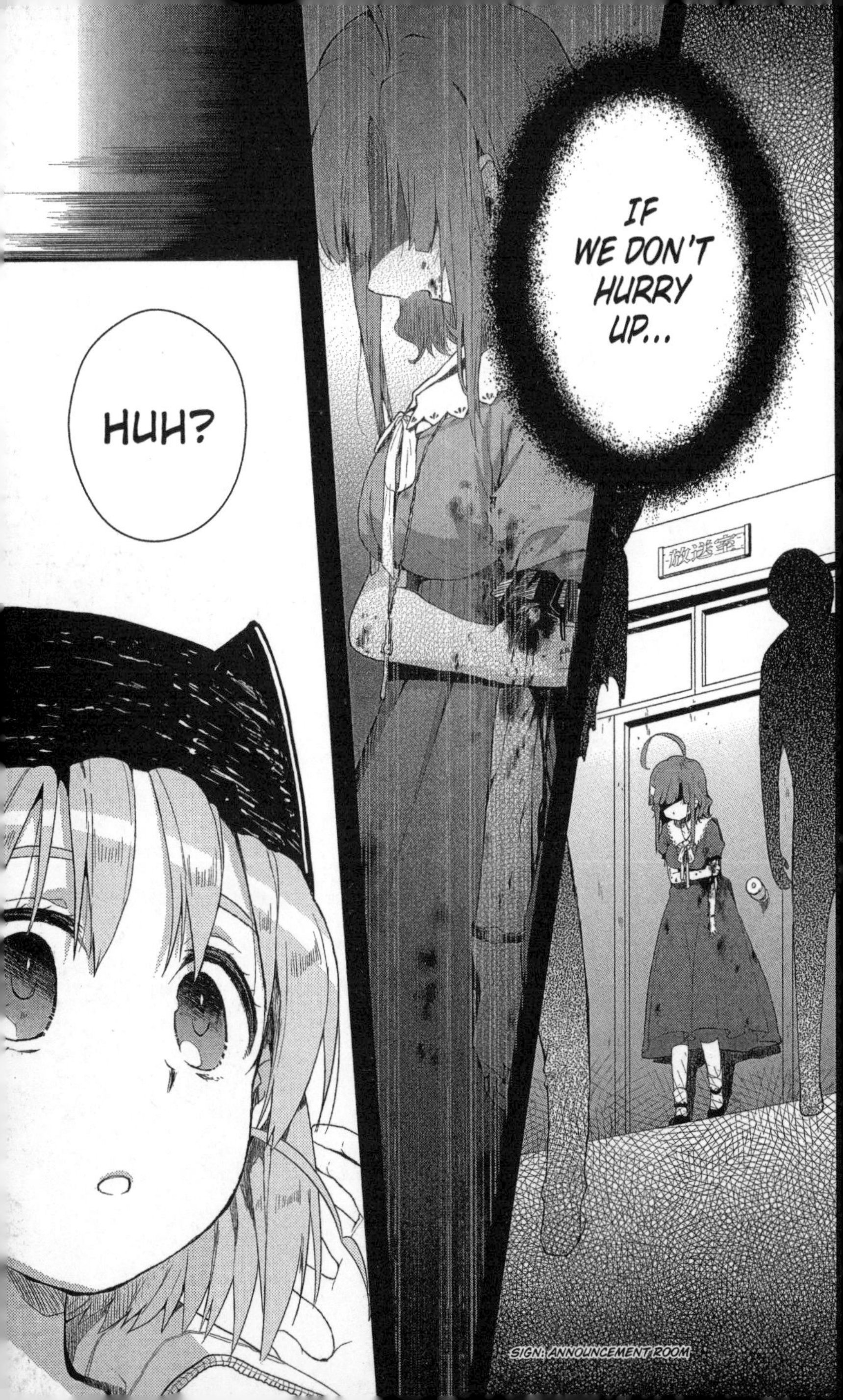
IF WE DON'T HURRY UP...
放送室
SIGN: ANNOUNCEMENT ROOM
HUH?

IT'S SOMETHING IMPORTANT.

SOMETHING SUPER IMPORTANT...

JUST NOW...

WHAT WAS THAT?

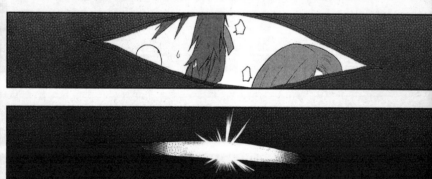

WHAT WAS IT...?

Chapter 6 Letter

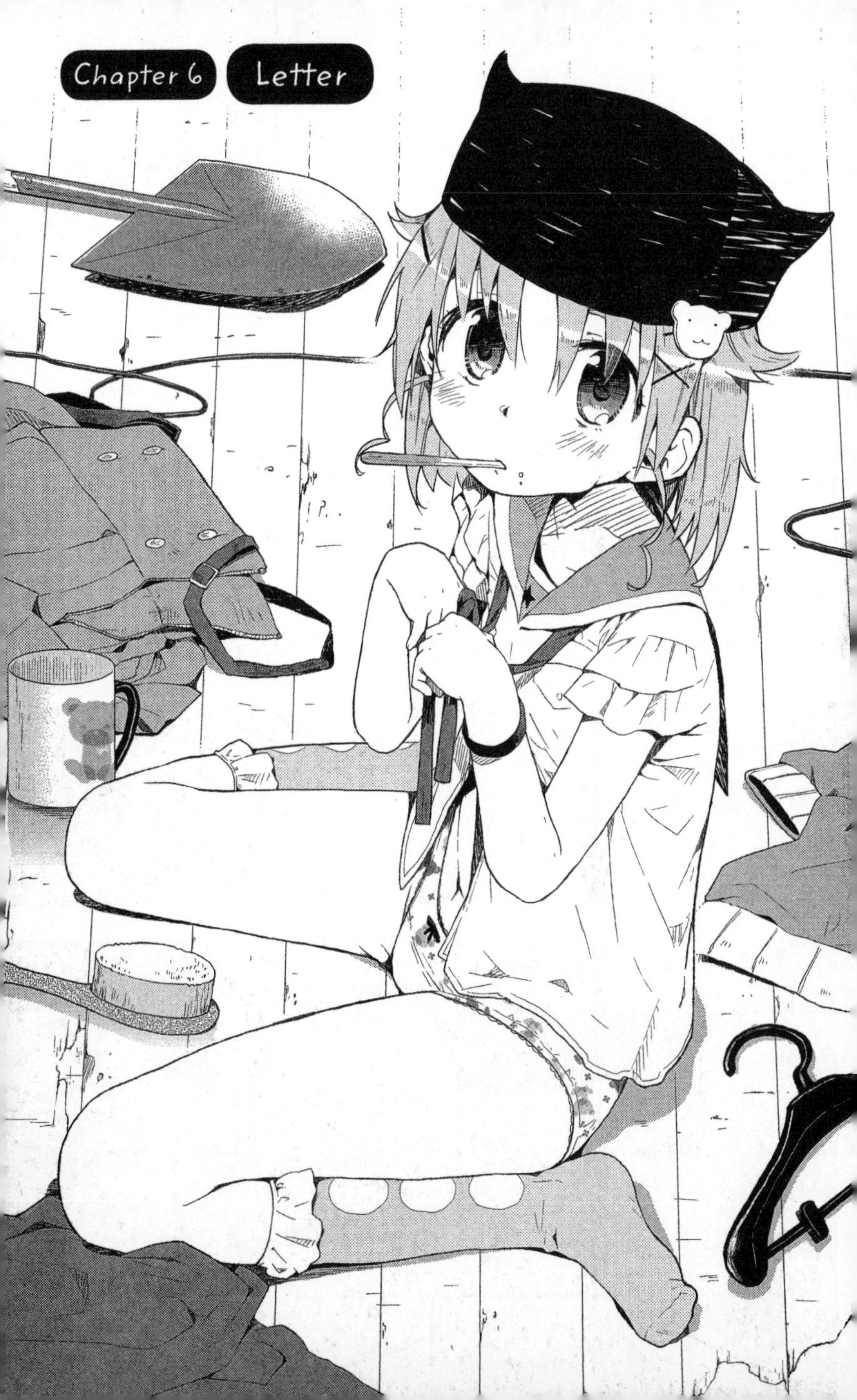

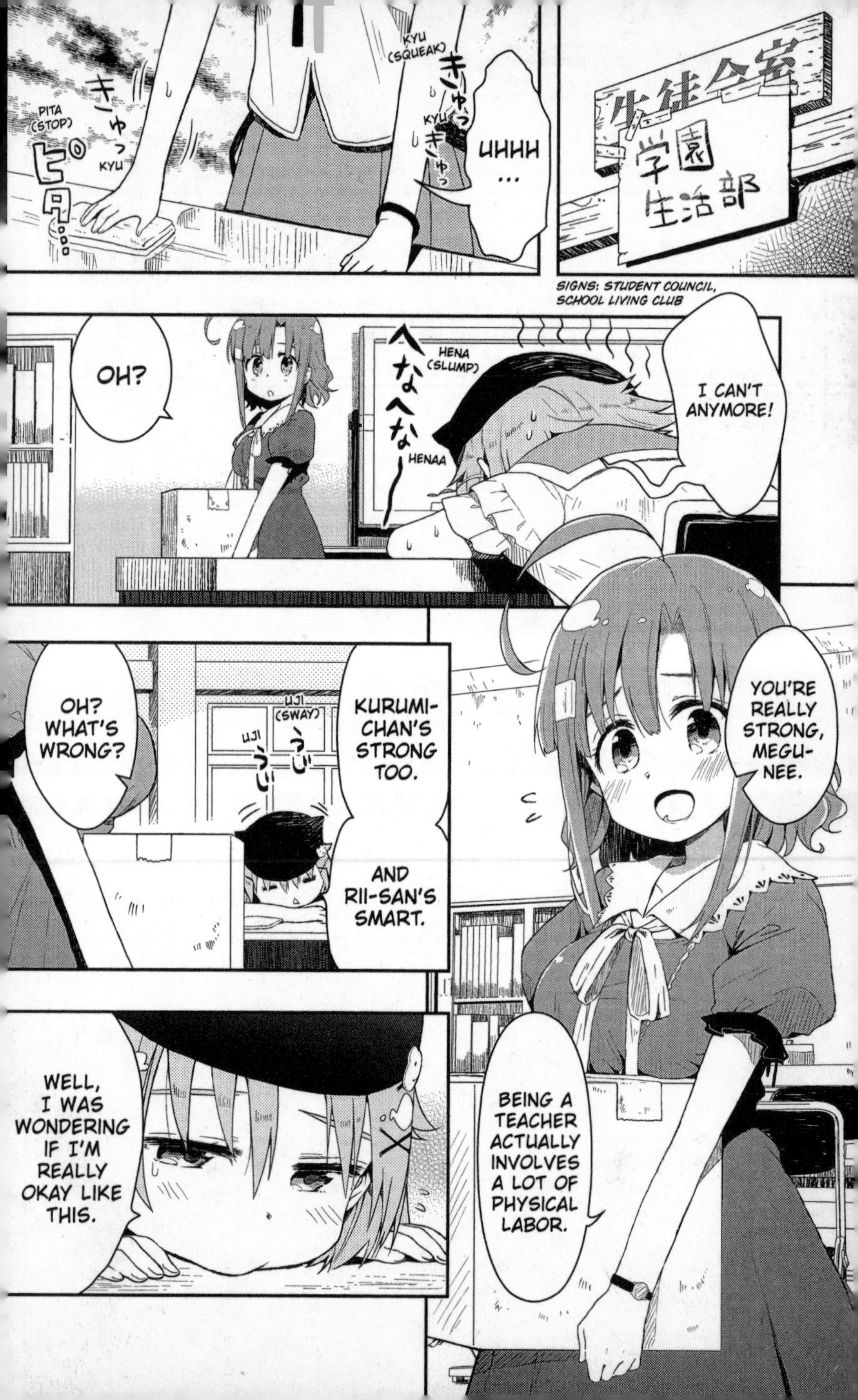
生徒会室
学園生活部
SIGNS: STUDENT COUNCIL, SCHOOL LIVING CLUB
UHHH...
KYU (SQUEAK)
きゅっ
KYU
きゅっ
きゅっ
KYU
PITA (STOP)
ピタ...
I CAN'T ANYMORE!
HENA (SLUMP)
へなへな～
HENAA
OH?
YOU'RE REALLY STRONG, MEGU-NEE.
BEING A TEACHER ACTUALLY INVOLVES A LOT OF PHYSICAL LABOR.
KURUMI-CHAN'S STRONG TOO.
AND RII-SAN'S SMART.
UJI (SWAY)
うじ
UJI
うじ
OH? WHAT'S WRONG?
WELL, I WAS WONDERING IF I'M REALLY OKAY LIKE THIS.

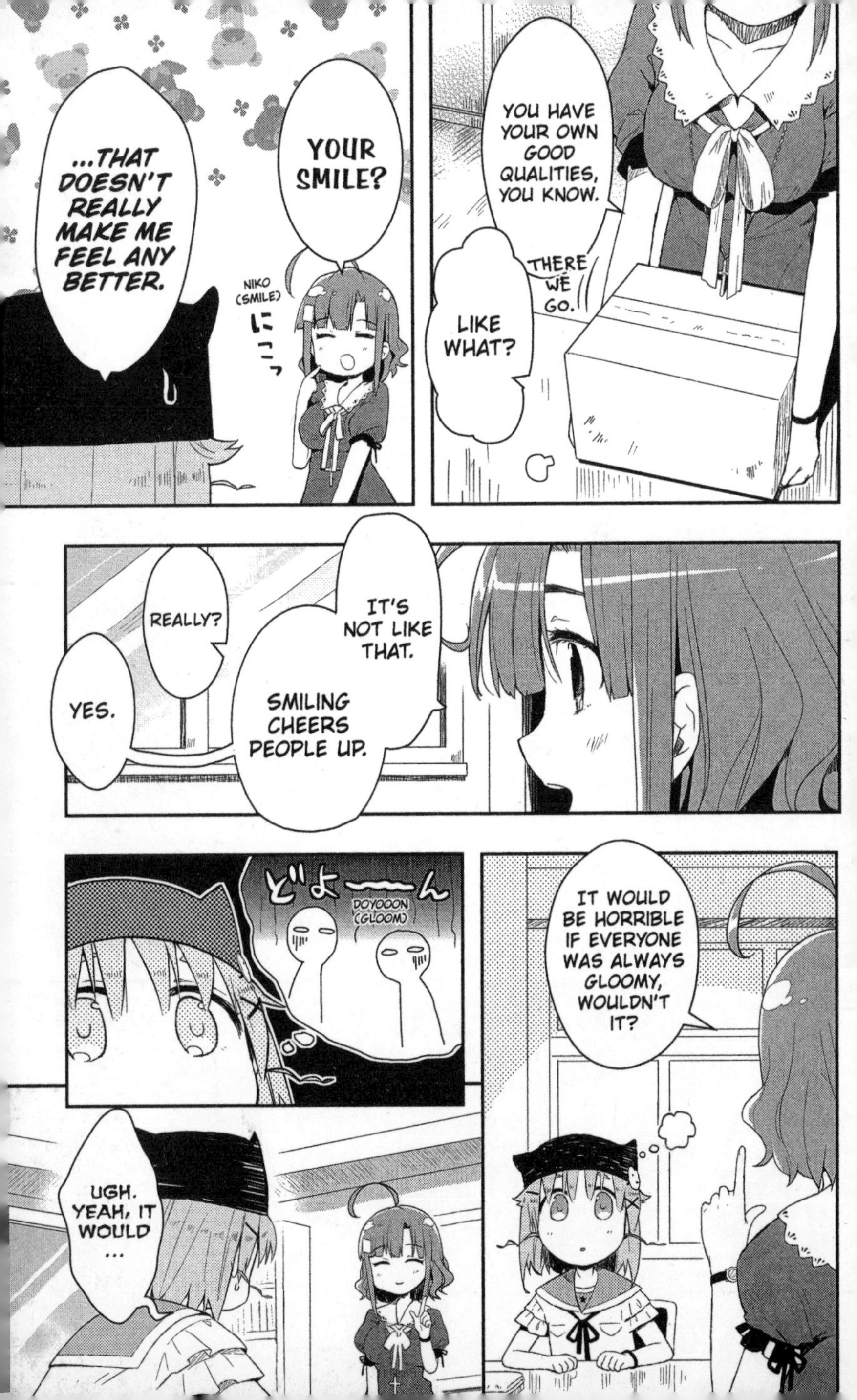
YOU HAVE YOUR OWN GOOD QUALITIES, YOU KNOW.
THERE WE GO.
LIKE WHAT?
YOUR SMILE?
NIKO (SMILE)
にこっ
...THAT DOESN'T REALLY MAKE ME FEEL ANY BETTER.
IT'S NOT LIKE THAT.
SMILING CHEERS PEOPLE UP.
REALLY?
YES.
IT WOULD BE HORRIBLE IF EVERYONE WAS ALWAYS GLOOMY, WOULDN'T IT?
どよーーん
DOYOOON (GLOOM)
UGH. YEAH, IT WOULD ...

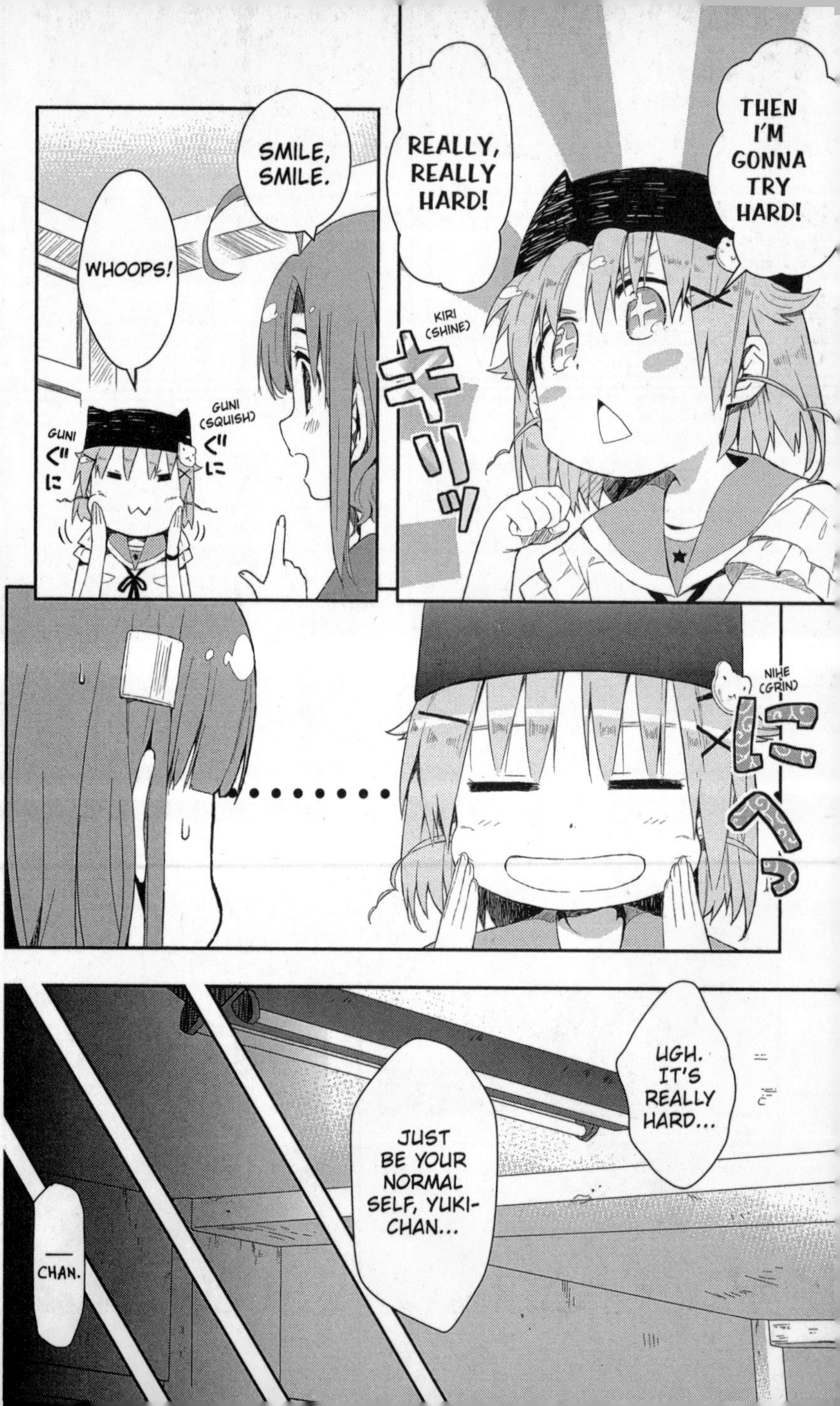
THEN I'M GONNA TRY HARD!
REALLY, REALLY HARD!
KIRI (SHINE)
キリッ
SMILE, SMILE.
WHOOPS!
GUNI (SQUISH)
ぐに
GUNI
ぐに
NIHE (GRIN)
にへへっ
....
UGH. IT'S REALLY HARD...
JUST BE YOUR NORMAL SELF, YUKI-CHAN...
— CHAN.

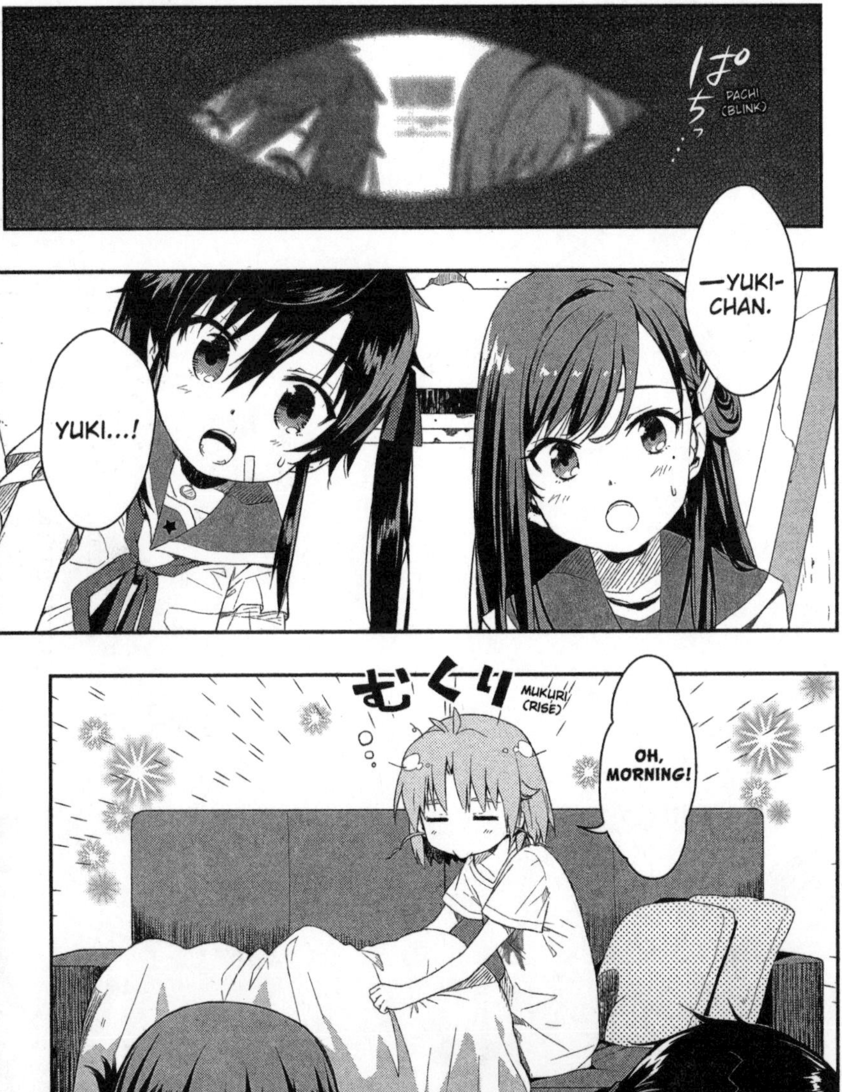
ぱちっ
PACHI (BLINK)
—YUKI-CHAN.
YUKI...!
OH, MORNING!
むくり
MUKURI (RISE)

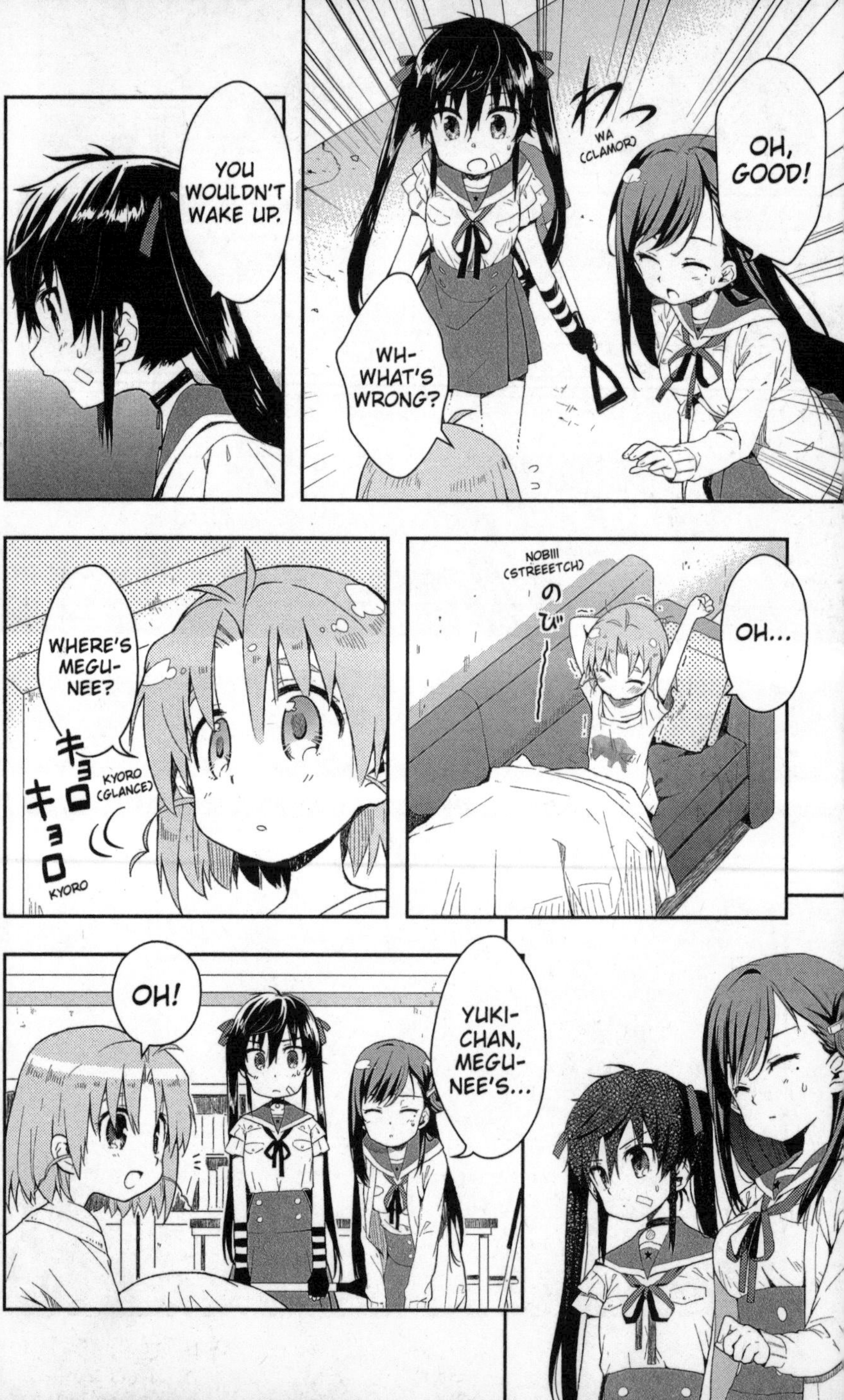
OH, GOOD!
わっ
WA (CLAMOR)
WH- WHAT'S WRONG?
YOU WOULDN'T WAKE UP.
OH...
のびー
NOBIII (STREEETCH)
WHERE'S MEGU-NEE?
キョロキョロ
KYORO (GLANCE) KYORO
YUKI-CHAN, MEGU-NEE'S...
OH!

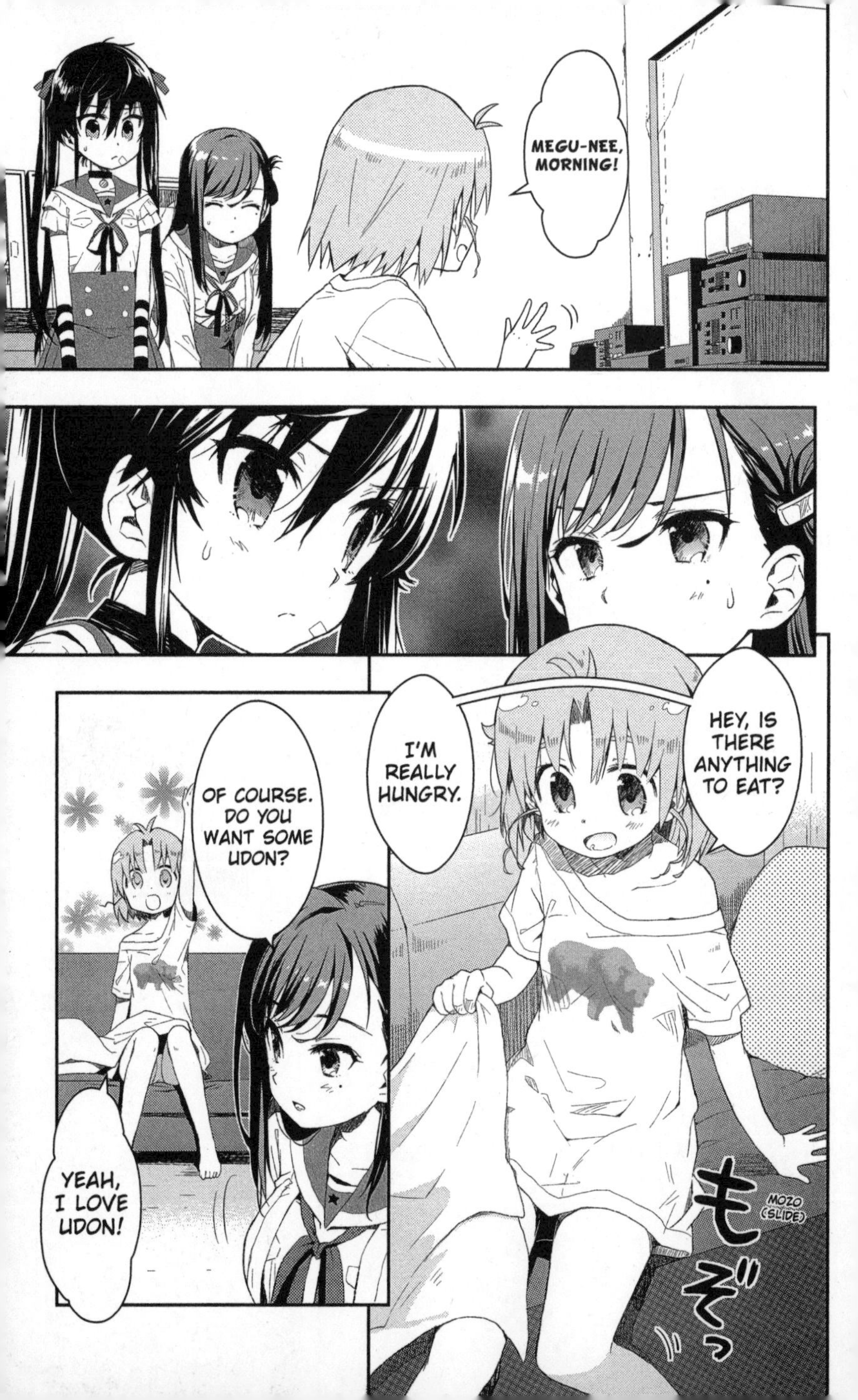
MEGU-NEE, MORNING!
HEY, IS THERE ANYTHING TO EAT?
I'M REALLY HUNGRY.
もぞっ
MOZO (SLIDE)
OF COURSE. DO YOU WANT SOME UDON?
YEAH, I LOVE UDON!

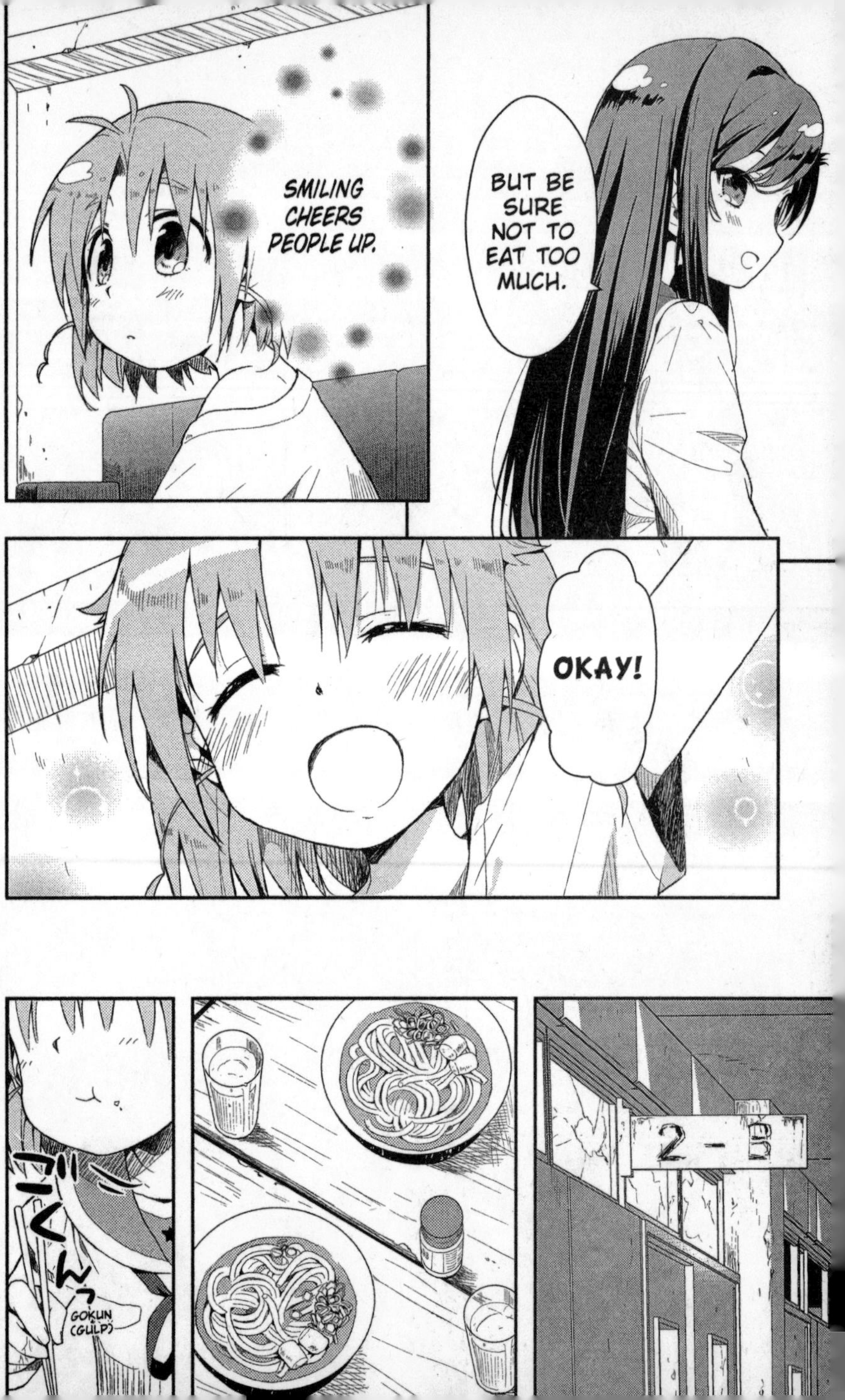
BUT BE SURE NOT TO EAT TOO MUCH.
SMILING CHEERS PEOPLE UP.
OKAY!
2-B
ごくん
GOKUN (GULP)

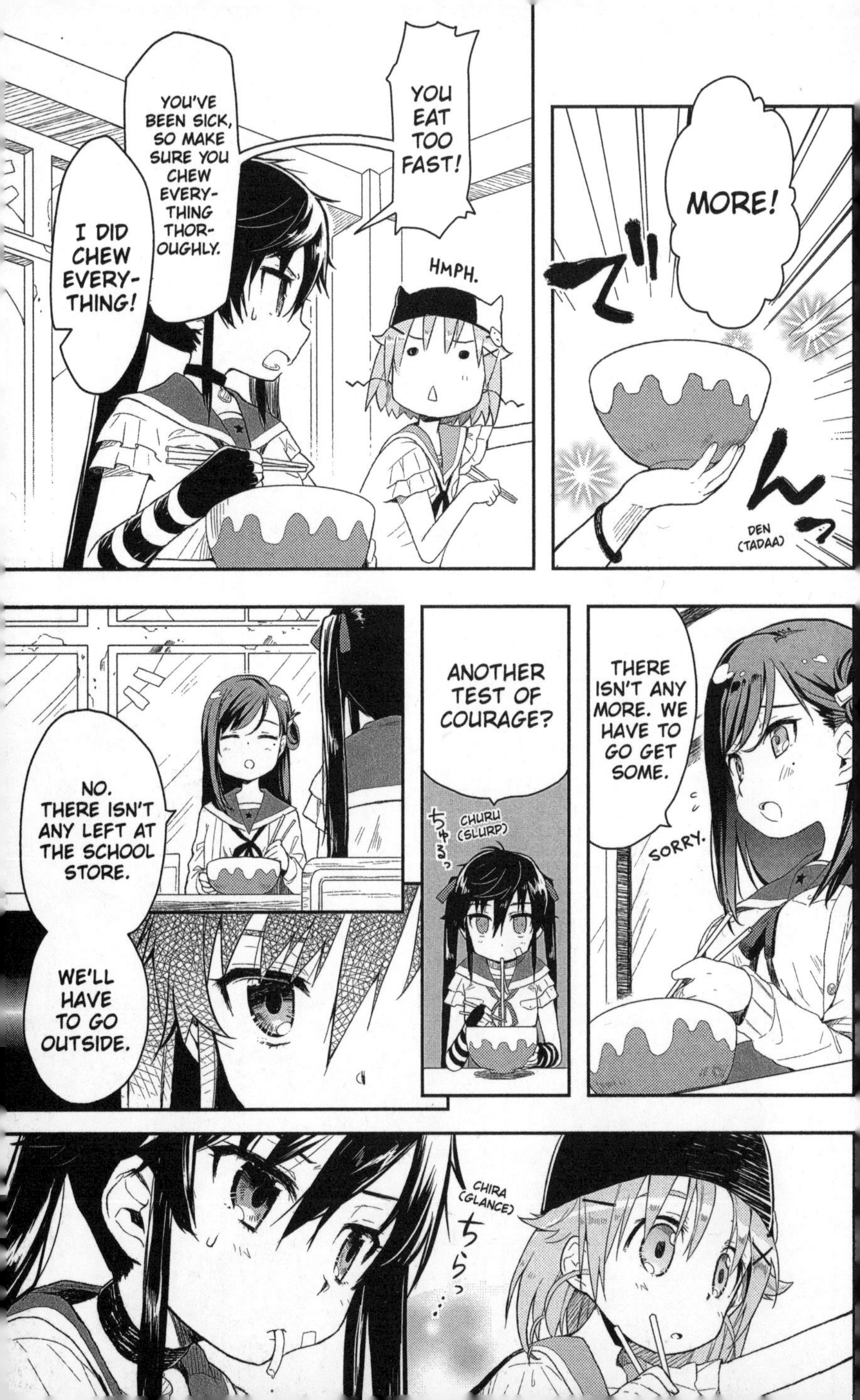
MORE!
でんっ
DEN (TADAA)
YOU EAT TOO FAST!
HMPH.
YOU'VE BEEN SICK, SO MAKE SURE YOU CHEW EVERY-THING THOR-OUGHLY.
I DID CHEW EVERY-THING!
THERE ISN'T ANY MORE. WE HAVE TO GO GET SOME.
SORRY.
ANOTHER TEST OF COURAGE?
ちゅるっ
CHURU (SLURP)
NO. THERE ISN'T ANY LEFT AT THE SCHOOL STORE.
WE'LL HAVE TO GO OUTSIDE.
CHIRA (GLANCE)
ちらっ

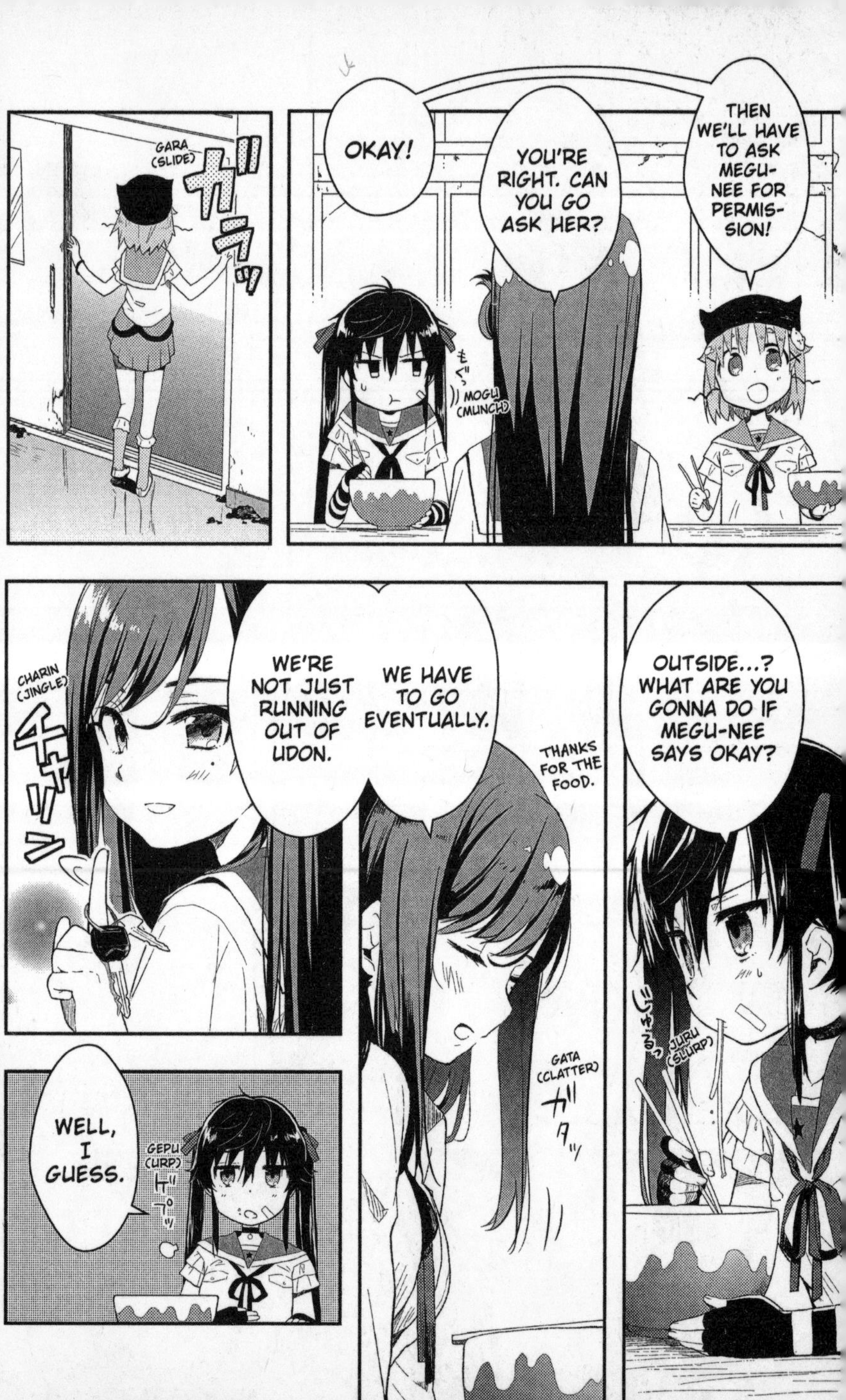
THEN WE'LL HAVE TO ASK MEGU-NEE FOR PERMISSION!
YOU'RE RIGHT. CAN YOU GO ASK HER?
OKAY!
MOGU (MUNCH)
GARA (SLIDE)
OUTSIDE...? WHAT ARE YOU GONNA DO IF MEGU-NEE SAYS OKAY?
JURU (SLURP)
THANKS FOR THE FOOD.
GATA (CLATTER)
WE HAVE TO GO EVENTUALLY.
WE'RE NOT JUST RUNNING OUT OF UDON.
CHARIN (JINGLE)
WELL, I GUESS.
GEPU (URP)

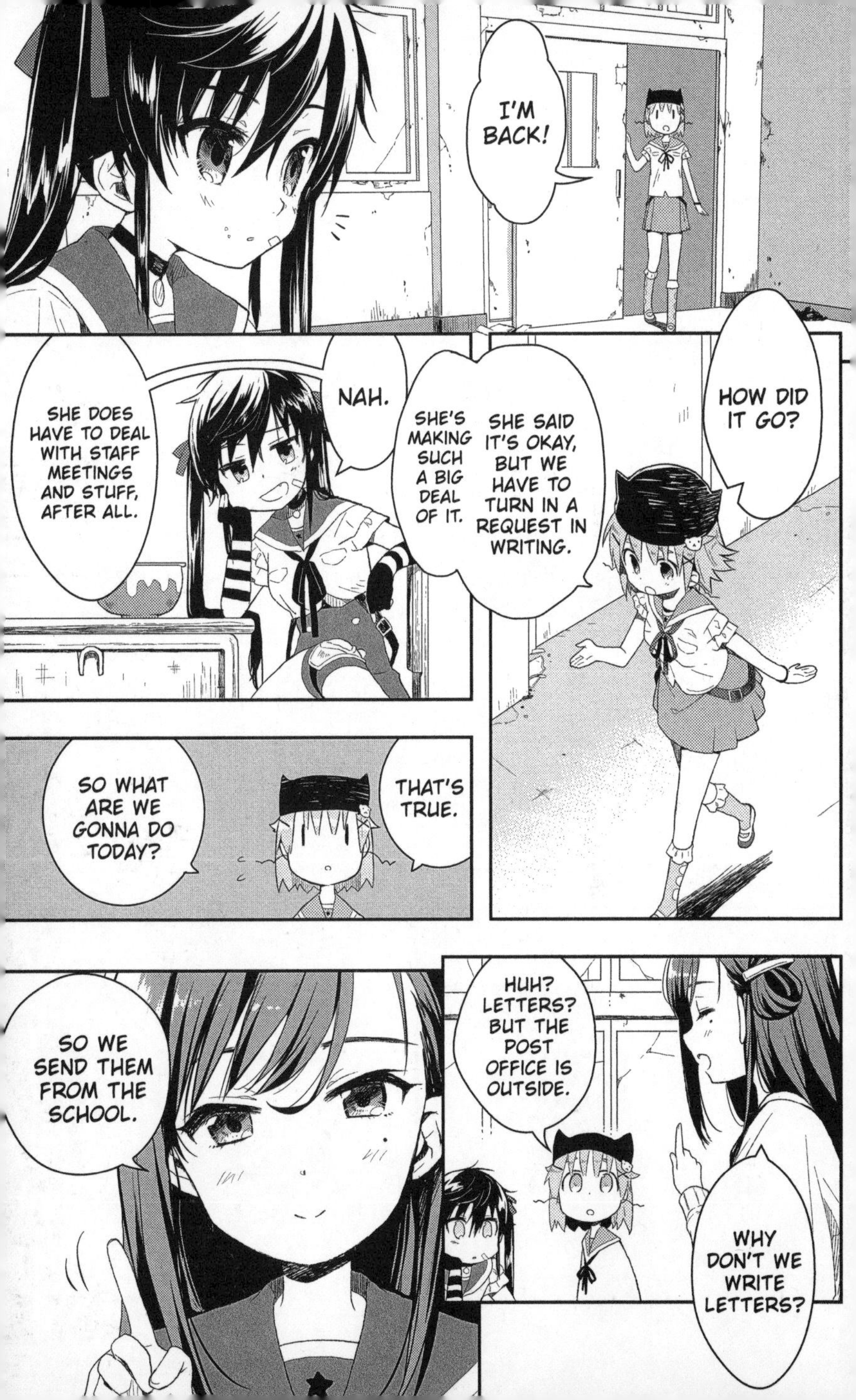
I'M BACK!
HOW DID IT GO?
SHE SAID IT'S OKAY, BUT WE HAVE TO TURN IN A REQUEST IN WRITING.
SHE'S MAKING SUCH A BIG DEAL OF IT.
NAH.
SHE DOES HAVE TO DEAL WITH STAFF MEETINGS AND STUFF, AFTER ALL.
THAT'S TRUE.
SO WHAT ARE WE GONNA DO TODAY?
WHY DON'T WE WRITE LETTERS?
HUH? LETTERS? BUT THE POST OFFICE IS OUTSIDE.
SO WE SEND THEM FROM THE SCHOOL.

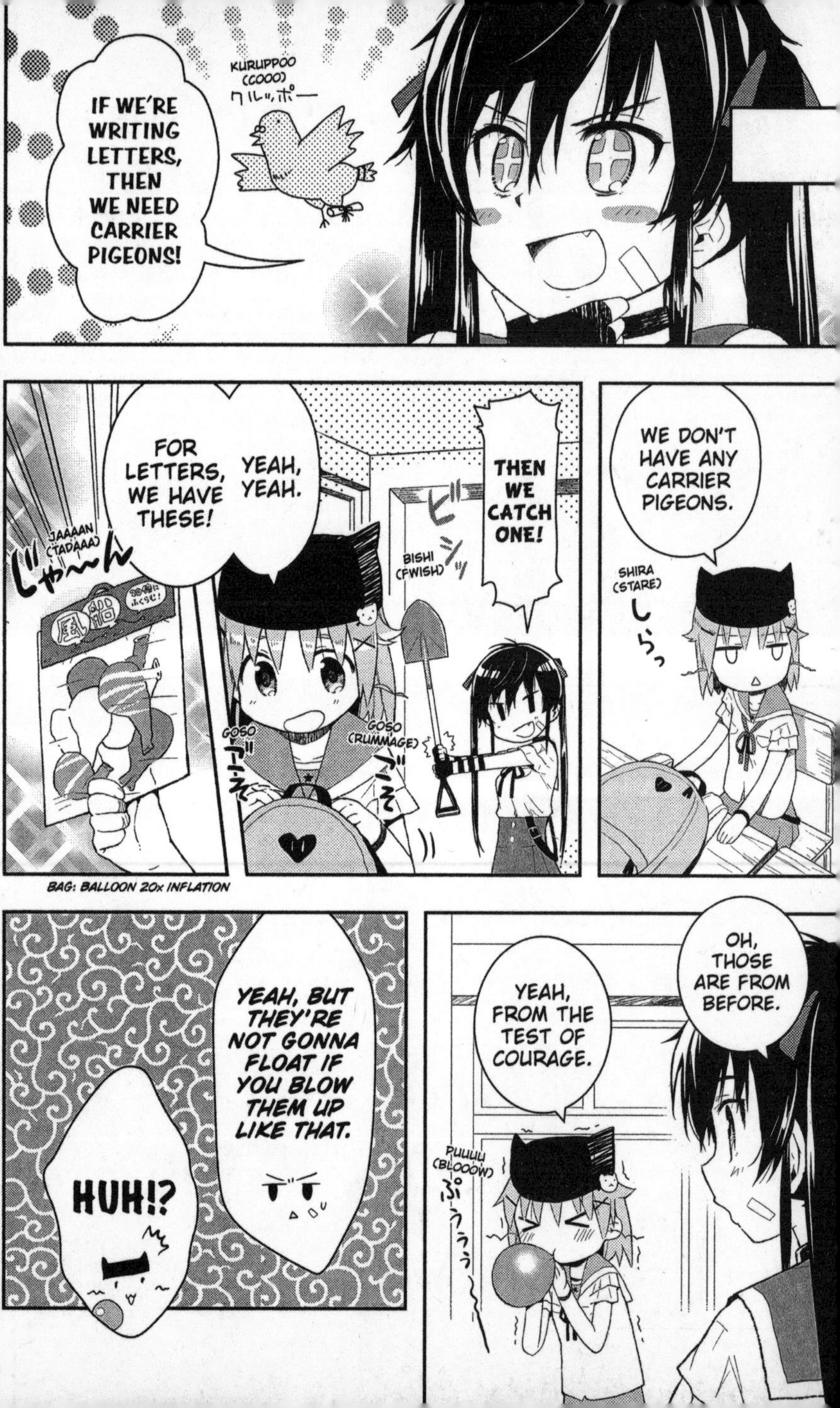
KURUPPOO (COOO) クルッポー
IF WE'RE WRITING LETTERS, THEN WE NEED CARRIER PIGEONS!
WE DON'T HAVE ANY CARRIER PIGEONS.
SHIRA (STARE) しらっ
THEN WE CATCH ONE!
BISHI (FWISH) ビシッ
YEAH, YEAH.
FOR LETTERS, WE HAVE THESE!
JAAAAN (TADAAA) じゃ〜〜ん
風船
GOSO (RUMMAGE) ごそ
GOSO ごそ
BAG: BALLOON 20x INFLATION
OH, THOSE ARE FROM BEFORE.
YEAH, FROM THE TEST OF COURAGE.
PUUUU (BLOOOW) ぷううう
YEAH, BUT THEY'RE NOT GONNA FLOAT IF YOU BLOW THEM UP LIKE THAT.
HUH!?

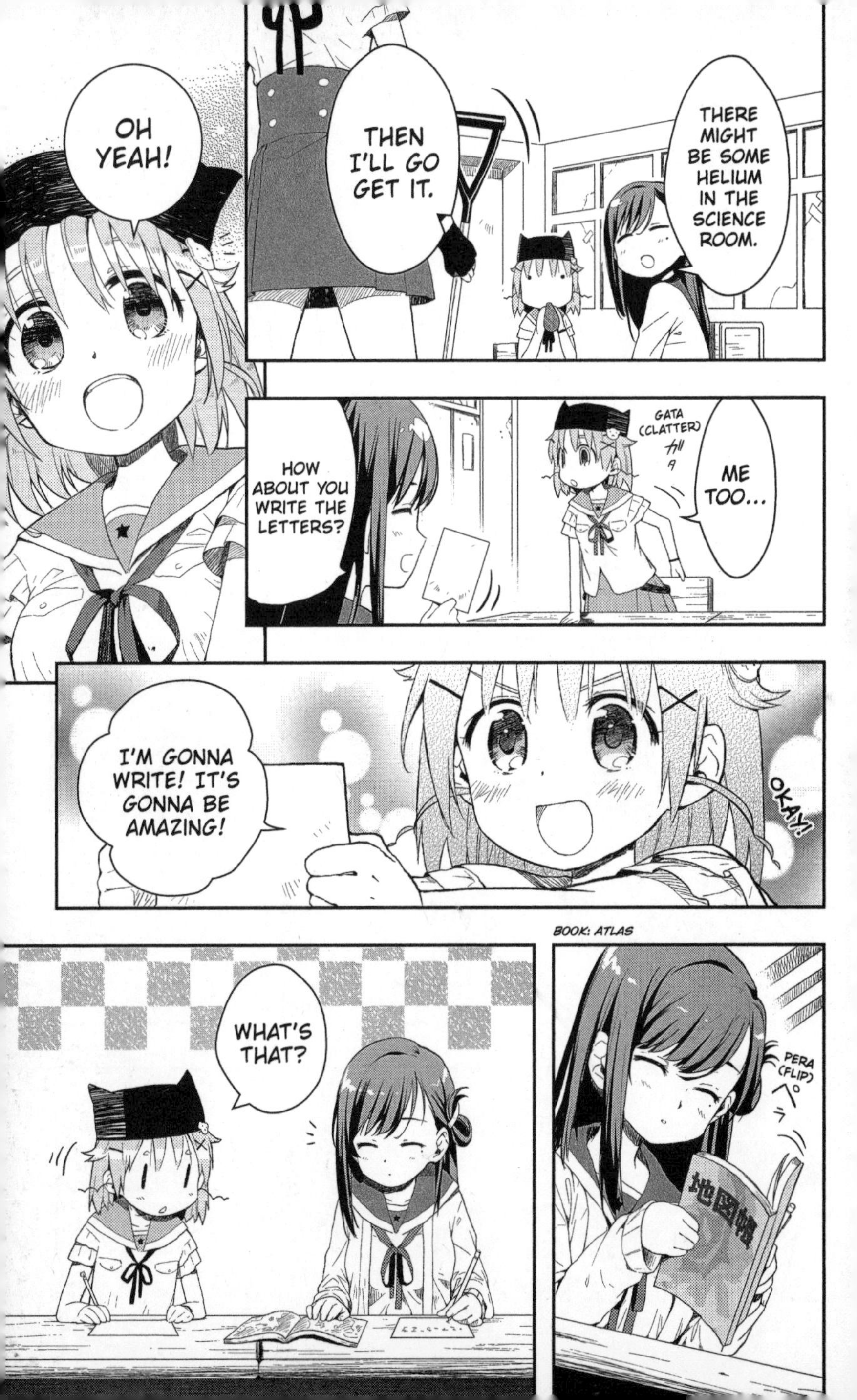
THERE MIGHT BE SOME HELIUM IN THE SCIENCE ROOM.
THEN I'LL GO GET IT.
GATA (CLATTER)
ME TOO...
HOW ABOUT YOU WRITE THE LETTERS?
OH YEAH!
OKAY!
I'M GONNA WRITE! IT'S GONNA BE AMAZING!
BOOK: ATLAS
PERA (FLIP)
地図帳
WHAT'S THAT?

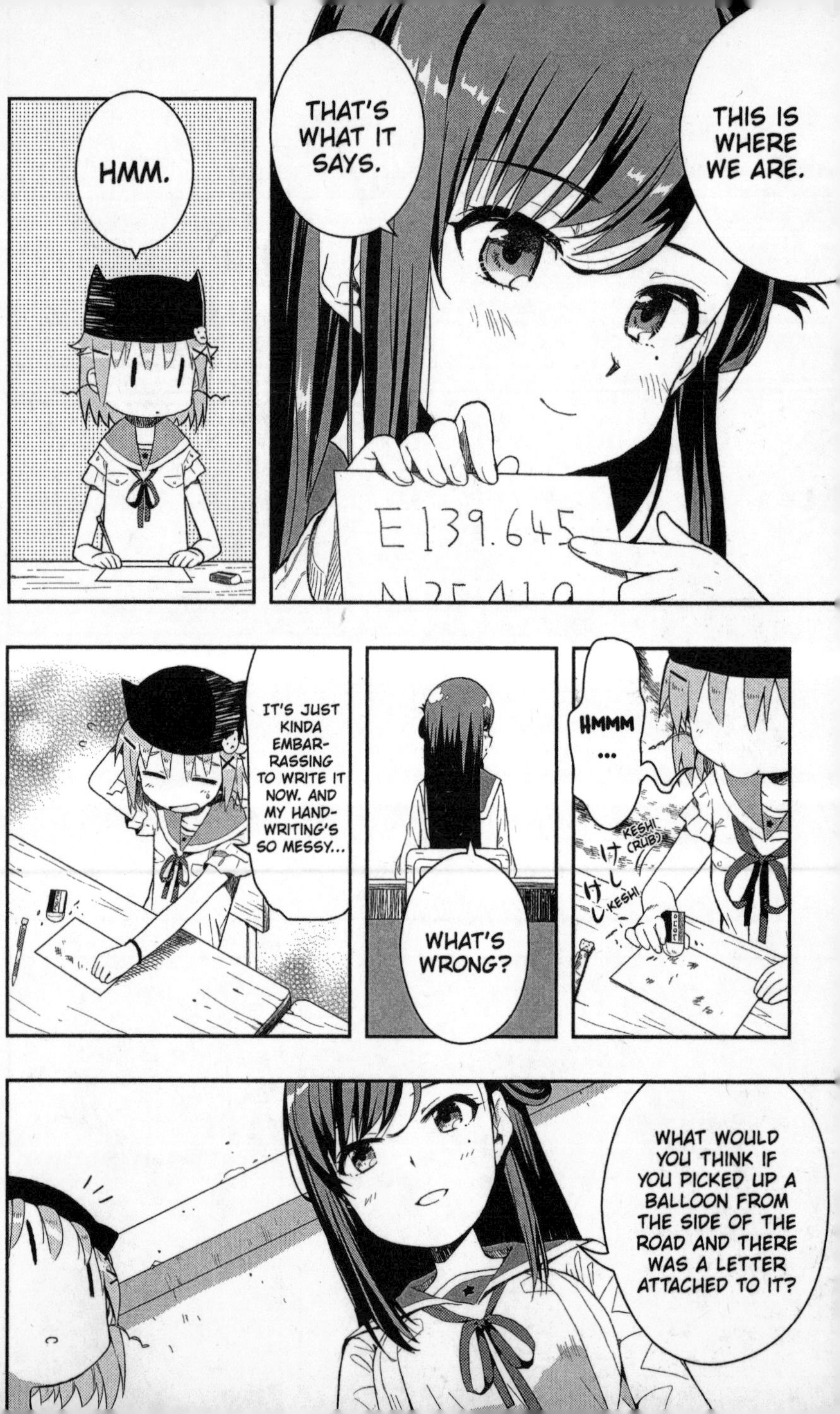
THIS IS WHERE WE ARE.
THAT'S WHAT IT SAYS.
E139.645
HMM.
HMMM ...
KESHI (RUB)
けし
けし
KESHI
WHAT'S WRONG?
IT'S JUST KINDA EMBARRASSING TO WRITE IT NOW. AND MY HANDWRITING'S SO MESSY...
WHAT WOULD YOU THINK IF YOU PICKED UP A BALLOON FROM THE SIDE OF THE ROAD AND THERE WAS A LETTER ATTACHED TO IT?

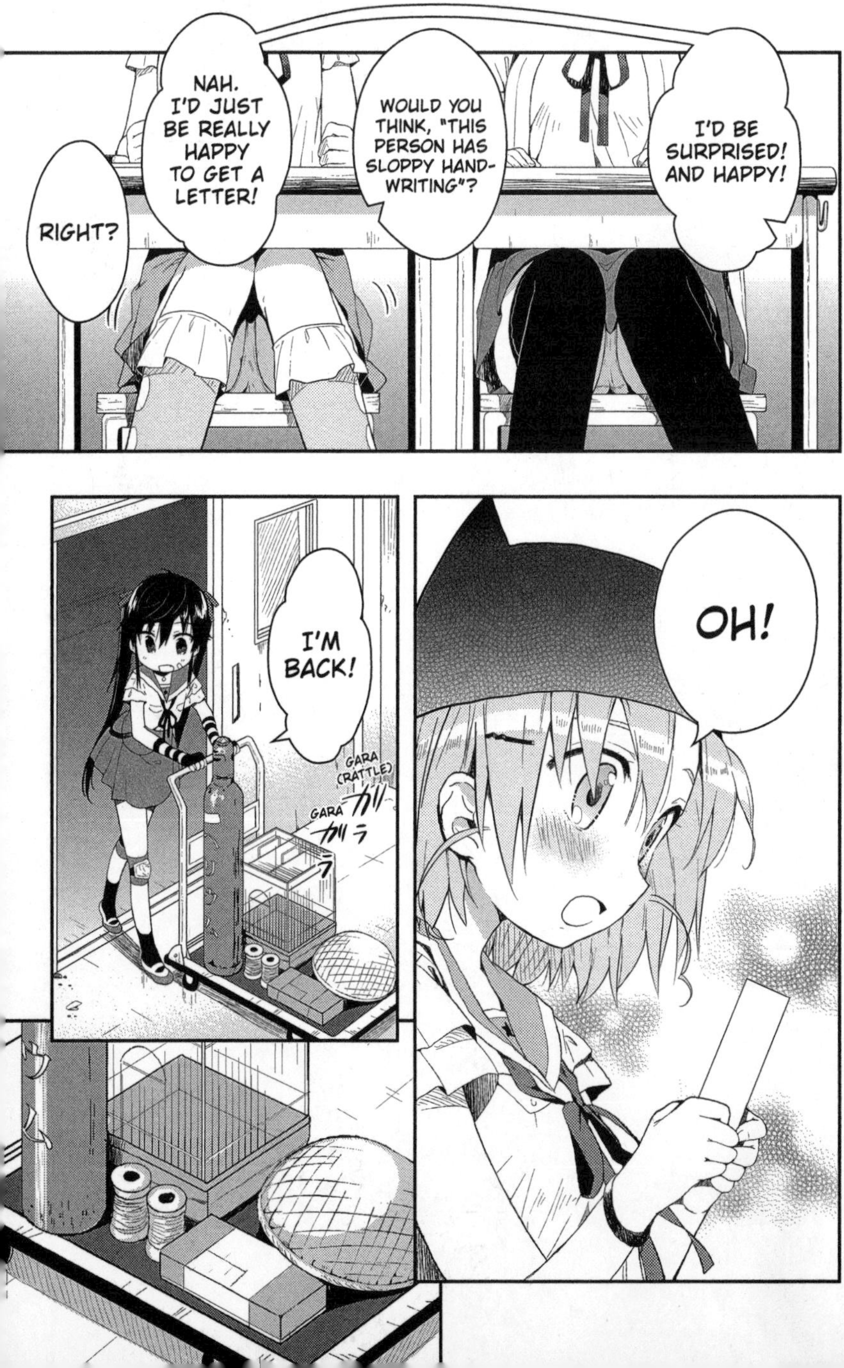

I'D BE SURPRISED! AND HAPPY!
WOULD YOU THINK, "THIS PERSON HAS SLOPPY HAND-WRITING"?
NAH. I'D JUST BE REALLY HAPPY TO GET A LETTER!
RIGHT?
OH!
I'M BACK!
GARA (RATTLE)
GARA

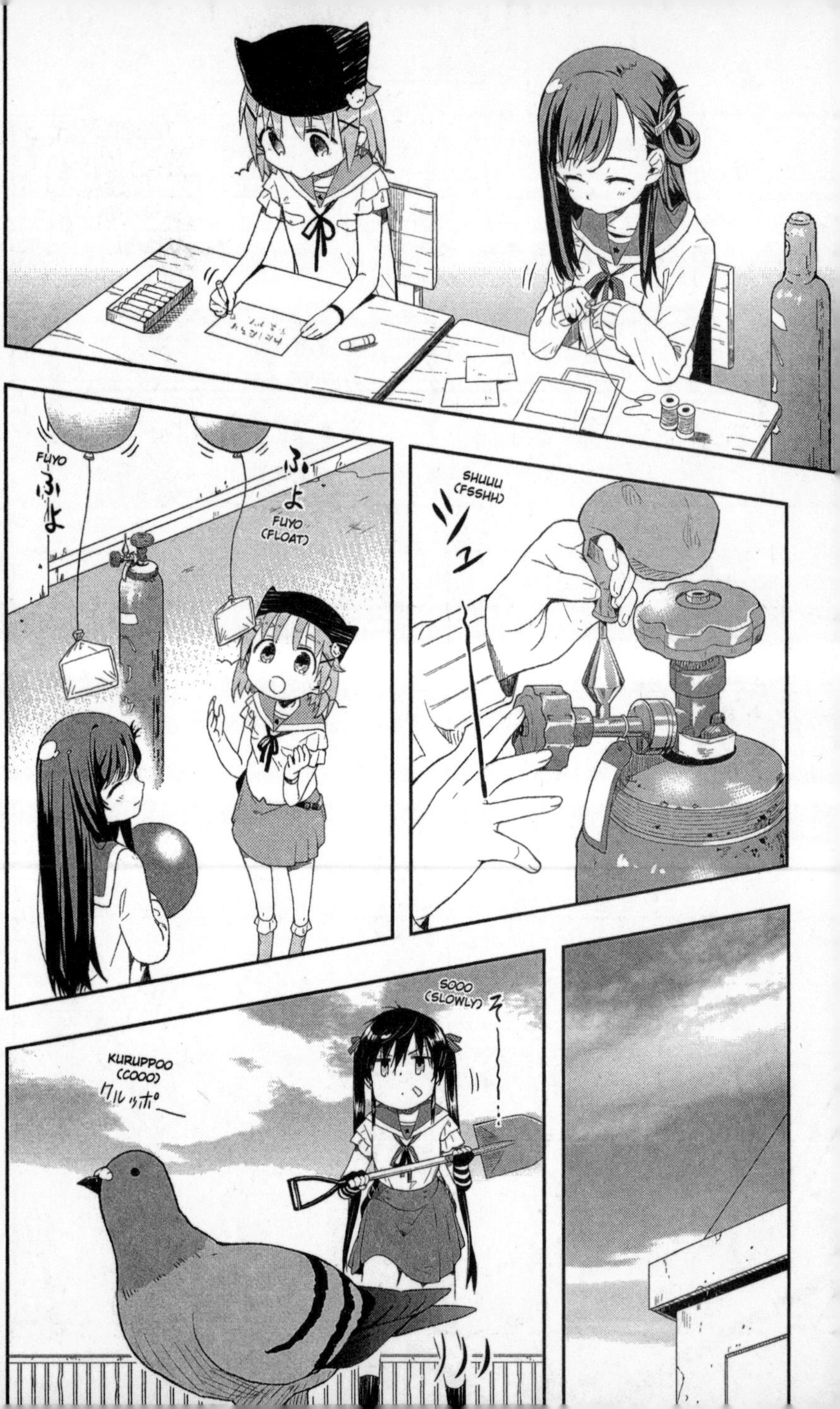
SHUUU
(FSSHH)
シュ
ふよ
FUYO
(FLOAT)
FUYO
ふよ
SOOO
(SLOWLY)
そ~~…
KURUPPOO
(COOO)
クルッポー

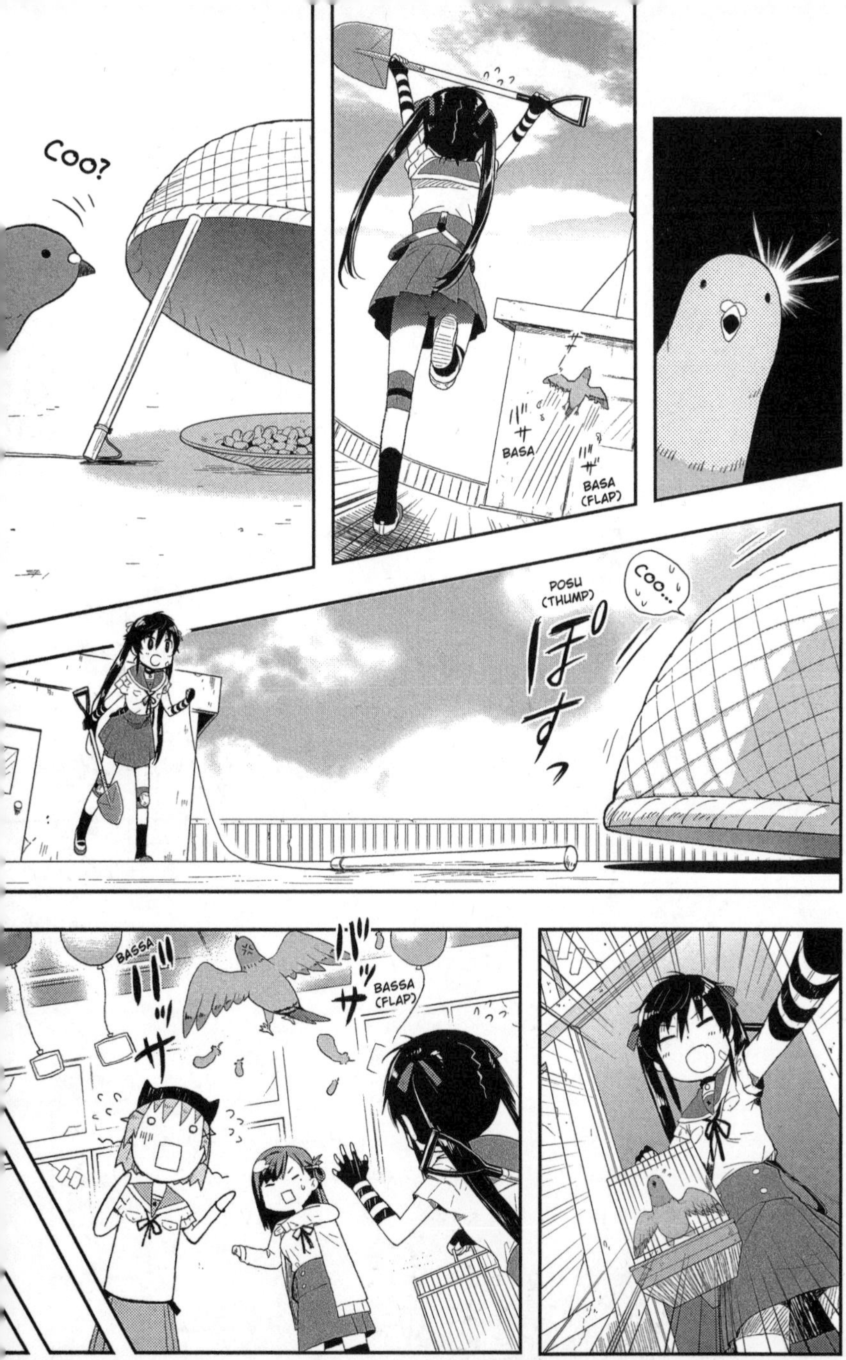
バサ
BASA
バサ
BASA (FLAP)
COO?
POSU (THUMP)
COO...
ぽすっ
バッサ
BASSA (FLAP)
BASSA
バッサ

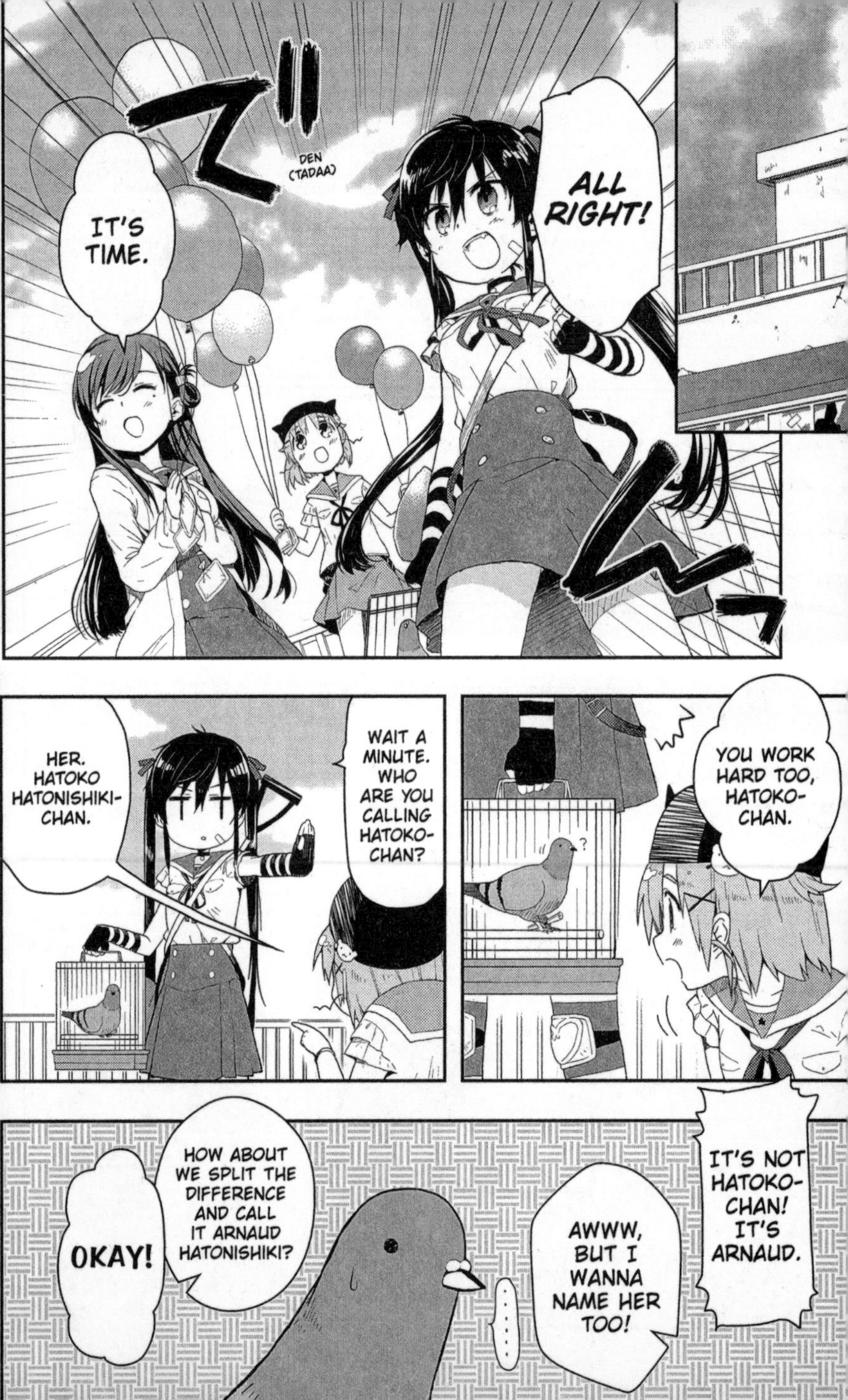
ALL RIGHT!
DEN (TADAA)
IT'S TIME.
YOU WORK HARD TOO, HATOKO-CHAN.
WAIT A MINUTE. WHO ARE YOU CALLING HATOKO-CHAN?
HER. HATOKO HATONISHIKI-CHAN.
IT'S NOT HATOKO-CHAN! IT'S ARNAUD.
AWWW, BUT I WANNA NAME HER TOO!
......
HOW ABOUT WE SPLIT THE DIFFERENCE AND CALL IT ARNAUD HATONISHIKI?
OKAY!

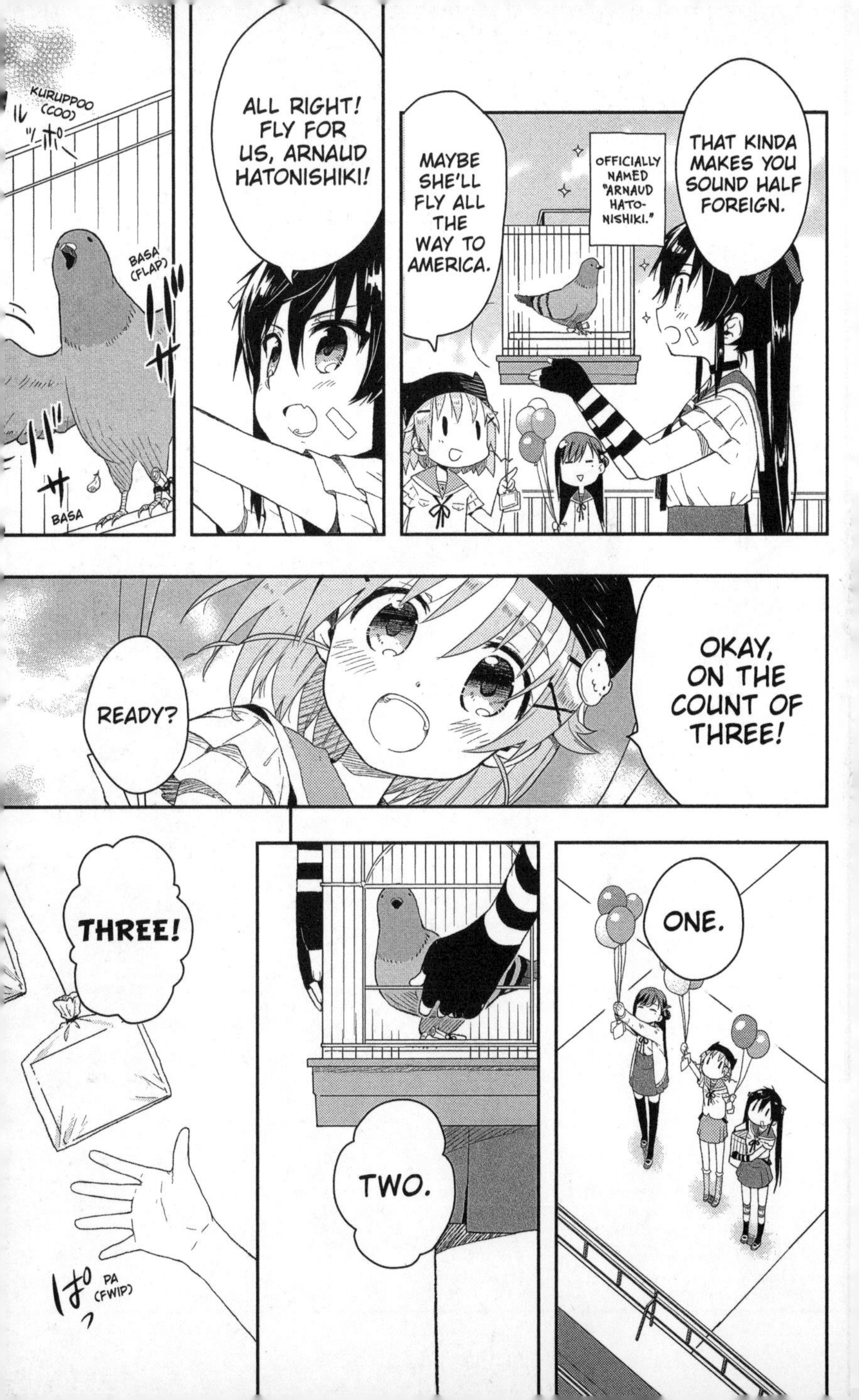
THAT KINDA MAKES YOU SOUND HALF FOREIGN.
OFFICIALLY NAMED "ARNAUD HATO-NISHIKI."
MAYBE SHE'LL FLY ALL THE WAY TO AMERICA.
ALL RIGHT! FLY FOR US, ARNAUD HATONISHIKI!
KURUPPOO (COO)
BASA (FLAP)
BASA
OKAY, ON THE COUNT OF THREE!
READY?
ONE.
TWO.
THREE!
PA (FWIP)

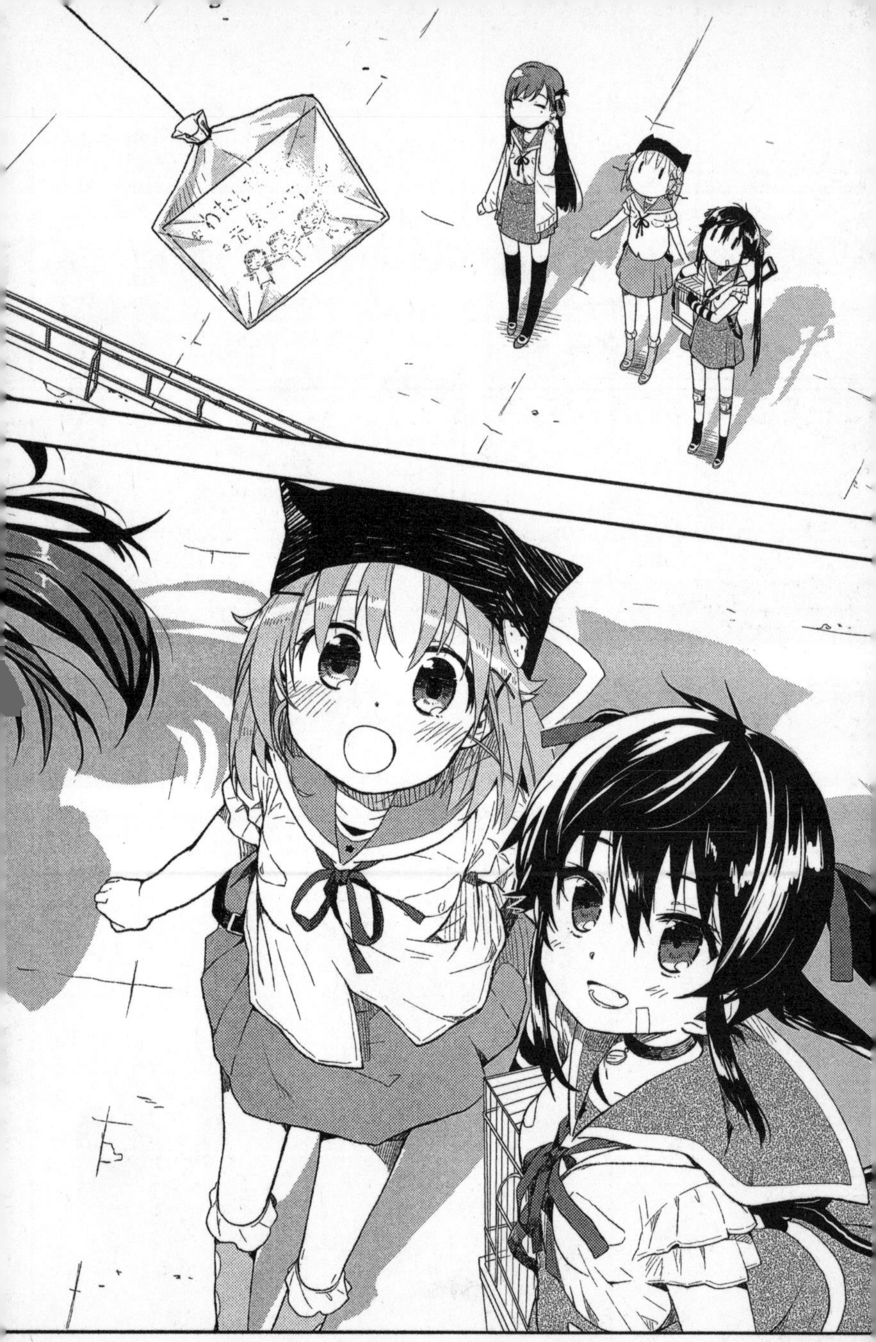

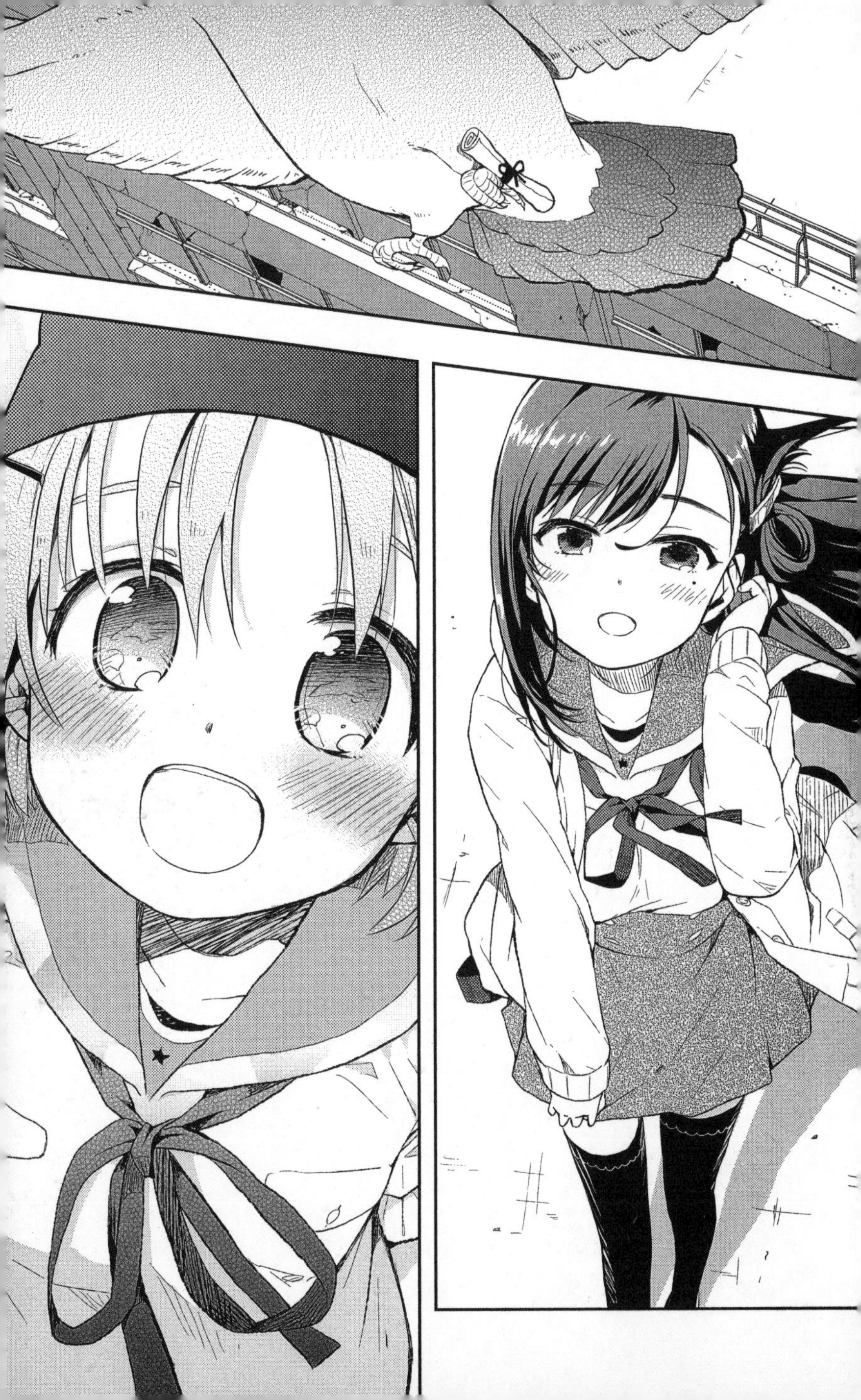

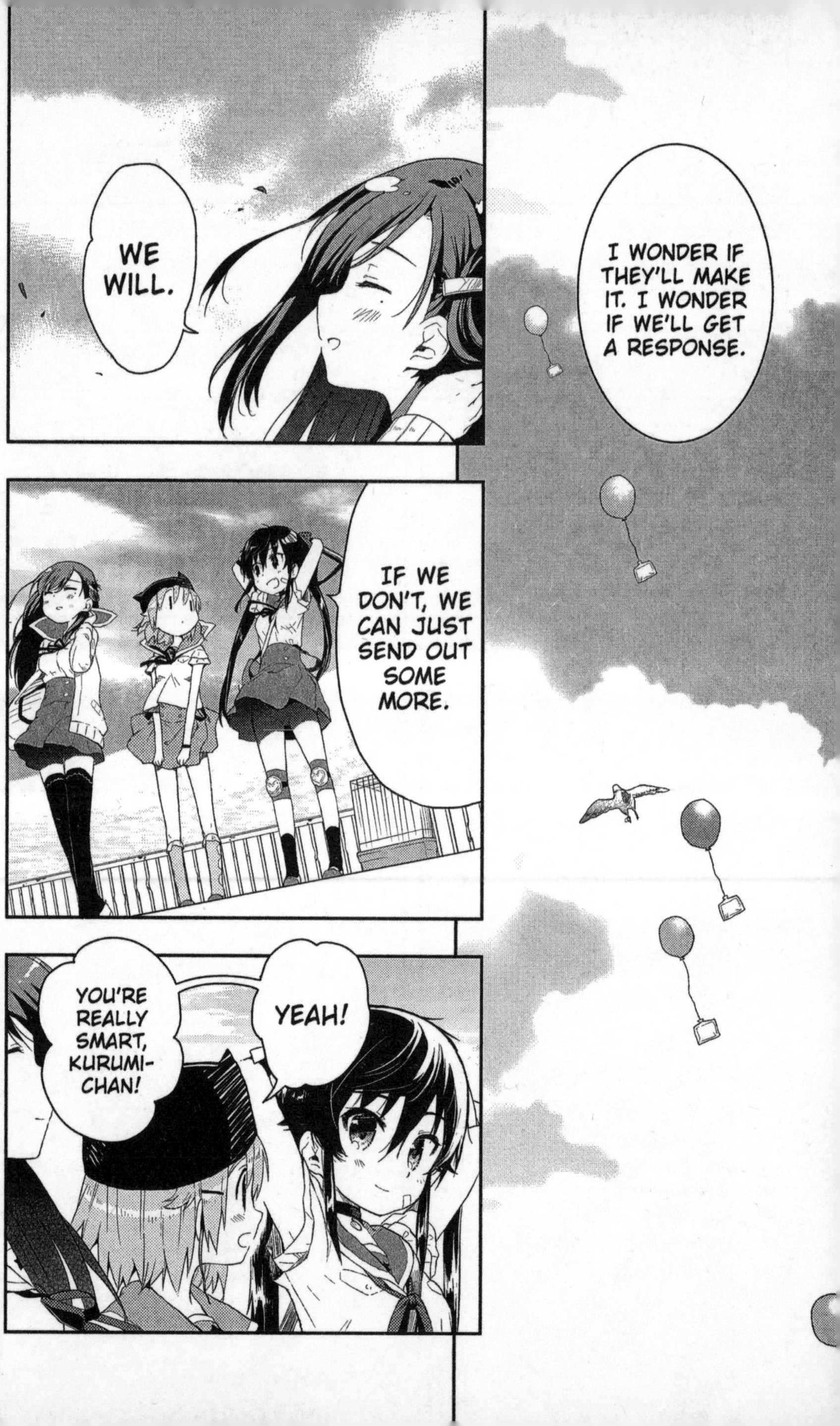
I WONDER IF THEY'LL MAKE IT. I WONDER IF WE'LL GET A RESPONSE.
WE WILL.
IF WE DON'T, WE CAN JUST SEND OUT SOME MORE.
YEAH!
YOU'RE REALLY SMART, KURUMI-CHAN!

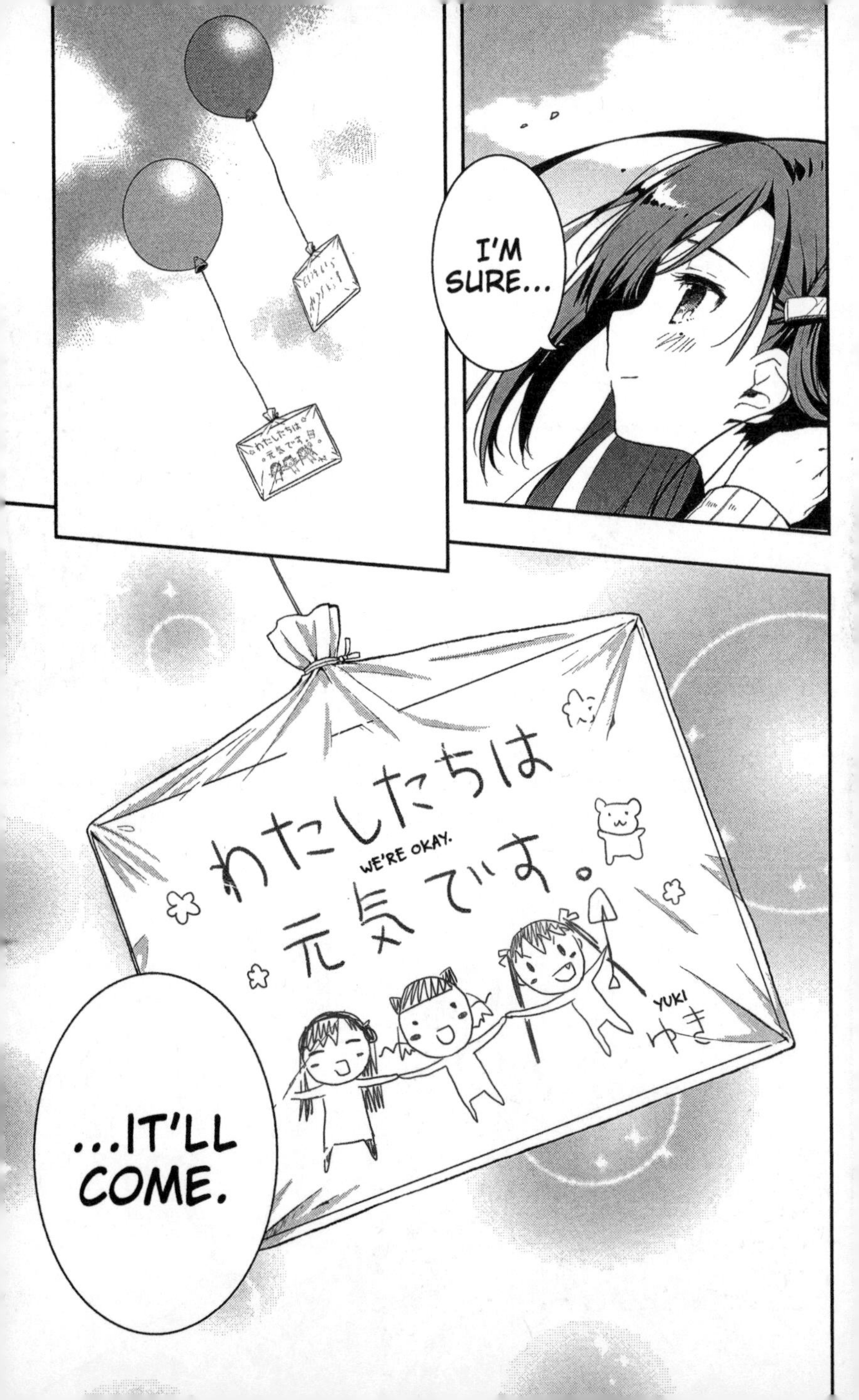
I'M SURE...
わたしたちは
元気です。
WE'RE OKAY.
YUKI
ゆき
...IT'LL COME.

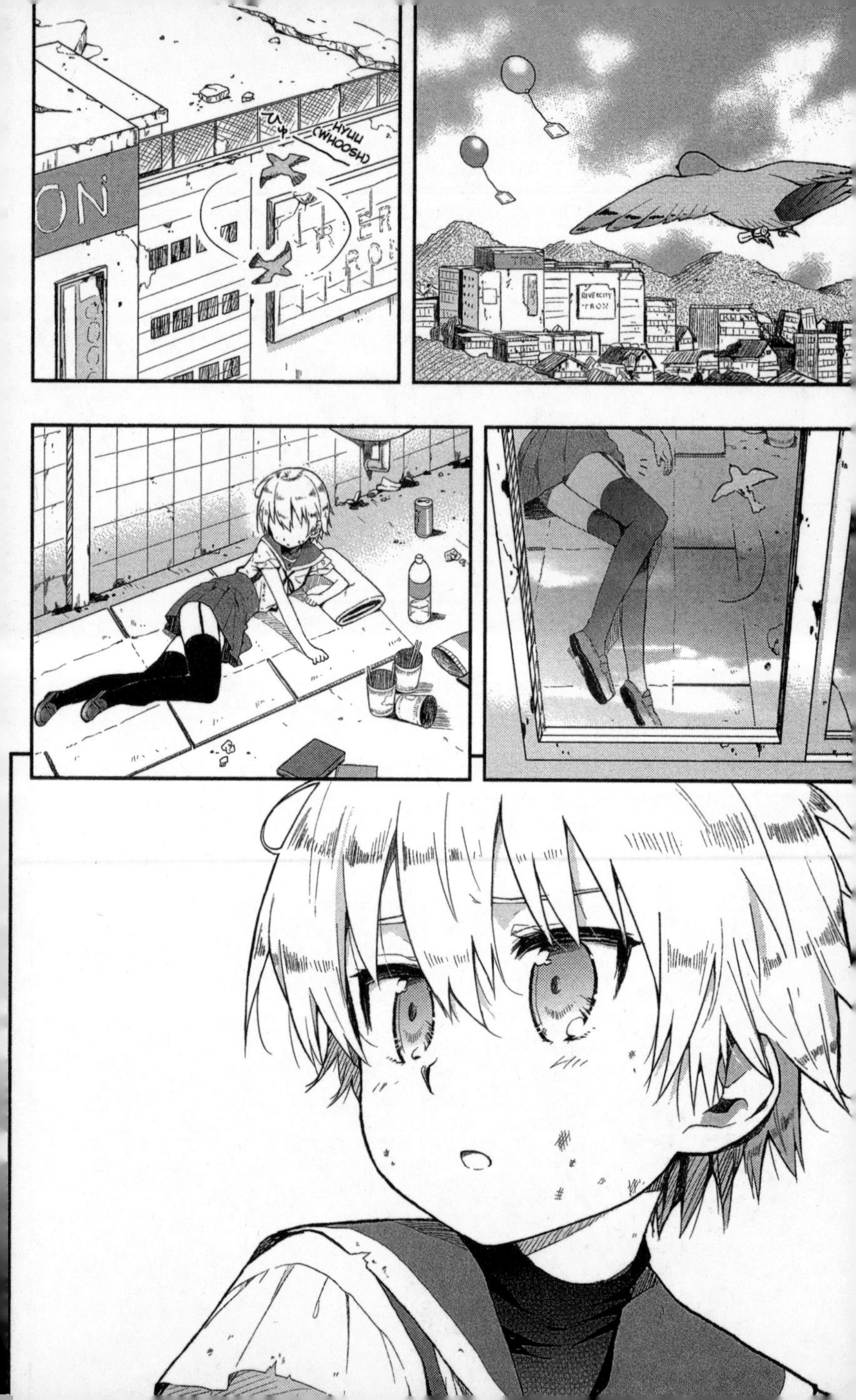
RIVERCITY TRON
ON
ひゅ
HYUU (WHOOSH)

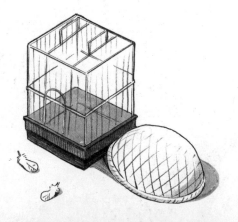

SCHOOL-LIVE!

Megurigaoka Academy Private High School

A.D.

Campus Information

Headmaster's Greeting

Our school's educational philosophy: "Independence and Autonomy."

The three years of high school are an invaluable time for young people flying toward the future. The entire meaning of school life is to prepare them for the adult society that awaits them, to give them all manner of different experiences, and to give them the power to carry on when they occasionally misstep. No matter how amazing their knowledge and skills may be, such treasures will remain unused without the will to wield them.

The founding principle of our school was "Independence and Autonomy," and we seek to provide an education that focuses the school, the family, and the student as one on fostering the student's ability to act in accordance with their own abilities.

A School that Is a Village

In order to uphold the principle of independence and autonomy, we at the academy view the school as a miniature version of society at large and have prepared various facilities to allow the students to gain a wide variety of experiences.

Megurigaoka Academy is a village, and as residents of the village, the students can try their hands at various jobs, always with the goal of becoming self-sufficient.

Education Sought After for the New Era

The importance of the spirit of independence and autonomy will never change, no matter what age we are in, but the desired focus of an education changes with the times. In these modern times during which the all-importance of academic credentials and the idea of lifetime employment have gone by the wayside, the ability to better oneself through an individualized plan, or perhaps the power to survive through raising others up, has become essential.

In order to give everyone the power to rise above the stormy seas of society, Megurigaoka Academy strives to provide a practical education.

Our entire staff awaits the enrollment of everyone who has read this pamphlet.

Megurigaoka Academy Headmaster
Jouji Andou

The History of the Institution

Surrounded by the history of Megurigaoka City.

The city of Megurigaoka in S Prefecture was long known as Dando, and people were quite close to the bounty of nature here. The city of Dando was known for its plentiful folklore, and the city is mentioned in books such as the classic *Snake Gods of the Impure Land* and the more modern *Devilish Thinking*. The city also kept a strong naval force, and H-shi, a professor of archaeology at K University, has compared the folklore of Dando to that of the West Indies and pointed out the possibility of a cultural exchange between the two places.

After the heartbreaking events of 1968, the worries of a further decline in population led the city of Dando to apply for a city development project. In 1979, the city changed its name to Megurigaoka and began to encourage corporations and local industries to set up business in the area, which has been the cornerstone of the community's current prosperity.

Megurigaoka, the name of both the city and the school, comes from the local rolling countryside and the desire to attain the cultural prosperity of ancient Rome brought by the people who visited the seven hills of Rome.

~721	The Ancient Records of Hajima were established around this time.
	The name Dando begins to be seen.
1889	The city of Dando is established.
	The city prospers through fishing and its navy.
1968	Half of the population of Dando is wiped out this year.
	Later on, this becomes known as Dando's nighttime.
1970	Dando applies for a city development project.
	The public is asked for ideas for a new city name.
1979	Dando's city development project is approved.
	The same year, the city's name is changed to Megurigaoka.
	Other proposed names included Ryuusei. (Dando's dawn.)
1984	This year, Dando's population rises to its highest since 1968.
	(Dando's morning.)
1987	Megurigaoka Academy Private High School is established.
1997	Tenth anniversary of Megurigaoka Academy Private High School.
2007	Twentieth anniversary of Megurigaoka Academy Private High School.

Tour of the Facility

At our school, which strives to function as a self-sufficient village, we have various facilities in the building that are necessary to allow the students to experience different aspects of living in society.

The vegetable gardens being bathed in sunlight.

Vegetable Gardens

The heart of independence and autonomy begins with food. Knowing this, our school is in the unique position of having vegetable gardens on the roof and in two other locations on campus, as well as keeping contract farms off campus.

These gardens are mostly tended to and harvested by students taking extracurricular courses or in the gardening club. The harvested foodstuffs are then cooked and fed to the students, while some portion is sold directly to the community under the popular Megurigaoka vegetables brand.

Water Purification System

Just as important to life as food is water. Our school draws water from the ground and the Kuchina River and passes it through our very own purification system to be used for such things as drinking or to fill the pool.

The purification system is powered by in-house generators, so the entire region could use the school as a base in case of a disaster.

Power Generators

Ranking alongside food and water in importance to modern society is power. At our school, the building is powered by both solar panels on the roof and hydroelectric turbines in the Kuchina River.

The distribution of this energy is decided by the student council. The extra power is sold back to the city, and this money, along with the savings on water rates because of the water purification system, is included in the budget for the Ryuusei Festival to teach the students the importance of saving energy even in school.

Computer Labs

In the modern age of Internet society, computers are not just tools for learning, but also great weapons, as well as the way to protect against such attacks. Our school has been using computers in learning since before the Internet existed, and we have been on the leading edge of computer education right up to the current day.

In our state-of-the-art computer labs, students learn not just the basics of how to use a computer, but also Internet literacy and security.

Student Kitchens

The majority of the vegetables from the school gardens are cooked in the student kitchens and then used in student meals.

To aid in this, the student kitchens are large, efficient, and outfitted with the latest equipment, matching the scope of the gardens.

In particular, all of the kitchens in the school are put to work for the Ryuusei Festival.

The school store, stocked with an abundance of goods.

Emergency Food Stores

A portion of the produce from the gardens is preserved in the emergency food stores in the basement. The food in the stores runs from rice and wheat to our own special pickled vegetables. The gardening club's signature ten-year pickled plums are only brought out for special events and celebrations.

Library

In the spirit of independence and autonomy, the management of the collection in the school's library is mostly left to the students (the library committee).

In addition to the various books needed for academic study, there is a system to add new books according to student polls and requests. The wide variety of texts, including manga and other recreational works, is quite popular.

School Store and Gardening Club

In addition to items for every area of study, the school store sells goods made by the students themselves in their club activities, starting with the uniforms made by the handicrafts club, and a portion of the proceeds from these goods is returned to the clubs as part of their budgets. The gardening club's prize vegetables are used as part of the established school lunches.

The library's collection runs from books necessary for learning to material for fun and practical use.

School Life

At Megurigaoka Academy, we put our efforts into a quality academic education as well as various extracurricular courses to provide experiences that teach the spirit of independence and autonomy.

Foreign Language Learning

Our school encourages students to succeed across national borders, so we offer classes in English and ten other languages, including French and Chinese, taught by native speakers that we have invited to our school.

Extracurricular Courses

At our school, we offer courses in all manner of subjects, not just those restricted to the classroom, and every year countless students make use of these courses.

We bring in experts from various fields to offer courses such as the robot course, where students build a hobby robot over the course of a year, or the anime course, where students produce a completed short-form anime. The most popular course, the natural experiences course, in which students catch fish in the nearby Kuchina River and cook them, attracts countless students every year.

Club Activities

Club activities at our school strive to promote exchange with the community. The sports teams as well as the cultural clubs are quite close with local residents, thanks to things such as the charity concerts put on by the guitar club and the brass band, and the sale of the gardening club's vegetables.

The Ryuusei Festival

The cultural festival, held every year in October, is the prime occasion for students to show the spirit of independence and autonomy, as well as the top reason students give for choosing our school.

The name of the Ryuusei Festival comes from the legend of a saint who defeated an evil dragon, and the story is performed by the drama club as the *Ryuusei Drama*. Every year the *Ryuusei Drama*, which interprets the legend in various ways, receives much praise from the community.

The Megurigaoka Academy School Song

Lyrics: Unknown (Old Folk Song)
Adaptation of Lyrics: Takashi Yushimoto
Song: Akira Shirai

First among the seven hills
is the saint whose blade glitters like the heavens.
Roiling in the Kuchina River
is the poison breath of the great nine-headed serpent.

Seven days and seven nights of fighting.
What fell from the heavens were tears of blood,
which soaked deep into the ground.
The remains of the fires were the true horror.

The sun travels over the seven hills.
Now the saint is no longer here,
but our incomparable saint's descendants
wield his sword in their hearts.

Hold courage fast in your heart.
Go, people of Megurigaoka.

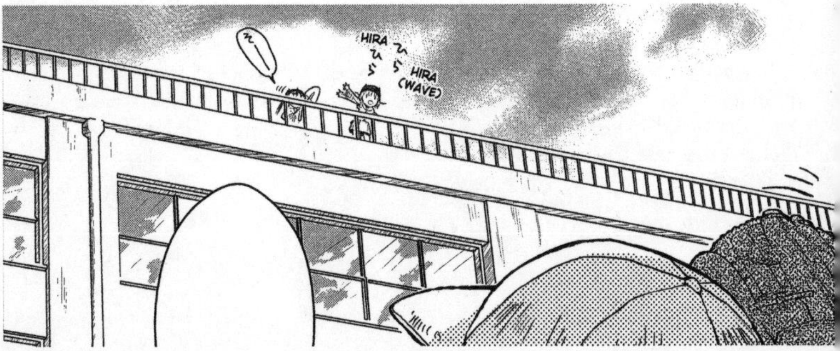
HIRA
HIRA (WAVE)

Megurigaoka Academy Private High School

~~2011~~ A.D.

Campus Information

Text: Norimitsu Kaihou
Editorial Assistance: Ryou Morise (Chronocraft)
Design: Shougo Iwahori (a-ism design)

Girls having a fun little tea party in their classroom while you can see the ruined city outside the window.

This is the sight that came to mind while I was chatting at dinner with my usual group of buddies.

Someone said that it was an interesting idea, and then I met Sadoru Chiba-san, who turned my hazy idea into something that made me go, "This! It has to be this!" And with so many connections just like that, and the help of so many people I couldn't name them all, this book came into being.

There really are so many people that I want to thank, but first my gratitude goes to the pioneers.

To Mary Shelley, Richard Matheson, George Romero, Tom Savini, and Brian Yuzna.

And to you, the person who picked up this book.

Thank you.

Norimitsu Kaihou

Next time
they're at a
shopping mall.
A mall!!

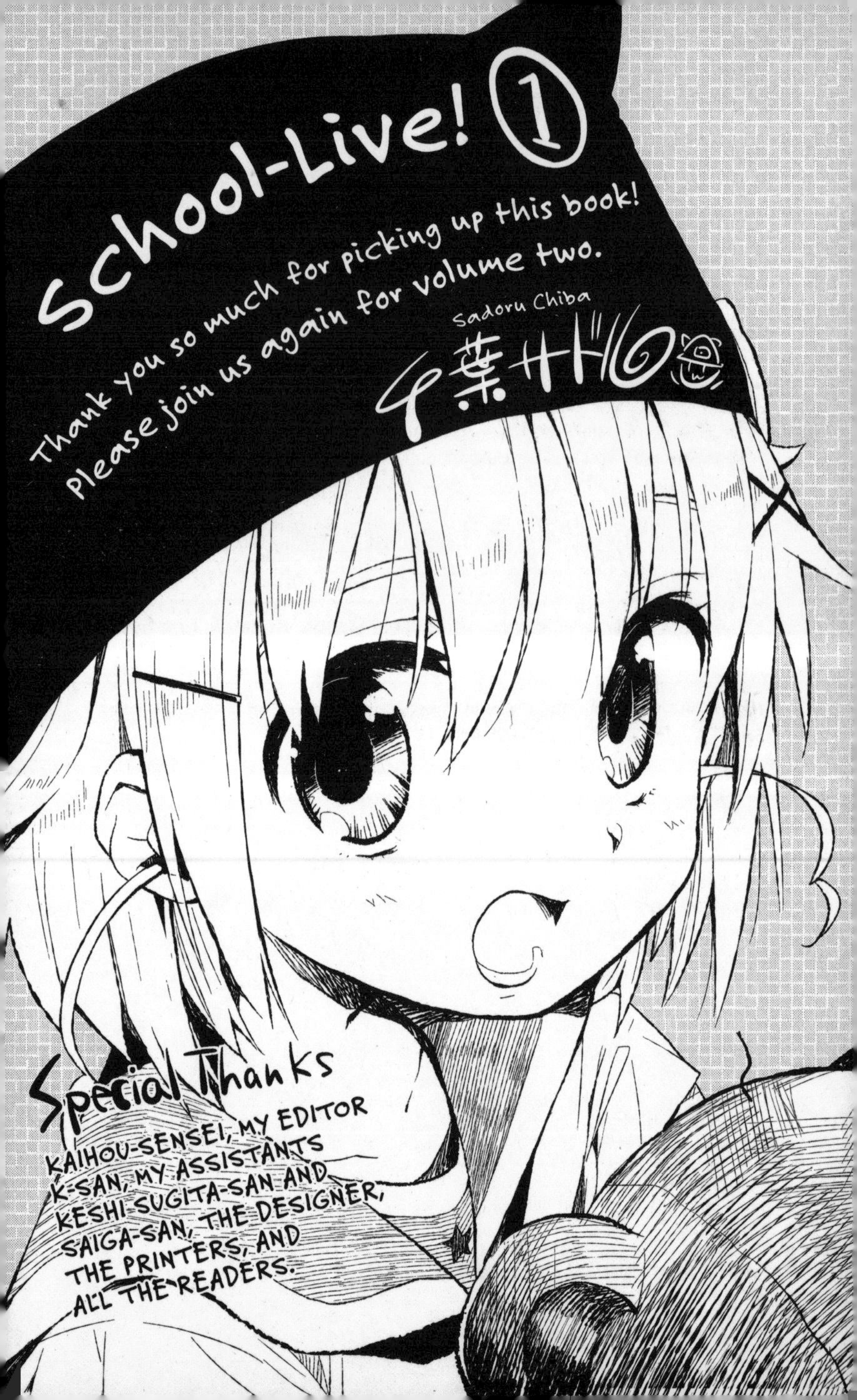
School-Live! 1
Thank you so much for picking up this book!
Please join us again for volume two.
Sadoru Chiba
千葉サドル
Special Thanks
KAIHOU-SENSEI, MY EDITOR
K-SAN, MY ASSISTANTS
KESHI SUGITA-SAN AND
SAIGA-SAN, THE DESIGNER,
THE PRINTERS, AND
ALL THE READERS.

Translation Notes

Common Honorifics:
no honorific: Indicates familiarity or closeness; if used without permission or reason, addressing someone in this manner would constitute an insult.
-san: The Japanese equivalent of Mr./Mrs./Miss. If a situation calls for politeness, this is the fail-safe honorific.
-chan: An affectionate honorific indicating familiarity used mostly in reference to girls; also used in reference to cute persons or animals of either gender.
-senpai: A suffix used to address upperclassmen or more experienced coworkers.
-sensei: A respectful term for teachers, artists, or high-level professionals.
-nee: Honorific derived from onee-san/sama ("big sister"). -nee when used alone after a name can mean closeness.

Page 58
Umakabo is a parody of *Umaibo*, a popular stick-shaped snack.

Page 74
All the manga titles on the shelf are parodies of other *Manga Time Kirara* titles, which is where *School-Live!* is being serialized.

Page 158
Hatoko Hatonishiki: Yuki is giving the pigeon the most straightforward name with *Hato* meaning pigeon and *nishiki* meaning beautiful.

SADORU CHIBA
IMITSU KAIHOU
(NITROPLUS)

Translation: Leighann Harvey

Lettering: Alexis Eckerman

GAKKOU GURASHI! Vol. 1
©Nitroplus / Norimitsu Kaihou, Sadoru Chiba, Houbunsha. All rights reserved. First published in Japan in 2012 by HOUBUNSHA CO., LTD., Tokyo. English translation rights in United States, Canada, and United Kingdom arranged with HOUBUNSHA CO., LTD through Tuttle-Mori Agency, Inc., Tokyo.

Translation © 2015 by Hachette Book Group, Inc.

Yen Press
Hachette Book Group
1290 Avenue of the Americas, New York, NY 10104

www.HachetteBookGroup.com
www.YenPress.com

Yen Press is an imprint of Hachette Book Group, Inc. The Yen Press name and logo are trademarks of Hachette Book Group, Inc.

The publisher is not responsible for websites (or their content) that are not owned by the publisher.

First Yen Press Edition: November 2015

ISBN: 978-0-316-30970-7

10 9 8 7 6 5 4 3 2 1

BVG

Printed in the United States of America